Police Management

ISSUES

**P
E
R
S**&
**P
E
C
T
I
V
E
S**

Edited by
Larry T. Hoover
Sam Houston State University

D0911275

Fred Toler, Executive Director
Texas Commission on Law Enforcement
  Officer Standards and Education
Austin, Texas

Jack L. Ryle, Director
Law Enforcement Management Institute
Texas Commission on Law Enforcement
  Officer Standards and Education
Austin, Texas

Darrel W. Stephens, Executive Director
Police Executive Research Forum
Washington, D.C.

Jamie L. Tillerson, Project Coordinator
Sam Houston State University
Huntsville, Texas

This anthology was produced by Sam Houston State University, Huntsville, Texas, under contract with the Texas Commission on Law Enforcement Officer Standards and Education. Publication is by a cooperative agreement with the Police Executive Research Forum. The views expressed in this publication are those of the authors and do not necessarily represent those of the PERF membership.

Police Executive Research Forum
2300 M Street, N.W., Suite 910
Washington, D.C. 20037

Contents

Preface

The theme that is interwoven throughout this anthology is the intractability of certain problems in police management. One will find reference throughout the book to "endemic issues" in policing. Every human enterprise entails perpetual problems not subject to an ultimate solution, which are, if not unique, at least peculiar to the particular enterprise. We have employed the term "endemic issues" to describe such problems in policing. Like some who believe in the ultimate perfectibility of human kind, there are those who believe that we can ultimately solve every problem in policing. We cannot.

No matter how hard we try we can never ultimately resolve the relationship between the police and the public in a democracy. On the one hand, we desire community input, indeed community control of the police. On the other hand, we wish to insulate law enforcement from partisan political influence, i.e., controlling the police in such a way as to serve the interest of one political party or interest group to the detriment of others. The issue of community alliance requires maintenance of a delicate balance between the two — and will never be ultimately resolved.

Similarly, there is no ultimate solution to the activity trap dilemma in policing. All organizations struggle with maintaining a clear focus on ultimate goals, attempting to ensure that means do not become ends in and of themselves, and, hence, actually displace desired goals. For example, probation agencies would like to be able to measure the ultimate effectiveness of probation officers in both supervising and counseling probationers. But because it is extraordinarily difficult to measure that ultimate effect, performance evaluation most frequently is based upon intermediate criteria that are really means to achieve the end, not ends in and of themselves. Too often criteria such as the quality of a probation officer's written reports totally supplant assessment of the degree to which the actions of the probation officer achieve desired ends. This "activity trap" phenomenon is replicated in organization after organization. It is thus not unique to policing. It is, however, endemic in policing. Measurement of ultimate goal attainment is ultimately impossible for police agencies as a whole, and hence, for individual members of the agency. The means to achieve desired ends vary dramatically from circumstance to circumstance and time to time within a given agency, not to mention across agencies. The currently popular term to describe the supplanting of goals with the measurement of means or activities is "bean counting." Certainly, agencies can strive to improve their performance evaluation systems, and, certainly, they can move beyond the simplest form of bean counting. But they will never be able to measure accurately and objectively the relative contribution of individual members to policing's ultimate mission. Thus, the activity trap is another one of policing's endemic issues.

As noted in the Foreword, this book is an outgrowth of the Texas Law Enforcement Management Institute's Executive Issues Seminar Series. The seminars are designed to offer police managers the opportunity to exchange views on long-term problematic issues. In searching for an appropriate framework around which such a seminar series might be organized, the idea of a matrix with a set of endemic issues on one axis and management perspectives on the other was developed. During a brainstorming session, Dr. Victor Strecher of Sam Houston State University, then Chief Elizabeth Watson of the Houston Police Department, Dr. Timothy Oettmeier of the Houston Police Department, and this author developed the conceptual matrix depicted in Figure 1. The enlarged focus on the "cell" at the juncture of community alliance and alternative futures illustrates the type of questions/issues that are contained in each of the thirty-six cells. The appendix contains a complete explication of the matrix.

The Texas Law Enforcement Management Institute Executive Issues Seminar Series has been organized around this matrix; each seminar addresses a single column or row in the matrix. With the addition of an introductory and conclusionary chapter, this book is likewise organized in terms of the matrix. After the introductory chapter, the next six chapters address sequentially the endemic issues listed, the subsequent six chapters each address one of the management perspectives. The anthology is thus not a mere random collection of interesting articles on police management. It is held together by a conceptual framework that addresses in a systematic way the underlying issues and management problems of policing the world's oldest democracy as we approach and enter the twenty-first century. We do not mean to suggest that there are not some additional endemic issues that might be addressed, or that there are not additional management perspectives that might provide useful insight. We would suggest, however, that the conceptual framework of the anthology provides a reasonably comprehensive look at important underlying issues and problems in police management.

Figure 1

Conceptual Matrix

MANAGEMENT PERSPECTIVES	ENDEMIC ISSUES					
	Matching Structure to Objectives	Community Alliance	Enriching Traditional Roles	Activity Trap	Creativity with Accountability	Stability amid Change
Alternative Futures						
Strategic Approaches						
Human Resource Issues						
Technological & Material Resource Management						
Organizational Communication						
Executive Responsibility						

	Issue: Community Alliance
Perspective: Alternative Futures	• What is the nature of the "community" and its values and preferences for law enforcement? • What is the proper "co-production" of crime control and order maintenance between law enforcement agencies, community groups, and individuals? • How will communities, and their law enforcement needs and desires, differ in the future? * Heterogeneous communities and their contradictory demands * Pluralism vs. assimilation * Politics vs. public policy input * Professional autonomy vs. public participation * Standardized vs. differentiated law enforcement * Integrity issues * Comparative perspectives

iii

Foreword

Addressing the long-term, intractable problems associated with policing a democracy is the goal of the Executive Issues Seminar Series provided by the Law Enforcement Management Institute, Texas Commission on Law Enforcement Officer Standards and Education. Highly respected, knowledgeable professional police administrators and academics were paired as facilitators in this series to stimulate discussion in a seminar setting to which law enforcement administrators holding the responsibility of bureau commander or above were invited. Care was exercised to ensure a retreat-like setting for each of the seminars with the intention of fostering understanding and an easy exchange of ideas as participants examine issues endemic to policing. In so doing, the interchange among police administrators has resulted in ideas, solutions, and observations vital to effective policing into the twenty-first century.

As plans were made for this series of seminars, high priority was given to enabling the candid discussion of these law enforcement managers as they examined each issue from various management perspectives. The cumulative experience and wisdom that subsequently evolved has enormous benefit potential for the police profession. To provide perspective to the participants' discussion notes and at our request, many of the facilitators agreed to add to these notes their own perspective. This collection is the result.

The seminar series itself would have been difficult to develop and present had it not been for a few very dedicated supporters. Without the seminar series and the participation of almost two hundred law enforcement managers, this collection would be meaningless. Larry T. Hoover, Ph.D., Professor of Criminal Justice, Sam Houston State University, and Jamie Tillerson, Program Manager, Sam Houston State University, planned, organized, and managed the series. The scholars charged with facilitating each seminar provided the ingredients for success and have made their written contributions to this collection. The participants (whose ideas and solutions are anonymously included) provided the impetus for this project. To all of you, we say thanks.

Jack L. Ryle

Acknowledgments

The conceptual framework that undergirds this book was initially developed by Timothy Oettmeier, Victor Strecher, Elizabeth Watson, and this author. Gary Cordner contributed substantially to its elaboration and refinement. I want to thank all of them for an invaluable contribution — an idea.

Each of the authors composed her or his work with short notice and under tight deadlines. The originality and insight of their work is particularly significant given the time frame allowed for completion.

Although not directly represented, the staff of the Texas Commission on Law Enforcement Officer Standards and Education were an important part of the book's development. The administrative support provided for both the Executive Issues Seminars (the genesis of the book) and the book project itself was an essential element of the book's publication. Among the staff participating in this respect were Fred Toler, Executive Director of the Commission, Steve Boriskie, Craig Campbell, Joe Gonzalez, and Edd Laine. In particular, I want to thank Jack Ryle, Director of the Law Enforcement Management Institute, for both administrative and conceptual contributions. The importance of his foresight and commitment to creating a management institute of national import cannot be overstated.

Darrel Stephens, Executive Director of the Police Executive Research Forum (PERF), has contributed as a facilitator for the seminar series, as the author of one of the chapters, and administratively. I am grateful as well to PERF as an organization for sponsoring the book and for its assistance in the publication process.

Finally, and most important, Jamie Tillerson, Program Manager at Sam Houston State University, was a genuinely essential part of the project. She was responsible for coordination of the seminar series, handled all administrative matters, and completed the composition and layout of the book. I am most grateful for her dedication and extra hours away from her family.

Chapter 1

Police Mission: An Era of Debate

Larry T. Hoover

Mission and Macrostrategy

It is difficult to develop a reasonably simplified statement of the police mission. Clearly, it is not mere enforcement of criminal statutes. Certainly, law enforcement is a common denominator among innumerable police activities, in fact the majority of police activities. But delivering death messages has nothing to do with law enforcement, standing by downed wires until a power company arrives has nothing to do with law enforcement, and many of the dispute resolution activities in which the police engage are at best tangentially related to law enforcement.

Thus, we end up substituting very broad descriptors of the police mission, for example, public service. The problem here is that these terms become so broad as to be meaningless. The terms don't really distinguish the police role from the functions of government generally, or offer any criteria for sorting the governmental functions that should be the purview of the police department from those that are the responsibility of other governmental agencies. Our best efforts tend to result in mission statements that are actually a list of ten to fifteen different *functions,* hardly a mission statement.

In this chapter it is argued that ambiguity with regard to the police mission is at the heart of current debate regarding "macrostrategy." There are now three macrostrategies competing for loyalty among police administrators and scholars:

- Professional efficiency model
- Problem-oriented policing
- Community-oriented policing

Differences among them are often thought to be subtle, but are in reality very substantial.   If seriously implemented, resource allocation varies dramatically by strategy. Each of the strategies is independently resource hungry. An agency that genuinely commits to crime-specific specialization under the aegis of the professional efficiency model must forgo community-oriented policing, and vice versa. The choice among strategies is arguably the most critical decision a police administrator makes. Further, the recent development of a premature affinity among scholars for one of the three choices, community-oriented policing, may foreclose unbiased evaluation of the other two, particularly problem-oriented policing.

It is the perception of mission that most influences police professionals in their choice of strategy. Unfortunately, differences in such perceptions are not well articulated. Most discussions of mission never move beyond "it's clearly not mere law enforcement, so how about 'to protect and serve.'" The lack of clearly defined mission boundaries leaves us wandering all over the map when the macrostrategy issue is raised.

Mission and Effectiveness

It should be understood that policing is not the only human enterprise that lacks clearly defined mission boundaries. Illustrations abound. For example, the organization that exemplifies flexibility and marketing diversity is Sears, Roebuck and Company. Initiated as a catalogue mail order house, the annual Sears WishBook is still a part of nearly every American child's Christmas. Early in this century, however, the company recognized the trend toward large retail store outlets and is still, with the exception of discount chains, the only national full-service department store. Using its chain of retail outlets as a base, Sears initiated directly related *services*, such as appliance and automotive repair. Sears, Roebuck and Company continues to develop enterprises in the service sector, such as Allstate Insurance, Caldwell Bankers Real Estate, a full-service optical department, Budget Rental Cars, and now even a stock brokerage firm. Regardless of what the future brings, Sears, Roebuck and Company will forever be cited as one of the most successful business enterprises of the twentieth century.

Does it possess a clearly defined mission?   There are certainly hallmarks of its philosophy that we all recognize, e.g., durability of goods, service after the sale, accessibility to even the smallest towns in America, but these characteristics do not constitute a mission. It is difficult to capture in a single mission statement distribution of a Christmas catalogue, selling eye glasses, and renting automobiles.

But Sears is cited here precisely *because* it is an exception. The overwhelming majority of private sector organizations operate within a narrowly defined sector of the economy. Indeed, the flurry of corporate acquisitions and mergers that occurred on Wall Street during the early 1980s, assembling conglomerates of unrelated enterprises under the umbrella of a single "financial corporation," is now disintegrating. The sixth principle of Peters and Waterman's *In Search of Excellence* (1982) — *'stick to the knitting'* — is proving valid. Those companies that stick to the business they know prosper best in the long run. And indeed even the icon of diversity in American business, Sears, Roebuck and Company, has recently seen its percentage of the retail sales market slip steadily, particularly to the onslaught of a small retailer from Arkansas who initiated a chain that initially focused on the needs of small towns in America, reminiscent of the specific mission of Sears, Roebuck and Company of one hundred years ago.

The point being made is that serving largely unrelated objectives is a difficult posture to maintain successfully for any organization. It can be accomplished for a period of time, occasionally even for an extended period of time. But organizations with diffuse missions tend to be both the exception and short lived.

In the public sector it is only the police that we ask to maintain such a posture. Other governmental agencies have a clearly focused mission, or at least a clearly focused central mission. For example, no one questions the mission of fire departments. They do take responsibility for some services ancillary to fire fighting. Since fire departments have to handle hazardous materials whenever they respond to an industrial fire, in most jurisdictions by extension they have been made responsible for hazardous materials problems wherever they occur in a community. In some communities fire departments also handle emergency medical services (EMS) response. Again, however, this extension of fire fighter training in EMS is part of their responsibilities on the fire ground, and the dispersion of fire stations throughout a community makes them a natural base for stationing ambulances. The clear central mission of every fire department, however, remains fire prevention and suppression.

Further, when one moves beyond our sister public safety agency, mission statements are even more tightly focused. Departments of sanitation, public works, public transportation, water, parks and recreation, and road maintenance all possess clearly defined roles. We all understand clearly what they do, and don't expect them to be doing anything else. The water department does not receive hundreds of phone calls a day for which it might ask, "What in the world do we do with this one?"

A Better Definition of the Traditional Police Mission

A significant part of the ambiguity surrounding the definition of police mission is the unfortunate use of the term "order maintenance" as synonymous with "conflict management." The so-called order maintenance function of the police is then held in contrast to the law enforcement function, i.e., order maintenance versus law enforcement. Characterized in this way, the two are co-equal but potentially conflicting police missions. Hence, we hear discussions that typically are as follows:

> It is symptomatic of our disproportionate identification with the crime control function that 90% of training is dedicated to law enforcement while 90% of the calls are order maintenance.

Are hundreds of police professionals associated with designing and authorizing training programs that are skewed? I would assert that they are not; instead, it is the characterization of order maintenance and law enforcement as contrasting missions that presents a skewed picture of the police role.

Order maintenance, modified by the word "temporal" is better viewed as **THE** traditional police mission, the raison d'être of police organizations. Temporal order maintenance can be thought of as maintaining the status quo, i.e., keeping society stable and functioning by acceptable rules, by using interventions with short-term effects. Order maintenance used without the word "temporal" is too broad. Government itself maintains order. The police are responsible only for temporal, or short duration, issues.

Consistent with the concept of a hierarchy of organizational goals, we can then think of the mission of temporal order maintenance as subsuming at least three strategic objectives: public service/public safety, conflict management, and law enforcement. Illustrations of the types of calls for service that generally fall into each of these three categories are contained in Figure 1.

Figure 1 also illustrates two other important phenomena. First, different intervention techniques are preferred depending upon the on-scene objective. The public service/public safety role is most often fulfilled by using social counseling. Comfort provided in delivering a death message, reassurance offered parents of a lost child, and warnings to children and citizens to stay back from downed power wires all fall under the rubric of social counseling. Conflict management, however, demands a different response. Here authoritative persuasion is preferred. Police officers still aren't literally enforcing the law in this role, but they do employ their authority as a "law enforcement officer" to add strength to their persuasive

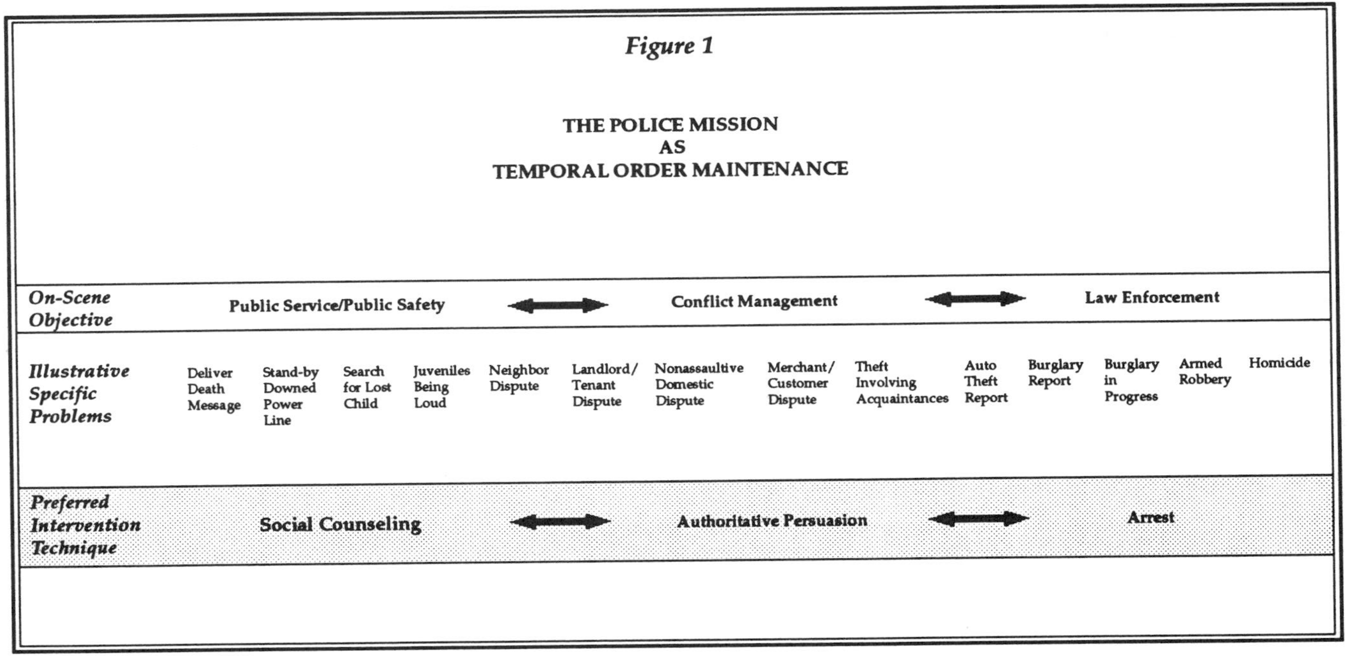

Figure 1

THE POLICE MISSION
AS
TEMPORAL ORDER MAINTENANCE

On-Scene Objective	Public Service/Public Safety				Conflict Management				Law Enforcement			
Illustrative Specific Problems	Deliver Death Message	Stand-by Downed Power Line	Search for Lost Child	Juveniles Being Loud	Neighbor Dispute	Landlord/ Tenant Dispute	Nonassaultive Domestic Dispute	Merchant/ Customer Dispute	Theft Involving Acquaintances	Auto Theft Report	Burglary Report	Burglary in Progress	Armed Robbery	Homicide
Preferred Intervention Technique	Social Counseling				Authoritative Persuasion					Arrest			

talents. They do not, however, respond to these calls intending to arrest anyone. Finally, there is that category of responsibilities that are indeed law enforcement, and here the preferred intervention technique is arrest. The police do not respond to a robbery in progress with any intent to counsel or persuade, only to take someone into custody.

The second phenomenon illustrated by Figure 1 is the fact that both the on-scene objective of the police and their preferred intervention technique are best represented as a continuum of responses, not separate categories. Hence a report of juveniles being loud isn't clearly either public service/public safety or conflict management. Likewise, a theft involving acquaintances, or even an auto theft report, isn't always law enforcement — many times these turn out to be conflict management situations. Furthermore, a problem that initially is likely to be a public service/public safety issue, e.g., a report of a lost child, may occasionally turn out to be a law enforcement issue, e.g., kidnapping. Likewise, a report of loud juveniles may be a fight over a drug sale. Hence, the police respond to a given situation with an assumed on-scene objective and with a preferred intervention technique, but both may change rapidly with further information. Indeed, the behavior of respondents at a scene often changes the preferred police intervention technique. In a conflict management situation a belligerent respondent may evoke an arrest intervention, despite the fact that the definition of the situation remains conflict management. Thus, a given on-scene objective may be achieved by various intervention techniques or combination of techniques. Clear, mutually exclusive, categorical objectives and intervention techniques do not exist. Instead a continuum of objectives and intervention techniques are intermingled, although patterns of association certainly are definable.

This makes sense if one recognizes that the overarching mission is temporal order maintenance. The police are at a scene fundamentally to maintain order, to keep the peace. As noted by Bittner (1990),

> peacekeeping occasionally acquires the external aspects of law enforcement. This makes it specious to inquire whether or not police discretion in invoking the law conforms with the intention of some specific legal formula. The real reason behind an arrest is virtually always the actual state of particular social situations . . . .

Peacekeeping, or temporal order maintenance, governs police response. But one must also not confuse law enforcement as an objective with arrest as a technique. It is such confusion that results in many scholars understating the importance of law enforcement as an element of policing. Law enforcement is not merely a technique. Arrest is a technique. Law enforcement is one of three primary strategic objectives subsumed by the mission of temporal order maintenance. There is a whole class of police activities focused exclusively upon this objective which have nothing to do with conflict management or public service/public safety.

This schematic also clarifies the issue of what constitutes "real" police work.   Real police work is performing the role of a *peace* officer. Peacefulness, or orderliness, is the overall mission. A disorderly situation begets a call for police service or proactive police intrusion. Disorder ranges from downed power lines to robberies in progress. There is, however, a hierarchical relationship among disorderly situations. As one moves from the public service/public safety class of situations through conflict management to law enforcement the threat to stable social order generally increases. Law enforcement situations usually result in greater harm and also possess the characteristic of being more generically threatening. Most public service/public safety and conflict management situations do not involve a general threat. Most also entail disorderly interactions among acquaintances (it may seem cold to think of delivering death messages in this way, but this task falls under this category). Because of the tendency for greater harm, and the more generic threat, the law enforcement role of the police predominates both resource allocation and public image. Nevertheless, it is but one element of keeping the peace.

Changing the Police Mission

Sometimes form follows function, sometimes function follows form, and occasionally they interact. In the past ten years in policing form and function have been interacting. Problem-oriented and community-oriented policing *techniques* have become macrostrategies that may actually change the police mission. Only by understanding this fact can one appreciate the depth of the current debate about these strategies. They are not merely a better way of doing things, they constitute doing different things.

Each strategy moves the police to a new role. The traditional mission has been *temporal* order maintenance.   Both problem-oriented and community-oriented strategies may solve short-term problems, but they also push the police toward structural and environmental interventions with significant community impact. Although there is considerable overlap, it is argued here that problem-oriented policing changes the police mission to sustained order maintenance, while community-oriented policing changes the role of the police to neighborhood management. If agencies are successful in implementing either or both of these macrostrategies, the police mission will have forever been changed. And changing the police mission in a democracy merits long and thorough debate.

Confusion Between Problem-Oriented and Community-Oriented Policing

The difference between problem-oriented policing and community-oriented policing is subtle but substantial. There has been an unfortunate tendency over the past five years to treat the two perspectives as if they were synonymous. Nothing could be further from the truth. The tendency to treat them alike emanates from several sources. First, both are suggested as radical and dramatic alternatives to traditional policing. Second, both use as the fundamental rationale for their implementation the failure of the professional model. Third, both arose as organized concepts during the mid to late 1980s. Fourth, there is considerable overlap among the advocates of the two concepts. The core proponent organization of problem-oriented policing is the Police Executive Research Forum. The core advocate group of community-oriented policing is Michigan State University. However, the individual scholars involved tend to be associated with initiatives and programs offered by each organization. Fifth, the actual street-level techniques employed under the aegis of one strategy overlap considerably those employed under the aegis of the other. An intervention designed to eliminate difficulties associated with rowdy teenagers monopolizing a neighborhood park can be called either problem-oriented or community-oriented policing.

Further, the distinction between problem-oriented and community-oriented policing becomes more blurred when problem-oriented interventions are employed at neighborhoodwide levels. Problem-oriented techniques that are focused upon a very specific situation, in particular, repetitive calls for service from a single source, do not constitute a philosophical or mission switch. However, when the police begin to initiate the reconstruction of housing projects, deployment of the city's sanitation department, or redrawing of zoning ordinances, a substantial change in mission has occurred. The police are no longer dealing with *temporal* order maintenance, but with long-term intervention in a community's infrastructure. The mission has changed from "temporal" order maintenance to "sustained" order maintenance. The police are operating at an intermediate level. Police interventions are longer term, and have a far more enduring impact, but are still limited to defined needs. The three objectives of policing remain the same — public service/public safety, conflict management, and law enforcement. The kinds of specific problems handled remain the same. But in addition to using social counseling, authoritative persuasion, and arrest, the police occasionally employ social referral, extended counseling, or effect structural or environmental changes to provide a longer term, enduring impact. See Figure 2.

A gray zone exists in this area between problem-oriented and community-oriented policing. But there is an important distinction. The

Figure 2

THE POLICE MISSION
AS
SUSTAINED ORDER MAINTENANCE

With Problem-Oriented Policing Intervention Overlay

	Public Service/Public Safety				Conflict Management					Law Enforcement				
On-scene Objective	Public Service/Public Safety				⟷ Conflict Management					⟷ Law Enforcement				
Illustrative Specific Problems	Deliver Death Message	Stand-by Downed Power Line	Search for Lost Child	Juveniles Being Loud	Neighbor Dispute	Landlord/Tenant Dispute	Nonassaultive Domestic Dispute	Merchant/Customer Dispute	Theft Involving Acquaintances	Auto Theft Report	Burglary Report	Burglary in Progress	Armed Robbery	Homicide
Problem-Oriented Intervention Techniques	A Few Instances Where Social Referral or Extended Counseling is Appropriate ⟷				Numerous Instances Where Social Referral or Extended Counseling is Appropriate ⟷				A Few Instances Where Structural or Environmental Intervention is Appropriate ⟷				Numerous Instances Where Structural or Environmental Intervention is Appropriate	

distinction between problem-oriented policing and community-oriented policing is one of duration. Problem-oriented interventions may involve modifying a community's infrastructure, but there is an end point to the intervention. Changes are made and the police "withdraw." It is an intermediate level of order maintenance responsibility. This is not so with community-oriented policing. The police come to a neighborhood, and are there to stay as generalist government agents responsible for the quality of life in the microcommunity. See Figure 3.

Taken to its logical conclusion, community-oriented policing changes the police mission from temporal order maintenance to neighborhood management. This is a far more profound change than that beget by the problem-oriented model. It is just as profound a change with just as profound implications as the change at the turn of the century at Sears, Roebuck and Company from a catalogue order house to a retail outlet. We do indeed still have the Sears WishBook, just as community-oriented agencies will still have temporal order maintenance responsibilities. But we no longer think of Sears as a catalogue order house. And like Sears opening of retail outlets, the change in mission to neighborhood management may either open new vistas of opportunity or a Pandora's box of pestilence and plague.

The subtle but overwhelmingly significant distinction between community-oriented and problem-oriented policing is almost never recognized. Community policing changes fundamentally the role of law enforcement agencies. While the difference between Figures 1 and 2 aren't extreme, Figure 3 represents a different kind of government agency. It is no longer responsible only for temporal or even intermediate order maintenance. Rather, if *true* community-oriented policing is fully implemented, the patrol officer of the future will be a neighborhood manager. Of equal import, many of the ardent advocates of community policing see the role of this neighborhood manager as an arbiter between her or his employer, a county or municipality, and the citizens on her or his beat. The fact that there are very few employers willing to give someone a paycheck to serve as a bureaucratic guerilla advocating a single special interest tends to be either overlooked entirely or quickly glossed over.

Reassessing the Professional Efficiency Model

If the professional model has its faults, it also has its strengths. The pervasive bias in favor of entrepreneurial organizations in American culture can backfire on enterprises where innovation is either impossible, impractical, or simply not desirable. Elements of policing fit this criterion. In a headlong rush to prove to other police administrators that he or she is at the cutting edge, a police chief would do well to pause and consider the traditional police mission — temporal order maintenance, or stated

Figure 3

THE POLICE MISSION
AS
NEIGHBORHOOD MANAGEMENT

With Community-Oriented Policing Intervention Overlay

On-scene Objective	Public Service/ Public Safety	⟷	Conflict Management	⟷	Law Enforcement	⟷	Family Assistance	⟷	Youth Guidance	⟷	Physical Structure	⟷	Government Social Outreach
Illustrative Specific Problems	Deliver Death Message		Neighbor Dispute		Armed Robbery		Chronic Welfare Dependence		Lack of Organized Sports Leagues		Substandard or Deteriorating Housing		Disseminating Information on AIDS
Community-Oriented Intervention Techniques	Numerous Instances Where Social Referral or Extended Counseling is Appropriate	⟷	A Few Instances Where Structural or Environmental Intervention is Appropriate	⟷	Sustained Structural or Environmental Intervention Services	⟷	Sustained Counseling Services	⟷	Sustained Counseling or Social Interaction and Recreation Services	⟷	Sustained Structural or Environmental Intervention Services	⟷	Sustained Counseling Services

differently, *keeping things the way they are.*   Innovative, creative entrepreneurship doesn't always fit this mission. More frequently, staid, standardized, routinized bureaucratic response will best accomplish the goal of temporal order maintenance. Police administrators need to consider carefully whether they wish to change the police mission before launching problem- or community-oriented policing. If they don't, the professional model may, in fact, be considerably better suited to fulfilling the mission of temporal order maintenance.

Analogies sometimes provide useful insight. Any analogy between policing and another enterprise has its limits, but one strikes me as particularly useful in understanding the match between police mission and police strategy. It is with the airline industry.

I routinely fly to Chicago. Inevitably, I board American Airlines Flight 300, departing Houston's Intercontinental Airport at 7:05 a.m. and arriving two hours and fifteen minutes later at Chicago's O'Hare. Other options are available, but my travel agent understands when I call and say that I'm going to Chicago again, it will be American Airlines Flight 300. The dynamics of this *a priori* decision are these:

- The basic issue is to get to Chicago's O'Hare on schedule. Business meeting plans are made assuming a scheduled arrival. About 80% of my decision is premised upon this issue. Regardless of all other considerations, the primary criterion is getting from point A to point B.
- The "no-frills" option available on this route is Southwest Airlines. I don't use it because I actually enjoy the coach class breakfast on American. However, I don't enjoy a breakfast with *all* the frills so much that I'm willing to pay for a first-class ticket.
- I'll bend by an hour or so on arrival time to stay on American Airlines because I'm hooked on their frequent flyer program. Besides, and I must admit to being mildly embarrassed to even admit this, they've managed to convince me through little perks and bonuses that I really am "someone special" to them, i.e., they've been successful in cultivating customer loyalty.
- I try to avoid Continental Airlines, because I'm from a blue-collar labor family and their past labor policies vaguely offend me.
- Finally, I'm reasonably tolerant of unavoidable delays. They irritate me, but I recognize, like 99.9% of the flying public, that delays are an inevitable part of flying. The weather certainly can't be controlled, and equipment malfunctions can't be eliminated even with aggressive

maintenance.   Nevertheless, at the time a delay is announced I'll be irritated. And at the least I expect airline personnel to be courteous and honest in telling me about the delay.

It should be noted, however, that I still don't enjoy flying. Probably the most salient issue is this respect is the cattle-herding phenomenon. I recognize, however, that given the exigencies of flying that current technology will economically permit, there isn't anything any airline can do about it.

The analogies with regard to policing are these:

- Despite analysis of calls for service indicating the predominance of conflict management calls, and despite the discussion in this chapter, the public regards the police role as crime control (just as the airlines' role is to get one from point A to point B). Police administrators would do well not to ignore this fact.
- The public appears willing to pay enough in taxes to get police services that exceed absolute minimums. There are some "no-frills" agencies, just as there are a few no-frills airlines.   But the substantial majority of agencies are sufficiently funded to provide some training to their officers, some crime prevention effort, and an Explorer Scout program. Few communities, however, are willing to pay first-class fares, buying everything a police agency can possibly provide. Rather, most agencies feel some strain on resources. And very, very few agencies are sufficiently funded to provide "first-class" neighborhood management.
- Many citizens will wait a while to talk to an officer they know rather than just any officer. Even these "frequent users," however, are unwilling to reschedule dramatically to stay with their favorite officer.
- The public wants to deal with an agency that reflects at least in a macro sense their personal philosophy. Like my avoidance of Continental, they'll avoid a department that isn't perceived as being in line with their world view by not reporting incidents.
- Analogous to airline delays, the public recognizes that in the big picture the police can't solve every crime, can't resolve every problem. Nevertheless, they'll be irritated when it's their problem that can't be resolved. Further, they expect that the police to make the best effort to solve

their problem; and, at the least, to be courteous and honest in
telling them that they can't.

It should be noted, however, that try as the police might, the substantial
majority of the public will never "enjoy" contact with the police. Just as the
airlines can't do anything about the herding phenomenon that makes air
travel tedious, the police will always be associated with "trouble."

At the risk of stretching this analogy to the breaking point, it is also
instructive to note what I expect of American Airlines once I show up to board
Flight 300:

- An accessible reservations clerk
- A window seat
- Prompt departure
- Quick coffee
- A breakfast that is at least lukewarm
- My luggage on the same flight
- The engine to stay bolted on
- Courteous staff (not gratuitous, not officious, not bubbly —
  especially not at 7:00 a.m. — just courteous)

In short, I want an efficient, competent — but very routine —
bureaucratic response. What I explicitly do not want is:

- Creative routing of my luggage through Tokyo
- An innovative seat assignment
- Imaginative flying at nonprescribed altitudes
- Novel food (particularly when I have no menu choices)
- Inventive landing techniques

A significant portion of policing should meet the same criterion — an
efficient, competent bureaucratic response — and nothing more. This is
particularly true if the mission is defined as temporal order maintenance.
For example, a large part of the police function is simple information
processing. These "take a report" calls, including minor traffic accidents, are
best handled by highly routine, standardized procedures. Further, the best
response to some types of calls is with a highly prescribed technique, e.g.,
delivering death message, or issuing traffic citations.

The problem is that a simple, efficient, prescribed bureaucratic
response isn't inherently exciting to academics, research organizations,
management consultants, and change-oriented police managers. Indeed, there
is a strong bias in the management literature in favor of entrepreneurial
organizations. Advocates of bureaucratic efficiency in policing are now

labeled "traditionalists," with all the negative connotations that the term implies.

But the reality is that classical bureaucratic efficiency is serving some organizations very well. Rensis Likert observed that Ray Kroc did not invent anything. The most successful food service enterprise the world has ever known was built, and continues to grow, on turn-of-the-century efficiency management principles. And whether I walk into a McDonalds in New York, Moscow, London, or Tokyo, the service and product will always be the same — standardization taken to the extreme.

Similarly, the airline industry has prospered in the past twenty years, passenger miles increasing several times over, by doing the basics better. The relevance of such comparisons to policing is, of course, limited. Police agencies differ not only in the public versus private dimension, but numerous others as well. Nevertheless, we need to be cognizant of the fact that success does not always require daily creativity.

Yet almost universally the professional model is disdained. I will readily concede that aspects of the model are either no longer necessary or no longer serving us as well as alternatives might. But not everything about the professional model should be discarded.

Take the issue of response time. The Kansas City Response Time Experiment included the finding that rapid response makes a difference in apprehension probability in only a small percentage of calls for service (Pate et al., 1976). Our reaction has been the classical overreaction discussed elsewhere in this chapter, that response time makes no difference. But that simply isn't true. First, even if it makes a difference in only a small fraction of law enforcement situations, we aren't at all sure what the deterrent effect might be. Second, on-scene arrests often clear numerous offenses, not just the immediate one. One on-scene robbery arrest may take an offender off the street who is committing several robberies a month. Third, the findings are directly relevant only to law enforcement problems. Those in which the on-scene police objective is public service/public safety or conflict management typically require reasonably rapid police response to maintain citizen satisfaction if nothing else. When a suicide is discovered in a residence it would be tacky, to say the least, to leave the body in place waiting for two hours for the police to arrive. Similarly, a report of a lost child shouldn't wait for hours for a response. Public expectations require reasonable response times (Williams, undated), regardless of the effect of response time on apprehension rates. The limits of research such as the Response Time Study, as important as it may be, are better understood when the police mission is understood as temporal order maintenance.

Unfortunately, response time, as well as numerous other elements of the professional model, are in disfavor because of their association with simplified measures of police efficiency. Herbert Simon (1945) argued in *Administrative Behavior* that efficiency is a completely neutral concept. It is neither inherently good nor bad. Mintzberg (1989) points out, however, that

> A management obsessed with efficiency is a management obsessed with measurement. The cult of efficiency is the cult of calculation. And therein lies the problem.

But too many police administrators and scholars throw out the baby with the bathwater. Obsession with superficial efficiency measures of elements of police operations does not require as a reaction eliminating the operations. There is a difference between overrating response time measures as a criterion of success and response time being meaningless.

Before we abandon the professional model we would do well to consider what it has bequeathed us. More educated and better trained personnel, sophisticated use of technology, better adherence to due process, far less corruption, and — yes — better response time are all the products of the Vollmer and Wilson legacy. Perhaps the legacy should not so readily be disdained because of some negative elements. Professional efficiency may not be such a bad idea.

Reassessing Crime-Specific Specialization

Closely associated with the professional efficiency model is an emphasis upon crime-specific interventions. A series of field experiments conducted in the 1970s regarding the efficacy of various interventions commonly employed by patrol and investigative divisions cast considerable doubt on the validity of such techniques. In particular the Kansas City Preventive Patrol Experiment (Kelling et al., 1974) and the RAND Criminal Investigation Study (Greenwood and Petersilia, 1975) undermined our confidence in the fundamental means employed by the police to interdict criminal events and apprehend criminal offenders. The creation of an illusion of omnipresence by random routine patrol was declared ineffectual by the Police Foundation. The RAND Corporation characterized detectives not as supersleuths in the Sherlock Holmes tradition but as clerks for the district attorney. These two studies were the blockbusters of the 1970s. What remained was a disjunctive list of crime-specific, narrowly focused, and labor-intensive techniques lacking systematic evaluation.

Undergirding the two blockbuster studies was the widely recognized observation that crime rates have little or no relationship to police-citizen ratios. Indeed, if any kind of police interventions made a difference, then one would expect to see at least isolated instances where simply more police would make a difference. When police forces are staffed at bare minimums, they are unable to do much more than respond to calls for service in the patrol division and follow up on the most serious offenses, in the form of clerking for the district attorney in the criminal investigation division. Since resources beyond minimums are likely to be focused on crime-specific interventions, one would assume that if some proactive interventions made some difference, then at least a slight positive correlation would exist between crime rates and police-citizen ratios. But a pattern of higher impact with higher numbers simply does not exist. Ratios among major cities are as high as 6.9/1000 officers in Washington, DC (4.9 in Detroit, 4.3 in Chicago) to lows of 1.6 in San Antonio and 1.7 in San Diego (Federal Bureau of Investigation, 1991). There are, however, no demonstrable relationships between these ratios and crime rates (Walker, 1989).

It should be emphasized that this fact standing in isolation does not *prove* that the police make no difference. Walker noted that the cause and effect relationship between police-citizen ratios and crime rates may in fact be reversed, i.e., high crime rates cause communities to hire more police, hence an inverse correlation often exists. The fact that no relationship exists may simply indicate that this is a highly idiosyncratic phenomenon, subject to influence by numerous social, political, and demographic variables. A single "for instance" is the use of one person versus two person patrol cars, which will dramatically affect the number of patrol *units* per citizen. Nevertheless, the lack of correlation, taken in conjunction with the Police Foundation and RAND Corporation findings, caused additional doubt to be cast on the efficacy of police crime-specific interventions.

A decade passed while police administrators and scholars searched for meaningful alternatives to preventive patrol and reactive investigations. Such efforts included Directed Patrol in Pontiac, Michigan, and New Haven, Connecticut; Split-Force Patrol in Wilmington, Delaware; Community Profiling in San Diego, California; Perpetrator and Location-Oriented Patrol in Kansas City, Missouri; and innumerable other efforts (Cordner and Trojanowicz, 1992). Evaluation results have been mixed.

Is it true then that in policing it can be said that "nothing works"? The quick and unequivocal answer is absolutely not. Again, an analogy may be helpful in understanding the issue. In 1974 the field of corrections was rocked by the publication of Robert Martinson's critique of the efficacy of rehabilitation (Martinson, 1974). The precise observation he made was:

> It is just possible that some of our treatment programs *are* working to some extent, but that our research is so bad that it is incapable of telling. . . .
>
> This is not to say that we found no instances of success or partial success; it is only to say that these instances have been isolated, producing no clear pattern to indicate the efficacy of any particular method of treatment. . . .

Martinson did not actually say that nothing works. However, to a public in the throws of a conservative political rollback the phrase "no clear pattern to indicate the efficacy of any particular method of treatment" was quickly shortened to "nothing works." The development of rehabilitative programming in corrections was essentially suspended, and what little programming existed in 1972 was either kept at minimal funding levels or even reduced.

It was clear to many correctional administrators and scholars from day one of the "nothing works" outcry that a modification of that position would eventually be necessary. For one thing, the evaluative research assessed by Martinson did not actually indicate that nothing works. In fact, evaluative research had indicated that tightly focused interventions aimed at carefully defined subgroups of offenders did have some effect. That is to say, Martinson was technically not wrong, but the overgeneralization of his findings certainly were. Research published over the past twenty years has unequivocally confirmed that some interventions have some effect for some offender groups. Unlike some medical interventions, no social intervention will ever achieve 100 percent effectiveness. There are no Salk vaccines for the wide range of deviant behavior we put in the category of criminality. Modest gains are, however, possible and certainly well worth the investment in rehabilitative programming.

The Kansas City Preventive Patrol Experiment was published the same year as the Martinson Report, the RAND Criminal Investigation Study a year later. Our tendency has been to do the same thing with the Police Foundation Study and the Rand Report as was done with the Martinson Report, i.e., to make a broader generalization that proactive, crime-specific, typologically focused interventions, by extrapolation, don't work.

The past twenty years has brought a more sophisticated view of both the promises and limits of rehabilitative intervention for convicted offenders. Focused interventions do reduce recidivism for selected groups of offenders by measurable amounts. Similarly, carefully focused crime intervention strategies may have some effects on some offense categories. This certainly appeared to be the case during the field interrogation experiment in San Diego, California (Boydstun, 1975). And in contrast to the pessimistic pronouncements of the RAND Criminal Investigation Study, decentralized investigative techniques in Rochester, New York, involving close cooperation between detectives and patrol officers appeared to improve clearance rates (Bloch and Bell, 1976).

Further, the research findings of the 1970s are to some extent contradictory. George Kelling would be quick to point out that the Kansas City Preventive Patrol Experiment tested one strategy and only one strategy, random routine patrol. No effort was made to ascertain the effect of field interrogations. But if indeed field interrogations are imbedded in routine patrol, i.e., are an inherent and routine part of routine patrol, then the picture is quite different. And indeed, I cannot think of a way to effect field interrogations without using the routine patrol strategy as its springboard. A contradiction in methodology may not exist between the two research experiments, but the policy implications of the field interrogation experiment certainly affect the policy implications of the Kansas City Preventive Patrol Experiment.

Similar implications exist for the RAND Criminal Investigation Study. Although methodologically sound and certainly offering only carefully drawn conclusions, the research was a cursory look at best at investigative strategies. It is a quintessential *prevailing modes/decisive effect* research study. Other studies have reached conclusions that are at definitive odds with the "nothing works" view of investigations (cf., Eck, 1983; Bloch and Bell, 1976). As noted by Eck (1992),

> Though detectives may not be as omnipotent as the public myth
> (and some detectives) would have us believe, detectives are not
> as unproductive as earlier research had suggested.

Thus, investigations — both reactive and proactive — may yield significant dividends. It is certainly premature to abandon the investigative process as a major element of policing.

We need another era of experimentation in policing. First of all, we desperately need to replicate the field experiments testing the fundamental strategies employed by patrol and investigation. We have a set of single site, single time frame, nonreplicated studies that are guiding the distribution of massive resources in the 1990s. Researchers and administrators in the field of physical science would be aghast. Many of the research findings are directly contradictory, others possess implied contradiction. In addition to replication of the experiments of the 1970s, evaluations of more specific interventions are desperately needed. Multiple site, multiple time frame, multiple agency experiments need to be conducted to measure the effect of specific interventions aimed at specific problems. We have only begun to test the efficacy of crime-specific strategies.

Jumping off the Community-Oriented Policing Bandwagon

Crime-specific interventions are associated in the literature with the professional model of policing. The professional model is then characterized as a failure, and the foundation for suggesting that it is time to consider dramatically different approaches to policing has been laid. A wealth of accumulated knowledge, a great deal of literature, and at least some research is rather cavalierly swept aside with that general assertion.

Community policing has become, in fact, a quintessential illustration of "politically correct thinking." Those who raise questions about the validity of its underlying premises or the lack of evidence that as a prevailing mode of policing it has a decisive effect upon the incidence of crime, citizens' fear of crime, or even citizen satisfaction are summarily dismissed either as traditionalists or "not really understanding what community policing is all about." When Gary Sykes, Director of the Southwestern Law Enforcement Institute, tried to recruit speakers for a national symposium addressing the pros and cons of community policing, he found it difficult to find individuals to speak on the negative side. With the notable exception of Victor Strecher's article (1991) in the charter issue of the Academy of Criminal Justice Science's Police Section newsletter *Police Forum*, one is hard pressed until now to find anything in the literature that really raised serious questions about the totality of the strategy. To do so is to risk being labeled regressive, retrograde, and perhaps even one of the Neanderthals of the field. The Rodney King incident in Los Angeles has not helped the situation. The major urban agency most identified with crime-specific intervention techniques has found itself subject to national ridicule. The premise that community policing is the wave of the future, the only way to go, and the right thing to do was reinforced a thousandfold by this single event.

But very recently there are some signs of doubt. Strecher's article (1991) was the first widely recognized opposing viewpoint, suggesting that history does not inevitably point in the direction of community policing. There is now even a handful of police administrators otherwise regarded as progressive who are daring to question, if not the desirability of community policing, at least the practicality of ever implementing it (Koby and Lucy, 1992).

I don't want to be misunderstood regarding the issue of dissent in community policing. The lopsidedness of the literature in favor of the technique is characteristic of any new organizational initiative. Inevitably, the advocates speak first, there is a period of experimentation, and critical analysis follows. Those who have not spoken to the issue are not necessarily scholarly or administrative wimps, but rather in most cases have deliberatively chosen to "wait and see." At the same time one cannot ignore the political correctness issue. The descriptive terminology associated with community policing has a progressive, democratic, enlightened valance. Terms such as neighborhood involvement, public communication, breadth of input, shared responsibility, responsiveness, long-term commitment, and — my favorite — coproduction all have a wholesome, democratic ring. Contrast this set of terms with those describing crime-specific interventions — covert operations, electronic eavesdropping, stings, decoy squads, stop and question, and, last but certainly not least, special weapons and tactics. Little wonder that city managers, always conscious of public relations, are quick to jump on the community policing bandwagon.

That bandwagon effect may be the downfall of what, for some communities, may be a very good idea, i.e., conversion of its police department to a department of neighborhood management. For just as the post-Rodney King Los Angeles Police Department will undoubtedly soften its rhetoric, its unit acronyms, and its tactics, so too simultaneously the reverse is happening in other communities. The once politically correct language of community policing in other locations is backfiring. In a growing number of communities, Houston and Tulsa are recent examples, the rhetoric of community policing is being equated to "soft on crime," and hence the basic strategy is being abandoned. Politically correct rhetoric is a two-edged sword. If the advocates of community policing don't soon modify their rhetoric, they may well kill their golden goose.

It is incumbent upon the advocates of community policing to define clearly its attributes. Those attributes, should not, cannot, and do not consist of

| Everything good about policing | = | community policing |
| Everything bad about policing | = | the failed and despicable professional model |

Assigning two officers out of a force of two hundred to a housing project for a six-month period to develop an array of approaches to help curb crime and disorder in that project, then proudly announcing to the world that this municipality engages in community policing is absurd. Abandoning rotating shifts or beats for semipermanent assignments, then announcing community policing has been implemented is absurd. When the chief of a five-person police department policing a community of 5,000 proudly announces that her or his department has been doing community policing all along but just didn't call it that it is absurd. Community policing is a dramatically altered deployment scheme that creates some opportunities, but precludes others. It isn't unquestionably, undoubtedly, and without debate "the right thing to do."

There may be those who are critical of my characterization of community policing as comprehensive neighborhood management. For those who believe it is an overstatement, listed below, mostly from Trojanowicz and Bucqueroux's *Community Policing* (1990), are some of the roles suggested for community police "outreach specialists":

- Coordinating family assistance
- Helping youngsters manage their lives and build self esteem
- Taking kids to the zoo, organizing softball teams, organizing fishing derbies
- Controlling gangs
- Helping solve the problem of the homeless

- Organizing neighborhood cleanup campaigns
- Initiating action to demolish abandoned structures
- Easing racial tensions and addressing minority crime concerns
- Assisting undocumented aliens, particularly Mexican nationals
- Assisting students, tourists, transients, and the elderly
- Disseminating information on AIDS

Indeed, in discussing what community policing offers, Trojanowicz and Bucqueroux (1990) note,

> By expanding police work to include addressing the full range of community concerns, including crime, fear of crime, social and physical disorder, and community decay, Community Policing gives police officers an expanded agenda that allows fuller expression of their full range of talents, skills, and abilities. And by making that all-important shift from seeing the police officer primarily as a crime-fighter to enlarging their role to that of community problem-solver, this not only opens up the scope of the job, but it changes the basic nature of the police response from an emphasis on dealing with individual crime incidents to attacking the underlying dynamics that detract from the overall quality of life in the community.

Make no mistake about it, the advocates of community policing foresee the police permanently placed within, in charge of, and managing neighborhoods.

Police departments do not have infinite resources available to them. One might legitimately ask of the list above, "Who can afford all this?" The list of good things for the police to do reads like the agenda of the Lyndon Johnson era War on Poverty. Community policing may well be the 1964 Great Society resurrected on the local level, and no more affordable than then.

Implementation of a neighborhood management mission will require that other initiatives be forsaken. In particular, the very real benefits that might be accrued from specialization cannot concurrently be harvested when grass-roots neighborhood support is being cultivated. The neighborhood management model is a resource sponge. Those who indicate otherwise have either never tried to implement the model or simply claim to be doing community policing anytime they smile at a citizen.

Indeed, superficiality pervades the current enthusiasm for community policing. Community-oriented policing does NOT consist merely of treating citizens with decency and respect. Did O. W. Wilson ever suggest that they be treated with officiousness and indifference? Further, depersonalization was not the *sine qua non* of the professional model. Rotating beats and shifts was a technique employed by some agencies to help clean out the residual corruption of the Prohibition Era. If it is true that corruption is not an inevitable result of the permanent beat assignments of community policing, then it is also true that nothing in the model of policing suggested by Vollmer and Wilson leads inevitably to the beating of Rodney King.

Real community policing techniques require substantial amounts of uncommitted patrol time. If current agency staffing is such that patrol officers are responding to a dozen calls per shift, community contact and interaction efforts are impossible. Hence, the implementation of community-oriented policing is frequently associated with concurrent implementation of call-for-service management programs.

Call-for-service management is often only a euphemism for providing less service to the public. Citizens not only have to wait longer to talk to a patrol officer at the scene but, in many instances, they won't ever see a patrol officer at the scene. Some incidents are simply declared outside the scope of police responsibility, e.g., taking property damage traffic accident reports, while other incidents are handled over the phone or by having citizens come to the police station (where there is never any public parking).

Despite the National Institute of Justice's evaluative work in Garden Grove, California; Greensboro, North Carolina; and Toledo, Ohio; it is still questionable whether the public will be happier under these circumstances. It is certainly true that a patrol officer responding to the scene of an auto theft can't do much at the scene but look at the empty parking space and note, "By golly you're right, your car isn't there any more." On the other hand, a citizen victimized by a $10,000 to $30,000 theft perhaps "deserves" to talk to a real live representative of her or his local *law enforcement* agency. Such a citizen might legitimately respond, when queried by her or his neighborhood community-oriented officer about what the police can do to improve the quality of life in the area, by saying, "Come when I call you."

Skepticism about the ability of community policing to deliver what's promised at national symposia abounds among patrol officers who have tried to implement it. It is interesting to note the duplicity illustrated by the reaction of a patrol officer's skepticism toward community policing. When promoting the value of community policing, advocates characterize working patrol officers as a talented untapped reservoir of insight and initiative. The characterization is almost "just turn them loose, then stand back." The professional model is depicted as a nemesis suppressing a bursting desire to self-actualize on the part of patrol officers.

But ten years after initiating neighborhood-oriented patrol efforts in Houston, at least 80 percent of the patrol officers involved remain strong skeptics. Most are outright cynics. Command staff indicate that at best 20 percent of the officers who have been involved in the neighborhood-oriented patrol effort are supporters. Indeed, skeptical managers point out that the 20 percent support may well represent individuals who have decided that the politically correct way to get ahead in the organization is to support the initiatives of central administration. Keep in mind these are not patrol officers who have merely received a one-hour orientation to community policing. They have had a great deal of training, have been to numerous discussion sessions on neighborhood-oriented patrol, and have been assigned to neighborhood-oriented patrol areas for a number of years. Why this degree of cynicism toward a program that hypothetically is designed to enrich the role of the patrol officer, providing her or him with enhanced responsibility and respect?

It is at this juncture that some advocates of community policing do an about-face regarding their attitude toward our average patrol officer. Suddenly these officers are retrograde Neanderthals who simply want to "cuff'em and stuff'em." Our enlightened but repressed worker becomes an unenlightened and repressive force in the agency.

There is, of course, some truth in both views of patrol officers. What we euphemistically called traditional policing conducted under the professional model was more often than not unchallenging and unfulfilling. Specialization has degraded the patrol role in many agencies to that of the security guard, "stay at your post and call a specialist if anything important comes up." There is indeed a quantity of repressed motivation, commitment, and enthusiasm waiting to be unleashed. There is also some truth in the view of patrol officers as unenlightened and authoritarian personalities. The pervasive negative elements of the national police subculture are well documented. The basic characteristics of the patrol officer role socializes individuals into dealing with all problems within at most an eight-hour time frame. The basic structure and role expectations preclude carry-forward of responsibilities beyond an eight-hour shift. Hence, "cuff'em and stuff'em" becomes a mindset.

On balance, however, I prefer to give considerable credibility to patrol officer skepticism. When I am told by patrol officers that "we are not social workers," I read more into the statement than the rejection of any intervention besides arrest. Indeed, as noted earlier, patrol officers routinely and preferably use techniques other than arrest to maintain temporal order maintenance. I think instead that the statement is a recognition of the underlying premise of this chapter — the ambiguity regarding the mission of the police at the heart of current debate regarding police strategies. Patrol officers involved in many community policing efforts recognize that they are not empowered to be neighborhood managers. They are not trained to be neighborhood managers. There isn't sufficient funding to make them neighborhood managers. They are not expected from a political perspective to be neighborhood managers. Indeed, if they tried to become neighborhood managers it is likely that reprimand or transfer would soon follow. Thus, under the rubric of community policing they are left to what Vic Strecher so aptly calls "schmooze." And they are rightfully cynical about schmooze.

Reassessing Community-Oriented Policing

The arguments presented here are not intended to imply that we reject the community-oriented model of policing. It may well be appropriate for some communities or even a large number of communities. But an evaluation can be made only after a clear definition has been established. A vague philosophy suggesting that we treat citizens responsively is a characteristic of any democratic model of policing, not just community-oriented policing. Importantly, the *relative* impact of community-oriented policing can only be assessed if comparative evaluations are possible with at least the two alternative models suggested here. And such assessment requires that we very clearly define what community policing is.

Community-oriented policing also needs to be debated on a philosophical level not subject to quantitative evaluation. There are overwhelmingly serious political implications to decentralized neighborhood management, with or without police involvement. The autonomy of the former republics of the Soviet Union is generally regarded as a welcome geopolitical change, the jigsaw puzzle balkanization of Yugoslavia is not. Decentralization isn't an automatic good. And there are certainly serious political implications to placing uniformed armed government agents with arrest authority in charge of neighborhood management.

Twenty-five years after the President's Commission on Law Enforcement and the Administration of Justice endorsed the professional model, a national bandwagon debasing nearly all the elements of that model is rolling through the country. It isn't so much the stated characteristics of the model clearly identified in *Task Force Report: The Police* that are being criticized, it is the hypothetical unintended consequences of those characteristics. History has a way of repeating itself. Twenty-five years from now we may be wondering why the unintended consequences of deploying armed neighborhood managers on every other residential block wasn't foreseen.

Reassessing Problem-Oriented Policing

For those who choose to reject the neighborhood management model, care should be exercised not to throw the baby out with the bathwater. Problem-oriented policing offers a clear alternative. Many techniques identified with community policing make intrinsically good sense, and are logically part of a problem-oriented approach. Chris Braiden in Chapter 4 describes the benefits of beat "ownership." I concur completely with his analysis. The time I remember best while serving as a patrol officer on the Lansing Michigan Police Department, and the time during which I am convinced I was the most effective, was when I was assigned permanently on midnights walking foot patrol Beat Four. From 10:00 p.m. until 6:00 a.m. between January and June of 1968 a twenty-two year-old neophyte but inspired college graduate staked out as his turf ten commercial blocks of East Michigan Avenue. He made it his business to know the people, the social interactions, what was normal, and what was not. That young officer changed his style considerably when he was rotated among automobile beats and around the clock.

Similarly, neighborhood communication and involvement certainly cannot be rejected. One may certainly legitimately debate the boundaries of police responsibility for managing neighborhoods, but one can hardly question the utility of encouraging communication and even empathy in realizing whatever objectives we choose for policing neighborhoods. Not every square block of a jurisdiction can be classified as belonging to a neighborhood, but there are certainly in every community large amounts of people and places that do constitute a real defined neighborhood.

Most important, the core concept underlying problem-oriented policing is sound. We should, however, debate the limits of police intervention into the infrastructure of a community. The Newport News experience is the best documented case of problem-oriented policing and serves well as an instructive illustration. There are three primary interventions reviewed in the case study and evaluation. (Eck and Spelman, 1987):

- Prostitution and robbery on Washington Avenue
- Thefts from vehicles in the shipyard parking lots
- Burglaries in the New Briarfield Apartment Complex

Each involved a different type of intervention, and, importantly, a different level of police intrusion into community infrastructure. See Figure 4.

The Washington Street robberies were handled by essentially coordinating and focusing relatively traditional types of police interventions. The thefts from autos in the shipyard parking lots involved the police on a different level of intervention, but not dramatically beyond past practice. It is unusual for the police to initiate legislation to help solve a problem, but not unheard of. It is less common to work directly with the city planning department. Finally, the New Briarfield endeavor represents a totally new role for the police. Here they became immersed in the community infrastructure, leading a coalition of city departments in an effort to raze and rebuild a housing project.

It is at this level of intrusion that caution needs to be exercised. The term "intrusion" is used deliberately here, because it connotes what should explicitly be recognized — the police are initiating a role new to their mission of traditional temporal order maintenance. Their role as agents of government is expanded dramatically. The issue is not whether the

Figure 4

INTERVENTION INTRUSIVENESS IN NEWPORT NEWS

Problem	Solution(s)	Level of Intrusion Into Community Infrastructure
Washington Avenue Robberies	Enforcement of Prostitution Ordinance Offender Probation Revocation Alcohol Licensee Premise Enforcement Visible Street Patrol	None to Nominal
Shipyard Thefts From Vehicles	Crime Analysis/Directed Patrol Prevention Efforts Initiated State Legislation to Upgrade Thefts to Felonies Initiated Planning for Security Redesign Participation With City Planning Dept. in Design and Location of New Parking Garages	Intermediate
New Briarfield Burglaries	Crime Watch Garbage Removal Abandoned Car Tow-Away Formed Coalition of City Depts. Legal Action Against HUD Improve Existing Structural Conditions Raze the Complex, Replacing it With a New Development	Extensive

miserable situation at the New Briarfield complex needed innovative and extensive government intervention. The issue is the initiation of a new role for police agencies. Perhaps it is true — indeed, probably it is true — that the police can best play the role of mover and shaker in New Briarfield situations. But we need to recognize that problem-oriented interventions are part of a continuum of police intrusiveness. There is an enormous difference between the Washington Avenue interventions and razing housing projects. Debate and discussion about the police role in modifying community infrastructure is needed.

Conclusion

Instead of approaching the twenty-first century with our minds made up about the model of policing that is best for a democracy, we ought to be encouraging experimentation with at least the three models identified in this chapter. As noted by Moore and Stephens (1991),

> One can seek to define the mission of a police department by trying to discover the unchanging essence of policing, or by thinking through the question of how particular police departments, embodying particular kinds of competences and capabilities, might make the greatest contributions to the quality of life in the communities in which they operate.

It has been suggested that the three models described in this chapter subsume three very different mission statements. A police department operating under the aegis of the professional efficiency and crime-specific model will focus on temporal order maintenance. Problem-oriented policing implies a mission of sustained order maintenance. Community-oriented policing requires full neighborhood management.

It is important that we not outright reject the professional efficiency and crime-specific model. It may well be the best model for a number of communities for either political or economic reasons. Even if "pure" forms of the model aren't appropriate for a given community, elements of it certainly merit consideration. Further, our large cities are a conglomerate of communities. There is no mandate requiring the same mission be pursued on every block.

It is equally important that problem-oriented policing be carefully distinguished from the community-oriented model. Sustained order maintenance is a dramatically different mission than neighborhood management. Both debate and evaluation of the problem-oriented model are stifled by its association with community policing.

Finally, and most important, it is time to jump off the community-oriented policing bandwagon. The lyrics of the siren song enticing police administrators to get aboard — *responsiveness, commitment, shared responsibility, involvement, open communication, and coproduction* — needs to be balanced against the martial beat of *omniscient, intrusive, and armed neighborhood control agent*. It is time for an era of open debate about police mission.

References

Bittner, E. (1990). *Aspects of police work*. Boston: Northeastern University Press.

Bloch, P. & Bell, J. (1976). *Managing criminal investigations: The Rochester system*. Washington, DC: The Police Foundation.

Boydstun, J. E. (1975). *San Diego field interrogation: Final report*. Washington, DC: The Police Foundation.

Cordner, G. W. & Trojanowicz, R. C. (1992). Patrol. In G. W. Cordner & D. C. Hale (Eds.), *What works in policing*. Cincinnati: Anderson Publishing Co.

Eck, J. E. (1983). *Solving crimes: The investigation of burglary and robbery*. Washington, DC: Police Executive Research Forum.

Eck, J. E. (1992). Criminal investigations. In G. W. Cordner & D. C. Hale (Eds.), *What works in policing*. Cincinnati: Anderson Publishing Co.

Eck, J. E. & Spelman, W. (1987). *Problem-solving: Problem-oriented policing in Newport News*. Washington, DC: Police Executive Research Forum.

Federal Bureau of Investigation. (1991). *Crime in the United States* [Uniform Crime Reports]. Washington, DC: U.S. Government Printing Office.

Greenwood, P. & Petersilia, J. (1975). *The criminal investigation process — Volume I: Summary and policy implications*. Santa Monica, CA: RAND Corporation.

Kelling, G. L., Pate, T., Dieckman, D., & Brown, C.E. (1974). *The Kansas City preventive patrol experiment: A technical report*. Washington, DC: The Police Foundation.

Koby, T. G. & Lucy, V. M. (1992). Two promising concepts in trouble. *Law Enforcement News*, XVIII, 352 (February 14, 1992).

Martinson, R. (1974). What works? — Questions and answers about prison reform. *Public Interest*, 35, 22-54.

Mintzberg, H. (1989). *Mintzberg on management*. New York: The Free Press.

Moore, M. H. & Stephens, D. W. (1991). *Beyond command and control: The strategic management of police departments*. Washington, DC: Police Executive Research Forum.

Pate, T., Ferrara, A., Bowers, R., & Lorence, J. (1976). *Police response time: Its determinants and effects.* Washington, DC: The Police Foundation.

Peters, T. J. & Waterman, Jr., R. H. (1982). *In search of excellence.* New York: Harper & Row, Publishers Inc.

Simon, H. (1945). *Administrative behavior.* New York: The Free Press.

Strecher, V. G. (1991). Histories and futures of policing: Readings and misreadings of pivotal present. *Police Forum,* Academy of Criminal Justice Sciences Police Section, 1(1) (January).

Trojanowicz, R. & Bucqueroux, B. (1990). *Community policing: A contemporary perspective.* Cincinnati: Anderson Publishing Co.

Walker, S. (1989). *Sense and nonsense about crime* (2nd ed.) Pacific Grove, CA: Brooks/Cole Publishing Co.

Williams, H. (undated). Commentary on the video *Foot Patrol.* Crime File Video Series. Washington, DC: The Police Foundation and Television Station WETA.

Chapter 2

Matching Structure to Objectives

Timothy N. Oettmeier

Introduction

The police managers of today find themselves working in a paradoxical environment. As is the case with any municipal department head, police managers are expected to "hold the line" on resource expenditures. However, as the competition for dwindling tax dollars escalates between local, state, and federal bureaucracies, the public is demanding more action to curb the escalating disorder, violence, and immoral behavior that has once again emerged in force to take over our streets and neighborhoods. Even though the public demands continued accountability and efficiency, they also expect their respective law enforcement agencies to take immediate action to reclaim their supremacy in the constant, ongoing battle against crime and disorder.

Management, consequently, is placed in a precarious position of having to balance a commitment between austerity and creativity. Austerity is reflected in the administration of no-growth, retrenchment, or cut-back operational strategies. Creativity is demanded by the increased volume and sophistication of today's crime and disorder problems. Quite simply, police managers are expected to perform minor miracles when in actuality it takes a magnanimous effort by them to just keep their heads above water.

There is no question that the nature and scope of this paradox varies from one city to the next. Each city contributes what they can to support their local law enforcement effort. As expected, the size of departments varies from one jurisdiction to the next. The differential is quite spectacular, ranging from a predominance of ten or less members on a force to New York

City's unbelievable contingent of 26,000 plus classified personnel. Despite this obvious difference, all police agencies share two distinct commonalties: the functions they perform and the manner in which their agencies are organized.

For the past several decades, police departments have clung to the premise that their primary responsibilities are basically reactive in nature. Management's task is to allocate resources and direct operations in response to increasing reactive demands. The organization is structured to support and maintain this narrow commitment.

However, given today's economic and environmental demands and the perceived ineffectiveness of current strategies, police managers are now confronted with having to think differently about the nature of police work. Instead of focusing attention on procedural concerns brought about by the demand to react to incidents, police managers are beginning to think in terms of addressing substantive issues or problems. Unfortunately, this change is slow to materialize, as evidenced by Goldstein's (1990) observations:

> Relatively little in the current organization and staffing of police agencies reflects a regular, continuing institutionalized concern for substantive manners.   Some agencies and administrators get closer than do others.   Some get involved when a problem becomes a crisis.   But the field as a whole has seldom taken a serious, inquiring, in-depth interest in the wide range of problems that constitute the business, nor does it have the tradition of proceeding logically from knowledge gained about a particular problem to the fashioning of an appropriate response (p. 15).

In laying the groundwork for problem-oriented policing, Goldstein is implying police managers must begin to think differently about the nature of police work; that there is more to policing than just reacting to and processing incidents.

A commitment to substantive issues cannot be easily attained without first overcoming a couple of obstacles. Chief among them is the organization itself. As police officers begin to flex their intellectual capabilities, they rapidly discover the debilitating effects the organizational structure places on them. Since organizations are generally designed to reflect functionality, creative officers should expect to be stymied by bureaucratic processes that support a different set of assumptions. According to Bieck and colleagues (1991), operational assumptions postulated within a heavily laden bureaucratic police agency tend to reflect the traditional mindsets people have about the patrol function.

A second obstacle centers upon the notion that structural characteristics (e.g., centralized authority, rigid chain of command, strict adherence to rules and regulations, closed to the community, etc.) of a bureaucratic police organization are designed to promote "administrative convenience." In other words, policies and procedures become the ends in and of themselves rather than a means to an end. Emphasis is placed more on the efficient performance of internal procedures than on the service delivery product. Bieck and colleagues (1991) cautions that while internal issues cannot be ignored the police must devote attention to questions that any service industry needs to address: "consumer" satisfaction, service effectiveness, the likely emergence of new problems, and concomitant demands for service.

When service objectives begin to change, they are apt to require accompanying administrative and operational adjustments to occur within the organization as well. These adjustments, brought about by role conflicts, cause stress and tension to occur among officers and management alike. Probably one of the most difficult tasks confronting personnel working within this type of environment is to attain consensus on roles and responsibilities.

What aggravates this dilemma under traditional thinking is the preeminence of "discensus" over consensus as to what officers could and should be doing. This confusion not only exists within the rank and file, but also extends to supervisors. The situation is compounded for supervisors as they experience confusion not only among their peers, but also with their officers and immediate superiors. Given Bieck and colleagues' (1991) observation about the changing service demands being placed on officers, the process of consensus building among and between officers, supervisors, and management will continue to experience aggravation.

A change in service objectives can also cause "structural stress" to occur within the organization. The quasi-military stature of police organizations is quite rigid and unforgiving. Klockars (1985) claims the quasi-military model is organizationally primitive in large part because of its reliance on hundreds of rules and regulations that promulgate control and because of management's desire to induce productivity through the use of punishment. Rigidity is also reinforced through the use of formalized communication channels that inhibit decision making. Illogical organizational configurations lead to replication of services and wasted expenditures of valuable resources. The inability of the organization to develop the capacity to acquire and process information keeps people uninformed and misinformed causing frustration and confusion.

If this stress is not alleviated, managers and supervisors will become lethargic and cynical; quick to point out that there is nothing more they can do. Officers, in sensing little support from above, will seek safety and comfort in doing just enough to get by. Thus, the status quo remains intact, the structural integrity of the traditional organization is no longer threatened, and the unsuspecting public is left receiving an inferior product.

While there is no one best method for avoiding this predicament, there are a few things police practitioners can come to understand and upon which they can act. First, police managers must understand how traditional functions within policing are evolving. They must recognize that as functional responsibilities expand for officers, there will be a commensurate change in management's roles. Second, management must integrate functional responsibilities within the organization in a manner that is consistent with being able to address community problems and concerns. Finally, organizational structures must be reconfigured so as to not impede management's ability to assist officers in the attainment of their respective objectives. The importance of reconfiguring structures cannot be understated, especially when the objectives are products of collaborative efforts between officers and the citizens they serve.

The Patrol Function in Transition

There has been relatively little disagreement over the fact that policing has been evolving over the past several decades. Kelling and Moore (1988) have classified this change process using a trichotomy that analyzes three different policing eras. While there is considerable debate as to the accuracy of their interpretation of the historical developments (see Strecher, 1991; Williams and Murphy, 1990) that led to their classification scheme, they did examine functionality across all three paradigms. The one constant function contained within the analysis of each of the eras was, to no one's surprise, crime control. What is surprising, however, is how police agencies have operationalized their commitment to crime control.

Historically, the primary reason for allocating police resources has been and, in many instances, continues to be based on the need to respond to calls for service. Crime control was addressed in tandem with handling calls for service through the use of the random, preventive patrol strategy. For years it had been assumed that there was an inherent link between random, preventive patrol and crime reduction.

Bieck and colleagues' (1991) insightful analysis of the patrol function attributes this link to the belief in several assumptions by police managers. The first assumption proclaims the police will intercept criminal activity as a direct result of their randomness and perceived omnipresence by the criminal. The second assumption centers on the belief that a highly visible presence of the police will deter criminal activity. A third and final assumption claims rapid response to all calls for service will have a measurable effect on crime.

Given these assumptions, one should not be surprised by management's oversimplified interpretation of the patrol function. As depicted in Figure 1, police officers are expected to perform two primary responsibilities: respond to calls for service and conduct random, preventive patrols. This traditional perspective contains a number of interesting characteristics.

Figure 1

Traditional Perspective

Random Preventive Patrol

Calls For Service

Reactive System - Incident Driven
No Planning Required
No Information Support Needed
Limited Role For Officers
"Management" is Control-Oriented
Strong Supervisor Required To Maintain Control
Officer Performance Based on Conformity & "Bean Counting"
Little Incentive For Change & Innovation
"Closed System" - No Link With Community

First, and foremost, it represents a reactive system driven by the need to respond to a mindboggling number of different incidents. Officers are expected to handle calls for service as expeditiously as possible and return to service to await another call. As they wait, they are expected to patrol an assigned area randomly in an effort to deter unknown or undetected criminal activity. Since it is extremely difficult to measure the unknown, the efficacy of this strategy is highly suspect.

This traditional perspective provides the officer with a very limited role. In fact, this role is very compatible with hiring practices that seek to acquire "automatons with brawn, not brains." Hence, there is no expectation for officers to know how to plan their daily activities, nor is there a need to provide officers with information support that would help in the decision-making process.

There is little incentive for innovation or change associated with this perspective. Because officers are not expected to think for themselves, they should not be expected to deviate from preprogrammed activities. This is reinforced through the use of a performance evaluation system that stresses "bean counting." Officers are expected to handle a lot of calls, write a lot of tickets, take a lot of reports, and drive a lot of miles. Work sheets or daily logs emphasize activities and numbers not outcomes or results.

This type of environment requires strong supervisors who can maintain control. Control is justified by the supervisor's lack of trust in their officers' individual and collective capabilities. Officers must constantly ask their supervisor's permission to do just about anything, which in turn, feeds the supervisor's belief that stringent control measures are justified.

Accordingly, if a supervisor wants the opinion of one of his or her officers, he or she will give it to him or her rather than solicit it. And heaven help the officer who generates a complaint of some type that would require supervisory involvement. Supervisors do not want to perform any "additional work" generated by a complaint even if it means there is a distinct possibility the investigation will lead to the exoneration of the complaint. Officers are expected to respect the supervisor's right to "privacy" and their right to determine when and how they will perform their responsibilities.

Research Initiatives

It wasn't until the advent of the 1970s that policing began to experience significant operational and managerial changes. Spearheaded by seed money from the Law Enforcement Assistance Administration, research efforts began to proliferate. The traditional assumptions regarding interdiction, deterrence, and rapid response were rigorously tested, evaluated, and found to be misleading.

The continued reliance on the use of random, preventive patrol began to raise doubts in the minds of police officers (in Kansas City) and astute managers. The notion that random patrol directly controlled criminal activity began to be contested as evidence by the work of Riess (1971). Riess claimed that in congested urban environments with numerous police vehicles present, the limited reliable evidence suggests that criminal events are most likely to be found by a unit other than the one assigned to that area, and that discovery is largely incidental to other ongoing police activities than the conscious outcome of random patrol. Furthermore, Bieck and colleagues (1991) claims that what patrolling officers do discover are likely to be the least serious types of incidents, many of which will probably be reported to the police anyway. Moreover, "95 percent of the time an individual will not be arrested by randomly, patrolling police during or immediately following the commission of a crime" (p. 64).

A multitude of field research was conducted in several departments during the 1970s. Led by the preventive patrol and response time studies in Kansas City, other strategies and concepts began to be tested. Directed patrol was studied in New Haven, Connecticut, in addition to Kansas City's Directed Interaction Patrol initiative. Of particular importance in these studies was the use of crime analysis information to guide and direct the efforts of the officers. The use of a split-force was tested in Wilmington, Delaware, as a means of examining the use of uncommitted patrol time. The restructuring of beats and the use of call stacking procedures were seen as important support considerations that provided the officers with time to address specific neighborhood problems and concerns.

The San Diego Field Interrogation experiment and the One-Officer, Two-Officer Patrol experiment provided insight into the use of a crime deterrence strategy and resource allocation concerns. San Diego was also the site where some of today's popular community-based policing strategies were initially tried. The use of permanent beat assignments and beat profiling techniques sought to affirm the importance of information gleaned from the neighborhoods that guided the officers in providing responsive service to a variety of citizen demands.

The RAND Corporation's study (Greenwood and Petersilia, 1975), The Criminal Investigation Process sought to describe "investigative organization and practices," including among other things, how detectives spent their time and how crimes were solved. Included within Greenwood and Petersilia's (1975) findings was the recognition that

> the single most important determinant of whether or not a case
> will be solved is the information the victim supplies to the
> immediately responding patrol officer. If the information that
> uniquely identifies the perpetrator is not presented at the time

the crime is reported, the perpetrator, by and large, will not be subsequently identified (p. ix).

The RAND study, coupled with research conducted by the Stanford Research Institute (which developed criteria to help determine if a particular burglary case would have been solved if assigned) led to a number of recommendations. According to Greenberg and Wasserman (1979) they included

- increased patrol officer involvement in the investigative functions;
- increased patrol officer and detective cooperation;
- utilization of some form of early case closure (procedures); and
- increased cooperation between the police and prosecutor.

Research Conclusions

Without a doubt, the 1970s could easily be classified as the decade of research for policing. Nowhere in the history of policing had more been attempted or achieved in learning about the nature, breadth, and depth of police operations. As noted by Oettmeier and Bieck (1987), the conclusions based upon the studies conducted in the 1970s proved to be insightful and straightforward:

1) The use of random, preventive patrol should be dismissed, and the use of preprogrammed, goal-oriented patrol strategies should be increased;

2) The addition of more officers to reduce police response time to all calls for service cannot be justified as a means to increase on-scene criminal apprehensions. Citizen reporting delays tend to negate the potential impact rapid police response would have on many types of calls;

3) Effective management of the patrol function is dependent upon intelligent management of the dispatch function. Logical and interdependent linkages exist between management of the dispatch function, management of the patrol function, and management of criminal investigations;

4) The development of crime and operational analysis procedures is vital in managing the patrol and investigative functions;

5) The use of patrol officers in activities other than performing routine patrol and "running calls" has been

underutilized. Meaningful incentives are needed to attract and retain good officers in patrol and must be developed by police managers;

6) Management must recognize that, as with the patrol officers, citizens also represent an untapped resource that can provide valuable assistance in helping the police perform their work;

7) To facilitate the development of stronger ties with the community, policies that require the frequent rotation of officers across shifts must be seriously examined;

8) Attention needs to be devoted to assessing or reassessing the purpose and function of beat structures. Rather than being traditionally defined as "patrol areas" (initially developed to equalize work load), emphasis needs to be given to reconfiguring beats around neighborhoods;

9) Patrol officers should be allowed to perform some follow-up investigations and obtain early case closures if sufficient time is available; and

10) Case management systems must be developed and implemented to fit the needs of various investigative functions (pp. 16-17).

In having reviewed some of the pertinent research findings governing police operations and having assessed the ensuing implications, it is not surprising that the findings from these studies made many police administrators nervous.

It was of no small consequence that it became exceedingly difficult for chiefs of police to defend the traditional rationale that had been used for budgetary increases for additional officers and more equipment. And the economic milieu of the 1970s with recession, inflation, fuel shortages, and "Proposition 13s" provided credence to elected officials who, in light of the research findings, sought justification to chop police budgets.

Many chiefs of police did not survive the momentum for change that began to build during the past decade. But for most of those who did they brought a different philosophy of municipal policing into the 1980s. Influenced by the events of the 1960s and the research of the 1970s, this philosophy contained an expression of values regarding human life, personal dignity, and individual rights. It also contained a change in emphasis that diminished the perception of police officers from being primarily "enforcement oriented" to becoming more receptive and open in working with the public to prevent crime and identify and suggest solutions for crime and noncrime citizen concerns (Oettmeier and Bieck, 1987, p. 17).

The Emergence of a New Perspective

If the 1970s was characterized by a commitment to research, the 1980s saw a commitment by police departments to reassess their relationship with the community. The notion of "community policing" began to sweep across the country like a grass fire. Because of its political popularity and perceived effectiveness, police chiefs were being asked to implement the concept within their own agencies.

Despite the popularity of community policing, there was (and still is) no agreed upon definition of what the concept represents. It has been referred to as a strategy, a program, a process, an ethos, and as a philosophy. In retrospect, it may yet be classified as a trend or a brief fad. Irrespective of its classification, the 1980s saw a pronounced commitment to the concept. It seemed as if "everyone" wanted to claim they were doing community policing, but no one was really sure what it was they were supposed to be doing.

Despite popular perceptions to the contrary, there has been no logical progression in the development of community policing. There is no definitive literary piece that accurately describes or substantiates the birth of community policing. Even Kelling and Moore's (1988) paradigm model comes under a scathing attack by Strecher (1991) on the basis of their misinterpretation of history. Because there has been no consensus on how to define community policing, departments have been left up to their own devices to determine how it should be implemented.

Absent this consensus, police agencies have experienced a "group grope" phenomenon. Management within these agencies sensed that something was amiss. They heard what other agencies were doing, but they were not sure just exactly what it was and how it differed from what their department was doing. They began to think in terms of who they could call or where they could send someone to observe "the program" in action. Of course, in their hearts, they were hoping their emissary would discover the proverbial "cookbook" of community policing and bring it home. Once home, management would rapidly digest the information and to no one's surprise, breathe a sigh of relief when they realized they had been doing community policing all along; they just called it something else. Thus, the agencies would continue conducting business with a false sense of assurance that they too were a community-based police organization.

The problem with this scenario is that most police agencies are not community-based police agencies. Goldstein (1979), for one, claims "the police have been particularly susceptible to the 'means over ends' syndrome" (p. 236). Management has continued to place more emphasis on improving the organization and operating methods than on the substantive outcome of their work. Goldstein (1990) contends, (that) focusing on the substantive, community problems that the police must handle is a much more radical step than it initially appears to be, for it requires the police to go beyond taking satisfaction in the smooth operation of their organization; it requires that they extend their concern to dealing effectively with the problems that justify creating a police agency in the first instance (p. 35).

As simple as this may sound, deciding just exactly how a police agency is supposed to embrace problem-oriented policing, in light of its commitment to community policing, caused much consternation and debate throughout the 1980s. Statements indicating one is "into problem-oriented policing but not community-oriented policing" exemplify the state of confusion.

Whereas Goldstein (1987) contends a basic prerequisite for realizing the potential in community policing is to develop a commitment to analyzing systematically the problems that the police are called upon to handle and to work for the development of more effective responses to these problems; police management has responded by creating short-term programmatic approaches or by establishing specialized community-oriented policing units.

Examples abound led by Flint, Michigan's, police department. They instituted a foot patrol strategy in which the patrol operation was bifurcated into motorized patrols and "community-based" foot patrols. In Maryland, Baltimore County's Citizen Oriented Police Enforcement program initially established a specialized problem-solving unit that coexisted with regular patrol units. In Madison, Wisconsin, an "experimental patrol district" was established for the expressed purpose of field testing new operational and managerial strategies that were consistent with the community-oriented policing philosophy.

The New York City Police Department implemented a Community Police Officer Program that sought to place "community police officers" in precincts with regular patrol officers. While the patrol officers handled the calls, the community police officers were allowed to work, without interruption to handle calls on localized crime and disorder problems. This program has not only been expanded to all seventy-five precincts, but a specialized experimental precinct has been targeted to field test the integration of responsibilities between regular patrol officers and community-oriented patrol officers.

The Houston Police Department also sought to isolate its experimentation with community-oriented policing. Initial exploratory efforts were limited to three of the city's twenty master police districts. However, Houston did not bifurcate its patrol force, nor did it opt to establish specialized problem-oriented enforcement squads. Houston's Neighborhood-Oriented Policing (NOP) concept calls for the formation of a cooperative agreement between police officers and citizens to work together in the prevention and control of crime in the city's neighborhoods. In having recognized both the need and importance to modify traditional management thought regarding a new and different approach in providing service delivery, NOP has acquired an additional overtone as constituting a management philosophy. According to Oettmeier and Bieck (1988),

> NOP provides a conceptual framework to direct a multiplicity of organizational functions designed to improve the quality of life in the city of Houston. As with any management philosophy, NOP is "results-oriented." Explicitly in focus, NOP seeks to integrate the desires and expectations of citizens with actions taken by the department to identify and address conditions that negatively impact the city's neighborhoods and, therefore, community life in general (p. 4).

The key to successful implementation of NOP in Houston is in having police officers recognize the multiplicity of organizational functions they are expected to perform.

To assist patrol officers in the department's transformation to institutionalize NOP throughout the organization, an "operational continuum" was developed (W. A. Bieck, personal communication, 1988). This continuum has been and still is being presented within a multitude of educational workshops, training sessions, and as a permanent part of the recruit training curriculum within the department.

The operational continuum consists of three functional components: a reactive function that focuses on immediate responses, a proactive function that focuses on tactical responses, and a "coactive" function that focuses on strategic responses.

The Reactive Function

This function is as viable now as it was several decades ago. Despite the rhetoric that police agencies should minimize their commitment to reactivity, it still represents the bulk of what the public expects police agencies to do. This function consists of several responsibilities to be performed by the patrol officer, all of which are critical to maintaining order and combating crime. Among them are handling calls for service, arresting criminals, enforcing local and state traffic ordinances, conducting initial investigations, and, when visibility is a necessity, performing random, preventive patrol. Of the five responsibilities, handling calls for service engulfs most of the officers' time.

With the implementation of numerous differential police response strategies (e.g., use of prioritization codes, call stacking procedures, supervisory override, and teleserve), departments are trying to accumulate more uncommitted time for the officers while simultaneously managing the call load so citizens continue to receive the service they expect. Goldstein's influence can also be felt in utilizing the analysis of repeat call information to isolate and analyze certain types of incidents. If a determination can be made as why these incidents persist, specific resources can be directed toward overcoming the causative factors.

Although there is open debate over just how much time an officer has available when not handling calls for service, the real challenge is encouraging the officers to direct their uncommitted time toward specific objectives rather than perform random, preventive patrol. For the past several years, it has been suggested that random patrol begets random results (Oettmeier and Bieck, 1987). Unless there is a specific need for visibility within a neighborhood or business area, officers are encouraged to proactively redirect their efforts toward specific objectives.

The Proactive Function

This function requires officers to develop directed or structured patrol strategies in response to identified crime and disorder problems that exist within or among neighborhoods. The objective of these strategies is to "proactively" initiate action to interdict criminal activity, which is accomplished by aggressively pursuing the suspect(s) through the use of multiple strategies.

Directed patrol strategies can be initiated by police officers, sergeants, crime analysts, and, in some instances, on the basis of information gleaned from citizens. Examples of directed patrol strategies include aggressive patrol tactics (e.g., saturation patrols, traffic stops, channeling, etc.), covert tactics (e.g., stakeouts, use of plainclothes, etc.), and surveillance (e.g., physical and electronic) tactics.

Directed patrol strategies not only require time, but also information and a commitment to short-term tactical planning. Information comes in the form of an analysis of crime patterns or trends from crime analysis units. For example, when a series of robberies or burglaries occur, if several victims have been raped or assaulted, or if violent acts are attributed to the actions of a gang of juveniles, the public expects that the police will first identify the transgressions and second will respond quickly and effectively.

As information about these problems is received by the officers, they have the option of developing a tactical plan(s) to combat the problem(s). Tactical plans can be initiated from two sources. First, a tactical action plan can be generated from crime analysts. Information, formatted to facilitate the planning process, consists of identifying a crime pattern(s) or trend(s), describing characteristics of the crime, and posing a series of questions to prompt supervisors and officers as they work to develop an appropriate field response. Detailed information is requested about the plan, results are documented, and feedback to the crime analysts is required once the plan has been implemented.

A second type of plan, sometimes called "patrol management plans" (PMPs), can be initiated from patrol officers. These plans require officers to identify problems, objectives, strategies, resources, and anticipated results before taking action (Oettmeier, 1985). Conceptually, the PMP is designed to help officers manage their time by requiring the development of a logical approach to identifying and resolving problems. The documentation provides the supervisor with a means of justification for implementation and accountability for the action taken.

A final proactive responsibility is the performance of follow-up investigations. Patrol officers should be allowed to take a more active role in conducting investigations. Greenwood and Petersilia's (1975) summary of the RAND study noted,

> Of those cases that are ultimately cleared but in which the perpetrator is not identifiable at the time of the initial police incident report, almost all are cleared as a result of routine police procedures . . . that is, they required no imaginative exercise of investigative experience and skills . . . . Investigative "special action" made a perceptible difference in only three types of crimes: commercial burglary, robbery, and homicide. In these crimes, we found that roughly 10 percent of the cases were solved as a result of nonroutine initiatives taken by investigators (p. 27).

This suggests there is no magical "waving of the wand" when it comes to conducting investigations. Nor does it bode well for requiring specialists to perform all types of investigations, especially since RAND claimed the responding officer to the initial scene of a crime is the key to successfully closing a case (Greenwood and Petersilia, 1975). Therefore, the performance of follow-up investigations must be an important part of an officer's repertoire of skills. Ultimately, as patrol officers become more adept in performing their investigations, more early case closures will result, thereby reducing the volume of follow-up work assigned to investigative personnel.

The proactive function incorporates the performance of four basic responsibilities: directed patrols, crime analysis, tactical planning, and follow-up investigations. Self-initiation is a common theme woven throughout each of these responsibilities. The police assume direct responsibility for taking action, whereas the public is viewed as a "passive observer."

However, despite knowing that crime patterns arise from a wide variety of conditions such as opportunity, citizen apathy, and victim vulnerability, a proactive response might not be sufficient. Academicians and practitioners alike suggest such problems can best be handled by a combination of the police, the public, and other public and private service organizations working together. Among the terminology describing this activity is coproduction (Skogan, 1985) or coactivity. This term was presented to the author at a time when efforts were being made within the department to operationalize NOP in a manner that did not dichotomize traditional patrol responsibilities from newly emerging responsibilities. The creation of this continuum and associated components has helped officers and managers alike understand NOP in a nonthreatening manner. (Bieck, 1988).

The Coactive Function

This function, which represents the third and final component of Bieck's operational continuum, can best be defined as an active outreach and systematic engagement between the police and the public for the expressed purpose of identifying and addressing localized problems of crime and disorder. Coactivity operates on the premise that once officers establish contact with the citizens, communication will ensue. Extensive, consistent communication focusing on the identification of crime and noncrime problems will eventually evolve into a relationship characterized by trust. As trust is formed, the willingness to exchange information increases (Sitz, 1987). This is important, as noted by Skogan, "because citizens hold a virtual monopoly over the key item necessary to succeed in combatting crime: information" (1985, p. 332).

Under the context of coactivity, officers and managers are expected to develop "strategic" or long-term plans in response to more complex and sophisticated crime problems. Unlike tactical planning, which depends upon the use of tactical crime analysis information, strategic planning is dependent upon strategic analysis. The strategic analyst obtains expertise on the basis of interaction; interaction between and among patrol personnel, investigators, other analysts, and the citizens.

The purpose of the interaction is to develop an "understanding as to why problems exist in neighborhoods." Strategic analysts will attempt to identify conditions that contribute to and perpetuate crime. Conceptually, this is quite different from determining what types of problems exist, which is the primary responsibility of the tactical crime analysts. According to Oettmeier and Bieck (1988),

> Strategic analysts will be interested in collecting and analyzing information which is traditionally not available within police

departments.   This type of information will provide insight regarding characteristics of problem causation existing within the neighborhoods.   This type of information will certainly prove useful in the planning and implementation of tactical responses and crime prevention; two activities strategic analysts should be involved in (p. 64).

Strategic planning is usually associated with addressing crime problems that do not necessarily lend themselves to short-term, tactical resolutions. The complex problems involving the acquisition, distribution, and use of illegal narcotics and abuse of prescription drugs demands long-term, coordinated efforts among many agencies. Auto theft is another sophisticated problem that cannot be readily addressed by singular actions taken by patrol officers. The problem of vice represents another area of application. Gambling, prostitution, pornography, and liquor law violations are well-organized crimes that require extensive planning and coordination of response efforts by the police.

The creation of tactical response units, whose responsibility is to plan and implement tactical operations designed to interdict citywide criminal activity, requires the use of strategic planning skills. These units focus on the problem of apprehending criminals who have committed multiple offenses throughout the city. Strategic plans can also be used to coordinate citywide tactical interdiction responsibilities. The use of covert activities requires elaborate planning and communication with patrol and investigative personnel to ensure success and minimize danger through inadvertent exposure.

Another critical coactive responsibility is self-direction on the part of the patrol officer. As officers become more familiar with their assigned area, their knowledge of what services are needed increases. Management must entrust and empower the officers to take definitive action in response to those demands. It also means the officers must begin thinking and acting like "managers."

The coactive function requires officers to be able to manage their own time and the utilization of available resources. Because uncommitted time periods are irregular, officers must become adept in knowing what they can legitimately accomplish within reasonable time frames. Complete success will be based on the department's ability to devise a system for managing calls for service.

Self-direction also requires an officer to manage the involvement of other officers and investigators to resolve crime problems within their respective neighborhood. Certain people may possess expertise that is needed in a given area. Officers are expected to contact these people, explain why they are needed, seek their assistance in addressing the problem, and learn how to coordinate their involvement (O'Keefe and Oettmeier, 1988).

It is through the responsibility of self-direction that a bond is formed between the officer and the citizens who reside and work in the officer's assigned area. This bond is characterized by a concomitant desire to identify and resolve neighborhood problems and concerns. The nature of this relation goes beyond interaction. It ascends to actual involvement and a commitment of resources by the public as they work with the police. It is through this partnership that a new functional perspective begins to emerge for policing.

This new perspective, depicted in Figure 2, seeks to combine the reactive (calls for service), proactive (directed patrol and follow-up investigations), and coactive (self-directed activities) functions. The utility of this perspective rests on the assumption that the demographic divergence found in cities defies categorical application of a single style of policing. Instead, an officer's role involves the performance of a multiplicity of functions, any of which can be required at any given time, in any given area. Although there may be times when a particular function may be emphasized over the others, it in no way diminishes the importance of the other functions.

This perspective is inextricably linked to the community through the interactive exchanges between the officers and the citizens. By developing a grass-roots process of close interaction, the department's method of establishing goals becomes directly linked to citizen's perceptions and expectations regarding localized needs. Being results-oriented, this perspective places a premium more on what is accomplished in the neighborhoods than it does on any particular style of policing. Furthermore, because of the potentially disparate viewpoints on given issues found among neighborhood residents, no one style of policing can serve most of the people most of the time (Oettmeier and Bieck, 1988).

Having recognized the evolution of the patrol function, the implications for management are overwhelming. It becomes incumbent upon management to facilitate the integration of these functions to ensure that the efficient delivery of services is consistent with neighborhood concerns and expectations.

Analyzing Managerial Implication of Change

Traditional management styles used within numerous police agencies across the country today could be characterized as reactionary in nature. There is little planning, coordination, or evaluation of efforts expended to accomplish specific short- or long-term results within respective communities. Officers generally work independently of one another with little, if any, discretionary decision-making authority. Officers seldom have the opportunity to become involved in strategy development or response

Figure 2

Emerging Perspective

Differential
Police
Response

Directed Patrol

Calls For Service

Self Directed Activity

Interactive Process Linked To Community
Information Driven
Role Expansion - Increased Responsibility
Absence of Random Patrol
Planning Required
Goal/Objective/Result Oriented
Accountability Based
More Sophisticated Management System Required
Less Militaristic Structure

implementation schemes; these activities are reserved for specialists or supervisors.

Interaction between the officer and their respective supervisor is minimal, usually initiated only on the basis of seeking clarification to a department policy or procedure or in asking permission to perform an activity deemed outside the officer's sphere of responsibility.

Traditional managers prosper within organizational milieus that place a premium on administrative responsibilities. The term management is probably a misnomer because the concept is operationalized through organizational compliance to written directives, policies and procedures, and rules and regulations.

First-line supervisors become the enforcement arm of control and are more apt to represent the epitome of a "walking encyclopedia of rules and regulations." They exude discipline, conformity, and control with an eye toward ensuring that their officers never make mistakes. Anything less is unacceptable, and immediately invokes sanctions that invariably brings about a "paper compliance phenomenon." Once again, the emphasis with the paperwork is on "dotting all of the i's and crossing all of the t's" than focusing on addressing the nature of the problem.

There is no question the concept of control is vitally important to policing and the public. But control only for the sake of control is debilitating to the organization and its people. However, if control can be redefined within the context of professional and organizational development, it can cease to be destructive. Tom Peters (1987) provides a glimpse of how this can occur by stating,

> Control is the knowledge that someone who is interested and cares is paying close attention. Real and effective control comes from a small number of simple rules (or measures) that are directly consistent with the organization's vision (p. 314).

In Peters' vision of effective management, control is not administration nor is it control via forms. Unfortunately, policing as a whole has yet to advance to this mindset. In many respects, it is not the fault of the individuals as it is a fault of the "system." For decades, policing has bred generation after generation of administrators who occasionally manage rather than managers who occasionally administer.

What the communities of tomorrow need are people who, in the truest sense of the term, are managers. They must be people who are visionary, who collect data, analyze it to identify problems, and respond efficiently and completely. The managers of tomorrow must be independent thinkers, who thrive on creativity and innovation. They must pride themselves on self-initiation and self-direction.

These managers must be obsessed with achieving qualitative results. They must realize the value of developing personnel within the organization. They have to understand the importance of system integration and synergism. Since the organization to which they belong will operate as an open system, these managers will be required to develop and maintain a global community perspective. Cultural diversity within the community will be a valued commodity within the organization and not a liability to be given little attention.

Because of their strategic focus, these managers will be required to work with and cooperate with other city agencies and city groups. There will be a willingness to be a part of a larger team effort for the betterment of the entire community.

The ability of these managers to get things done will depend more on the number of networks in which they are centrally involved than on their height in the hierarchy. Naisbitt (1982) pointed this out quite some time ago when he claimed, "the failure of hierarchies to solve society's problems forced people to talk to one another — and that was the beginning of networks" (p. 191). He goes on to claim that "networks offer what bureaucracies can never deliver — the horizontal link" (p. 196).

In examining the horizontal link, Kanter (1989) states "that managers will add value (to the organization) by deal making, by brokering at interfaces, rather than by presiding over their individual empires" (p. 89). Every manager in tomorrow's emerging police agency must be able to think cross-functionally. This is necessary because every organizational entity has a strategic role that contributes to other facets of the department. Thus, it comes to no one's surprise that "in a network environment, rewards come by empowering others, not by climbing over them" (Naisbitt, 1982, p. 204).

Kanter (1989) also suggests that "as managers spend more time working across boundaries with peers and partners over whom they have no direct control, their negotiating skills become essential assets" (p. 89). As alliances and partnerships are formed, joint planning and decision making become commonplace. Unfortunately, these cooperative efforts place managers in positions of vulnerability. Since they are more personally exposed, there will be a need to build a bond of trust that makes the partnership operate smoothly. These collaborative efforts, claims Kanter (1989),

> often bring together groups with different methods, cultures, symbols, even languages; good deal making depends on empathy — the ability to step into other people's shoes and appreciate their goals . . . . Effective communication in a cooperative effort rests on more than simple exchange of information; people must be adept at anticipating the responses of other groups (pp. 89-90).

It becomes incumbent on future managers to begin installing, what Peters (1987) calls, "horizontal management." This style requires managers to practice relationship management, to visit with and listen to the concerns of the citizens receiving the services, and, perhaps most important, to reward the people on the front line for doing a good job.

The importance of these managerial implications cannot be overstated. If functional responsibilities from expanded roles are to be integrated within the organization, managerial styles and practices must change. Managers must move away from building internal empires and protecting "precious turf." They must resist trying to outlast change because of personal disagreements and begin thinking in terms of what is good for the entire organization and the people to whom the organization was established to serve.

Probably the most formidable task confronting tomorrow's police managers is reconfiguring organizational structures to enhance their management style and facilitate the integration of the officers' functional responsibilities. If this task is not addressed, bureaucratic structures will continue to plague management's attempt to help officers attain their stated objectives.

Reconfiguring Organizational Structures

When one thinks about how a police department is organized, the first thing that comes to mind are "boxes." Police departments are depicted using lines and boxes. Although simple in form, these symbols are recognized as being synonymous with bureaucracies. Bureaucratic organizations, claims Brown (1986) are inefficient, the problem arising from multitiered hierarchies and elaborate regulations. Information flow becomes restricted and cumbersome as the number of levels and personnel increase. There is little cross-networking as most communication emanates from the command staff, which all too quickly becomes overloaded. Thus, the speed and accuracy of information becomes unreliable, thereby prohibiting effective decision making.

Even though it can be argued that organization structure must exist as a necessary means of solving problems (March and Simon, 1958), it eventually becomes problematic, undermines adaptability and vitality, and creates the incapacity to respond to the changing environment (Brown, 1986). Accordingly, it would behoove police managers to begin thinking about how they could change the structural configuration of their organization to avoid these pitfalls. More important, these adjustments will help facilitate the emergence of new operational and managerial perspectives.

New organizational configurations should be collateral in nature. They should facilitate the sharing of responsibility irrespective of who reports to whom. Attempts to determine who is at fault, if things don't go just right, or disclaiming responsibility when personal differences of opinions exist must be replaced with a commitment to help people understand so they can become productive team members. This is important to the vitality of an organization since it is always subject to change. People must always be willing to learn new things and adapt.

Coincidentally, as organizations change, they too are learning. A learning organization obtains and uses new knowledge, tools, behaviors, and values. It happens at all levels in the organization. According to Bennis and Nanus (1985),

> Individuals learn as part of their daily activities, particularly as they interact with each other and the outside world. Groups learn as their members cooperate to accomplish common goals. The entire system learns as it obtains feedback from the environment and anticipates further changes. At all levels, newly learned knowledge is translated into new goals, procedures, expectations, role structures, and measures of success (p. 191).

The "learning organization" is incompatible with the bureaucratic configuration of police organizations.

Common sense dictates that wholesale changes to present configurations are very risky. Keep in mind, that within every bureaucracy there are those who have not only survived, but prospered. It is highly unlikely they will be openly receptive to changing a system that has benefited them personally. Therefore, change should be handled carefully. Any new adjustments should be designed to coexist with traditional organizational configurations. An example of how this can occur can be seen within the Houston Police Department.

In fall 1989 the Houston Police Academy emerged from a semi-dormant state (recruit training had been closed down for three years) to a full-service support center for the department. Rather than reestablish the previous organizational structure that supported traditional bureaucratic responsibilities, a new configuration was developed to support present functional needs as well as to prepare for optimal growth and future development.

Academy personnel recognized managerial effectiveness could not be achieved in isolation. Success required a commitment to teamwork. And teamwork requires a desire and willingness to work together on behalf of all involved parties. Toward this end, a managerial triad was established to administer the operations of the Houston Police Academy. As noted in Figure 3, this triad consists of a management team, a staff advisory group, and an administrative support group.

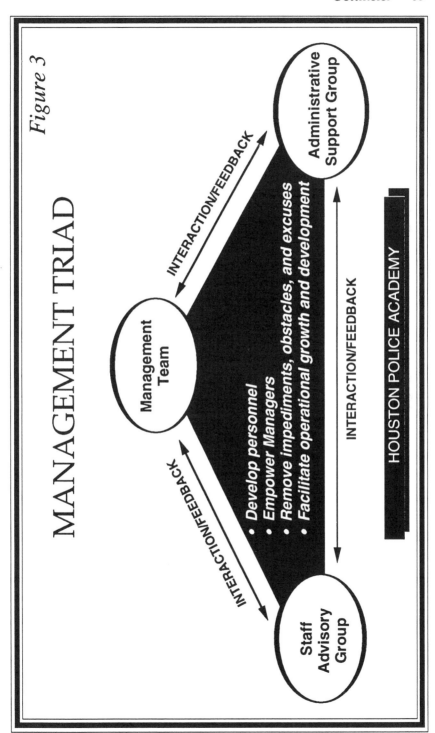

Figure 3

MANAGEMENT TRIAD

This managerial alignment provides a unique check and balance system within the academy. Officers are a part of the decision-making process by virtue of oversight responsibility. The officers are able to express their viewpoints and concerns without fear of distortion. This type of expression also provides a foundation from which growth and development can occur for the officers. If they desire to pursue ideas, develop programs, or modify existing ones, they have the latitude to do so.

Managers are entrusted with the responsibility of directing and supervising the affairs of their respective units. Equally as important though is their responsibility for managing the entire academy operation. This includes, but is not limited to, developing and administering the budget, identifying and addressing problems, and maintaining open lines of communication throughout the organization.

Administrative duties have been isolated and reassigned so as to minimize their debilitating effects on the operation of the academy. By effectively controlling administrative impediments, more time can be spent pursuing programmatic growth and development opportunities.

Each component of the management triad is briefly described below:

Management Team

The team consists of managers from each of the academy's operational units. The team has been entrusted with the responsibility of managing operational functions and addressing issues that affect the academy's day-to-day affairs. Since each manager has an obligation to contribute to the betterment of the academy as a whole, each person has access to any operational unit. Thus, if questions arise as to the effectiveness of any given unit's performance, all managers have an opportunity to work with the manager in charge to make the necessary improvements.

The management team does not defer or delegate decision making to the director of the academy unless an impasse is reached. The director is an equal member of the team. All managers are expected to work through their daily problems by consulting each other for advice. If problems arise, each manager has a series of options with which to pursue resolutions. Each manager is expected to consult with another manager(s); work with the administrative support group; or, as is frequently the case, seek advice from the management team as a whole.

Staff Advisory Group

This group consists of police officers who serve as representatives from each of the operational units within the academy along with a representative from the management team. The group's primary responsibility is to oversee the entire operation of the academy. In a very real sense, the staff advisory group serves as a "quality control check" for the academy. This means they have complete access to any operational or administrative issue within the academy that is in need of attention as determined by the group or other components of the triad.

The staff advisory group has the authority to study existing or emerging academy problems, programs, or future needs. They can form research committees or groups at will. They are encouraged to seek counsel or assistance from personnel within the academy, the department, or personnel from the corporate or academic communities.

Administrative Support Group

This group consists of civilian and classified managers who are primarily responsible for handling administrative functions and issues that affect the operation of the academy. By removing administrative impediments and obstacles, the operational managers are able to make more effective decisions. By handling administrative inquiries from other department personnel, managers and officers do not become distracted from running their respective operations.

The administrative support group is also entrusted with the challenge of analyzing opportunities for growth and development within the academy. This parallels the work of the staff advisory group, but is done so independently. Information gained from this process is provided to both the management team and staff advisory group personnel for review and commentary before a decision is made regarding adoption and implementation.

If the functional responsibilities associated with the managerial triad are to be performed effectively, a different type of organizational configuration is needed. The traditional structure depicted using interconnected boxes arranged in hierarchical manner has been abandoned. It has been replaced by a configuration consisting of a free-flowing series of integrated circles. See Figure 4. This type of configuration supports a managerial style characterized by integration, continuous interaction, and teamwork. Decision making is shared and group projects are standard as authority is equally distributed among managers and officers alike.

A unique attribute of this configuration is the creation of community liaison councils. The purpose of establishing these councils is to ensure that a continuous flow of fresh information permeates the mindset of the managers. Thus, each operational unit is required to establish their own council. Council representatives consist of personnel from the community who possess relevant skills and knowledge that are valuable to the development of the academy's ongoing operation and future development concerns. People with this expertise are asked by the unit managers to meet on a predefined

Figure 4

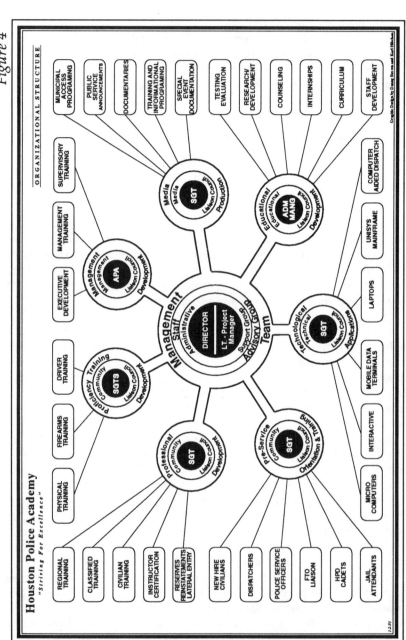

schedule to discuss problems or issues confronting the unit. Requests are made to contribute ideas toward the growth and development of that unit as well as the academy as a whole.

This type of community input is unique in the annals of police training. It signifies to police trainers and educators that community involvement can be of value beyond traditional classroom participation as an instructor. It allows police personnel to capitalize on other professionals' expertise and experiences. It also offers opportunities for new challenges to be addressed by academy personnel as they strive to build excellence within their programs and the academy operation as a whole.

Managers in any police organizational unit must be effective communicators. They must be adept at establishing information networks that will help them make sound decisions. They must work to develop the knowledge, skills, and abilities of their personnel. As consummate opportunists, the managers are expected to take calculated risks, indulge in creative endeavors, and challenge traditional assumptions. This type of organizational configuration will facilitate the performance of these managerial responsibilities. In return, the managerial triad, with its components working in tandem, ensures the attainment of organizational objectives.

Conclusion

The Houston Police Academy experience represents just one example of how organizational configurations can be altered to support evolving managerial styles while simultaneously facilitating the integration of emerging functional responsibilities. Although the application occurs within a support unit, similar steps can be taken to improve the efficiency of line units. Police departments in Madison, Wisconsin; New York City; and Portland, Oregon; are already pursuing these steps; albeit, each is at a different phase in their respective development.

What these departments and others have recognized is the need for change. It is not a question of change just for the sake of change. More important, there is an understanding of the value of building an organization that will become more responsive to dynamic and culturally diverse communities. As the demand for services continues to grow, organizations must become more flexible or they will run the risk of becoming obsolete, serving only to address their own means. Redesigning organizations so they will become less bureaucratic and more responsive to the needs and demands of our fast-paced society may loom as one of the biggest tasks confronting the police managers of today and tomorrow.

References

Bennis, W. & Nanus, B. (1985). *Leaders: The strategies for taking charge.* New York: Harper & Row Publishers, Inc.

Bieck, W. H. (1988). Internal communication, Houston Police Department.

Bieck, W. H., Spelman, W., & Sweeney, T. J. (1991). The patrol function. In W. A. Geller (Ed.), *Local government police management* (pp. 59-95). International City Management Association.

Brown, W. J. (1986). Structural reform in municipal policing. *Canadian Police College Journal,* 10(2).

Goldstein, H. (1979). Improving policing: A problem-oriented approach. *Crime and Delinquency,* 25(2), 236-258.

Goldstein, H. (1987). Toward community-oriented policing: Potential, basic requirements, and threshold questions. *Crime and Delinquency,* 33(1), (January).

Goldstein, H. (1990). *Problem-oriented policing.* New York: McGraw-Hill Inc.

Greenberg, I. & Wasserman, R. (1979). *Managing criminal investigations.* Washington, DC: U.S. Department of Justice, Law Enforcement Assistance Administration, National Institute of Law Enforcement and Criminal Justice.

Greenwood, P. W. & Petersilia, J. (1975). *The criminal investigation process.* Santa Monica, CA: The RAND Corporation.

Kanter, R. M. (1989). The new managerial work. *Harvard Business Review.,* (6), (November-December).

Kelling, G. L. & Moore, M. H. (1988). The evolving strategy of policing, *Perspectives on policing.,* (4).

Klockars, C. B. (1985). Order maintenance, the quality of urban life, and police: A different line of argument. In W. A. Geller, *Police leadership in America -- crisis and opportunity* (pp. 309-321). New York: American Bar Association, Praeger Publishers.

March, J. G. & Simon, H. A. (1958). *Organizations*. New York: John Wiley & Sons Inc.

Naisbitt, J. (1982). *Megatrends: Ten new directions transforming our lives*. New York: John Wiley & Sons Inc.

O'Keefe, J. & Oettmeier, T. N. (1988). Field training implications of Houston's neighborhood oriented policing initiative. *The Field Training Quarterly*, The Houston Police Department, 2(4), 11-18.

Oettmeier, T. N. (1985). *The D.A.R.T. conversion report*. Houston: Houston Police Department.

Oettmeier, T. N. & Bieck, W. H. (1987). *Developing a policing style for neighborhood oriented policing: Executive session #1*. Houston: Houston Police Department.

Oettmeier, T. N. & Bieck, W. H. (1988). *Integrating investigative operations through neighborhood oriented policing: Executive session #2*. Houston: Houston Police Department.

Peters, T. & Austin, N. (1985). *A passion for excellence: The leadership difference*. New York: Random House Inc.

Peters, T. (1987). *Thriving on chaos: Handbook for a management revolution*. New York: Alfred A. Knopf Inc.

Reiss, A. J., Jr. (1971). *The police and the public*. New Haven, CT: Yale University Press.

Sitz, D. (1987). *Lesson plan for orientation training*. Houston: Westside Command Station, Houston Police Department.

Skogan, W. G. (1985). Making better use of victims and witnesses. In W. A. Geller (Ed.), *Police leadership in America — Crisis and opportunity* (pp. 322-339). New York: American Bar Association, Praeger Publishers.

Strecher, V. G. (1991). Histories and futures of policing: Readings and misreadings of pivotal present. *Police Forum*, Academy of Criminal Justice Sciences Police Section, 1(1), (January).

Williams, H. & Murphy, P. V. (1990). The evolving strategy of police: A minority view. *Perspectives on Policing*, Washingtion, DC: U.S.

Department of Justice, Office of Justice Programs, National Institute of Justice, 13, (January).

Chapter 3

Community Alliance

David L. Carter

> *The [city] manager and the mayor both told me to get the community involved with the police; they said they would support me 100 percent. So I organize this community meeting, advertise it extremely, try to sell it as a public responsibility, and only twenty-two people show up. And then, most of them are "too busy" to do anything. How do [the manager and mayor] expect me to involve the community in policing responsibilities if the "good citizens" seem to care less about it. That's one big reason why I'm not the chief any more.*

> Former Chief of Police (Virginia)

The Context

The relationship between the police and community in America has been like a flesh wound that would not completely respond to treatment. As we apply salves to the wound and treat it carefully, it begins to heal. Then, without warning, we turn our head and re-injure the wound, once again looking for medications and "wonder treatments" that will cure the injury with finality. In the 1950s we experienced the beginning of the police-community relations (PCR) movement, healing the wounds of public mistrust. As progress was being made, re-injury occurred with the aggressive response of the police during the riots of the 1960s. Of recent, the community-oriented policing (COP) movement has appeared as a potential "wonder treatment" for police-community alliance, only to be traumatized by the videotape of the Los Angeles police officers beating Rodney King — an incident that rekindled festering concerns about our brothers' keepers in communities across the country. The Los Angeles riots following the Rodney King verdict once again moved the issue to the national political agenda.

Making the police and community allies in a "war against crime" as well as the goal of increasing the quality of life in a community is something that both want. Yet obstacles appear to present themselves continually when initiatives are made to strengthen the relationship. These obstacles — endemic issues — have been the constant Achilles heal that both the police and community have attempted to resolve through a variety of programs and dialogue. This chapter attempts to identify the more prevalent issues, describe reconciliation initiatives to resolve the issues, and explore current movements related to stabilizing a reciprocal police-community relationship.

While a wide array of research is discussed in this chapter, there has been no attempt to address the *caveats* and subtleties involved in each of the studies. Rather, the intent is simply to provide an analytic overview of the issues, responses, and trends that permeate the realm of community alliance.

The Theory

A fundamental theoretical issue in the police-community alliance is the *social contract*. Our constitutional form of government mandates that the ultimate authority for law lies with the people. As such, the citizens empower the government to create police forces that, acting in concert with the community, will maintain order in society. Thus, *social contract* essentially means that the police derive their authority from the community. In accepting that authority, the police agree to perform their function in a manner consistent to community social and moral standards as well as within the standards of law. The community, in exchange, agrees to support the police (fiscal support, legal support, emotional support) as an institution responsible for maintaining the sanctity of community standards. Moreover, while the police have the authority to restrict behavior and exercise *reasonably* intrusive practices *with just cause*, they remain accountable to the public. Police behavior should reflect both the *letter* of the law and the *spirit* of the law (i.e., a recognition of applied police discretion). An inherent recognition of the social contract is that authority and responsibility rest with the community, *and* the police are accountable to the community.

The evolution of our society has drawn us away from these basic principles. Populations have grown, policing has become both more complex and more "professionalized," and technological advances have touched virtually every aspect of our society. These, among many other social development dynamics, have made the police (as well as other elements of government) become *institutionalized* — that is, they tend to act as social entities in and of themselves, regardless of the obligations to their "roots." This phenomenon has resulted in increased isolation and alienation between the police and community.   Certainly, the nature of the police-community alliance must be different today than it was two centuries ago, but that alliance — an alliance with constitutional and social origins — must be fulfilled.

Community alliance is a broad conceptualization of efforts to enhance the relationship, communications, and reciprocity between police authority and responsibility and the needs of the public. This chapter explores issues, obstacles, and remedies that have encircled the goal of a homeostatic community alliance.

The Issues

Why has there been such difficulty in developing and maintaining a stable alliance between the police and the community? The answer, in a nutshell, is that it is the "nature of the beast." This dissonant relationship is a function of the nature of the policing responsibility in a free society. There are a number of endemic issues — problems that do not appear to be "resolvable" — that have permeated the police-community relationship. This section will explore some of the more prevalent issues that have placed a strain on the alliance between the police and community.

Excessive Force

Some people don't listen to you unless you're rough.   A good thumping also shows the . . . . whose boss.
Police Officer (California)

Whenever any police officer uses excessive force, it undermines the public respect for all of law enforcement.
Police Officer (Florida)

There is, perhaps, no single issue that stirs emotion in the police-citizen relationship so fervently as the use of excessive force (Carter, 1984, 1985). It was recently emphasized in Los Angeles how quickly the tide can turn. The Los Angeles Police Department (LAPD) has enjoyed a reputation as a professional law enforcement agency that is well trained and proactive in dealing with crime problems — a reputation that, perhaps, was much stronger in the public's mind than in that of the law enforcement community in general.

LAPD, and Chief Gates in particular, have been credited for beginning the Drug Abuse Reduction Education (D.A.R.E.) program, a school-based antidrug education program that has become a fixture in schools nationwide. In addition, because of the gang and violence problems Los Angeles has experienced, the department initiated a number of programs such as "street sweeps" in the Rampart and Newton Divisions of LAPD as proactive means to deal with these problems. These activities received widespread support from citizens and even gained notice from the White House in both the Reagan and Bush administrations.

Within this framework of a professional image and wide public support for both the LAPD and Chief Gates, the Rodney King incident occurred. Across the country the videotaped images of LAPD officers beating and kicking a black man enraged the public — including President Bush. The fire heated up when transcripts of officers' messages on the Mobile Digital Terminals (MDTs) were publicized containing racial slurs and comments about the routinization of excessive force as a tool of the officers. Immediate calls were made for Chief Gates resignation and The Christopher Commission was created to investigate this and related incidents.

The salient point to note was that while the public had shown strong support for the LAPD and its programs, the support was tenuous. Following the telecast of the King videotape, there were virtually no comments that this was an anomalous incident; rather the public focus was on the horror of officers using excessive force. The reader is cautioned that there are many dynamics involved in this illustration, yet for the current discussion one should note the fragility of the alliance between the police and community. The community, as illustrated in this case, wants the police to be proactive in dealing with such things as drugs and violence. Yet, that proactivity *must* be tempered by constitutional controls.

Moreover, an undercurrent of the Rodney King incident, the alliance (or lack thereof) the police have established with the *different* communities it serves (c.f., Manning, 1978), was aptly demonstrated by attitudes and actions of various groups in the south central Los Angeles riots. While critical of the police in this case, the middle- and upper-class white communities in Los Angeles tended to view the incident as being the exception to the rule. However, the poorer and minority communities charged that this behavior was commonplace. It was argued that this was a discriminatory action by the police that had become institutionalized as a means to deal with crime in Los Angeles.

Important lessons in community alliance learned from this incident first focuses on the fragility of the police-community relationship. Furthermore, different types of alliances must be established with different communities. While law enforcement provides a great deal of lip service to this need, action is not always forthcoming.

Corruption

Free meals, discounts, and things like that aren't corrupt.   It's the way the public shows its appreciation for the police.
                                                    Field Training Officer (Missouri)

Corruption is counter to everything we stand for — yet it seems we can't escape it.
                                                    DEA Agent (District of Columbia)

Law enforcement has experienced a notorious legacy of corruption from informal individual graft to institutionalized cases of bribery and manipulation (Dombrink, 1991). The "professionalism movement" in policing — notably in the 1970s — addressed the issue of corruption by aggressive internal investigations, more careful hiring practices, upgrading of standards, better supervision, and generally increasing the quality of management. However, in recent years, law enforcement has experienced a "new generation" of corruption as a result of the vast amount of money in the illicit drug trade (Carter, 1990a, 1990b).

Certainly, when corruption occurs there is a loss of public confidence in the police because, by its very nature, officers have abrogated their oath of office. In essence, they have intentionally violated critical responsibilities mandated through the codification of the social contract. Efforts to enhance the police-community alliance are met with cynicism and skepticism because the public has already been betrayed through the abrogation of duty.

Fortunately, serious cases of corruption are not widespread. However, there are corruption-related problems on a less visible scale, which offer significant obstacles to community alliance — the issue of *gratuities*. There is a pragmatic debate of whether the acceptance of gratuities is corrupt behavior. From the common definitions of corruption, the acceptance of a gratuity — free meal, clothing discounts, and the like — is not corruption unless there is actual or expected favorable behavior by the officer extended to the person providing the gratuity *is a result of the gratuitous act* (Barker and Carter, 1991).

From a philosophical perspective the situation is somewhat different. Many citizens perceive the acceptance of gratuities as corrupt behavior. Public comments are all too common such as, "He'll never get a ticket; he gives cops free meals all the time." This perception can be as damaging to community alliance as the serious cases of corruption because the same dynamics of mistrust and perceived abrogation of duty occur.

Ironically, citizens themselves also contribute to "the gratuity problem." They frequently provide the opportunity for a gratuity through the offer (regardless of their motives). In many ways this is a "chicken and egg" issue: whose expectation for a gratuity comes first, the citizen's or the officer's? This is one reason corruption remains an endemic issue to policing.

Rudeness

I'm not rude. I'm direct. Any more questions?
> Police Detective (New Jersey)

A police officer must ***always*** *be humane and civil to* ***every*** *member of the public.*
> Police Chief (Wisconsin)

One of the most common complaints against officers — or "beefs" as it is colloquially known — is that an officer was rude. These accusations rarely come from persons arrested for serious crimes, but come from citizens receiving traffic citations, people reporting crimes to the police, or from persons simply asking directions. As in any case there are two perspectives related to the rudeness of officers. From one perspective, officers must understand their obligation to explain, even tolerate, inquiries from citizens, particularly when some type of official action is being taken against the citizen. From another perspective, citizens should try to empathize with the types of questions and demands placed on officers that become trying with repetition.

As one illustration, when I was a police officer I was repeatedly interrupted at dinner by citizens asking questions — directions, information about vehicle registration, and so forth. It seemed that every meal was peppered with these interruptions and a quiet meal was impossible to obtain unless I stayed in my patrol car. I rationalized that mealtime was "my time" and that the citizen interruptions were rude transgressions. I then started "evasive actions" to deal with these interruptions. As citizens approached, they would be ignored as I wrote reports or "listened" to the two-way radio. When a conversation could not be avoided during mealtime, it was usually terse with the clear communication of displeasure with the interruption. Despite receiving a citizen complaint about this rudeness, I rationalized that the behavior was warranted because personal mealtime was being interrupted by the citizens — and Internal Affairs agreed!

This experience was revisited recently while I was in a major midwestern city. Unable to locate a street, I saw a police officer eating a hamburger. Not thinking about my own meals as a policeman, I approached the officer to ask directions and was immediately — *rudely* — rebuffed with a comment something to the effect of "Can't you people leave me alone long enough to eat a hamburger?" *Deja vu.* My immediate reaction was hostility toward the officer's rude behavior; then I recalled my own experiences and realized the damage *I* had done to community relations in Kansas City.

Rudeness is an endemic problem in policing because it is an endemic problem in human nature that is magnified by the nature of the police-citizen relationship. Small, seemingly inconsequential, moments of rude interactions can maintain the fabric of conflict that will continue to serve as an obstacle in the police-community alliance.

Authoritarianism

Cops are king of the mountain — you have to be to stay in control.

Police Sergeant (Alabama)

Police authority is a heavy responsibility that becomes part of your personality.

Police Trainer (Missouri)

The literature is replete with research documenting the authoritarian personality characteristic of police officers (see Barker and Carter, 1991). Some research indicates that policing attracts persons with an authoritarian personality while other research suggests that authoritarianism is produced by occupational socialization. Regardless of its source, authoritarianism is clearly present in the police persona. Pragmatically, this has beneficial elements. The interrogation of a suspect, handling a crime scene, conducting an investigation, maintaining control at a traffic accident, and resolving a domestic dispute are all situations that police officers will be involved in and all which require a degree of authoritarianism. However, this characteristic can become dysfunctional if it emerges too strongly in situations requiring cooperation, compromise, or capitulation.

Dealing with the community, particularly in departments adopting the community policing philosophy, requires "tempered authoritarianism." On the one hand, officers will need to maintain the authoritative personality structure yet be able to relinquish this characteristic in the appropriate situation.

Many officers are able to accomplish this quite easily; many others have greater difficulty. The authoritativeness of officers, particularly when it is *not* tempered in the appropriate circumstances, is a pervasive obstacle to community alliance. Authoritative behavior directed toward citizens is interpreted as a manifestation of the ability of the police to restrict the public's freedoms. Since such restriction is counter to the "freedom philosophy" embraced by Americans, authoritarianism represents a critical obstacle to a homeostatic community alliance.

Politics

Politics is for politicians; it has no role in professional law enforcement.

Police Chief (Michigan)

You can't be a successful chief unless you are a successful politician.

Police Chief (Illinois)

Traditionally, politics has had a negative connotation. Perhaps it relates back to the "spoils era" wherein political patronage was commonplace and incompetent and/or corrupt persons were appointed as police chief. Similarly, traditional views of "glad handing" (or "schmoozing" — a term I particularly like) with influential citizens and elected officials as a means to convert them to one's views, as well as developing "favors" or obligations, was viewed as distasteful. This type of political maneuvering in the spoils era certainly had negative elements and did impart undue favoritism (in all realms of government, not just the police).

The political process has evolved and so has the police executive's role in that process — attitudes toward politics have not evolved at the same rate (as indicated by the two quotes above). It must be recognized that the police exist in a political environment that has different dimensions. At the executive level, police chiefs must be able to present budgets and negotiate policy changes within the political process. In some cases, chiefs — such as Neil Behan (Baltimore County, Maryland), former chief Joe MacNamara (San Jose, California), former chief Gerry Williams (Aurora, Colorado), and Keith Bergstrom (Tarpon Springs, Florida) — have become more aggressively political to influence legislation at the state and national levels on gun sale laws.

As a legislator from Missouri told me, ". . . politics are part of a legitimate and respectable process that is inherent in a democratic form of government." It is not a process of corruption, but one of education and informing law makers and decision makers. I am not so naive to suggest the process is pure, but this is a pragmatic view.

As police departments adopt the community policing philosophy, the role of politics becomes even more prevalent for the line-level officer. The need to interact with different units within the police department, different departments within the governmental structure, and different community constituencies require the educational and influencing skills characteristic of good politics. Unfortunately, this can be a two-edged sword for which the officer must make careful judgments.

In Flint, Michigan, for example, one officer's activism reached the degree to which he led a protest march (in uniform) in front of city hall. Needless to say, the city fathers were less than pleased with this officer's political activities. In another case, (also in Flint) an officer had become such a strong advocate for a neighborhood, citizen groups protested when the department attempted to transfer the officer to another assignment. In the latter case, the political process interfered with the department's administrative prerogative to assign personnel.

At the other end of the spectrum, if a chief or line officer becomes too enmeshed in the political process, he or she may be viewed as being too aggressive. In these cases, it may be perceived that the police department is going beyond its assigned role — a factor that can upset the delicate equilibrium of politicization and, at the extreme, lead to charges of an attempted "police state." In some respects this has occurred in England and Wales.

When the provincial constabularies were reorganized into forty-three regional police forces, English citizens expressed concern that they would lose a voice in the police role. This concern was countered with a control and funding structure that gave the policing regions input by both citizen advisors and some funding controls. Currently, there is a move by some chief constables and staff members in the British Home Office to explore the feasibility of creating a single national police force to replace the forty-three regional forces. The primary purpose would be to increase efficiency although it is argued that effectiveness would also increase. The community has generally opposed this move, even if it would save money in financially strapped Britain. The Queen's subjects simply feel that a national police force would make the police too powerful with too much political influence.

In the United States, the autonomy enjoyed by local governments would most likely not be relinquished to any notable extent to increase efficiency or effectiveness. Concern for a police state reflects, among other things, the boundaries of community tolerance for politics by police officers.

Responding to Public Needs

We can't do everything the public wants — we simply do not have the resources.

Police Official (New York)

We pay the bills. When the public shouts, the police should jump.

Citizen (Colorado)

A common perspective by the police is that analysis of reported crime and calls for service dictate the activities the police must perform. As professional law enforcement officers, the police are aware of community needs — the traditional view is that the public does not understand what they need. While there is a ring of truth to this, there is also an element of elitism (and institutional authoritarianism). As observed by Madison, Wisconsin, Police Chief David Couper (1988), "How can we possibly know what the public wants unless we ask them?" The public, it appears, wants to have input in what the police do, yet the police know best.

When the police, in good faith, pursue activities that do not necessarily fulfill community desires, then a chasm in the alliance occurs. If the community calls remain unanswered, the chasm will widen. Many of the activities the community wants the police to handle are typically viewed as "minor problems" by law enforcement — problems that consume scarce resources yet don't "put bad guys in jail."

For example, research through the National Center for Community Policing at Michigan State University has consistently shown that among the priorities the public wants the police to handle are barking dogs, abandoned cars, and trespassing juveniles. These types of incidents certainly do not have the *machismo* influence as do assaults and robberies nor do they have the headline appeal of drug busts and serial murderers. Yet, these minor incidents can touch many more citizens on a *daily* basis whereas the more serious crimes will affect a limited number of citizens for a limited time. As a result, the minor cases — which the police usually disdain — may have a greater overall effect on the quality of life in a community.

Given the broader reach of the quality of life problems and the citizen's demands to address these problems, the police should respond to these issues with the same resolve devoted to the more serious crimes. When the police do *not* respond and, even worse, tell the public that their problems are "minor" or "not important," the police-community relationship will become even more taxed.

Public Paradox

> *Cops are a necessary evil. I don't really trust them.*
>
> Citizen (Michigan)

> *I thought I knew what police officers did. Then I went on a "ride-a-long" — how eye-opening! That gave me much more respect for the police.*
>
> Citizen (Florida)

A theme that has underscored each of the issues discussed above is the public paradox as related to the police function. This paradox is an inherent element that makes the endemic issues unresolvable. The paradox is that our system of government guarantees freedoms and cherishes individual independence, free from government interference. The police represent a force that may lawfully deprive a person of those freedoms as well as lawfully invade the sanctity of one's privacy (within the realm of due process of law). While citizens recognize the need for these police powers (as per the social contract) the powers nonetheless run counter to the basic freedom ethic of Americans. As a result, a conflict in the alliance — albeit frequently subtle — typically remains between the police and the public.

Perhaps this paradox is most overtly demonstrated in traffic enforcement. A traffic stop by a police officer is a temporary deprivation of freedom. It also symbolizes a formal institutional action to penalize a person for not following prescribed rules of behavior and movement. While citizens recognize the need for traffic regulations and their consequent enforcement, the action nonetheless represents a point of frequent conflict between the police and community. Moreover, this is aggravated when compounded by rudeness of the officer and/or clear exhibition of an authoritarian attitude.

This paradox, inherited from the essence of the social contract, stands clearly as the most pervasive endemic issue in the police-community relationship — it also contributes to robust checks and balances that are necessary in our governmental system.

The Responses

Just as there are clearly identifiable endemic issues in the police-community alliance, there have been significant investments of energy and resources to resolve these problems while concomitantly attempting to fulfill the policing mandate. Conceptually consistent with the social contract, these initiatives — or responses — require efforts by both the police and community.

Civilian Review Boards

Why should civilians review police officers' decisions like a Monday morning quarterback? They don't understand what we do or what we face.

Police Officer (California)

Citizens are the ultimate authority to whom we are responsible.
We are obliged to have them review complaints about police
behaviours.

Police Inspector (Britain)

Primarily (but not exclusively) because of concerns about excessive force by officers, the movement toward civilian review boards began. The intent of civilian review was to maintain overt citizen involvement in the social contract with police by reviewing complaints against officers. The idea being that the general attitudes of citizens about the propriety of police actions would be introduced into deliberations of complaints against officers.

Among the well-documented attempts at civilian review are the Philadelphia Police Advisory Board; the New York City Civilian Complaint Review Board; the Kansas City, Missouri, Office of Civilian Complaints; the San Jose, California Ombudsman; Berkeley, California Police Review Commission; the Chicago Police's Office of Professional Standards; the Dade County, Florida, Independent Review Panel; the Portland Police Internal Investigations Audit Committee; and the McAllen, Texas, Police Human Relations Committee. Each of these attempted to provide some type of citizen input either directly into the complaint review process, as an audit process, or as an appeal process. Even in the most cooperatively formalized cases, civilian review has had mixed results. As observed by West,

There is obviously not "one best model." ... Rather, factors such as community attitude and support of the police, the presence of police malpractice problems, allegations of police department cover-ups, and the sociopolitical environment of the community must all be considered in a complaint review program (1991, p. 399).

While police departments have been generally resistant to civilian review, evaluations of these programs have found that the citizens tend to be highly supportive of the police. In many cases, civilian review has been more lenient toward misconduct of officers than have police managers (West, 1991). One reason for this is the selection of persons who provide civilian review; they are typically supportive of the police and are not truly representative of the community — particularly the poor and minority communities. This lack of representation and the supportive attitude may also be misleading if interpreted to be the sentiments of the community *in toto*.

Neighborhood Watch

> *Neighborhood Watch is a joke — it's a way to fool the public that the police are helping them.*
>
> Citizen (Kansas)

> *Neighborhood Watch is one of the best things the police have done for this city.*
>
> Citizen (Michigan)

Certainly, the intent of Neighborhood Watch was not to establish a strong police-community alliance — it was viewed as a means to help prevent burglaries and increase the probability of apprehension of criminals. The concept evolved to also include safe havens for children and to address other crime-related problems (such as vandalism) that may be present in the neighborhood.

An obvious inherent element in Neighborhood Watch is to involve the community in crime deterrence and apprehension strategies.   The organization of structured groups on a neighborhood basis not only increases the acquaintances among those within the neighborhood but also provides a forum for the police to address the community on crime prevention techniques or other issues that may arise.   As such, it increases the quality of the relationship between police and community that ultimately helps address incongruities manifest by the endemic issues. The beneficial consequences of Neighborhood Watch exceed the initial goal of the program by providing an additional avenue to strengthen the police-community alliance.

Crime Stoppers

> *I'm not convinced Crime Stoppers can really live up to its promises. It relies too much on chance to be really effective.*
>
> Criminal Justice Professor (Ohio)

> *Crime Stoppers is surprisingly effective. It not only gets citizens involved in criminal apprehension, it increases their awareness about crime in the community.*
>
> FBI Agent (Virginia)

Like Neighborhood Watch, Crime Stoppers was designed as a crime suppression and apprehension program with no explicit intent to ally the police and community. Crime Stoppers is a joint venture between citizens, the media, and police to locate and identify persons responsible for committing serious crimes (typically when there is a limited amount of evidence for investigators). Selected crimes are highlighted weekly through descriptions and re-enactments on television (or radio narrations). Citizens may make anonymous calls to report information they may have on the "focus crime" or any other crime. Selected crimes or information may also have a cash reward.

Does Crime Stoppers work? Both of the views expressed above are accurate. Crime Stoppers is very probabilistic: A person must have seen (and observed) some information about a crime *and* that crime must be selected to be aired on a Crime Stoppers program *and* that person must also see the program *and* recognize it as the crime he or she observed *and* finally report that crime to the "hotline." Despite these delimiting probabilities, Crime Stoppers has been surprisingly successful nationwide. This suggests that citizens are aware of criminal occurrences and are sufficiently concerned about crime to both watch the program and make the report to the police.

An inference one may make as an unstated result of Crime Stoppers is that the program has served as an electronic means to develop community alliance. While it lacks the traditional elements of face-to-face contact and individual "bonding" between officers and members of the community, it nonetheless provides an avenue of understanding and involvement that can support other community alliance efforts.

Volunteers

Citizen volunteers are a pain.

Police Chief (Texas)

Our volunteers have been a God-send.

Police Chief (Michigan)

For a variety of reasons related to constrained resources, community relations, and community activism, police departments began using volunteers to assist in a wide range of organizational functions. At one end of the spectrum, volunteers were used as "reserve" or "auxiliary" officers to assist in law enforcement activities. Even these programs vary widely — some reserve officers are used simply for traffic control while others, such as in Kansas City, Missouri, and San Bernardino County, California, provide reserve officers full police powers and responsibilities. At the other end of the continuum of volunteers, departments use citizens to do odd jobs at the department on an irregular or unscheduled basis.

Volunteers can be a valuable resource for a police department both because of the money saved in salaries and because of the expertise that can be gained from the volunteer. For example, the American Association of Retired Persons (AARP) has a structured process for soliciting, screening, and training volunteers to work with a police department. Relying on retired accountants, psychologists, teachers, lawyers, and other skilled persons can provide the department with expertise that may not otherwise be available.

An obvious additional advantage to volunteers is the community alliance role. They can provide a "citizens perspective" of issues as well as serve as a sounding board for policies and practices. It is hoped the volunteers will also serve as a community resource on matters relating to the police department.

The operational and community alliance roles for volunteers have great potential to increase the favorable profile of the police department. Unfortunately, most organizations do not take complete advantage of the opportunities afforded through volunteers, instead there is a tendency to treat them as interlopers in the sanctum of policing. This attitude, directed toward those who won't help the police through volunteerism, will likely have a negative effect on the police-community relationship.

Crime Prevention

> *The reality is that we can't prevent any crime.   The so-called "crime prevention" programs simply* **displace** *crime.*
> Criminal Justice Professor (Florida)

> *I didn't really believe it at first, but this stuff [crime prevention] really works!*
> Deputy Sheriff (Florida)

The sociologically based concept of crime prevention was a generally long-term approach aimed at youthful offenders. The hypothesis was that potential criminal behavior would initially manifest itself in youthful behavior. As such, juvenile delinquency was a precursor — an early warning sign perhaps — to adult criminality. Thus, in order to prevent future crime, one needed to identify youthful offenders and change their behavior. There are both theoretical and pragmatic limitations to this hypothesis, however, the basic premise appears to ring true. Unfortunately, because of legal, financial, and practical restrictions, the fruits of this hypothesis cannot be tested. Certainly, however, research in this vein contributed to greater thought about ways to *prevent* crime, not just apprehension.

The 1970s saw a tremendous growth in the "physical crime prevention" movement. As a very pragmatically oriented approach — sometimes simply known as "locks and bolts" — physical crime prevention initially relied on the premise that the more difficult it was for a burglar or thief to get access to and steal property, the less likelihood there was that the intended crime would be committed. The concept grew to include programs such as Operation

Identification wherein the premise was that a thief was less likely to steal property if it was known that the property was clearly marked and recorded, thereby making it more difficult to "fence" the goods. Other variations of this crime prevention theme grew with popularity among police departments. (For a comprehensive discussion of crime prevention see Rosenbaum, 1986).

From a theoretical perspective this movement relied on a probable fallacious assumption that a crime would be *prevented*. In fact, the likelihood is that a crime would still be committed, just not at the initially intended location — the phenomenon of *displacement*. Despite this theoretical concern police departments embraced the concept because as long as the community had been comprehensively canvassed with crime prevention surveys and "protections," displacement to another jurisdiction was fine.

Just as police departments embraced the concept, so did the public. The program seemed logical and it provided physical evidence of some behavior designed to reduce the probability of crime and, consequently, reduced the fear of crime. As in the case of Neighborhood Watch, these crime prevention programs provided an avenue for the police to open doors to the "law-abiding" community and perform a service they wanted. This, too, helped relieve some of the pressures associated with the endemic issues of community alliance. While there are many positive aspects of physical crime prevention, it lacks the depth to deal with problems to any substantive degree. Instead, it provides a cushion on which concerns about victimization and fear of crime may rest.

Police-Community Relations

> *[PCR] is nothing but hand holding and knee patting.   I guess somebody's got to do it, but I'm glad it's not me.*
> Patrol Officer (Missouri)

> *If it wasn't for good police-community relations, [the police department] would really be hurting after these lawsuits.*
> Police Captain (Texas)

With its roots at the National Center for Police Community Relations at Michigan State University in the 1950s, led by Louis Radelet, the PCR movement attempted to resolve the antagonism between law enforcement and citizens by opening lines of communication. While the initial ideas of PCR were to develop a means to exchange information, PCR evolved into a programmatic emphasis to teach officers about communications with the public; teach the public about the challenges and enigmas of police work; and develop reciprocal empathy about the plight of each group in their daily relationship.

The PCR movement was the first initiative that truly attempted to reach the community. The initial focus was to identify community leaders as a focal point for establishing a liaison with citizens. Positive relations between the community leadership and the police, it was theorized, would "trickle down" (to borrow a Reaganomics term) to community members. At the outset, PCR was largely one-sided — its focus was predominantly on changing the community view of the police and to make citizens more supportive and understanding of police actions (President's Commission, 1967). By the 1970s virtually every police department of any size had a PCR unit (or officer) and courses on PCR had become a staple in law enforcement and criminal justice college curricula (Radelet, 1986).

As the movement matured, the focus on PCR become somewhat more reciprocal. It was felt that police officers needed to learn more about the social-psychological dynamics involved in their relationship with the community. Moreover, PCR needed to be practiced by *all* officers, not just those assigned to a PCR unit. As a result, emphasis was also being placed on police training as a means to get all officers to have a more communicative — sometimes civil — attitude toward the public. Particularly in the late 1970s police departments also regularly incorporated crime prevention programs and Neighborhood Watch with the PCR unit. It was felt that this was an additional step to help the police and community communicate as well as to make an effort to reduce crime (Radelet, 1986).

PCR was the first comprehensive effort that attempted to resolve the endemic issues inherent in community alliance. The movement recognized that disequilibrium existed between the police and community and it developed programmatic strategies to address this dissonance. The goal of PCR was to establish an effective dialogue between citizens and law enforcement and, consequently, develop better support for the police as well as enhance police accountability to the public as conceptually proffered in the social contract.

Without question, the greatest focus of PCR efforts were on minority communities for this was where the greatest disequilibrium existed between the police and the citizens. The need for better relations with minorities became evident in the 1960s. With the force of the Civil Rights Movement punctuated by civil disturbances and protest marches, it became evident changes had to be made in police practices. The National Advisory Commission on Civil Disorders, the National Commission on the Causes and Prevention of Violence (1969), and the President's Commission on Law Enforcement and Administration of Justice (1967) all cited problems in PCR — particularly excessive force, deprivation of constitutional rights, rudeness, insensitivity to minorities, and discriminatory practices. As a remedy to these and other strains in the police-community relationship, each of these commissions recommended that police departments develop aggressive PCR programs.

The PCR concept is by no means dead, but it is being rethought. Concerns emerged from police executives that PCR did not delve deep enough. Despite the intent, PCR appeared to have become a veneer for police inadequacies — a predominantly *reactive* method to deal with problems. The proactive elements of PCR were limited and generally shallow.

Based on the evolving body of research on police practices and the increasingly apparent limitation of PCR programs, practitioners and theoreticians alike felt that the endemic issues of policing in general — not simply those related to community alliance — were not being effectively addressed. This is the framework from which the embryo of community policing was conceived.

Community Policing

> *[Community policing] is nothing more than social work. I became a cop to put bad guys in jail, not just to wave and grin.*
> Police Officer (Colorado)

> *Community policing saved my career. It's rewarding, it's fun, it's positive, and I put lots of people in jail as well as make lots of friends in the community. I love it!*
> Police Officer (Indiana)

Community policing emerged most evidently as a result of the experiments of the Neighborhood Foot Patrol in Flint, Michigan; the Citizen-Oriented Police Experiment in Baltimore County, Maryland; and the Problem-Oriented Policing in Newport News, Virginia (Trojanowicz, undated; Eck and Spelman, 1987). It must be recognized that community policing is a philosophy, not a tactic. It is a proactive, decentralized approach to policing, designed to reduce crime, disorder, and fear of crime while also responding to explicit needs and demands of the community. Community policing views police responsibilities in the aggregate, examining consistent problems, determining underlying causes of the problems, and developing solutions to those problems. (Trojanowicz and Carter, 1988; Eck and Spelman, 1987).

Because community policing is a philosophy, it (ideally) permeates each unit of the organization. It strives for the *depth* that PCR never achieved by involving a wide range of community members in the policing responsibility as well as designing operational policies that seek to *solve problems*. In many ways, community policing represents a formalization of the social contract by the police through the development of shared responsibility for community problems and attempting to address the issues that most directly concern the community.

Reviews of community policing experiments in Flint, Michigan; Newport News, Virginia; Baltimore County, Maryland; McAllen, Texas; Ft. Pierce, Florida; Aurora, Colorado; Houston, Texas; and other cities appear very favorable. Law enforcement appears to be more effective, officers more satisfied, and the community alliance strengthened. It has been suggested by some that community policing has become "the accepted" way of policing in America. However, the concept is still new, too many variables are untested, and the long-term effects of community policing policies is not known; simply stated, more research is needed (see Klockars and Mastrofski, 1991). Despite the unknowns, the potential for community policing appears bright. Based on the brief legacy of research in policing and what we have learned through other initiatives with community alliance, the *zeitgeist* for a more responsive and holistic philosophy appears to be embodied in community policing.

The Emerging Stability

While the endemic issues of policing cannot, by their nature, be completely resolved, they can be managed. Conflict will always exist, but good faith efforts will reduce the negative effects of the problems. In fact, it may be argued that the conflict inherent in the endemic issues is good — as noted previously, it is a form of checks and balances.

One element of emerging stability, as discussed above, is community policing. The impact it has had on the field thus far is the most significant *philosophical* change ever to occur in American law enforcement. Despite the spread of community policing and the spectacular growth of literature on the philosophy, it is by no means the norm of policing in this country. Moreover, there are no definitive evaluations to pass judgment on the operational soundness of the philosophy or the operational policies emerging from the philosophy's implementation (see Chapter 1). Despite these *caveats*, there can be no doubt that at this early point in community policing's development, it seeks to not only provide more efficient and effective police service, it also *directly* addresses the endemic issues that plague the community alliance.

Other developments are occurring in law enforcement, which also contribute to a more robust alliance. Coincidentally, these same factors support both the philosophical and operational precepts of community policing.

Values

Values are designed to be *beliefs* and *principles* by which the police department fulfills its responsibilities. They represent the department's commitment — its "social contract" — to the community. In the past few years an increasing number of police departments of various sizes and in different locales have articulated formal value statements (e.g., Alexandria, Virginia; Houston, Texas; Madison, Wisconsin; McAllen, Texas; Newport News, Virginia, among others). These values serve as the standards against which all police behaviors are held.

Included in virtually all the police department value statements are factors such as:

- The adherence to the Constitution and democratic values.
- The commitment to rigorous law enforcement using a wide variety of policing resources to deal with crime.
- The pursuit of crime prevention.
- Understanding the nature of crime problems in neighborhoods as well as responding to the needs and concerns of citizens.
- The commitment to an open and honest relationship with the community.
- The pledge that police employees will perform their tasks with integrity and professionalism.
- The solicitation of citizen participation in policing tasks.
- The commitment to participating in programs that incorporate shared responsibility with the community.

Formalized values serve as an institutional pledge to the community. If these standards can be manifest into not only policy but also the working persona of every police officer, then a stronger alliance will be established and the effect of the endemic problems will be minimized.

Higher Educational Levels

Since the 1967 recommendations of the President's Commission on Law Enforcement and Administration of Justice for police officers to have a college education, a great deal of research has been conducted on the effects of higher education on police behavior.

In sum, it has been found that the college experience

- Develops a broader base of information for decision making.
- Provides additional years and experiences for increasing maturity.

- Inculcates responsibility in the individual through course requirements and achievements.
- Through general education courses and coursework in the major (particularly a criminal justice major), permits the individual to learn more about the history of the country and the democratic process, and to appreciate constitutional rights, values, and the democratic form of government.
- Engenders the ability to handle difficult or ambiguous situations with greater creativity or innovation.
- In the case of criminal justice majors, permits a better view of the "big picture" of the criminal justice system and a fuller understanding and appreciation for the prosecutorial, courts, and correctional roles.
- Develops a greater empathy for minorities and their discriminatory experiences — this understanding is developed both through coursework and through interaction in the academic environment.
- Engenders understanding and tolerance for persons with different lifestyles and ideologies, which can translate into more effective communications and community relationships in the practice of policing.
- Makes officers appear to be less rigid in decision making, to tend to make their decisions in the spirit of the democratic process, and to use discretion in dealing with individual cases rather than applying the same rules to all cases.
- Helps officers to communicate and respond to the crime and service needs of the public in a competent manner, with civility and humanity.
- Makes officers more innovative and more flexible when dealing with complex policing programs and strategies, such as problem-oriented policing, community policing, and task force responses.
- Equips officers better to perform tasks and to make continuous policing decisions with little or no supervision.
- Helps officers to develop better overall community relations skills, including engendering the respect and confidence of the community.
- Engenders more "professional" demeanor and performance.
- Enables officers to cope better with stress and to be more likely to seek assistance with personal or stress-related problems, and thereby be more stable and more reliable employees.
- Enables officers to adapt their styles of communication and behavior to a wider range of social conditions and classes.

- Tends to make officers less authoritarian and less cynical with respect to the milieu of policing.
- Enables officers to accept and adapt to organizational change more readily. (Carter and Sapp, 1990; Carter et al., 1988).

The proportion of police officers who have received higher education has progressively changed since 1960. Whereas the average educational level of officers in 1967 was 12.3 years — barely more than a high school diploma — the current average level is 13.6, or well into the junior year of college (Carter et al., 1988). Not only is the level of education increasing among police officers, but it is also steadily rising for the public.

It may be inferred from the research on higher education that a better educated police force would address the tasks of policing with greater professionalism, greater civility, and greater humanity. If these factors alone could be accomplished, the goal toward a strong community alliance would make a geometric leap forward.

Increased Work Force Diversity

As noted previously, the greatest (and most serious) conflict between the police and community has centered on relations with racial and ethnic minorities. There is no doubt that discrimination has occurred both during the exercise of police power and during the police employment process. As a result of the civil rights movement, court decisions, and greater awareness of past discrimination by police leaders, contemporary police executives have made great strides in increasing the racial, ethnic, and gender diversity of America's police forces. While complete parity has not yet been accomplished, law enforcement has made notable accomplishments.

The findings of a Police Executive Research Forum study showed that minority representation in American law enforcement agencies approximates the general population. Moreover, educational levels of minorities in law enforcement are virtually the same as those of white officers (Carter and Sapp, 1990; Carter et al., 1988). On a related note, the same study found that 12.8 percent of all sworn police officers are women. While no empirical evidence was found on a national level, there are indicators that in 1970 women composed less than 2 percent of all sworn officers. Obviously, this amount of change in two decades is substantial. Further, it was interesting to note that women officers average a full year more of college compared with men.

As the work force approaches the representativeness of a community's racial and ethnic composition, it also increases its representativeness of mores and values. This, in turn, will both decrease levels of conflict and increase the strength of the alliance.

Changing Police Management Styles

Kelling and Moore (1988) provide a concise discussion on how the management of law enforcement has evolved through three eras: the political, reform, and community-based.   The political era reflected patronage and general incompetence. During the reform era, efficiency, rigid controls, and autocracy were central themes in police management. The community-based era, where law enforcement is currently emerging, reflects the philosophy and values as described previously in this chapter related to community policing and values. Clearly, as it has been noted, this style of management is more conducive to a strong community alliance.

Within this era — and even more recently — another management movement is emerging: Deming's quality management. (For greater detail on this topic, see Couper, 1991.) The focus of quality management is to serve the needs of the organization's *customers* — in the case of law enforcement, this would be the citizens. Fundamental to the quality management philosophy is answering the questions:

- Does the police service meet the customer's desires?
- Can the police service be presented more efficiently?

The premises of quality management argue that an organization must address the needs of both internal and external customers. Moreover, it is argued that most individual performance measures are counterproductive because they inspire individually centered conflict and competition rather than a quality customer-oriented service.

From the limited perspective of community alliance, suffice it to note that if citizens are viewed as *customers* of police service and efforts are expended accordingly, then a stronger bond would likely develop between the police and community.

Media Merger

There has traditionally been a conflictual relationship between the police and the media. Law enforcement would argue that the media want information to which they do not have a right, that the media are too critical of the police and fail to show the "police side" of controversies, and that media exposure compounds serious investigations. On the other side, the media argue that the police are too secretive and tread on the freedom of the press.

Since many public opinions about the police are strongly influenced by the media — both the news and entertainment media — the severity of the endemic issues as well as the strength (or weakness) of community alliance are related to media portrayals of the police. Because of concerns on both sides of the issue, the police-media relationship is stabilizing.

Police executives are establishing policies to work more cooperatively with the media and are opening doors, where possible, to media inquiries and interviews. As a result, a more trusting bond is developing wherein both sides may provide "give and take" to meet needs unique to their own responsibilities.

Not only is this occurring with the news media, but the police and entertainment media are also working more closely with programming such as *COPS*, *Top Cops*, and *America's Most Wanted*. While media foci will always address the more sensational and intriguing issues — that is how an audience is drawn — a cooperative relationship will permit this portrayal in a more realistic light.

The Epilogue

Community alliance is like fishing: You have to start with commitment, go to the right place, use the correct bait, have patience, be willing to change your strategy, and seize the opportunity at the right moment. Your efforts may not always result in "a keeper," but when the "big one" bites, it is enjoyable and rewarding. It is also an ongoing effort — never quite finished and always striving for a better catch.

The discussion of research was admittedly selective in this chapter in order to present critical findings related to the endemic issues that compound an effective community alliance. The topics were intended to serve not as answers, but as guideposts for further discussion and administrative contemplation.

While assumptions and conjecture were plentiful, there is one statement that can be made with granite-like resolve: Regardless of innovation, energy, and effort on behalf of the police, there will never be a completely harmonious community alliance. When the community stops questioning the police, then we should begin questioning ourselves.

References

Barker, T. & Carter, D. L. (Eds.). (1991). *Police deviance* (2nd ed.). Cincinnati: Anderson Publishing Co.

Carter, D. L. (1984). Theoretical dimensions in the abuse of authority by police officers. *Police Studies*, 7(4), 224-236 (Winter).

Carter, D. L. (1985). Police brutality: A model for definition, perspective, and control. In A. Blumberg & E. Niederhoffer (Eds.), *The ambivalent force* (3rd ed.) (pp 321-330). New York: Holt, Rinehart and Winston Inc.

Carter, D. L. (1990a). An overview of drug-related misconduct of police officers: Drug abuse and narcotic corruption. In R. Weisheit (Ed.), *Drugs and the criminal justice system*. Cincinnati: Anderson Publishing Co.

Carter, D. L. (1990b). Drug related corruption of police officers: A contemporary typology, *Journal of Criminal Justice*. 18(2).

Carter, D. L. & Sapp, A. D. (1990). The evolution of higher education in law enforcement organizations: Preliminary findings from a national study. *Journal of Criminal Justice Education*, 1(1) (Spring).

Carter, D. L., Sapp, A. D., & Stephens, D. W. (1988). *The state of police education: Policy direction for the 21st Century*. Washington, DC: Police Executive Research Forum.

Couper, D. C. (1988). *What is quality policing?* METAPOL Computer Bulletin Board Network. Staff Item 33. Washington, DC: Police Executive Research Forum.

Couper, D. C. (1991). *Quality policing: The Madison experience*. Washington, DC: Police Executive Research Forum.

Dombrink, J. (1991). The touchables: Vice and police corruption in the 1980s. In T. Barker & D. L. Carter (Eds.), *Police deviance* (2nd ed.). Cincinnati: Anderson Publishing Co.

Eck, J. & Spelman, W. (1987). *Problem-solving: Problem-oriented policing in Newport News*. Washington, DC: Police Executive Research Forum.

Kelling, G L. & Moore, M. H. (1988). The evolving strategy of policing. *National Institute of Justice/Harvard University Perspectives on Policing*. Washington, DC: National Institute of Justice.

Klockars, C. B. & Mastrofski, S. D. (Eds.). (1991). *Thinking about police: Contemporary readings* (2d. ed.). New York: McGraw-Hill Inc.

Manning, P. K. (1978). The police: Mandate, strategies, and appearance. In P. K. Manning & J. Van Maanen (Eds.), *Policing: A view from the street*. Santa Monica, CA: Goodyear Publishing Co.

National Advisory Commission on Civil Disorders. (1968). *Report*. Washington, DC: U.S. Government Printing Office.

National Commission on the Causes and Prevention of Violence. (1969). *Law and order reconsidered*. Washington, DC: U.S. Government Printing Office.

President's Commission on Law Enforcement and Administration of Justice. (1967). *Task force report: The police*. Washington, DC: U.S. Government Printing Office.

Radelet, L. (1986) *The police and the community* (4th ed.). New York: Macmillan Publishing Co.

Rosenbaum, D. P. (Ed.). (1986). *Community crime prevention: Does it work?* Beverly Hills, CA: Sage Publications Inc.

Trojanowicz, R. (Undated). *The neighborhood foot patrol program in Flint, Michigan*. East Lansing, MI: National Neighborhood Foot Patrol Center.

Trojanowicz, R. & Carter, D. L. (1988). *The philosophy and role of community policing*. East Lansing, MI: National Center for Community Policing.

West, P. (1991). Investigation and review of complaints against police officers. In T. Barker & D. L. Carter (Eds.), *Police deviance* (2nd ed.). Cincinnati: Anderson Publishing Co.

Chapter 4

Enriching Traditional Roles

Chris R. Braiden

First Word

An explanation is necessary here so that I don't anger the very people I want to champion. Throughout this paper I use the term "Grunt." I do so intentionally, out of respect. That is why I capitalize the word. A Grunt, quite simply, is the one who delivers — as opposed to packages — the goods. In the conventional police organization, all players do not contribute equally. There are too many packagers, and not enough deliverers. In fact, I see this freeloading by too many on the backs of too few as the primary obstacle confronting fundamental change in conventional policing.

Grunts are the people who produce the "moments of truth" upon which the fundamental success of the organization depends. I borrow this term from the chief executive officer (CEO) (can't remember his name) of Scandinavian Airlines. A moment of truth occurs when a person or a policy of the organization makes contact with a customer. In the policing context, citizens know little — or care — about Uniform Crime Reports, clearance rates, strategic plans or standard operating procedures, but they can give you a graphic description of their encounter with a Grunt, for whatever the reason.

I believe the Grunts of policing have been neglected and their work demeaned. They are the Cinderellas; they do the most work but reap the least rewards. On the other hand, the specialists are the ugly step-sisters; they do the least work but reap the most rewards. Grunts run the most risks, too; it takes real effort to die in the line of duty — or run afoul of Internal Affairs — in an office. The Grunt produces the fundamental product that sustains the organization but management has become mesmerized with the package. I think the idea was put best by the guy who was talking about quality control in his company. He said, "I'll tell you all you need to know about quality control and I'll tell it to you in one sentence. Quality Control is the guy on the loading dock who decides NOT to throw the . . . box into the back of the truck." He's a Grunt. Right now, in policing, the Grunt is throwing the box into the back of the truck too often. We need to discover why.

Figures Policing

For a long time I have been looking outside policing to try to understand things inside better. I am trying to look beyond law and crime. For too long, policing has tried to exist as an island in a sea of societal and human problems. It has pursued crime as if it has a definitive start and finish. Someone once said that crime is the only problem we consider solved when we charge someone. I realized long ago that true policing cannot be divorced from poverty, bigotry, illiteracy, hate, racism, unemployment, and all of the other failings of human nature because their consequences make up the reality of policing. The flight to the suburbs has left most cities with core slums. The gap between the poor and middle class continues to widen. Money still talks, the poor being the overwhelming favorite to become either a criminal or a victim of violent crime. One third of all Canadian children now live with one parent. These are the realities around which any intelligent examination of policing must begin. All are beyond our control and are immune to law enforcement, yet that is how we have been reacting to them.

I enjoy reading, but not fiction. I need to know I am learning as I read and so along the way I have read many biographies. In understanding my world of policing, I think I have learned more from Ed Deming than anyone else. Dr. W. Edwards Deming is now eighty-nine years old, but still very active and sharp as a tack. His doctorate is in mathematical physics. He was a catalytic figure in the success of American industrial productivity during the Second World War. He went to Japan in 1950 at the request of the scientific community and spent many years living there before returning to the United States. In that country, he is credited with the success of their industrial miracle that redefined "made in Japan" from junk to excellence. The production system in Japan is structured around Deming's theory of Statistical Quality Management (Deming, 1986). They considered him a god in that country and indeed their annual award for industrial excellence is named after him.

By now you probably think Braiden has lost his marbles trying to apply Deming's theory to policing, but just hang in there for a bit. Dr. Deming was giving a lecture to an MBA class at Utah State University in

1985. His subject was running a company on figures. Here is what he had to say:

> Some of you are students of finance. You learn how to figure and you learn how to run a company on figures. If you run a company on figures alone, you will go under. How long will it take your company to go under, get drowned? I don't know, but it is sure to fail. Why? Because the most important figures are not there. Did you learn that in your school of finance? You will, ten or fifteen years from now, learn that the most important figures are those that are unknown, and unknowable.
>
> What about the multiplying effect of a happy customer, in either manufacturing *or in service*? Is he in your figures? What about the multiplying effect of an unhappy customer? Do you know that figure? You don't, and if you run your company without it, you won't have a company. What about the multiplying effect of doing a better job along the line?

Deming was talking about Grunts and their work. Even though his theory is built around statistics, he knew that in the final analysis ordinary people have to deliver the product. The conventional model of policing is only interested in known figures: uniform crime reports, clearance rates, response times, arrests, and charges. But these things only speak to *quantity*; they tell us nothing about quality. All of them can be reduced to numbers. Two hours spent writing tickets can be quantified; an hour with a wino bent on suicide cannot.

As a consequence of this short-range focus, specialized units — and people — in policing have multiplied like rabbits over the past two decades and their work has been glamorized. But these latter do not produce moments of truth, or contribute equally. In fact, they often slow down and create work for the Grunts. For example, detectives used to do their own legwork and make their own arrests. Now they "coordinate" others to do it for them in the form of surveillance teams and take-down teams.

In policing, we need to create new heroes. Management needs to reassess its priorities — and reward systems. If we do, I forecast the dawning of a new day for the Grunt, a better service to our constituents, and a reassessment of personal resumés. And it all has to do with ownership.

The Start

Ownership, whether it be of things, time, or destiny, is a powerful force in the human psyche. Lack of it brought down communism and the

Berlin Wall and got rid of the Ceausescus all in a single weekend, things that the United Nations, NATO, kremlinologists, sovietologists, countless politicians, and international conferences could not do over the span of forty years. When two or three people a week tried to get over the wall, they could be shot. When a million climbed up from both sides, the senselessness of the wall was over.

A political system that ignores the elementary humanism that people want to own things will leave half its national crop in the field to rot. Every year in the former U.S.S.R. 30 percent of everything produced never reached market. On the other hand, farmers who own their land don't leave a grain. The flaws of communism and conventional police management have much in common, I think. Both deny the human spirit.

By the time we reach the age of ten, we want our "own" room that then becomes far more important than the rest of the house. As soon as we get our first driver's licence, there is a universal urge to "own" our own car. Even though it's an old "clunker," it's ours! And it doesn't seem to matter that we could still drive the old man's, which is probably nicer.

And then when we get married, there is that same compulsion to own our own house, however humble it may be. Who washes a rented car or paints a rented house? No one, but the minute we become owners of either, one of the first things we do is wash the car or paint the house. It is well documented by observers of human behavior that self-employed people work much harder than those employed by others. We will invest in ourselves quicker than in others. It is just the way of the human animal. That is why profit-sharing is so common in free enterprise.

Everyone has heard of the late Ray Kroc of McDonald's fame. He parleyed a single hamburger stand into a multibillion-dollar miracle. In fact, it was no miracle; it was just that Ray Kroc understood people. His "big-stick" was the franchise. He sold them. He realized that people work hardest when they are working for themselves and so he shared the wealth by letting people own a piece of the action. Ray Kroc knew that in the short term, he could have made more money by retaining total control of the enterprise and hiring salaried managers to operate individual outlets. That was the conventional approach at the time. But because Ray Kroc knew people, he also knew that in the long term, that approach would fail.

Ray Kroc's miracle could not happen in the former Soviet Union, doing things their way. In fact, by introducing his franchise system in Moscow some years ago, he might have contributed more to the downfall of communism than presidents and prime ministers! It would be interesting to know how much time Gorbachev spent sitting in McDonald's in Moscow before he came up with *perestroika*. That is why the August coup failed. Freedom, once tasted, is addictive. Freedom is simply ownership of our destiny.

And so it is with policing. Understand humans and the flaws of convention jump out at you. Surely it is a given that policing is labor intensive. The vast majority of police work in the broadest sense, the stuff that consumes 90 percent of the average workday, is done by people. Therefore, it seems clear to me that if we are ever to make significant improvements in the quality of our product, it will have to come through the minds, hearts, and sweat glands of the people doing the work. Ed Deming had this to say on the subject, "The quality of any product is primarily a function of human commitment" (Deming, 1986). This being the case, it seems elementary to me that if I want to get quality work from people, I had better figure out what turns their crank on — and off.

The Emperor's New Clothes

I remember so well the little story I used to read to my two sons when they were small. It was about an emperor who had a huge ego. He already had the finest wardrobe in the empire (I think he was related to Imelda Marcos) but like all egocentrics, he was never satisfied. Two shysters knew about the emperor's ego and proceeded to sell him a very unique new suit of clothes — made of material only brilliant people could see. Of course, the emperor saw the "material" as did his advisors, generals, and ministers.

When the new suit was finally delivered and modeled, the royal sycophants fawned so much over the emperor's brilliant choice of material that he decided to have a parade through the empire so that his fortuitous subjects could share in his good fortune, too.

The parade day was a very special one. The morning broke with brilliant sunshine and, of course, everyone along the parade route was "brilliant" too because the word had gone out about the uniqueness of the material in the suit.

The emperor was having a grand time as he rode along to choruses of cheers from his intelligent subjects until he rode by a little six-year old boy who said, quite simply, "Mommy, the emperor has no clothes on." A hush fell over the crowd. The child's mother, with reddened face, turned to her friend, humbled, and said, "He's right, the king is naked." The child's honesty, like a refluent wave, spread along the parade route until what had been cheers of praise turned to shouts of derision as the emperor galloped furiously back into his castle surrounded by his "brilliant" lackeys amid a shower of bottles, stones, and boots.

Policing, I think, has much to learn from this little story. We are in great need of people of character who will blow the whistle on some of the senseless things we do, as a matter of routine. Sadly, most chiefs have surrounded themselves with obsequious bureaucrats who routinely provide them with echoes of their own opinion on every issue. A free mind is a rare thing in policing; a free spirit even rarer. All of us, at every level of the organization, routinely do things that are patently senseless, we grumble, and then continue to do them. I am convinced that the primary reason police officers — everywhere — are a crotchety lot is because we are routinely forced to do senseless things. For every minute we spend on the task, we spend five on the process writing about what we did. Surely no one still believes that aimlessly driving around in a police car for six or seven hours a day serves any purpose other than to pollute. Surely no police administrator still believes that rigid central control with its standard operating procedures mentality can give you quality work. Surely no one believes that enthusiasm, imagination, or creativity can be ordered up or made a matter of policy. Surely no one still believes that policing is a separate entity from poverty, illiteracy, racism, human frailty, or misery. Mark Twain was right when he said, "The human race is a flawed race. It is the only species that can blush, and the only one that needs to."

Surely no one still believes that prisons correct or that the criminal justice system is effective. The criminal justice system, at best, is a treatment, not a cure. Cures to crime, if there be any, still lie ahead of us. Poverty spawns one type of crime; wealth, another. Drugs, our worst plague, go where the money is: North America and Europe. How much of the Colombian coke is sold in Colombia or any other poor country? Ironically, the poorest countries exert some control of the richest through drugs. There has always been an underground economy. During the Depression it was gambling; in the prohibition years, it was booze. Why is the United States, with the highest standard of living on earth, perhaps the most violent? All crimes are committed by humans, and until a way is found to force human beings to change significantly personal behavior, the jury on this issue will remain out. One thing alone is certain; there will always be crime just as there will always be rain, sunshine, and garbage. Only the amounts change. All that is new about crime are statistics and the media. The human animal, since the dawning of the species, has had a need for a high. We may get rid of crack cocaine, but something else will replace it.

The Problem

The "I'm All Right Jack" Factor

I believe the main reason why many people in policing simply function in a robotic fashion as they mope their way through the day is because there is no sense of ownership between them and their work; they don't see themselves as part of the problem, or the solution. For the typical police officer, there are two work worlds. One world houses the brass and policy; they live in the other. To them, these two worlds are like ships passing in the night, oblivious to each other. The theory is that decisions are made in one to be carried out in the other. In reality, the daily decisions of management have nothing to do with the daily work of the Grunt where it is presumed there is a generic police product to be dished out by a stranger to a stranger. As a result, in the daily routine of the Grunt, there is no sense of involvement or achievement. He or she is like the long-range artilleryman; someone hands him a shell and he just fires it, with no thought as to where it might land. Once it leaves the muzzle, his job is done. And so you get the "name, address, and telephone number" mentality.

Specialization by Function

Many people disagree with me. They claim that because of all the specialized units that exist in the professional model of policing there is infinitely more ownership than ever before.

They are right, but it is ownership of the *wrong thing*. When the ten year old owns his own room, he loses interest in the rest of the house. The sixteen year old will wash his own car, but not the old man's (unless he or she is paid). With ownership, agendas shift, horizons shrink. What is important to people changes. Ownership can be a blessing or a curse, depending upon to what it is attached.

The old adage "In the bosom of every solution lie the seeds of a new problem" applies here. People are motivated by self-interest; that is why it is so hard to create a sense of commonwealth in communities today. Privacy is the primary concern. When we buy a new house, the first thing we do is build a fence around it because everything we need is within. In middle-class North America, people don't need community; so, generally speaking, they don't contribute to it. When is the last time someone borrowed a cup of sugar? It is only when it can be demonstrated that people need community that they will begin to focus beyond their own backyard.

My hypothesis is that this same human fact affects policing. The conventional organization chart has become a collection of disparate — and sometimes — discordant empires; fixation is on individual backyards. Everyone is busy flitting from one specialty to the next in the interests of "career." Fleshing out resumés has become the name of the game because it is believed that is how the boss got where he or she is. The universal perception is that reward is attached to the office, not the pavement. The average police officer believes that doing a good job along the line is meaningless to the boss. In the meantime, the contents of the "in" and "out" baskets consume the day and exhaust the energy of the bosses, only to be faced again the next day. In most agencies no one is up on the balcony looking down on the dance floor and pulling things together. And so empires drift and agendas conflict. Ray Kroc would never let this happen. Franchises would be lifted.

Today most organizations have twice as many boxes on the organization chart compared with the chart from twenty years ago — Edmonton's has tripled over that period. But what improvement in product quality has resulted?   None that I can see.   On the contrary, this preoccupation with specialization has done more harm that good.   It has reduced peacekeeping to a jumble of law enforcement functions.   What has come to be known as the "professional" law enforcement model is, in reality, a corruption of the original mandate of policing.   The Oxford Dictionary defines policing as "A better state of society."   Sir Robert Peel described his model this way, "Policing by, of and for the people in the interests of community welfare and existence."   Peel's model is the forerunner of urban policing in North America.

Ex-Chief Justice Warren Burger, in his retirement speech, had this to say about the entire criminal justice system, "The entire legal profession, lawyers, judges, law teachers, have become so mesmerized with the courtroom contest, we have forgotten our fundamental mandate — healers of conflict."   The same has happened to policing.   Gradually, it has been made over into a product that more reflects the personality of the conventional police bureaucrat than the needs of the people who consume it.   Conventional policing is bureaucracy based; it needs to be community based.   Peel formed his police to *replace* soldiers; convention *emulates* them.   Every police chief, by virtue of their position, is a monopolist; their product is the only ticket in town.   Effectiveness and monopoly are opposites.   Effectiveness means "doing the right things."   Henry Lloyd said, "Monopoly is business at the end of its journey."   Police agencies get a free ride and so there was no need to be effective.   For a quick mental flash of what monopoly does to the quality of any product, picture the difference between a Lada automobile built in East Germany and a Mercedes Benz built in Germany.   And so, like communism, the setting is ripe for drift from what the consumer needs — to what the producer wants.

The professional model of policing has given us specialization by function.   It breaks the art of peacekeeping into a myriad of disconnected law enforcement functions: traffic, drugs, vice, fraud, or crime prevention, to name a few.   It focuses on the symptoms and so we never get to the real problem — dysfunctional families.   As Henry Thoreau so aptly put it, "There are a thousand people hacking at the branches of evil but no one is striking at the roots."   For instance, it is common for detectives from different specialties to be working cases involving the same suspect or family but not collaborate because their specialties keep them apart.   And then these specialties often sprout families of their own.   Within the generic term of traffic, one might work in hit and run, traffic flow, or selective enforcement.   In crime prevention, one might be assigned to school liaison, neighborhood watch, or race relations.

There are numerous flaws to this approach, and I will treat them in order.

The Zealot

If one is blessed with an energetic, dedicated worker who spends every day of every week mentally and physically immersed in their specialty, focused on the narrow at the expense of the broad picture, over time, the importance of their function blots out the purpose of the exercise. Eventually, people become obsessed with the *efficiency* (doing things right) of their function at the expense of the *effectiveness* (doing the right things) of the organization (Bennis & Nanus, 1985). Efficiency produces law enforcement, effectiveness promotes problem solving. The two definitions of "right things" begin to part company. But there is a fatal flaw here; no amount of efficiency can replace a lack of effectiveness. If we are doing the wrong thing, it matters little how well we do it. Peter Drucker described the phenomenon beautifully when he said, "There is nothing so useless as doing efficiently that which need not be done at all" (Drucker, 1973).

Some parts of the conventional organization chart are cosmetic, they need not be done at all. They are there to mollify the public; our job is to protect them, even when they don't want us to. Police are not in the business of service as is a hairdresser, where customers always get what they want. Our role more resembles that of a doctor: customers get what is best for them. Hence, most police managers have developed an amazing tolerance for ineffectiveness because they concentrate so much on efficiency. They repeatedly send out efficiency vibes by focusing on the process and so they get more of the same. Fixation on efficiency leads inexorably to obsolescence because people become rooted in convention; no one moves the ball. The ball of police management hasn't moved in thirty years.

As well, with the passage of time, another "virus" develops. This dedication to the cause of the function often becomes counterproductive to the original idea. Bertrand Russell had this to say on the subject, "Organizations have a life of their own independent of their founder. The most striking of these is the Catholic Church, of which Christ would be astonished." Mark Twain expanded the same sentiment to include all Christians; he said "If Christ came back today there's one thing he wouldn't be — a Christian."

Being Catholic, I have often wondered how we can reconcile the grandeur of Rome and basilica all over the world — even in the poorest countries — with the memory of a man who was a simple carpenter, lived with his mother, and never owned a house and whose fundamental message was "Do unto others. . . ." I cannot imagine magnificent edifices being built to the memory of Mahatma Ghandi or Mother Teresa. I picture Christ the same way. We are told that Christ drove the money lenders out of the temple.

Well, today the Catholic Church in Canada alone is a $500 million a year business. God only knows how much the rest of "religion" makes in Christ's name. That's drift for you. I think too many religious bureaucrats have set themselves up as brokers through whom we sinners must pass on our way to heaven, whatever we perceive it to be.

So too would Sir Robert Peel and the average citizen be astonished if they ever saw the inner workings of a conventional police organization today. They would wonder at the logic of it all. This just seems to be the way of things when people get their hands on something; we have this animal compulsion to make it into our own likeness.

Production-Line Mentality

The opposite of the zealot is the plodder, the result of the standard operating procedures mentality. These people will give you enough of their specific product in order to stay out of trouble. They are the inevitable product of the drudgery of routine labor that ultimately dulls the brain and saps the spirit. You get what you order up. Sadly, bright people literally chain their brain at the gate coming in, function through their shift, and pick it up again on the way out. We go out of our way to hire the brightest people we can find, and then we teach them to follow orders like soldiers. This approach is fostered by the military mindset of bureaucrats who believe that there must be a set-piece for every activity; where the past mistakes of the most inept and dishonest among us provide the spawning ground of policy that then blankets everyone. This means that *people's failure — not success* drives the organization; the focus is always on failure and punishment. Oddly enough, these plodders are often very creative in their leisure time. Someone once said, "Tell me what you think about and I'll tell you who you are." Whenever I need a bright person to help me on a project, I don't look at their resumés, I check out their hobbies. I try to find out as much as I can about their activities *off* the job. If I am looking for imagination and creativity, a person's automobile will probably tell me more than his resumé.

This set-piece mentality conjures up visions of the production-line approach to quality workmanship that was thrown out years ago by most successful organizations. Unfortunately, because of monopoly, police leadership has not been in the vanguard of creative thinking; most thinkers are quickly "neutralized," one way or another. Convention rewards conformity; convention sets process above task.

Tunnel Vision

During my quarter-century in policing, I have watched the impact of specialization by function on the organizational chart. Its way of dealing with problems is to create a new box, put a few people in it, and announce the birth of whatever. In Edmonton we have grown from 40 boxes in 1970 to 121 in 1988. Predictably, human nature comes into play and trips us up, again. If you call something, something, long enough, for sure it will eventually become it. Over time, those involved will identify solely with their specific function and, more important, lose sight of the cause of the organization. I turn to Peter Drucker for corroboration on this point; he said, "The degenerative disease of specialization is tunnel vision" (Drucker, 1973). My experience in policing tells me the man is right on the button. Organized around the professional model, people do develop ownership — but only of their particular function that obliterates all else.

I come back to Ray Kroc once more for help. Kroc sold franchises, but not unconditionally. He didn't sell the farm. He retained enough control to ensure that no franchise strayed too far from the mother ship. He clearly understood that the success of all depended upon the reputation of all. If individual franchises do not maintain a certain standard, they are gone. Individual franchises are not allowed to lose sight of the cause — a quality Big Mac in Montreal, Minneapolis, or Moscow. This is exactly the opposite of the specialization by function model; tunnel vision is rewarded. There is no supreme cause that obligates all to each other.

The damage done by this specialist approach doesn't end there, however. The term "specialist" has a certain ring to it; it smacks of importance. But what does it say to the nonspecialist, the Grunt in the Front. Well, it tells them that they are not specialists, and so must be of a lesser sort. The immigrant phenomenon repeats itself here. I know, I was one. No one wants to be low rung on the status ladder. The last wave of immigrants can't wait for another to arrive so that they can move up a step on the status ladder and a little farther away from the slums. Being specialists and proud of it, they can now look down their nose at the Grunts, who only do ordinary things.

The Dumping Factor

Then there is the dumping factor. Most people, if allowed, will solve their problem on the backs of others. Many specialties started out in support of the front end, however, with the shift in definition of "right things," they invariably end up creating work for the very people they were supposed to be helping. Whenever a bureaucrat or specialist solves a problem, that "solution" will usually translate into more work for the Grunt. Amazingly often, these specialists end up coordinating others in doing work originally assigned to them. Crime prevention specialists will give lectures and make promises that the Grunt will have to fulfill. When we instituted neighborhood foot patrol in Edmonton, we almost needed a stick to beat detectives away from dumping their work onto the constables working the beat. In fact, one robbery detail detective implored me not to move a beat from a particular neighborhood because "he wouldn't be able to handle his files if I did." I did. If allowed to pass the buck, most of us will.

One fundamental rule should be entrenched in all police organizations — *Solve your own problem!* If it were, I predict most problems would disappear overnight.

Crime Prevention?

Over the past two decades, there has been a great proliferation of crime prevention units in police organizations. These units are usually staffed by people who, soon after becoming police officers, decide they don't really like arresting drunks but do like the pay and permanency so they stay, but dodge the bullet. They become crime prevention specialists, usually attired in suits with a briefcase who specialize in giving lectures, invariably to the converted, about crimes they will probably never encounter and who are urged to call the cops with their slightest worries. Unfortunately, these people are noticeable by their absence in the neighborhoods most in need of their services. Such programs as Neighborhood Watch and Block Parents don't exist in inner cities. Most violent crime does. Relentlessly, these people churn out millions of pamphlets and posters, buttons, and balloons, and in the process have probably been responsible for clear-cutting an entire mountain in British Columbia. Pamphlets are the penicillin of crime prevention units.

As a consequence, fear of crime has become an industry in its own right. There is money to be made by scaring people. Doctors and dentists copped onto that long ago. Most of the people who install burglar alarms and put five locks on their doors live in the safest neighborhoods. Burglar alarms, usually installed at the urging of these specialists, generate massive amounts of unnecessary work for the Grunt because 98 percent of incidents they are called to when an alarm goes off are false. In Edmonton in 1990, there were 11,000 false intrusion alarms that constituted 42 percent of our high-priority dispatches for that year. The private sector installs them, reaps the profit, and the public police (the Grunt, of course — not the specialist) services them. And so another job is dumped.

Empire Building

Then there is the "empire-building" phenomenon. Parkinson's Law says that when a new position is created, the work will grow to fill it until it takes two people to do what didn't need to be done by anyone in the first place. In policing, people justify budgets and promotions by the size of their unit. But these "new" people have to come from somewhere. They do —

invariably from patrol. For instance, the Edmonton Police Service had 545 constables assigned to patrol divisions in 1980 when the population was 505,000. Today, with a population of 605,000, the reported crime rate 44 percent higher, and the complement of the service essentially the same, there are 468 constables assigned to patrol division. In the interim, several new specialized boxes appeared on the organization chart and several others grew in size.

The Flight From the Front

I have long believed that with most things in life, there is the theory of what is supposed to be and the reality of what is. One thing is certain in policing; we are stuck with things as they are and so I try to focus on the realities of society. Generally, it is thought that people become police officers to help others. Unfortunately, the reality of specialization by function has led to what I call the "flight from the front." No one wants to work in patrol any more where your opportunity to help someone is greatest. Taking calls for service, the "Big Mac" of policing, has become the lowest rung on the status ladder. No one wants to do it. Let me support that statement with hard figures.

The Edmonton Police Service has at this point in time 1,088 police officers. In 1988 242 applied for transfer to 6 of our specialized units while less than 5 applied for transfer from specialized units to patrol. In 1990, and only up to November of that year, 489 had applied for transfer to the same six specialized units while less than 5 asked to go to patrol division. The only parallel I can think of was the exodus from East Berlin after the wall came down, and we know why they were leaving. Can there be a stronger message? For whatever reason, few want to do the work we all joined up to do. Few are interested in community welfare and existence because they perceive the rewards to be elsewhere.

Of course, we learned the same thing years ago when we were kids playing hockey; no one wanted to be goalie but who is the most important player on any successful hockey team? What the Roman, Aurilius, said 1,700 years ago is indeed very true, "Our lives become what our thoughts make them." In their minds, these people are specialists, not police officers. They see themselves as functionaries who perform a task; they do not serve people. They live out the forecast of Ron Zemke, a service improvement expert who said, "Left to our own devices, we pay more and more attention to things of less and less importance to our customers." It is common to have specialists working at a time when high-priority calls are outstanding but they will neither volunteer — nor be dispatched — to take those calls. It's not their job. People will simply have to wait until a Grunt comes free.

In summary, I believe this to be the inevitable outcome of specialization by function. People become specialists first and police officers second. In the police psyche, specialists are more important than Grunts and so the work that comprises 90 percent of total output becomes subordinate to the other 10 percent. That needs to be turned around. The ownership phenomenon does occur, but of the wrong thing. But this should not be a revelation to anyone; it happens in private industry, too. Raymond Smith, CEO of Atlantic Bell (1989 revenues of $11.5B), described the same problem he encountered when he took over in 1989. He said, "In a large business, the most important determinant of success is the effectiveness of millions of day-to-day interactions of human beings. If these contacts are contentious, turf-oriented and parochial, the company will flounder, bureaucracies will grow and internal competition will be rampant." My experience is that policing has become a bunch of disconnected jobs with competing priorities; it needs to be a peacekeeping vocation.

But what to do?

The Answer

A Core Value

Whenever I take on a new job, I need to have a clear focus of the bottom line: what is the object of the exercise? What is the one thing that dominates all else? I suppose what I am talking about is a core value. Successful individuals, families, institutions, and businesses all seem to have one, *and they never lose sight of it.* To me, a core value serves as a beacon that prevents drift from the cause of the family or the organization. Although people may take different routes, they all arrive at the same destination. The primary task of the chief is to provide leadership that rises above unit and section goals. He or she does that by being up on the balcony, pulling things together, and keeping everyone focused on the cause.

Public policing exists for a cause: to make community life and the life of the individual safe and secure for people and their possessions. But people come before possessions. Wealth must never dictate who gets police service. Indeed, research and experience tells us that the poor need us the most. The cause, in turn, needs to be represented by a core value. Conventional policing does not meet this test. There doesn't seem to be a cause or a core value that is supreme above all others. Law enforcement is *not* a cause, or even a core value; it is a function. Certainly, convention has goals and objectives but these need a "faith" to guide them. When there is no core value, there is bound to be drift from the cause. To correct that drift, we must start with a core value, entrench it and then evaluate or reward all actions and everyone based on that value. If this is done, I forecast the collapse of many organization chart boxes, a shift in career paths, a reassessment of resumés, and, most important, the emergence of a new hero in policing, the Grunt.

Finally, a core value must be visible to — and attainable by — all, regardless of their individual assignment. In Edmonton, for several years our primary goal has been community policing. Quite apart from what I say on this issue later on, that term is too blurry to be a core value. There are no hard edges to it; it seems to mean all things to all people. Second, it must be something that the guy working in traffic, stolen auto detail, narcotics, etc. can apply to his or her daily chores. I was able to convince my chief that we needed to hammer out a core value that reduced community policing to harder terms. The Executive Officers' Team had a one-day retreat for that sole purpose; we settled on "committed to community needs" as our core value. We then put this suggestion to everyone in the organization and asked for others. After all those suggestions that were received were considered, "committed to community needs" represented the thoughts of the majority and so it is now our core value. I will demonstrate its universality later.

Ownership of Turf

Those of us who are charged with the responsibility of leading others in the workplace would do well to contemplate the words of John Steinbeck, who said, "I find it necessary to contemplate man as an animal before I can understand him as a man." I have learned that whenever I want to institute a new idea, at home or at work, I always start out with the human element. I believe people willingly accept change only when an idea sells itself, and they accept it on their terms. For problem-oriented policing to become a reality, I advocate replacing specialization by function with ownership of turf. Let me explain.

I am convinced that my city is not just a glob of 605,000 people. Rather, it is a collection of villages stuck together that are as unique as if they were villages in the conventional sense. And it has ever been thus. Think about what Plato said of his city 2,400 years ago, "Any ordinary city is, in fact, two cities; one for the rich and one for the poor, each at war with the other. And in either city, there are smaller ones. You would make a great mistake if you treated them all alike." Contemplate the difference between inner cities and suburbia; nevertheless, conventional policing treats all villages alike. I will continue to use the word "village" to describe my idea.

The ideal is to give ownership of a village to an individual police officer so that everything of a policing nature in that village "belongs" to that person. This general principle must, of necessity, remain flexible because the needs of all villages are not the same. Indeed, many villages in a typical city don't need much policing while others require intense attention for different reasons. In some cases teams of people need to be assigned to a village but the one constant will be ownership of the problems of that village through permanent assignment. What has to happen is the reverse of convention. *Instead of the Grunt being co-opted by the specialist, the specialist will be co-opted by the Grunt, when appropriate, to deal with village problems.* The Grunt becomes the surgeon with everyone else in support.

I do not advocate doing away with specialization entirely. Recently, my wife had a serious automobile accident and required major surgery; I did not want our family doctor doing it. Logic dictates that significant specialization remain and even new ones sprout that will differ from organization to organization, but the guiding principle must be, *generalize where possible, specialize where necessary.* In the generalist work environment, the ownership phenomenon stays, but the focus of it shifts from the function to the core value. *People become peace officers first and specialists second.* People must look beyond law enforcement to the core value. Everyone is now driven by the commonweal of their village. Their daily work becomes, and remains, a natural microcosm of the macrocosm (I love these computer words!). The "right things" to do are the same for all. By applying the core value to their village, individuals remain connected — and contribute — to the cause of the organization. Over time, a common ownership develops between the producer and consumer of the police product, supported whenever necessary by the police specialist, to achieve the things of utmost importance to that village in the interests of overall community welfare and existence.

Some will say this is naive thinking. So be it. Emerson said that nothing great is ever achieved without enthusiasm; he also defined enthusiasm as the child in us winning out over the adult. Innocence goes hand-in-hand with enthusiasm. Wasn't the little boy naive to blow the whistle on the emperor's stupidity? Were not the Wright brothers naive too to think their flimsy contraption would work? But where would flight be today if they had said, "We ain't running off this hill until we see a stealth bomber"? Obviously, there were skeptics 400 years ago too because here is what Francis Bacon had to say on the matter way back then, "As the birth of all living creatures are ill-shapen, so too are all innovations which are the births of time." The present of everything is at once half dead and half pregnant with the future.

I am not dumb; I don't subscribe to the old adage, "He ain't heavy, he's my brother." Sometimes my brother weighs a ton if I have to do all the carrying. I played rugby too long to believe everyone in a scrum pushes; some use it as a rest period. There are only so many Mother Teresas out there, and I'm not one of them. But I do subscribe to the sensible saying, "I'll scratch your back if you scratch mine." Most people will contribute to a common cause, if there is a common pay-off. That is why it is smarter for *five neighbors to build a common fence together than five separate ones alone*; they can buy in bulk and everyone will do a good job on every fence because they know they will reap what they sow. Besides, it's more fun.

Neighborhood Foot Patrol in Edmonton

I have tried to practice the principles of ownership in policing and learn as I go along. I have also tried to practice what Fred Hertzberg said about motivation in the workplace. He said, "The only way to motivate people is to give them meaningful work, control over it, resources to do the job, then get out of their way" (Herzberg, 1968).

In Edmonton we have individual police officers assigned permanently to twenty-two villages. They are on foot, have their own store-front offices manned by volunteer citizens and because they carry pagers, most of their daily work is dictated by the needs of their village. We started in 1988 with the busiest twenty-one officers. At the outset we asked for volunteers, got forty-four and chose twenty-one whose length of service averaged nine years. Their role, quite simply, is to take care of as much of the daily policing needs of their village as possible and work back through the specialized units for whatever help they need. *They are decentralized, are not part of a specialized unit, work shifts, and respond to all levels of calls for service in their village.* I knew from the outset that the success of the enterprise would depend upon the people doing the work. I needed people who would bring their brain through the gate with them. Our patrol personnel work ten-hour shifts; most specialities work eight. Foot patrol work eight. By volunteering, these people were agreeing to give up 48 days off a year, yet every single volunteer was from patrol. Not a single specialist volunteered. This is what people will do to get ownership of their work. There is lots of motivation in policing, it is simply dormant.

The initiative has been evaluated twice, technically by the Canadian Research Institute for Law and the Family (CRILF) through funding from the Federal Solicitor General, and, more informally, by a local author who was contracted to work with the people on the beat and to write a documentary of what the product looked like through the eyes of the people providing and consuming the service: the cop on the beat and the neighborhood resident. This latter work was funded by a grant from the Charles Stewart Mott Foundation of Flint, Michigan. Both evaluations have been published and are available.

They show unequivocally that a common ownership does develop, and indeed after a relatively short period of time. Unlike the specialist who encounters the same task, but not the same people on a continuing basis, this police officer is forced into ongoing contact with the same customers on a broad range of issues so that a common motivation to "do something" about the problem develops. If they don't face it today, both officer and resident will have to face it tomorrow. Unlike many of their fellow officers, these people thoroughly enjoy their work, bring their brains through the door with them, and use them.

The Family Doctor Approach

Let me use the Canadian health care system to illustrate what I am trying to get across. I equate specialization by function with the specialist medical doctor. Let's use the example of an orthopedic surgeon who specializes in hip replacements. This person will be very interested in our hips but oblivious to the rest of our body. They work on hips, not people. Once the hip is fixed you are passed on to someone else. Your paths are not likely to cross again and so there is little interest in you as a whole person. A "one-night stand," so to speak. As a consequence, the surgeon develops certain talents, at the expense of others. Health care research reveals that few malpractice suits emanate from careless scalpel work. Most are the product of poor bedside manners; usually demeaning treatment of the patient during the hospitalization process (Peters and Austin, 1985).

Contrast the doctor-patient relationship of the hip specialist with the family doctor. The relationship changes dramatically because the family doctor is responsible for the general health and well being of a village; a small group of perpetual customers who happen to live in a particular neighborhood. This is not a one-night stand; it's a marriage. The doctor needs his or her patients to come back and so he or she must treat them well. If he or she mistreats one member of a family, he or she will lose all. Over time, the doctor becomes very accountable and knowledgeable about the whole patient because he or she treats everything except that which requires emergency or specialist care.

So it is not surprising that the *good* family doctor inevitably becomes one of the most trusted, respected, and informed people in the village. Eventually, people turn to him or her for things that have nothing to do with health in the medical sense. People will share with him or her matters known to no other.

Policing should build its nonemergency service delivery around the family doctor idea, as much as possible. I think that most good family doctors recognized long ago that they don't control health; such things as lifestyle, heredity, smoking, booze, and sitting on our butt in front of the television filling our face with too much junk food can render the finest doctors in the land impotent. Doctors know about disease and sickness but these things only happen when health breaks down. The good family doctor knows that his or her practice must go beyond handing out pills and giving needles or he or she won't have much of a practice. He or she must get beyond the known to the unknown figures if he or she wants to stay in business because people can change doctors easily. In fact, most cities have too many doctors, that is why the health care system threatens to bankrupt the nation.

Surely the reality of policing is the same. Most of our work is made, or unmade, in the family, yet the common cry has been, "Let's not make a family problem a police problem" — as if we had any choice. One thing seems clear, kids who are cared for or cared about don't get into much trouble, kids who are not, do. Lev Tolstoy said, "All happy families resemble each other but each unhappy family is unhappy in its own way." Today I believe our family unit is more unhappy, in more ways, than at any time in history. Therefore, by definition, there is more police work than ever before.

I said early that I need a clear target to aim at when I take on a new job. Here is my target. I am convinced that the majority of police service an individual, family, or business requires is best provided by a single police officer they know, respect, and trust. We know that information is the lifeblood of policing and that ordinary people have a lock on it (Trojanowicz and Bucqueroux, 1990), but they won't give it to strangers. People don't bare their soul to the family doctor on the first visit either. Second, just as it takes time for the doctor to get to know the general health of the patient, it will take time for the police officer to get to know the health of the neighborhood and its people. Specialty by function cannot give you this; ownership of turf can, and the future model of policing must be built around it.

Who "Owns" the Bike?

I must tell a little story here to illustrate what I mean by ownership in the policing sense. One day several years ago, I noticed a bicycle chained to a post right in front of our headquarters building on 96th Street, which is in our city center. I watched this bike for four months throughout the winter. It was obvious from the start that it was either stolen or abandoned. At the time, we had twenty-one people assigned to foot patrol in the conventional sense who worked out of headquarters. No one was assigned to any particular beat on a permanent basis but headquarters was "home" to everyone. This beat assignment was a specialized unit; they worked in pairs and had no particular job description. Their job simply was to be seen. In fact, it was these positions I used to staff our neighborhood foot patrol two years later. Of course, it was considered a "plum" job because they didn't have to take calls for service. Some of our best young constables worked it. Every day it was necessary for these people to walk past that bike going to and from their beats. Each must have walked past the bike one hundred times, yet no one did anything about it. I think I know why.

I can just see it now as they walked out the door of headquarters each morning and upon confronting that confounded bike, Mick would say to himself, "Oh, Pat will take care of it." Of course, each time Pat encountered the bike, he would say the same thing to himself about Mick. The end result was that nobody took care of the bike because it wasn't their problem. No one "owned" the village that 96th Street is in.

Why do I feel so sure about this? Because I see this phenomenon repeat itself daily in my home. I have two sons, not bad kids, but for years I have watched them step around, over, and sometimes through stuff that belongs to the other. I have even seen them wash one of two dishes left in the sink because "they didn't dirty the other one."

If anyone wants to know the reality of what goes on in policing, don't study policy or management, get into the heads of the people doing the work. My good friend Herman Goldstein figured that one out years ago; that is why he understands the Grunt so well.

To Care and to Try Hard

There is something else I have learned during my years in policing that supports the ownership approach. For three years, I was the commander of the South Side Division that comprises about 250,000 people and 175 police officers. During that period, I received about three hundred letters from citizens, generated by the work of police officers, good and bad. The former outnumbered the latter about two-to-one. All, however, had a common theme. Every letter spoke about the extent to which the officer "cared" about or "tried hard" to solve a problem. Either he or she did or didn't. Not one complained that we had not caught the bad guy or recovered stolen property. In fact, most seemed to understand and accept that what the police can do about crime in the general sense is limited. They seemed prepared to accept the fact that most crime is the product of a multitude of things, most of which are beyond our control. They do, however, expect us to care, and to try hard for the short period of time we are dealing with them and their problem. And they have every right to.

I call these "moments of truth" letters. But really, all that people are asking is that we "police others as we would have them police us." Don't police officers expect the doctor, mechanic, barber, bank teller, and dentist to care and to try hard when they are working on their behalf? In fact, my experience tells me that cops are the most demanding customers on God's earth when they are on the receiving end of a product or service. When they sell a car they want the highest buck; when they buy, the lowest.

As police administrators, we cannot always deliver on a promise to reduce crime, no matter how hard we try. We can, however, deliver on a promise to care and to try hard about people's problems. It is against these efforts — these moments of truth — that the ultimate success of the entire organization will be measured.

Community Policing

I must dwell on the subject of community policing here a while. Community policing is perhaps the most topical issue in policing today. It is also misunderstood by most. It seems to mean all things to all people. Volumes have been written and library shelves are bending under the weight. One thing seems certain; whatever it is, everyone seems to like it. Many people are hitchhiking on its wave of popularity. I don't like hitchhikers; they remind me of the guys who lean on scrums. They are more interested in advancing their own cause than that of policing. They apply community policing to everything they do *outside* of fundamental patrol work. Often, all it means is changing the sign on the door of bureaucracy. Many polarize community policing from conventional policing. They seem to think the two are opposites of each other; that taking calls for service is the opposite of problem solving and that you must do one or the other, but not both. This is a critical error. How can the family doctor know about our health if he or she doesn't treat the aches and pains along the way? Community policing is what convention is supposed to be, but is not. Let me explain.

Imagine the reaction if the Canadian Medical Association announced that they were embarking upon a new way of doing business called patient-based health care! How would we react if the Canadian Teachers Association announced they were moving to student-based model of education? To suggest that community policing is new is to suggest that up until now, we have been policing someone else. When one goes fishing, there is no need to say "fishing for fish." Fishing says it all. So does policing. The adjective "community" is redundant; so are the arguments for and against community policing. In fact, those arguments make the point better than I can that we have seriously drifted from our original mission because we now have to use the qualifier "community" to identify what we are talking about. Simply put, community policing is what we should have been doing all along. For me, that community policing is the cause is a settled issue; what the problems are and how they should be attacked in a given community is another matter.

In support of my assertion, consider the following passages:

- The power of the police is dependent upon public approval of the police's existence, actions, and behavior.

- It is necessary to secure the willing cooperation of the public in maintaining order and securing peace.

- The test of police effectiveness is the absence of crime and disorder, not the visible evidence of police action in dealing with them.

- A relationship must be maintained at all times with the public that gives reality to the historic tradition that the police are the public and the public are the police. The police are simply members of the public who are paid to give full-time attention to duties that are incumbent upon every citizen, in the interest of community welfare and existence.

All the above are taken from Peel's Principles upon which the London Metropolitan Police was founded 162 years ago. All urban policing in North America, whether we like it or not, was fashioned after that model.

Regardless, people continue to define community policing as a new thing. My position is that they are wrong on both counts. It is neither new, nor is it a thing. The mandate of policing has not changed; bureaucrats' perceptions have — wildly. As evidence of the confusion that exists, recently I read a quote by a senior Canadian police official who said, "We have been in policing for hundreds of years, we have only been in community policing for a short time." There is only policing as it was intended to be, as it has come to be, and as it needs to be, community by community.

So let us get rid of the notion that we have a new product on the shelf, which is why it can never be realized as an add-on to the conventional model. Unfortunately, most efforts to implement it simply create a new box on the edge of the organization chart, put a few people in it and announce the birth of community policing. It is not an hors d'oeuvre or dessert, it's the main course.

Many organizations claim to be "into" community policing. From what I have seen, I'm skeptical. In most cases, copious policy is written and lectures given by bosses to Grunts but little structural or intellectual change at the management level results. In most cases, the Grunts were simply urged to "go forth and problem solve," while everyone and everything around them remained *in situ*. Before anything else happens, the heads of the brass have to be retooled before we worry about the feet of the Grunts. There is no point in putting a new paint job on a car if the engine is shot. Tom Peters said it best, "Radical improvement in the way we do business will only follow from radical improvement in the way we organize ourselves" (Peters and Austin, 1985). Experience has shown — and I accept it implicitly — that the most effective way to change behavior is to move people into a new organizational context that imposes new roles, responsibilities, and relationships upon them. Literally, you have to move the body before the brain begins to think differently. It is imperative that organization restructuring occurs *first* to accommodate community policing. If it is superimposed on convention, convention will win out and we will have a repeat of the team policing debacle of the 1970s.

Community Policing and Detectives

I don't want to dwell on community policing in this paper because it is not the object of the exercise, but there are a couple of points I must clear up before I leave the topic. I have the opportunity to travel extensively in my policing career across the continent. Few people seem to be able to link community policing and detectives. Here are a couple of scenarios that might help.

Suppose a robbery squad detective has two files to work on; a bank robbery in the business section of the city and a wino mugging outside a slum liquor store.

For the bank, the financial loss is infinitesimal ($1,500 average in Canada) and is insured, and the clerk, although traumatized, can escape to suburbia at the end of the day, probably never to see that person again. If things get too bad, the clerk can move to another branch, even change jobs if necessary. Witnesses too can escape the trauma the same way as the clerk because they never have to return to the scene of the crime if they don't wish to. Experience (in Edmonton, at least) shows that violence is rare in a bank robbery.

For the wino, the loss is total, perhaps his welfare or pension check. He probably lives within blocks of the crime scene so he cannot escape the trauma. He and his mugger probably know each other because the mugger probably lives in the neighborhood, too. He might even have been attacked by this person before but was afraid to report it; because he is destitute, he cannot escape. Those who witnessed the attack probably live close by, know the mugger, and will suffer the same trauma because they cannot flee the slums either. The wino probably suffered some physical injury, and the mugger, will continue to prey on the slum dwellers until he is stopped.

If the detective applies community policing values, he will decide which gets priority by looking at the *community damage* caused by both. Conventional policing would say, work the bank file first. Community policing would say, work the wino file first.

How would community policing apply to an auto theft squad? This way. An expensive Mercedes owned by a judge is stolen. An old school bus owned by an inner-city church group is stolen. Both end up on a detective's desk on Saturday morning. He must decide which case takes priority. Here are some things that would help him decide.

The Mercedes is insured against theft and the judge owns several other vehicles. Judges don't work on weekends. The church bus is not insured against theft, the church has no other vehicles, and they have planned a trip the next day for a bunch of inner-city kids.

Conventional policing would say, work the judge's case first. Community policing would say, work the church bus case first.

Conventional policing stops short of the mandate; it stops at the "what" of the work. Community policing takes it one step beyond, to the "why" of the work. It is because we have not consistently asked ourselves why we do things that we have ended up with functions in place of a cause.

Challenge me to apply this thinking to any box on the organization chart, from the chief to the janitor, and I could do it. It is simple. It all has to do with "constancy of purpose" (Ed Deming again) and priorities. All we need do is manage policing the way we manage our families and our personal lives; apply the same priority rationale at work as we do at home. Generally speaking, people who have reached the executive level in policing are relatively successful in their personal and family lives; their finances are in order, there are strong values in the home and decisions are based upon the commonwealth of the entire family; sometimes even the extended family. Mortgage takes precedence over exotic vacations and so on. If we apply the same value judgments at work that we do routinely at home, we would not be in the pickle we are in. If we were as prudent with the public dollar as we are with our own, policing wouldn't need the bureaucratic garage sale that is discussed next.

A Bureaucratic Garage Sale

Garage sales are very sensible. They achieve two things: get rid of junk that is either broken or out of style and free up a few bucks with which to buy new things. Let us apply this logic to the task at hand. The typical conventional police agency is in great need of a bureaucratic garage sale. Some of the boxes on the organization chart need to be eliminated, merged, or renovated so as to free up resources to do new things.

As I see it, the conventional police organization is like a fifty-year-old house. When it was built, it was new, strong, and in vogue but with the passage of time, two things happened. Parts of it rotted, and it went out of style. What is needed is an imaginative renovation job. Translated, the conventional police organization needs to be gutted and rebuilt around community welfare and existence; law enforcement must be relegated to component status.

We need to start out with a few mavericks and give them freedom to attack convention. But first, there must be vision, and then there must be leadership.

Vision

They can, because they think they can.
                    (Virgil)

I think vision is best described in the story of Michelangelo and the little boy. One day, as Michelangelo commenced to sculpt a large block of marble, a little boy sat down to watch. He came every day thereafter until, finally, the artist had finished a beautiful statue of David, which prompted the little lad to ask, "How did you know he was in there?"

There is a great lesson in this little story, and it is about vision. I'm sure that Michelangelo didn't know that particular statue of David was in there when he started. In fact, at the outset he probably used big, ugly hammers and chisels but as the work progressed, his instruments became more precise and his strokes more deft.

Like Michelangelo's block of marble, in the policing scenario the vision will take hold slowly, probably amidst great grumbling — even obstruction from people in key positions. Most causes attract more critics than champions. It will be a time reflected in the adage, "When the going gets tough, the tough get going." It is a huge plus if the chief is one of those mavericks because he or she will have to articulate, teach, live, and make the vision compelling to others. Eventually, he or she will have to create a cadre of people with diverse talents and then give them ownership of individual pieces of the whole. But the conventional bureaucrat will be no help to him or her this time; we are talking about a new breed of cat.

Vision is a thing of the future, but you only get there by the works of each day. I am sure that Michelangelo shed much sweat before David emerged. Plan, but, for God's sake, get started. We don't need all of the answers up front; in fact, many cannot be discovered until some preliminaries are complete. General George Patton was good at getting started; he said, "A good plan violently executed today is better than a perfect plan next week." For some, vision has "another world" aura to it, but don't be fooled. Its motivational power is hard, slogging work. Visionaries are perpetually battling to have their visions seen; many never succeed in their lifetime but we build statues to them a century later.

Leadership in Monopoly

The responsibility of power requires resisting and then redirecting a pervading condition.
                    (Anonymous)

Leadership in smooth times is easy. Managers and bureaucrats can play the role and get away with it. Leadership in policing during the 1950s, 1960s, and 1970s was never really tested because there was no particular crisis, at least in Canada. No one was paying much attention to us, budgets routinely increased by 10 percent annually, and departments grew in size. But all of that has changed now. We have discovered that the crime rate was also growing, despite the extra bodies and money being thrown at the problem. Now, next to politicians, policing is the most studied occupation on the continent. As a consequence, policy makers won't buy the "more bodies and more guns" argument anymore.

Crisis distinguishes true leaders — quickly. Winston Churchill, arguably the finest leader of this century, was *persona non grata* for the twelve years before the start of the Second World War. There simply was no need for a Churchill in Britain during that period; Chamberlain of "peace in our time" fame could fill the chair and get away with it. Bureaucrats crumble at the approach of crisis, leaders are pumped by it. People like Churchill put meaning to the phrase, "Necessity is the mother of invention." They see it as a chance to "strut their stuff," to rise above the pack.

But Churchill had a war going for him. Motivation was no problem. Motivation was no problem for Ray Kroc either; one's own franchise and its money-making capacity would cause the laziest among us to work hard, long hours. On the other hand, policing exists only for the cause. Motivation is tougher for a police chief than it was for Churchill or Ray Kroc. In policing, people get paid the same for sitting on their butt as they do for busting it. Moreover, the cause is like vision, a thing of the future. It is like a post-dated check; the work must be done now but the pay-off comes later, if at all. I was reading recently that annually, 85 percent of the research and development dollars spent by the Fortune 500 companies end in failure, yet they continue to do these efforts. The Wright brothers had to take their run off that hill, first, before they got their answer. Therefore, because motivation is so much harder to come by in our world, leadership in policing is more difficult than in the private sector. It is also more important.

Because vision and mission are future events, leaders must intellectually live in the future. To achieve this, daily routine must be delegated. But the chief cannot be a recluse; he or she must also stay in touch with the present. He or she can only do this by perpetually being in contact with the Grunts, teaching, inspiring, and even goading people to see the cause. Whenever I visit a police agency, the first thing I check is how much the "In" and "Out" baskets dominate the chief's day. This will give me a good indication whether the chief is a leader or a bureaucrat. On top of all else, there is the constant need to reexamine the original mission in the light of society's changes around policing so as continually to refocus and keep the core value current. This is exactly what *has not* happened in policing. O. W. Wilson's management philosophy was put in place in the 1950s and 1960s, for reasons that suited those times. But that model is still there in its original form notwithstanding its flaws uncovered by experience and the societal changes that have occurred in the interim. Evaluation of management decision making in policing is nonexistent. Once instituted, things become entrenched, therefore, the inevitable incremental changes that needed to occur, didn't. This is why we need the garage sale.

Pervading Condition

I chose the passage that opened this chapter for a reason. There is a pervading condition in policing. It is called apathy. Apathy flourishes whenever people "turn off," for whatever reason. People turn off when they feel "shut out." When people feel shut out, their mental energy finds another outlet. Most police officers I know feel shut out and so have found outlets other than policing for their mental energy; consider how many have jobs on the side — next to fire fighters, probably more than any other occupation. All of this is the legacy of three decades of the standard operating procedures management system in what is arguably the most unpredictable job in society. In most organizations today, we don't have peace officers, we have soldiers following orders. If the few remaining people who bring their brains through the gate with them ever stop doing so, we're in deep trouble. From where I sit, we are getting the job done, in spite of ourselves but I truly see crisis looming on the horizon. We need a few good leaders — fast — who have the courage to make the hard decisions and redirect this pervading condition. Most senior officers I know are quick to demand autonomy but rarely pass it on to others. Many are haughty and dictatorial. Most think they are sharing power when all they are doing is dumping the legwork on done deals. This had better change because Grunts are not buying their snake oil anymore. Power has two components: responsibility and the authority to carry out that responsibility. Power, like knowledge, is useless unless it is shared. Autocratic bureaucrats invariably end up lonely and up to their armpits in alligators because those around them provide only opinion echoes while abdicating their responsibilities. This is the pervading condition that afflicts policing today at all levels.

The End

I started this paper with ownership and ended up with leadership. I think they are one and the same. To me, it is self-evident that you cannot have one without the other. Leadership is the one thing we cannot have unless we are prepared to give it away by sharing power. True leaders have many talents but the most important one is the ability to recognize talent in others, and then liberate it. True leaders are forever creating new heroes around them. I have read that the biggest difference between Winston Churchill and F. D. Roosevelt was that Churchill was always championing young politicians while Roosevelt was busy silencing those around him.

The best example of making others heroes is captured in the words of Eugene Debs, founder of the railroad unions in the United States who said, "I am not your leader. I don't want you to follow me, or anyone else. If you are looking for a Moses to lead you out of the capitalist wilderness, you will stay right where you are. I would not lead you into the promised land if I could, because if I could lead you in, someone else could lead you out." I came across Deb's quote twenty years ago when I read his biography, *Adversary in the House* (Stone, 1948). It is one of the best books I have ever read, and I recommend it highly to anyone interested in true leadership, the kind that walks the talk.

In the home and in the workplace there are two things I have tried to provide for my children and the young people with whom I work. They are *roots* and *wings*: roots in strong values and wings in a free mind. I have tried to give my sons solid roots in a good home with values, but I don't want them to cling to me. I don't want them to clone me; that is why I gave them distinct old Irish names, Declan and Conor, both of whom were free-spirited warriors in Gaelic folklore. They didn't like it when they were younger but I think they now understand. I want them to explore thought and life around them, as I have, and to discover whatever it is God intended them to be. I think knowing that they have an intellectual nest to come home to in the form of someone who truly respects their individuality will make them better explorers, and they will return to the nest more often. I have encouraged them to read about the great people of history, especially the philosophers, to learn from them, even admire them, but through it all I have tried to teach them to be their own heroes. I want them never to stop testing their wings. As I look around me, I find it sad that so many of us seem more afraid of life than death.

In the workplace, I have been fortunate to have had numerous command positions and to have headed up several project teams. I don't change hats when I come to work. I try to apply the same philosophy at work as I do at home. In both venues, I try to practice what I preach in this paper, and I can tell you that it works. I have watched "washed-up" veterans flower and come to life because someone trusted them and gave them a piece of the action. I have watched conventionalists, once nudged them past the griping stage, pull asunder routine operating procedures and come up with simple, logical alternatives. I have watched Grunts work on weekends and even reschedule their family vacations just to stay on something they had got their teeth into as part of our project. I have watched people bury hatchets on personal differences and pull together in a common cause because each was dependent upon the other, and in the process discover a new side of each other. And all of this has made my job easy. In my own life, I have adhered to something I read long ago: *do what you can where you are with what you have*. It might have been Roosevelt who said it. I have always tried to be my own hero while absorbing everything I could learn from the great thinkers. I have always tried to make things happen in my sphere of control and in the process, I escaped the pervading condition. I am grateful for that.

Last Word

Time to sum up and bring things to a close. This paper has wandered but it is essentially about ownership in the workplace. Ownership is central to the human psyche. Once installed, ownership becomes the dominant factor so it better be attached to the right thing. It will attach to the wrong thing unless there is a core value that is visible to — and attainable by — all. The core value must be entrenched alongside ownership in the psyche of the organization so that the two become as one. The core value must epitomize the cause of the organization. Once the core value is entrenched, everyone and everything must be measured according to it. Humans are central to quality policing. Quality policing cannot be ordered up or bought. It cannot come from things. It is a product of the human mind. People will only give it to you when they bring their brains to work with them. They will do that only when they feel a commitment to the cause. They will only have commitment to the cause when they feel ownership for it. Ownership is central to leadership; they go together. The vital component of leadership is hero creation.

I have tried hard and long to understand my world of policing. Perhaps it is different from yours but I doubt that the fundamentals are. I truly believe that whatever the future of policing holds in store for us, it must be fashioned around the ownership that I have tried to describe here.

I suppose I could have saved everyone the trouble of reading this whole piece by starting out with this fundamental truism by Mark Twain (but that would be no fun), "Almost any man worth his salt would go to war to defend his home, but no one ever heard of a man going to war for his boarding-house."

References

Bennis, W. G. & Nanus, B. (1985). *Leaders: The strategies for taking charge.* New York: Harper & Row, Publishers Inc.

Crosby, P. (1984). *Quality without tears: The art of hassle free management.* New York: McGraw-Hill Inc.

Deming, W. E. (1986). *Out of the crisis.* Cambridge, MA: Massachusetts Institute of Technology.

Drucker, P. F. (1973). *Management: Tasks, responsibilities, and practices.* New York: Harper & Row, Publishers Inc.

Herzberg, F. (1968). One more time, how do you motivate employees. *Harvard Business Review,* (Jan/Feb).

Peters, T. J. & Austin, N. (1985). *A passion for excellence: The leadership difference.* New York: Random House Inc.

Stone, I. (1948). *Adversary in the house.* Sydney: Invincible Press.

Trojanowicz, R. & Bucqueroux, B. (1990). *Community policing: A contemporary perspective.* Cincinnati: Anderson Publishing Co.

Chapter 5

Activity Trap

Dennis R. Longmire

Introduction

As citizens increasingly demand accountability within public sector agencies (Kemp, 1990), there may be a tendency for agency executives to routinize the agency's activities so much that its employees become driven by evaluation procedures rather than the agency's particular mission. In law enforcement agencies, this possibility is best exemplified by tendencies of some departments to establish quota systems for traffic officers requiring that they issue some minimum level of traffic citations during a given period of time. Policies such as this instill requirements on personnel that have no clear connection to larger programmatic goals. They are indications of the activity trap facing many public sector agencies today.

On a more general level, the evaluation of police effectiveness through measures of variations in crime rates may also indicate that police agencies have fallen prey to the activity trap. Counting the relative increase or decrease of crimes reported to the police may result in some vague measure of police activity but just what the police are (or are not) doing to help cause fluctuations in crime rates is not necessarily represented by such a count. Wycoff (1982) argues forcefully for the development of enhanced measures of police performance based on observations of what the police actually do and the resulting consequences of their behaviors. She also advocates the use of individual level performance measures rather than aggregate level measures because "individual measures provide the most useful information about ways of changing, shaping, and managing the organization" (Wycoff, 1982, p. 12). Hatry (1970), on the other hand, cautions against reliance on individual level performance measures of police productivity.

In a recent study examining the attitudes held by supervisory level police officers toward the performance appraisal procedures used in their departments, Walsh (1990) reported that 87 percent (*n* = 106) of his sample did not find the particular system in use to be of any value in assessing the actual effectiveness of an officer's job performance. In light of this finding, the performance appraisal system itself might be viewed as an "activity trap" in that supervisory officers are going through the motions of an evaluation with little real expectation that the outcome of the process will enhance their supervisory abilities. In this context, the "activity trap" involves the victim of its power in activities that take on value and meaning only to the extent that they satisfy some formal or bureaucratic requirement. Little real or known value comes from such activities.

Specifically what should be measured to determine police effectiveness is debatable and has been the subject of almost continuous discussion since the dissemination of the results of Project STAR (Smith et al., 1974) which sets forth detailed performance objectives for all components of the criminal justice network including the police. For recent examples of these discussions, see Brandl and Horvath (1991); Conner and Richards (1991); Falkenberg and colleagues (1991); Gardner (1990); Petersilia and colleagues (1990); and Snow (1990). It is not the purpose of this chapter to provide a listing of possible productivity measures. Simply calling attention to the value of program evaluation for police decision making will suffice at this time.

In addition to helping agencies avoid the "activity trap," program evaluation provides a mechanism through which agencies can experience "planned change." Whisenand and Ferguson (1988) suggest that "strategic planning" is one tool available for police managers to use in their quest for enhanced leadership. Although not always discussed together, both strategic planning and program evaluation will enable the progressive police manager to respond effectively to changes in their environment.

The Inevitability of Change

Change is inevitable and will influence every existing element of life, even the structural arrangements in society referred to as "complex organizations." From the highly automated production line of the factory to the intense decision-making procedures in the executive boardroom, changes are inevitable. Whisenand and Rush (1988, p. 276) discuss the influence of rapid change on police management and call for the development of "change masters" in law enforcement leadership.

Application of the Darwinian principle of "the survival of the fittest" to the organizational environment leads to the conclusion that the ability for an organization to respond effectively to change determines its "survivability." The strongest organizational structure is the one most able to adapt to changes in the environment just as the "fittest" creature in the physical ecosystem is the one most able to adapt to changes in the physical environment. In general, an organization's ability to respond to changes in the environment is determined by the amount of research and development conducted under its auspices. The research and development division of most private sector organizations is a primary and integral dimension of the organization's formal structure. The goals and objectives of the organization are determined by directors and boards who take seriously the results of their research division and who call on their researchers to be constantly looking into the future offering insights into how their particular market is likely to change over the next several years. Such information is critical to any successful strategic planning initiative, and the successful organization is the one that is able to remain flexible enough to continue to meet the demands of a changing market.

Public sector organizations are woefully underdeveloped in the areas of research and development, program evaluation, and strategic planning. Perhaps as a result of their dependence on the "whim and fancy" of members of the various committees involved in highly politicized appropriations procedures, chief administrators of public sector organizations often find themselves trying to retrofit their goals and objectives to their budgets. Largely bureaucratic in nature, the typical public sector organization is *reactive* to changes in the environment rather than being more *proactive* by anticipating changes and initiating new strategies to deal better with the changing environment.

Within the criminal justice component of the public sector, the reality of change in the environment is readily apparent. The nature of criminal offending behavior has become increasingly violent in recent years. Drug distribution networks and adolescent gang organizations have become much more problematic in our nation's major urban areas. Even rural communities have become prey to the illicit drug industry. The growing number of elderly citizens increases their representation among the population being served by the criminal justice network, resulting in increased numbers of elderly victims as well as increased numbers of elderly offenders for the network to process. Added to these changes are changes in the nature of crime itself such as the development of new computer-enhanced ways to defraud citizens and taxpayers out of millions of dollars.

Each component of the criminal justice network has also experienced recent changes in the cultural composition of its employees. The network is now more fully represented by employees from different ethnic and cultural backgrounds than ever before in history. Every component of the network has both men and women occupying positions of authority and supervision where not long ago, women were prohibited from holding some positions simply because of their gender.

And there have been changes in the way each component of the criminal justice network does its job. As the social and political environment changes, so too do our expectations of what we want our police, courts, and postadjudicatory agencies to do. How well informed our agency officials are of the necessary changes depends largely upon their leadership's attentiveness to the changes in the environment and their ability to formulate strategies to respond to the environmental changes. Responsive leadership demands an openness to change and a willingness to remain constantly in touch with the goals and objectives of the agency one is working within, always being willing to try something new.

In times characterized by rapid and dramatic change it is important that organizations continue to commit resources to their research and development departments. When in the throes of change, what better tool is there to help the organization's leadership remain in touch with the environment than a strong and active research division? Within the criminal justice sector of public agencies there has been a steady decrease in the commitment of federal funds to research and development activities since the 1980s. In fact, in 1980 the Office of Justice Programs (then known as the Office of Justice Assistance, Research, and Statistics) committed 5 percent of its total budget to research, evaluation, and demonstration projects. In 1990 only 2.9 percent of its budget was allocated to support such efforts (Maguire and Flanagan, 1991, p. 15).

The purpose of this chapter is twofold, and both purposes are related to the need for criminal justice agencies in general and police agencies in particular to become more responsive to change. First, and of primary importance, is a call for increased awareness of the importance and value of research and development within the leadership of the law enforcement sector of criminal justice. The most familiar language to use in criminal justice when talking about research and development is "program evaluation." One of the goals of this chapter is to help convince the leaders in policing to become more receptive to the use of evaluation research to enhance their service delivery. A second but related goal of this chapter is to propose "comprehensive evaluation" as a model for evaluation that will result in an enlightened leadership within the law enforcement community. Through the use of comprehensive evaluations, executive level law enforcement officials will be committed to planned change resulting from a critical assessment of the environment. As a result, the enlightened leader will go beyond proactive change and will become *responsive* to the environment, exercising a positive influence to enhance the delivery of services that will meet the needs of the constituency being served.

Before focusing attention upon the police component of the criminal justice network, it will be instructive to examine the different ways correctional and police agencies have responded to changes in their environments. Understanding *why* agencies shift priorities or change goals can help to put the value of research into perspective. The experiences along these lines of the corrections and policing components of the criminal justice network have been quite different and it will be instructive to examine briefly some of the differences.

Change in America's Correctional Practices: "Nothing Fails Like a Little Success"

Within the corrections component of the criminal justice network, the change process has been beautifully captured in Dinitz's (1978) essay, "Nothing Fails Like a Little Success." The title almost says it all. The history of corrections has been a history of reform and change aimed at efforts to enhance the ability of postadjudicatory agencies to reduce the likelihood of future criminality among offenders. Much of the change implemented in corrections was first initiated through efforts to produce more humane custodial environments, and historical analysis shows that conditions in our nation's prisons and jails have become more humane and less brutal in comparison to the conditions characterizing our earliest prisons.

After prisons were recognized as being more humane, researchers interested in corrections focused attention upon the prison's ability to reform and/or rehabilitate the law violator. Due largely to the dominance of positivistic science in the late 1930s continuing through the late 1960s, prisons became "treatment facilities" or "correctional institutions," whose primary purpose was to provide offenders with necessary employment skills combined with a renewed commitment to prosocial and anticriminal value systems (Morash and Anderson, 1978). Such reform efforts led to increased discretion in the sentencing process with indeterminate sentences representing the hallmark of the rehabilitative model of corrections. Accordingly, an offender's sentence would be determined by his or her responsiveness to the many treatment programs being offered under the prison's auspices. As a result of this movement, prison systems around the nation introduced sophisticated inmate classification systems accompanied by a myriad of different programs ranging from cosmetic surgery to inmate support groups. Results from some very early research studies showed decreased recidivism rates for some offenders, and prison rehabilitation programs were introduced in virtually every prison system in the nation.

It is important to note that the "rehabilitative model" of corrections was introduced throughout the nation's prison systems without strong empirical evidence that offenders were indeed being rehabilitated through the programs. By the middle of the 1960s, a new group of prison reformers, once again motivated by humanitarian ideals, questioned the fairness of the indeterminate sentencing model (American Friends Service Committee, 1971). These reformers were among the first to rely upon the results of empirical evaluations of existing rehabilitation programs to support their argument against the corrections model. There was little good evaluation research to be sampled, however, the most exhaustive effort to evaluate the collective results of program evaluations in the area of corrections resulted in a resounding conclusion that "nothing works" (Martinson, 1974). To be fair, the conclusion drawn from the research concluded that there was so little good evaluation research that it was impossible to say that anything being done under the auspices of rehabilitation was working.

Out of the critical work following the now famous Martinson Report came a new correctional reform movement referred to as "the justice model" of corrections. Under this model, the indeterminate sentence was replaced by fixed and determinant sentences set, in the most extreme circumstances, by legislative guidelines requiring that sentencing officials justify any deviations from the fixed sentences set forth in legislation. The goal of the justice model was to ensure equity in the sentencing process, and early research efforts reported decreased sentencing disparity as a result of such reform efforts.

Once again, the initial success of the justice model's reforms were offset by change. The population of prisons grew tremendously under this new model. Such growth was caused, in a large part, by the legislators' tendencies to pass sentencing bills that pander to the public's cry for more severe punishments. More severe punishments resulted in longer minimum sentence lengths and, in some instances, the eradication of parole. Prison officials found themselves trapped in an unresolvable dilemma. They could not control the flow of inmates at the front end of their system because the courts, under strict sentencing guidelines, set the length of an offender's sentence. Nor could they control the flow of inmates at the back end of their system because of reduced sentencing flexibility and/or the loss of parole as an early release option.

As stated earlier, the title of Dinitz's (1978) essay so eloquently captures the history of prison reform in the United States: "Nothing Fails Like a Little Success." Early reform efforts were initially well responded to, followed by a full-scale implementation of new program guidelines based upon the innovative models. Once implemented on a grand scale, the flaws and imperfections of the reforms show themselves clearly reflecting major failures in some instances.

Change in America's Policing Practices:
"Nothing Succeeds Like a Little Failure"

Like the history of prison reform, the process of change in the law enforcement sector of the criminal justice network has been long and varied. Unlike in corrections, however, changes in policing were not the result of "little successes." Instead, the evolution of policing from the early roots of a constabulary system to the highly professionalized model of policing in operation today, results from what might be characterized as "little failures" in institutionalized police practices. With each "failure," the police community initiated reforms aimed at improving the delivery of services resulting in the highly complex system of law enforcement found in most communities today. Like the experience in corrections, early police reforms were, for the most part, not driven by empirical research and/or program evaluations.

The earliest forms of policing in the United States relied heavily upon citizen involvement and support. In fact, prior to the professionalization of law enforcement duties, responsibilities for the job of the police official rotated among the adult men living in a given community. Early policing in the United States was quite "decentralized," "geographically dispersed," and "highly personalized" (Sykes, 1986, p. 504). As a result, the quality of police services varied considerably from one jurisdiction to another and even varied within jurisdictions depending upon who "had the watch" on any given evening.

By the late 1700s urban centers throughout the United States had begun to hire a force of "quasi-professional watchmen" to improve upon the consistency of quality control. These watchmen were employed by private entrepreneurs whose principle concern was the security of their manufacturing plants and factory warehouses. By the middle of the 1800s, available police services had been, in most instances, taken over by city governments, but they were tightly controlled by "urban machine politics" (Bittner, 1990, p. 5). The quasi-professional movement had resulted in failure evidenced by widespread reports of police corruption and general inefficiency. This system of policing remained in use, however, through the entire period of prohibition (from 1920-1933) resulting in considerable disenchantment with the quasi-professional police force that had been established.

August Volmer led the cry for increased professionalism of the nation's law enforcement community as a way to reform the corrupt spoils system that had flourished under prohibition. The first to call for a college education as a requirement for all law enforcement officers, Volmer was indeed a man before his time. For the moment, let it suffice to note that the professional model most heavily influencing the earliest efforts to professionalize the police was the highly formalized military model of professionalism. Coming directly out of the informal system of a quasi-professional yet highly political police structure in the early to middle 1900s, the regimented, militaristic model of professionalism emerging in the middle 1930s represented a welcome change. The widespread corruption and inefficiency reported by the now famous Wickersham Commission in 1931 produced changes in the organization of policing that lasted, almost unchanged, through the 1970s.

The structure established in response to the "little failures" of the quasi-professional model of policing was the institutionalization of a quasi-military model of policing. Highly bureaucratic in nature, this system of organization attempted to govern corruption through the promulgation of detailed regulations requiring rigid conformity to the policies and procedures set forth in the departmental codebooks. Bittner (1990) summarized the impetus for the new "quasi-military professional" model for policing nicely when he stated that "it is no exaggeration to say that through the 1950s and 1960s the movement to 'professionalize' the police concentrated almost exclusively on efforts to eliminate political and venal corruption by means of introducing traits of military discipline" (p. 138). As a result, discretionary decision making by the police officer, under the quasi-military model of professionalism, was taboo.

As one of the most outspoken critics of the quasi-military model of police professionalism Bittner (1990) observed that "truly professional police officers" would not need to be treated like "soldier-bureaucrats" (p. 146). Klockars (1985) summarizes the key features of the "true professional" model of policing by noting that such officers will (1) recognize the need for developing "selective enforcement policies"; (2) rely primarily upon "research and professional expertise" to formulate such policies; and (3) have the ability to "be given broad, discretionary, selective enforcement powers" in order to implement properly the department's policies.

As this brief comparison between correctional reform and police reform demonstrates, both components of the criminal justice network have undergone extensive changes since their earliest conceptions. While correctional reforms seem to have been initiated as a result of "little successes," police reforms have been characterized as resulting from some "little" (and not so little) failures. In relatively recent history, the major instances of police corruption so characteristic of policing in the 1920s and 1930s has been replaced with a more controlled system of law enforcement. The civil rights movement of the 1960s resulted in considerable change in the composition and attitude of police officers in America. Today's police community is more culturally diverse and better educated than at any time in our history (Carter and Sapp, 1990).

In the final analysis, reforms in policing have been more heavily imbued with the language of "professionalism" than have reforms in corrections. Exactly what is being called for under this concept is unclear, however, it is generally agreed that specialized educational requirements and reliance on informed decision making are important dimensions of any "profession" (Volmer and Mills, 1966; Worden, 1990).

Program Evaluators as Catalysts for Change in Policing

General Role of Evaluation Research in the Systematic Change Process

Rossi and Freeman (1989) present a concise history of what is commonly referred to as evaluation research in the United States. In their overview, they note that the period following World War II represented a boom period in program evaluation since the ability for scientific researchers to enhance the war effort were generally recognized and respected. By the close of the 1950s social scientists were influential in the development and monitoring of numerous public sector programs ranging from evaluations of crime prevention programs to the assessment of the effectiveness of different community organization activities. During the 1960s evaluation researchers improved upon their research methodologies, and their activities began to include social experimentation as well as more traditional survey techniques. By the 1970s the collaboration between the research community and public sector agencies had expanded considerably.

The involvement of scientifically trained researchers in public policy activities, via program evaluation, has not been wholeheartedly embraced in all public sector agencies. In its formative years, the discipline of criminology and criminal justice was intimately connected with the practical field and much of the research conducted under the discipline's auspices had considerable pragmatic value. In pursuit of acceptance within the more pure academic and scientific community of the university, the discipline lost much of its relevance by pursuing research with more theoretical and conceptual value than practical merit (Petersilia, 1991).

Program evaluation is not a new concept to policy analysts and public agency heads and it is generally recognized that monitoring the relative success and failure of programs is paramount for responsible stewardship of agency resources. Both academic criminologists and agency heads working in the field of criminal justice have long recognized the need for increased use of program evaluation strategies (Hatry et al., 1973; Glaser, 1973) and the call for better collaboration between the academia and agency is indeed timely (Glaser, 1990; Gilsinan, 1991; Johnson, 1990).

The time is now ripe for a revivification of emphasis on pragmatic research. Kemp (1990) observes that public sector agencies are entering an era of increased accountability and will have to adopt new models for planning that enable them to "optimize their human and financial resources" (p. 15). At the root of these new models is the need for increased knowledge about what works and what doesn't work in public sector agencies' efforts to provide services to the citizenry.

Specific Examples of Evaluation Efforts
Which Have Changed Police Practices

The law enforcement community has a rich history of program evaluations that have influenced the delivery of police services nationwide. Goldstein (1990) distinguishes between two periods of police research the first of which was initiated in the 1950s and included studies inquiring into the nature of policing. These early studies provided a firm basis for an understanding of what police officers actually do in the conduct of their jobs. The second period of police research, according to Goldstein, grew out of the political and social crises of the 1960s and early 1970s and focused upon needs assessments aimed at improving the quality of services being provided under the auspices of the law enforcement community.

The RAND Corporation, one of the leaders in criminal justice evaluation research, has published the results of an extensive analysis of the influence federally funded criminal justice research has had on criminal justice practice in general (Petersilia, 1987). In their analysis, they focused particular attention on the major areas of influence researchers have had on policing, prosecution, sentencing, and corrections. Also, their study examined the influence of federal funding on the development of new and improved technologies geared toward enhancing the delivery of criminal justice services.

In the area of policing, Petersilia (1987) concludes that program evaluation has "influenced major changes in the way police departments operate" particularly in the areas of "patrol operations, criminal investigation practices" and the development of "specialized offense and offender operations" (p. 7). Below are summary comments reflecting the ways policing has been influenced by research in each of these areas. These comments are drawn largely from Petersilia's (1987) chapter entitled "The Influence of Research on Policing."

Research Influencing Patrol Operations

A series of studies funded by the National Institute of Justice (NIJ) challenged some of the basic assumptions that had driven decisions concerning resource allocation for police patrol practices. The most widely known of these studies was the Kansas City Preventive Patrol Study conducted and reported by a research team working under the sponsorship of the Police Foundation (Kelling et al., 1974). Their research showed that random preventive patrol practices achieved no appreciable effects on citizen's perception of safety or on the actual crime rates in the community. Similar studies were conducted in different cities with the same results.

Consequently, police resources nationwide were diverted away from preventive patrol and reallocated to support other police activities.

Another area of evaluation research conducted under federal sponsorship examined the traditional assumption that police effectiveness is largely determined by the police's ability to respond quickly to calls for assistance. Under the general context of numerous Differential Response Time Studies, it was concluded that "because of the time citizens take to report crimes, the application of technological innovations and human resources to reduce police response time will have negligible impact on crime outcomes" (Van Kirk, 1978, p. 24, as cited in Petersilia, 1987, p. 11). Similarly, in Wilmington, Delaware, a study of the Management of Demand System was conducted to determine whether crime rates and citizen attitudes changed when "noncritical" calls for service were handled in a less timely manner than normal. The results of this study showed no increase in crime rates and no reduction in citizen satisfaction with police services (Cahn and Tien, 1981). As a result, considerable resource reallocation within the police community was encouraged and implemented.

Research Influencing Criminal Investigation Practices

In the middle 1970s the Stanford Research Institute (SRI) and the RAND Corporation independently conducted studies to evaluate the effectiveness of the traditional criminal investigation procedures being used in law enforcement agencies nationwide (Greenberg et al., 1975; Greenwood et al., 1977). Both research efforts concluded that traditional "police investigations played a relatively minor role" in solving crimes (Petersilia, 1987, p. 15). Consequently, the NIJ established regional training workshops to promulgate improved investigation practices. Largely as a result of these studies, it was determined that patrol officers play a significant role in the effectiveness of crime investigation and that more training and responsibility in this area needed to be given to them.

The RAND and SRI studies also resulted in improvements in case screening procedures at the law enforcement level helping decision makers discern which cases can be solved and which ones cannot. In general, the results of research in the area of criminal investigation have radically changed the way police departments allocate resources to the investigation process.

Research Influencing the Development of
Specialized Offense and Offender Operations

Another area of policing that has changed as a result of evaluation research is the development of specialized police operations designed to focus on particular crimes and criminal offenders. Petersilia's (1987) research cited the general work examining the effectiveness of different styles of police intervention in spousal assault cases as a classic case of this type of research. Research consistently showed that police need to pay special attention to calls involving spousal abuse and that "arresting the suspect appears to be the most effective means of intervening to break the pattern" of assault (Petersilia, 1987, p. 22).

Similarly, research has been conducted affirming the traditional police suspicion that only a small proportion of offenders contribute to a large proportion of the crimes known to the police. Under the auspices of career criminal units many police departments had developed special investigation and patrol units to try to identify and arrest such offenders. The best known example of such a program is the Repeat Offender Project (ROP) initiated in 1982 in Washington, D.C. This program was evaluated by the Police Foundation, which concluded that it resulted in significant success in tracking and arresting serious law violators (Martin and Sherman, 1986). More recently, research has suggested that law enforcement efforts can be enhanced by focused attention on "hot spots" or areas in a community that have disproportionately higher levels of reported crimes (Roncek and Maier, 1991; Sherman et al., 1989). One can also argue that the entire concept of problem- and community-oriented policing evolved out of research efforts showing that police effectiveness can result from the innovative and non-traditional allocation of police resources.

It is safe to conclude that the law enforcement community has benefited considerably from evaluation research activities. As Goldstein (1990) concludes in his discussion of the role research has played in changing police practices, the progress that results from change that results from police research "belies some of the criticism commonly directed at the police field as being totally resistant to change" (p. 11). Program evaluation, whether examining specific programs and practices already in existence or focusing on experimental programs designed to test innovative techniques, can provide the progressive law enforcement administrator with improved techniques to deal with the ever changing problem of crime.

Avoiding the Activity Trap Through Comprehensive Program Evaluations

Bureaucratic agencies have a strong reputation for encouraging or positively reinforcing the activity trap by routinizing activities and rigidly formalizing procedures. Program evaluation provides one mechanism to help agency leaders avoid this trap. By embracing the use of evaluation research, public sector agency heads can monitor and determine the relative effectiveness of the programs conducted under their auspices. Much has been written delineating the different techniques of program evaluation. Berk and Rossi (1990) provide an extensive guide to the literature on program evaluation and social policy research. Those interested in a more technical discussion of evaluation methodologies are referred to the sources cited in that guide.

Program evaluation strategies may include sophisticated experimental studies aimed at determining the impact of different program services on some outcome measures as well as relatively straightforward measures of the financial costs associated with particular program functions. It is common to recognize that evaluation studies may include efforts aimed at diagnosing service needs; tailoring new or existing programs to fit particular needs; monitoring ongoing programs to determine the level of their continued appropriateness; impact assessments measuring the success or failure of programs in achieving stated goals and objectives; and efficiency studies including cost-effectiveness and cost-benefit analyses (Rossi and Freeman, 1989). Any one type of program evaluation used may help public sector agency heads avoid the problems of the activity trap discussed in the opening section of this chapter. Research provides agency heads with information about what their agency is doing. This information, if tied to action programs, will offset tendencies toward the mindless routinization of agency activities so stereotypically characteristic of public bureaucracies.

In an address to a group of students graduating from the University of Munich, the "father of bureaucracy" and its foremost critic, the German scholar Max Weber (as cited in Klockars, 1985, p. 132), cautioned against the power of political bureaucracies to corrupt the good intentions of those working within their structures. Weber offers the combination of "passion" and "perspective" as counterbalances to the inherent problems of bureaucracies. In this context, Weber argues that a strong conviction to the real goals of an agency (passion) combined with a firm understanding of how the agency fits into the more general social structure (perspective) will give the professional bureaucrat the ability to overcome the tendencies of bureaucracy to corrupt them.

More recently, another German scholar, Jurgen Habermas (1984), offers an alternative approach that he argues will help to overcome the structural problems inherent in formal organizations in particular and societal organizations in general. Habermas argues for what he refers to as "communicative action" as a means for all humans to better integrate their actions with the reality their actions are trying to represent. Although not discussing the activity trap directly, the insights provided by both Habermas and Weber help to direct attention toward knowledge development as a way to avoid the pitfalls of bureaucratic life. Weber's plea for perspective demands that public officials continue to know how their agency's goals and objectives fit into the more general goals of society.

Habermas's advocacy for communicative action involves the agency official in critical knowledge development.

In the language of program evaluation, the general attitude being advocated by both Weber and Habermas calls for public officials to embrace the evaluation process for its ability to ensure both perspective and communicative action.   Rossi and Freeman (1989) use the term "comprehensive evaluation" to characterize program evaluation efforts that are designed to "1) analyze the conceptualization and design of interventions; 2) monitor program implementation; and 3) assess program effectiveness and efficiency" (p. 44). A simple program evaluation may be designed to accomplish any one of these functions, comprehensive evaluations achieve all three. In the present context, police programs introduced, monitored, and assessed through comprehensive evaluation procedures will be directed by both perspective and communicative action.

The first element of comprehensive evaluations requires the *analysis of ideas* leading to the development of particular programs. Through this process, researchers are called upon to work with agency officials to help identify alternative strategies to provide desired services. In the law enforcement component of the criminal justice network, police officials relying upon this technique will be required to conceptualize and articulate clearly the reasons they are attempting to implement any particular action. For example, if a department decides to focus special investigative efforts on particular types of crimes, it would be incumbent upon the chief to formulate clear objectives for the program, to provide information supporting the decision to pursue this course of action, and to articulate some clear and unambiguous purpose for the program.   Through this process, both perspective and communicative action will emerge.

The second element of comprehensive evaluations takes into account the adage "the best laid plans of mice and men . . .," and recognizes the inevitable need to make adjustments in proposed programs. The researcher, at this stage, actively monitors the program implementation process and communicates the need for alterations in the proposed model discerned through the monitoring process. At this stage, the researcher must practice communicative action in the research process. It is imperative that policy makers be informed of problems discovered in early reviews of new programs so that the programs can be fine-tuned to better meet the intended purpose. Critically enlightened researchers at this stage are a must for successful comprehensive evaluations and their monitoring activities will help provide perspective and communicative action.

The final stage of comprehensive evaluations involves the researcher in the more traditional role assumed by program evaluators.   The determination of whether or not a program has fulfilled its stated goals or purposes is a common activity for evaluation researchers but this stage also requires the researcher to determine the relative degree of programmatic efficiency. Simply noting that the particular objectives of a program have been met (or not met) is not sufficient for a full comprehensive evaluation. By addressing both questions of effectiveness and efficiency, program evaluators are required to put the particular program into a broad organizational context. Ideally, in the context of criminal justice research, the relative levels of effectiveness and efficiency will be addressed at the departmental level as well as the systemic level. A full comprehensive evaluation of police programs will, therefore, require the examination of how particular programs fit into the department's structure as well as how they fit into the larger criminal justice network. Accordingly, both perspective and communicative action will be realized.

In a recent article delineating the value of different personnel and agency evaluation methodologies available for use in police agencies, Gellar (1991) uses the term "performance measurement" to refer to efforts to assess the degree to which police agencies are performing some useful functions. In this context, he argues for the use of departmental level performance measurements much in the same way Rossi and Freeman argue for the value of comprehensive evaluations. Gellar (1991) encourages police executives to rely heavily on performance measurements in making policy decisions. He concludes that evaluation procedures "contribute substantially to improved service and police ability to adapt to changing conditions" (Gellar, 1991, p. 360).

Enlightened leadership in any public sector agency will embrace comprehensive evaluation or performance measurement as an ultimate goal to assist in decision making. As such, the decisions made will be responsive rather than being either reactive or proactive. They will respond to anticipated needs yet, through the processes of program monitoring, impact assessments, efficiency assessments, and even cost-benefit analysis, the programs will be dynamic, constantly changing as new information about them are integrated into practice.

Program evaluations such as those advocated here are not scientifically neat in that the researcher is not expected to remain uninvolved or objective throughout the course of the research endeavor. As new information becomes available concerning particular dimensions of a program, it is expected that the program will be changed. In a purely scientific context, such action would contaminate the experimental design and invalidate the research findings. Some may even challenge the ethics of such active involvement in the setting being evaluated by researchers (Kimmel, 1988). In the final analysis, however, public sector agencies cannot afford to fall prey to the activity trap lest they lose public support and confidence. Comprehensive evaluation efforts will ensure that they do not and within the law enforcement component of the criminal justice network, community support is critical for the continued survival of both organizational level programs and individual level officers themselves.

Comprehensive evaluation must become a more frequently used tool by police leaders in the future.

References

American Friends Service Committee. (1971). *Struggle for justice: A report on crime and punishment in America.* New York: Hill and Wang.

Berk, R. & Rossi, P. (1990). *Thinking about program evaluation.* Beverly Hills, CA: Sage Publications Inc.

Bittner, E. (1990). *Aspects of police work.* Boston, MA: Northeastern University Press.

Brandl, S. & Horvath, F. (1991). Crime-victim evaluation of police investigative performance. *Journal of Criminal Justice,* 19(3), 293-305.

Carter, D. & Sapp, A. (1990). The evolution of higher education in law enforcement: Preliminary findings from a national study. *Journal of Criminal Justice Education,* 1(1), 59-85.

Cahn, M. & Tien, J. (1981). *An alternative approach in police response: Wilmington management of demand program.* Washington, DC: U.S. Department of Justice, National Institute of Justice.

Conner, P. & Richards, C. (1991). Evaluating detectives' performance. *The Police Chief,* (September), 51-55.

Dinitz, S. (1978). Nothing fails like a little success. *Criminology,* 16(2), 225-238.

Falkenberg, S., Gaines, L., & Cordner, G. (1991). An examination of the constructs underlying police performance appraisals. *Journal of Criminal Justice,* 19, 351-360.

Gardner, J. (1990). Automated performance evaluations. *Law and Order,* (October), 97-99.

Geller, W. A. (Ed.). (1991). *Local government police management* (3rd ed.) Washington, DC: International City Management Association.

Gilsinan, J. (1991). Public policy and criminology: An historical and philosophical reassessment. *Justice Quarterly*, 8(2), 201-216.

Glaser, D. (1973). *Routinizing evaluation: Getting feedback on effectiveness of crime and delinquency programs*. Washington, DC: U.S. Government Printing Office.

Glaser, D. (1990). Science and politics as criminologists' vocations. *Criminal Justice Research Bulletin*, 5(6), 1-6.

Goldstein, H. (1990). *Problem-oriented policing*. New York: McGraw-Hill Publishing Company.

Greenberg, B., Elliot, C. V., Kraft, L. P., & Procter, H.S. (1975). *Felony investigation decision model: An analysis of investigative elements of information*. Menlo Park, CA: Stanford Research Institute.

Greenwood, P., Petersilia, J., & Chaiken, J. (1977). *The criminal investigation process*. Lexington, MA: D.C. Heath and Company.

Habermas, J. (1984). *The theory of communicative action, Vol. 1*. Boston: Beacon Press.

Hatry, H. (1970). Wrestling with police crime control productivity measures. In J. Wolfle & J. Heaphy (Eds.), *Readings on productivity in policing*. Washington, DC: The Police Foundation.

Hatry, H., Winnie, R., & Fisk, D. (1973). *Practical program evaluation for state and local government officials*. Washington, DC: The Urban Institute.

Johnson, K. (1990). Impact of university-government partnership in criminal justice: A linkage model for the 1990s. *Journal of Criminal Justice Education*, 1(2), 167-194.

Kelling, G., Pate, T., Dieckman, D. & Brown, C. (1974). *The Kansas City preventive patrol experiment: A summary report*. Washington, DC: The Police Foundation.

Kemp, R. (1990). Cities in the year 2000 the forces of change. *The Futurist*, (Sept.-Oct.), 13-15.

Kimmel, A. (1988). *Ethics and values in applied social research*. Beverly Hills, CA: Sage Publications Inc.

Klockars, C. (1985). *The idea of police*. Beverly Hills, CA: Sage Publications Inc.

Maguire, K. & Flanagan, T. (Eds.). (1991). *Sourcebook of criminal justice statistics 1990*. U.S. Department of Justice, Bureau of Justice Statistics. Washington, DC: U.S. Government Printing Office.

Martin, S. & Sherman, L. (1986). *Catching career criminals: The Washington, D.C., Repeat Offender Project*. Washington, DC: The Police Foundation.

Martinson, R. (1974). What works? Questions and answers about prison reform. *The Public Interest*, 22-54.

Morash, M. & Anderson, E. (1978). Liberal thinking on rehabilitation: A workable solution to crime. *Social Problems*, 25(5), 556-563.

Petersilia, J. (1987). *The influence of criminal justice research*. Santa Monica, CA: The RAND Corporation.

Petersilia, J. (1991). Policy relevance and the future of criminology: The American Society of Criminology, 1990 Presidential Address, *Criminology*, 29(1), 1-15.

Petersilia, J., Abrahamse, A., & Wilson, J. Q. (1990). A summary of RAND's research on police performance, community characteristics, and case attrition. *Journal of Police Science and Administration*, 17(3), 219-226.

Roncek, D. & Maier, P. (1991). Bars, blocks, and crimes revisited: Linking the theory of routine activities to the empiricism of "hot spots." *Criminology*, 29(4), 725-753.

Rossi, P. & Freeman, H. (1989). *Evaluation: A systematic approach*, (4th ed.). Beverly Hills, CA: Sage Publications Inc.

Sherman, L., Gartin, P., & Buerger, M. (1989). Hot spots of predatory crime. *Criminology*, 27(1), 27-55.

Snow, R. (1990). How am I doing? Performance evaluation for small police departments. *Law and Order*, 61-64, (December).

Smith, C., Pehlke, D., & Weller, C. (1974). *Role performance and the criminal justice system, Volume II, Detailed performance objectives*.

Sacramento: California Commission on Peace Officer Standards and Training.

Sykes, G. (1986). Street justice: A moral defense of order maintenance and policing. *Justice Quarterly*, 3(4), 497-512.

Van Kirk, M. (1978). *Response time analysis: Executive summary*. National Institute of Law Enforcement and Criminal Justice, Washington, DC: U.S. Government Printing Office.

Volmer, H. & Mills, D. (Eds.). (1966). *Professionalization*. Englewood Cliffs, NJ: Prentice Hall.

Walsh, W. (1990). Performance evaluation in small and medium police departments: A supervisory perspective. *American Journal of Police*, 9(4), 93-109.

Whisenand, P. & Ferguson, F. (1988). *The managing of police organizations* (3rd ed.). Englewood Cliffs, NJ: Prentice Hall.

Whisenand, P. & Rush, G. (1988). *Supervising police personnel: Back to the basics*. Englewood Cliffs, NJ: Prentice Hall.

Worden, R. (1990). A badge and a baccalaureate: Policies, hypotheses, and further evidence. *Justice Quarterly*, 7(3), 565-592.

Wycoff, M. (1982). Improving police performance measurement: One more voice. *The Urban Interest*, 4(1), 8-16.

Chapter 6

Creativity With Accountability

George L. Kelling
Elizabeth M. Watson

Creative police reformers of the 1990s are moving policing in new directions. These changes have been broadly labeled as either *community-* or *problem-oriented policing*. While these models have some distinguishing characteristics, their similar orientations include (1) determination of neighborhood or community priorities; (2) partnership with the community in solving problems; (3) integration of police with other neighborhood and community resources; (4) a reemphasis on the peacekeeping and order-maintenance functions of police; (5) a focus on problems rather than incidents; (6) the establishment of personnel and accountability systems that recognize the full range of police functioning and discretion; and (7) increased police accountability both to neighborhoods and the community. A primary *method* of community- or problem-oriented policing is problem solving. Although this method may vary in cities, it includes the following steps: identifying problems, analyzing problems, developing responses, and evaluating outcome. (In the San Diego Police Department, for example, this model is referred to as SARA: Scanning, Analysis, Response, and Assessment.)

Most of these changes are based on what Herman Goldstein (1990) has called the new "common wisdom" about the police. This common wisdom includes

- The police do much more than deal with crime; they deal with many forms of behavior that are not defined as criminal.

- The wide range of functions that police are expected to perform, including dealing with fear and enforcing public order, are appropriate functions for the police; from the perspective of the community, they may be as important as the tasks police perform in dealing with behavior that is labeled criminal.

- Too much dependence in the past has been placed on the criminal law in order to get the police job done; arrest and prosecution are simply not an effective way to handle much of what constitutes police business. And even if potentially effective, it may not be possible to use the criminal justice system in some jurisdictions because it is so overloaded.

- Police use a wide range of methods — formal and informal — in getting their job done. Law enforcement is only one method among many.

- Police, of necessity, must exercise broad discretion, including discretion in deciding whether to arrest and prosecute in situations in which there is ample evidence that a criminal law has been violated.

- The police are not autonomous; the sensitive function they perform in our society requires that they be accountable, through the political process, to the community

While this common wisdom has permeated the elites of police and police scholars, it has not become the dominant mode of thinking among rank-and-file police officers, the unions that represent them, prosecutors, and judges, or, for that matter, criminal justice scholars whose primary interest in police focuses on their role in the criminal justice system — criminal investigation, interrogation, and arrest. For example, community- or problem-oriented policing is still rejected by many as soft policing. This position is not uncommon among those who resist the repositioning of police departments from traditional, reform policing, to community- or problem-oriented policing. A recent study of the Houston Police Department conducted by Cresap Management Consultants during the tenure of one of the authors as Houston's Chief of Police (Watson), for example, begrudgingly acknowledged that community policing had much to commend it, yet concluded that "community policing had reduced overall effectiveness, including response time" (*New York Times*, 1991). Informally, one hears of police being converted into the "grin-and-wave" squad, "hobby bobbies" (in England), community relations officers, and the most despised of all, social workers

(*New York Times*, 1991). Assertions are made, ostensibly to upbraid advocates of 1990s reform, that crime control is the core function of police, and that community- and problem-solving policing saps attention and energy from that primary concern. This idea — that community- and problem-solving strategies are soft on crime is the central focus of this paper. This paper argues that those who make the "soft on crime" argument wittingly or unwittingly misrepresent the nature of the crime problem in American society and how society ought to deal with it. At its most sophisticated level, this view of the crime problem was epitomized in the report of President Johnson's Crime Commission, *The Challenge of Crime in a Free Society.* In this view, rather than being a local governmental agency accountable to neighborhoods and communities through their political processes, police are the front end of a criminal justice system gaining authority from criminal law and their own professional knowledge.

Undergirding this criminal justice, law enforcement model are a set of images and metaphors. These images and metaphors, having been assiduously marketed by professional police and criminal justice agents for a generation, are widely accepted in both lay and professional circles. The crime problem is street crime — murder, rape, assault, robbery, and burglary. Criminals are predatory strangers who depredate innocent children, women, the elderly, and others who are vulnerable (Kelling and Stewart, 1991). The first line of defense between these evil-doers and the weak and innocent is law enforcement, the "thin blue line." Anthony V. Bouza, formerly of the New York Police Department, Deputy Chief of the New York City Transit Police Department (TPD), and Chief of the Minneapolis Police Department, gives voice to these images, "(T)he citizen . . . fears, and rightly, the wrath of the Vandals and Visigoths within our walls. Sporadic outbursts of violence . . . serve as periodic reminders of the beast kept at bay by the 'thin blue line'" (Bouza, 1985). If police fail and criminals successfully prey on good people, police are viewed as the front end of a criminal justice system comprising police, prosecutors, judges, and correctional officials, whose purpose is to arrest criminals and process them through this system. The role of citizens in all of this is to "support your local police," report crimes, and be good witnesses. Combined, these images compose the law enforcement model of policing and the criminal justice system model of crime control.

To begin, concentrating on street crime — murder, rape, assault, robbery, and burglary — is not without validity. These crimes shatter civic life; because of their fear of predatory crime by strangers, citizens are reluctant to leave their homes, move through city streets, or use public transportation and parks. Commerce and industry are driven from neighborhoods, communities, and cities, taking with them jobs and the cities' tax bases.

Second, the idea of predatory criminals is not without merit. Many criminals are unscrupulous and seize opportunities presented by the guileless minding their own business.

Moreover, police concentrate on street crime because of society's broad consensus that murder, rape, assault, robbery, and burglary are heinous crimes worthy of serious police and criminal justice agency attention. Early twentieth century vice and blue laws got police into a lot of trouble. If police enforced them, they met the wrath of ethnic minorities; if police didn't enforce them, they met the wrath of urban reformers. Few disagreed, however, that street crimes were evil and deserved the serious attention of police. For reformers who were trying to build a broad constituency for their ideas about the legitimate business of police, concentrating on street crimes appeared closer to political neutrality and was safer.

Finally, as Egon Bittner has pointed out, earlier reformers, such as O.W. Wilson, concentrated police on street crime because they believed that street crime required less sophisticated personnel than financial or corporate crime:

> Though not made explicit, it was quite well understood that the crime control activities assigned to the police were directed to what might be called residual crime. A large variety of other law enforcement agencies divided the tasks of dealing with crime taking place in banks, offices, boardrooms, government agencies, and so forth, which is almost entirely nonviolent and demands sophistication on the part of both the perpetrator and law enforcement . . . . The salience of so-called street crime, which frequently involves acts of violence, in the perceived police mandate dictated the definition of the person suitable to wage the struggle against it. The strengths sought in recruits were the "manly virtues" of honesty, loyalty, aggressiveness, and visceral courage (1990).

A current expression of the theme that city police have limited capacity is found in Houston's Cresap report: "And the report finds that while the concept of community policing requires a range of complex skills, it is unlikely that the department can recruit a force in which most officers have these skills, particularly at current pay levels" (Cresap report, 1990). This idea has been picked up by some academics as well.

So valid reasons exist to concentrate on street crime. It is a serious problem; many criminals are predatory; a broad political consensus supports strong action against it; and early reformers believed that city police were better suited to deal with street crime than other forms of crime or problems. Yet the popular and professional images and metaphors that define the nature of the serious crime problem — random victimization by strangers — woefully distorts its true nature. By oversimplifying the nature of street crime and the problem of fear, these images have fostered a set of police and criminal justice priorities that are only partially responsive to the nature of the problem or the demands of citizens.

The Nature of Street Crime

Even a cursory examination of violent crimes provides a good example of how the metaphors that undergird the street crime problem distorts its reality. Using 1987 as an example, of the estimated 5,660,570 violent crimes committed in the United States (rape, robbery, and assault), 2,439,290 (43 percent) were committed by nonstrangers. In more detail, 46 percent of the estimated 140,890 attempted and completed rapes, 20 percent of the 1,030,460 attempted and completed robberies, and 48 percent of the 4,489,220 aggravated and simple assaults were committed by nonstrangers (U.S. Dept. of Justice, 1989). Of the 17,859 murders, 57 percent were known to be committed by nonstrangers, 13 percent by strangers, and in 30 percent of the cases the relationship was unknown (U.S. Dept. of Justice, 1988). It is widely believed that a good proportion of burglaries are committed by nonstrangers as well. Furthermore, as noteworthy as these statistics are, we have every reason to believe that estimates about crimes that occur between nonstrangers are gross underestimates. Police tend to underestimate the severity of domestic incidents (Lagan and Innes, 1986). Victims often do not report crimes by related offenders because they view their victimization as private matters or fear reprisal (Klaus and Rand, 1984). Many affluent victims turn to a family physician or attorney for assistance or redress. And estimates from national probability samples include protocols that lead to underestimating crimes between nonstrangers (Klaus and Rand, 1984; Weingart, 1989).

Street crime, then, is more complicated than the imageries of "beasts at bay," "public enemies," or strangers. It is not only the predatory behavior of persons who are so predisposed, but includes criminal activities by people who are familiar with each other. What forms do such criminal activities take?

- A roommate who has moved out and is owed back rent by his partner returns with a gun and demands the exact amount he is owed.

- A mid-level drug dealer believes that he is being cheated by one of his "mules" and shoots him.

- A mother frustrated by the constant whining of her child slaps him again and again until he sustains serious injury.

- A separated husband breaks into his former home and steals "his" jewelry — jewelry that he had earlier bought for his wife.

- A high-school student's girlfriend believes that she has been insulted by another young man. The student stabs the other youth.

- A college student takes a fellow student on a date. After the date, she says no to intercourse. He forces intercourse knowing she "really wants it."

- A husband beats his wife because she aggravates him, knowing she "needs the discipline."

In each of these cases, one or both of the parties feels aggrieved by the other and believes he or she has a problem: Property is not returned, insults are put forth, sexual urges are not gratified, children or wives will not stop their aggravating behavior, a "business person" (drug dealer) is cheated, or money is owed. And, as Weingart (1989) has pointed out, problem solving or "private debt settlement" action is taken, not because the aggressor *can* take action, but because the aggressor believes he or she *ought* to take action. One is afflicted. His or her antagonist has teased, cheated, or been insulting. Justice, equity, and prestige demand a dramatic gesture. The adversary "deserves" retribution. The solution to the problem is some criminal action that "solves" it or reestablishes equity in the mind of the aggressor.

Thus, despite the prevailing view that dealing with thugs and processing them through the criminal justice system is simpler and less ambiguous than, say, dealing with corporate or financial crime, the problems enshrouded by the phrase "street crime" are fraught with complexity and ambiguity. Police, for example, have been loath to intrude into the affairs of families. This disinclination reflects important values: Belief in the right to maintain private lives free of governmental interference runs deep in society. Yet, many of the critical issues society and police are now confronting — date rape, spousal abuse, child abuse, violence in inner-city neighborhoods — are exactly those that place police in the middle of family, sexual, and neighborhood relationships.

Moreover, the importance of dealing with such problems cannot be overstated: The repercussions of criminal action by nonstrangers are grave. Because relationships with nonstrangers — friends, relatives, lovers, schoolmates, and the like — persist over time, such victimizations are often multiple and regularly intensify into more and more serious episodes. Victims often suffer repeated abuse and constant terror. Many victims internalize the reasons for their plight and suffer from guilt, believing they get what they deserve. Other suffering ranges from having to move, change schools, get a new or unlisted telephone number, to being ostracized from a family, kinship, or social network.

Also, by definition, nonstrangers are part of some social network — family, neighborhood, or school group. Crime within these institutions interferes with their functioning and threatens the values that they bring to society: Families fail to nurture; schools fail to educate; and houses and neighborhoods become destinations of terror and hurt instead of places of refuge.

Moreover, victims often become perpetrators, perpetuating cycles of violence. The abused child often later becomes the abusing parent (Dennis, 1980). The attempts of the Houston Police Department to prevent such outcomes, and the Cresap report's reaction to those efforts, will be discussed later in this paper.

This reluctance to intervene in private disputes notwithstanding, the construction that those who argue for getting "tough on street crime" have put on the nature of street crime has distracted police and other criminal justice professionals, as well as the media and general public, from developing a full picture of the nature of the crime problem (Kelling and Moore, 1988). The consequence has been that police have either left serious problems untended or responded to them as incidents and on an *ad hoc* basis, rather than as serious problems requiring careful analysis (Goldstein, 1979). Rhetoric to the contrary, those calling for getting tough on crime are merely arguing for continuation of practices that address an extraordinarily narrow definition of what constitutes crime control.

The street crime problem is complicated by even more than non-stranger victimization, however.

The Nature of Fear

Since 1982, one of the authors (Kelling) has argued that policy makers, police, and academics should take more seriously the problems of disorder and fear. James Q. Wilson and Kelling first put this forward in an *Atlantic* article titled "Broken Windows" (Wilson and Kelling, 1982).

In this article we developed a line of thought that originated during the 1960s, but that remained out of the mainstream of police, criminal justice, and criminological thinking: Disorder, as well as serious crime, creates citizen fear (Biderman et al., 1967). The authors argued that people act on these fears and that these fears have tangible consequences for neighborhoods and communities. Fear, stimulated by disorder, not just street crime, drives citizens from alleys, streets, parks, public transportation, and cities. Second, we argued that these fears are not unrealistic for disorder leads to crime. They used a metaphor to express this: broken windows. Just as an unrepaired broken window is a sign that no one cares and leads to increased and more serious vandalism, untended disorderly behavior is also a sign that no one cares and leads both to increased amounts of disorder and to serious crime.

These arguments were intuitively appealing, both to police and citizens, especially citizens active in community crime-control organizations. Coincidentally, when "Broken Windows" was published, I was observing the activities of neighborhood anticrime groups in Boston. Not knowing that I was one of the authors, citizens regularly gave me copies of the paper, admonishing me, "If you want to know what our neighborhood problems really are, read this." Police, especially those who worked with neighborhood groups, responded with equal enthusiasm, recounting their frustration. They wanted citizens to concentrate on computer listing of crimes in their neighborhoods; citizens wanted to talk about "minor issues" like youths drinking in parks and unseemly prostitutes instead.

Intuitively appealing though the "Broken Windows" ideas may have been, their policy implications were unclear. The idea that disorder leads to serious crime was a hypothesis that needed to be tested. The link between disorder and fear was firmly established empirically, yet it raised a policy debate. Is it legitimate for police to target scarce police resources on fear? Research in Newark, New Jersey, and Flint, Michigan, gave ample evidence that citizen fear of crime responded to foot patrol, and additional research in Houston, Texas, and Newark indicated that other tactics could be used to reduce fear as well. Nonetheless, the question of the legitimacy of such efforts remained.

Other important policy issues were raised, as well. Police had *abandoned* order maintenance efforts, at least officially, for a good portion of this century. Many police managers were extremely reluctant to return to a problem and set of activities that appeared to be as ambiguous as disorder and maintaining order. Superficially, at least, murder, rape, and robbery seemed to be far less ambiguous than disorder.

Even more fundamental was that the "Broken Windows" argument ran counter to a set of ideologies that had developed during the 1960s and 1970s. During this era, individualism, personal choice, and rights dominated political, legal, mental health, and criminal justice discourse. Raising the issue of disorder — the fear it caused and the need to regulate certain types of street behavior in the name of *community* rights — was outside the mainstream of academic and policy makers' thinking about the crime problem.

Typical of academic thinking is Christopher Jencks' article "Is Violent Crime Rising" in *The American Prospect*. Jencks, after examining Uniform Crime Reports and National Crime Surveys, concludes that aggregate levels of violent crimes haven't worsened much since the 1970s. Inferred, by the cover title "Crime Panic," is that the increasing level of fear is misplaced given the stable levels of violent crime since the 1960s.

Jencks attributes increased public concern about crime, first, to media concentration on New York and Washington, D.C. — cities that have experienced increases in violent crime — and, second, the experiences of middle-aged persons who grew up in suburban areas during a relatively placid era (prior to the decade when violent crime did increase — the 1960s) and who now work in cities where they are exposed to urban violence. I take his first point about media presentation of crime, but with some serious qualifications. Drawing conclusions about the crime problem from aggregate statistics can be terribly misleading. For example, several years ago Northeastern University researcher Glenn Pierce noted that if one looked at aggregate statistics, Boston did not have a gang problem. (This has changed since.) Telling that to citizens who lived in one small neighborhood, however, would have been absurd. They had a terrible gang problem, which since has spread. Likewise telling persons in particular neighborhoods that they are not having an increasing problem with violent crime, even in a cities like Kansas City, Dallas, Fort Lauderdale, or Milwaukee, is absurd. Neighborhoods are being devastated by violence.

Jencks' latter interpretation of the origin of citizen fear — their experiences when they go into cities — is hardly plausible, however. Relatively few middle-aged suburbanites, even in New York or Washington, D.C., experience violence — at least stranger violence. Whether newly moved to cities or not, they *experience* disorder: Panhandling, aggressive prostitutes, menacing youths, drunks blocking the sidewalks, graffiti, street vendors selling "hot" goods, obscenity, emotionally disturbed persons exposing themselves — a litany of incivilities. Concern, the "Crime Panic," the raw *fear*, has its origins as much in these incivilities as from serious crime. To the extent that fear is experienced based (rather than based on media exposure) for the vast majority of Jenck's middle-aged suburbanites, it is based either on experience of violence in their relationships with friends, neighborhoods, and family or on their experience with disorder. Again, this is not new. We have known about this since the 1960s. Yet academics, like police, prefer to deal with official statistics about crime rather than the experiences of citizens.

Wesley Skogan's new book, *Disorder and Decline: Crime and the Spiral of Decay in American Neighborhoods* adds urgency to the need to rethink the crime problem and crime control methods (1990). Until Skogan's book, the supposed link between disorder and crime was based on common sense and anecdotal experience rather than empirical findings. *Disorder and Decline* tests the "Broken Window" hypothesis and examines empirically the relationship between disorder, fear, crime, and neighborhood life. The findings confirm that disorder accompanies and is causally linked to serious crime.

> The evidence suggests that poverty, instability, and the racial composition of neighborhoods are strongly linked to area crime, but a substantial portion of that linkage is through disorder. . . . (Direct) action against disorder could have substantial payoff . . . . These data support the proposition that disorder needs to be taken seriously in research on neighborhood crime, and that both directly and through crime it plays an important role in neighborhood decline. "Broken windows" do need to be repaired quickly.

It is important to understand the thoroughness of Skogan's research. Skogan used two methods: surveys and field work in forty neighborhoods in six cities. Citizens were surveyed about conditions in their neighborhood, what they feared, what actions they have taken to defend themselves, and their personal victimizations. Independently, observers measured noted signs of disorder: vandalism, graffiti, gangs, drug dealing, drunkenness, and other such conditions.

Because Skogan both queried residents about disorderly conditions and observed neighborhood conditions, he was able to establish independently the extent to which persons with different personal characteristics — age, race, sex, social class, etc. — might have vastly different definitions of disorder. The importance of this, of course, is the extent to which class or racial distinctions might shape definitions of disorder. The findings were striking: Regardless of background, a strong consensus exists about what constitutes disorder, that it is frightening, and that something should be done about it.

Focus groups that Kelling observed in New York City while consulting with the Metropolitan Transportation Authority (MTA) about the problem of disorder in New York's subway system further confirm this broad consensus. These focus groups and marketing surveys demonstrated that potential riders were discouraged from using the subway because of their fear of disorderly persons. Moreover, to establish the public acceptability of aggressive order maintenance activities by subway police (these will be discussed later), focus groups were conducted with working class persons who use the subway, which presented scenarios in which police took various forms of action to deal with disorder. The responses of citizens were startling and uniform. They were virtually unanimous in identifying the behaviors to which they objected and in their support of police order maintenance activities. Indeed, most group members would have supported levels of police aggressiveness beyond those proposed by police. The group members simply were fed up with the indignities they had to face day after day.

Skogan found not only that disorder is linked to fear and crime, and that citizens generally agree about what constitutes disorder, he noted as well that disorder demoralizes neighborhoods and reduces their capacity for self-defense:

> Disorder may undermine in several ways the capacity of communities to preserve the conditions they value. Disorder may foster suspicion and distrust, undermine popular faith and commitment to the area, and discourage public and collective activities. Disorder may also undermine individual morale and the perceived efficacy of taking any possible action. Since there is little that individuals seem able to do about many forms of disorder, they may feel disheartened and frustrated, rather than motivated to do more, even to protect themselves.

And finally, as Nathan Glazer first pointed out when he wrote about graffiti in New York's subways in his 1979 *Public Interest* article, untended disorderly conditions not only demoralize citizens and neighborhoods, they undermine public confidence in government. If government cannot solve minor problems like vandalism and graffiti, the belief goes, it certainly cannot do anything about serious problems.

In other words, not only is disorder a problem in itself, untended disorder cascades rapidly into serious problems. When drinking youths swear at people in parks, strangers intimidate others who will not "spare some change," scantily clad prostitutes intimidate families and embarrass fathers in front of their children, and drunks sprawl on the stoops of apartments blocking doorways, the sense of civil community is destroyed. Once a certain breakoff point is reached, citizens abandon their parks, desert their local stores and shop instead in protected suburban malls (protected, by the way, by private security, but I will discuss this more later), desert public transportation, and finally leave cities entirely. Citizens become fearful to stand up for their own and other persons rights. And when citizens' "moral reliability" (Lewis and Salem, 1986) and sense of mutual obligation are lost, potential troublemakers are encouraged and emboldened, they become increasingly outrageous, other trouble-makers gravitate to the area, and community is lost. At this point, too often reached in too many communities, the admonition of the Cresap report to the Houston Police Department that "at least two measures — response times to calls for service and effectiveness in solving crime — should be used to evaluate the Department as a whole" is a cruel hoax on citizens. As Jane Jacobs pointed out as early as 1961,

> The first thing to understand is that the public peace — the sidewalk and street peace — of cities is not kept primarily by the police, necessary as police are. It is kept primarily by an intricate, almost unconscious, network of voluntary control and standards among the people themselves, and enforced by the

people themselves. In some city areas — older public housing projects and streets with very high population turnover are often conspicuous examples — the keeping of public sidewalk law and order is left almost entirely to the police and special guards. Such places are jungles. No amount of police can enforce civilization where the normal, casual enforcement of it has broken down. (Jacobs, 1961)

Conventional wisdom has dominated popular and professional thinking about the crime problem. It is serious crime by strangers. This tragic oversimplification both ignores a good proportion of serious crime, crime carried out by nonstrangers solving problems, and disorder that creates fear and leads to serious crime. The policies that are derived from such oversimplification are equally problematic.

Crime Control and Law Enforcement

In late 1989 the last New York City subway train covered with graffiti was removed from service and cleaned. This was a stunning victory. In 1984 virtually every inch of every train, inside and out, was covered by graffiti. During the fifteen years before then, graffiti had come to be seen as an insoluble problem. Special efforts by the Transit Authority, the mayor, the TPD, and the courts had been doomed to failur. Glazer, writing in the *Public Interest* on subway disorder, and documenting it as a criminal justice problem, saw it as unsolvable as well (Glazer, 1979).

The means by which this victory was accomplished are complicated and are reported elsewhere in detail; however, of interest here is the 1989 story in the *New York Times* (Sloan-Hewitt and Kelling, 1990). For years, as graffiti spread throughout the system and then prevailed as the default decor of subway trains, transit police responded to the problem of graffiti by identifying graffitists and arresting them. Annually, or whenever asked about the graffiti problem, police hauled out their arrest data. They were impressive. Arrests increased every year. Thus, ironically, by Cresap's standard in Houston, transit police had been successful until 1984. They solved graffiti crimes and made arrests, lots of arrests. Lost in this was that *the problem was progressively worsening despite solving crimes and making arrests*. Ironically, once subway officials devised the clean car program, arrests for graffiti immediately dropped and stayed relatively low throughout the five years. By Cresap's standards, however, despite solving the problem, police were less successful: *Arrests were declining*.

To be fair to transit police, they were not alone among police in pointing to clearances (solving crimes) and arrests as achievements. For generations, police had touted crime solving and arrests — along with the levels of reported crime — as primary indicators of their efficiency and success. Moreover, Cresap did not invent response time as a measure of police success; until the 1970s, police had advertised low response time as a measure, again, of police efficiency and success.

The reasons why police used measures of success like crime solving, arrests, Uniform Crime Reports, and response time included their ostensible objectivity, the need to find measures of accomplishment that police could communicate easily to the general public, their apparent "scientific" basis, and their universality in policing (so police departments could measure their success over time and between cities, or so earlier reformers believed). But the selection of these measures of efficiency and success also signaled a shift in police strategy from a broad service orientation that encompassed crime control to law enforcement, not only a far narrower concept of policing, but also a far narrower concept of crime control. So pervasive is this orientation to crime control that, for many, law enforcement has become synonymous with policing.

Another example: Recently in Buffalo, New York, neighborhood residents protested police handling of a series of eleven rapes. After the third rape, police determined that a serial rapist was attacking young girls on their way to school but kept that information to themselves. Five months and eight rapes later, outraged parents and neighborhood residents discovered that police had withheld information about the rapist and his mode of operation from them. Defending departmental action, the chief of detectives claimed that if residents had been notified, the resultant media sensationalism would have interfered with the department's investigation. Even though parents and residents were horror struck that information that they could have used to protect their children had been withheld from them, the police official's response to them made it clear that he believed the Buffalo Police Department was doing its job. And by police measures, they were. They were investigating the crimes for the purpose of making an arrest.

To be fair, police departments use other tactics as well in situations such as those in Buffalo, for example, increasing patrol and/or using undercover officers. Notice how narrow use of such tactics for prevention is, however. In the case of uniformed patrol, prevention rests on the "thin blue line" — the limited number of police officers who ride around in cars attempting to create a sense of omnipresence or to come upon the assault or rape in progress. Neither of which experience, research, or, now, common sense suggest these tactics accomplish very well. Moreover, the purpose of undercover officers is certainly preventive, but think about this for a moment, as well. While uniformed personnel are posted to create a sense of police presence to keep something from happening, plainclothes police attempt to give the impression that police are *not* there in hopes that the *criminal initiates the criminal act* and can be arrested with the proverbial "smoking gun." This certainly can prevent the *next* girl from being assaulted and raped (through incarceration, to put this in criminal justice terms), but imagine the terror and trauma of the girl who would experience the attack and the subsequent chaos involved in capturing and arresting her assailant.

Consider an alternative approach. The first responsibility of police is to prevent another child from being raped. Certainly, we want the perpetrator arrested, as a means of preventing other rapes and in the name of justice. In addition to investigating the crime and increasing patrols, however, police could have mobilized parents, children, neighborhood residents, and school and other officials to take individual and/or group preventive action. Moreover, serial crimes traumatize children. Aware of the danger of a sexual predator, children are emotionally victimized. Many are grieving for their friends and schoolmates. They need reassurance, information, and understanding. Schools and parents need advice about how to handle these fears. Compounding the dangers, events like serial rapes strain relations in neighborhoods and communities. Suspicions spoil neighborliness and trust at a time when it is most required.

Yet given current definitions — ala Cresap's definitions — of the basic business of police, officers who mobilized the community, allayed the anxiety of children, and restored and strengthened neighborhood social bonds might have been doing worthwhile things, but they would be operating outside of the core competencies of a contemporary police department. *Real* police work would have been riding around in cars responding to calls for service and arresting people, regardless of the ultimate outcome. *Success* would be defined as making an arrest, not as preventing rapes or restoring the community. This is not merely a hypothetical issue. The Houston Police Department's (HPD) initial success in preventing domestic homicide ran into exactly such criticism: The HPD was not doing *real* police work — investigating homicides.

Unlike the Buffalo Police Department's approach to its problem with serial rapes of children, the HPD decided in 1989 that its first responsibility was to prevent the next domestic homicide. It hosted a public summit concerning domestic abuse and assault. Reflecting on its own performance, the HPD decided that traditional police responses to domestic disputes — responding to incident after incident and conducting *post hoc* investigations — were inadequate. A preventive approach was devised.

The department created a Family Violence Unit and staffed it with part-time sworn officers and full-time civilian counselors. In-service training was provided to all police officers in early problem identification. Counselors visited homes in which there was a history of domestic violence. Unit members visited schools and other community institutions and provided public education about the nature of the problem and community resources to deal with it, and follow-up investigations of reported offenses were given high law enforcement priority.

The results? In 1991 22 percent more charges of criminal abuse were filed with the prosecutor's office; referrals to the Houston Area Women's Center increased by 120 percent; the number of women killed by intimates or family dropped by 12 percent; and the number of men killed by intimates or family dropped by 50 percent. This was despite the fact that Houston suffered from its highest murder rate in history in 1991 — up 11 percent from 1990.

Yet, an early draft of the Cresap report recommended that the HPD should discontinue its efforts to prevent homicides and emphasize follow-up investigations. When one of the authors (Watson) protested, Cresap softened the recommendation. Nonetheless, the authors of the report grumbled, "(T)he Department recently instituted a counseling program for victims of domestic violence at a time when the vast majority of aggravated assaults are not even investigated." Typically, the focus of the Cresap authors was on *method* not *outcome*.

Another example of preventive policing, again from the New York City transit police. Currently, although not a formal experiment, the TPD is conducting the first natural experiment with the policy implications of "Broken Windows." It will be recalled that "Broken Windows" argued, and Skogan's research supports, a causal link between disorder and serious crime. The policy implications that flow from this are, of course, that order maintenance activities of police should have a beneficial impact on the level of serious crime.[1] The opportunity to test this hypothesis, at least at the level of a natural experiment, occurred in 1989.

In 1989 subway ridership in New York City began a precipitous decline. Certainly, New York's declining economy contributed to the decline. Nonetheless, MTA survey results suggested that disorderly behavior in the subway contributed to this decline, as well. Disorder took two forms. The first was farebeating. Farebeating and associated scams include jumping over turnstiles; "coin sucking" (blocking the token receptacle and sucking out a deposited token); and, most outrageously, disabling all the token receptacles, holding open gates, and collecting fares from persons entering the system. During rush hours, this latter maneuver often results in bedlam, with confused passengers being channeled to one gate and confronted by an intimidating youth or youths collecting fares. In some cases, the situation became so chaotic that angry, yelling, and pushing passengers were backed up clear into the street. Some youths attacked the token receptacles themselves, having developed a technology for quickly springing the door of the receptacle. Hundreds or thousands of tokens were stolen in a matter of seconds. The thieves then either fled into the subway or street. (Vaults on the turnstiles finally halted this crime.) Losses from the various fare scams and thefts range from $60 million to $120 million a year, not to mention the indignation, demoralization, and fear paying passengers and on-site transit staff, especially toll-takers, felt.

The second form of disorder was broadly identified as "homelessness" — and like the term "farebeating," the term "homelessness" was a euphemism for a range of objectionable behaviors. The offensive behaviors, committed by both homeless and others who were not homeless, included aggressive panhandling; public urination and defecation; obstructing passenger movement by lying in corridors, passageways, and on trains; behaving in drunken and stuporous ways; and other forms of uncivil behavior.

Significant increases in felonies, primarily robbery, accompanied public concern about the disorder. In April 1988, 1,041 felonies were reported; in April 1989, 1,276; and in April 1990, 1,472. Police concentrated their efforts on robbery, giving grudging and spotty attention to farebeating and disorder, despite surveys indicating they were the public's primary concern. Attempts to concentrate activities on disorder and farebeating were opposed by the Patrolman's Benevolent Association; as had the Boston police union, they wanted to concentrate on serious crime. For many officers, attempts to involve them in more aggressive order maintenance was a blow to their professional pride. One officer, aware that I helped devise some of the order maintenance plan, angrily challenged me, "Where did you ever get the stupid idea that police should deal with minor s---? Our job is fighting crime." The best that the transit police could manage in dealing with farebeating and disorder was several false starts.

Nonetheless MTA and New York City Transit Authority concern about ridership levels and farebeating, the financial impacts of which threatened the future of the subway system, finally forced police to take seriously disorder and farebeating. Chief William Bratton, newly hired as chief of the transit police, moved to reposition the TPD. Robberies would be given attention, but no more than disorder or farebeating.[2]

Implementing these efforts was given considerable attention. Some of the details of the history of this effort have been published in another place and will not be repeated here (Kelling, 1991). Nonetheless, implementation efforts in the TPD took into account officers' work preferences; Bratton's communications emphasized farebeating, disorder, and robbery; training was developed using the same themes; district commanders were carefully oriented and made to understand that their evaluations would rest on their success in handling disorder and farebeating, as well as robberies; commanders who had earlier attempted to deal with disorder were given "fast track" promotions; Bratton spent considerable time, night and day, in the subway checking farebeating and disorderly conditions; and, within budgetary constraints, outcomes were evaluated. Based on these painstaking efforts, officers responded by increasing their activity: arrests increased by 67 percent. More interestingly, issuances of summonses increased 53 percent and ejections from the system nearly 300 percent.

It is, of course, too early to determine the final results. Moreover, funds were not available to evaluate systematically the outcome. Nonetheless, since the initiation of efforts in the summer of 1990 to control farebeating and disorder in the subway felonies have declined every month.   Overall, felonies declined over 14 percent when the first six months of 1991 are compared with the first six months of 1990.

Moreover, similar patterns resulted when Chief Joseph Flynn of the Long Island Rail Road (LIRR) enforced similar rules in New York's Penn Station in June 1990.   Crimes against passengers (larceny, assault, and robbery), which had averaged about twenty a month, dropped immediately to under ten a month and have stayed at that level since.[3]

But most interesting, although all transit police activity levels are up — arrests, summonses, and ejections — and felony crimes are down, *felony arrests have declined during the same period.*

Moreover, although the numbers are very small, the same trend has been noted by the LIRR Police in Penn Station.

Be sure, I am not arguing that these data represent hard social science evidence that order maintenance activities reduce felonies, especially robberies.   Not enough time has gone by, the data may be spurious, and no serious research has been conducted.   Moreover, the relevance of order maintenance activities in subways and other public facilities to street situations is debatable.   Nonetheless, the data raise interesting issues.   The efforts in New York's subways and Penn Station represent the most open and aggressive order maintenance efforts that I know of in any city.   Many cities are moving toward increased order maintenance activities in the form of passage of curfews and antipanhandling ordinances and other "chunks" of authority to increase the ability of police to regulate disorderly conditions and persons.   In both cases, felonies, especially robberies, have declined *while felony arrests have declined.*   This issue begs research and experimentation

The issue here, however, is that the crime problem comprises problems of disorder, fear, nonstranger crime, and stranger crime.   Yet, crime fighting, despite the experiences and demands of citizens, remains narrowly targeted on a small subset of these problems.

Conclusion

Loss of control over public places — streets, parks, and public transportation systems, but especially streets — has been the dominant domestic problem during the second half of the twentieth century.   It shows no sign of abating.   Reflexively, when we think of regaining control of the streets we think of serious street crime — murder, rape, assault, robbery, and burglary — and public agencies of criminal justice — police, prosecutors, judges, and correctional and prison officials.   This formulation is partially correct.   As this paper argues, it is also largely incorrect.

Despite the limitation of this formulation — street crime and public agencies of control — many politicians, police and criminal justice officials, media elites, and criminal justice and criminological educators continue to behave as if it were true. It is kept in place by powerful ideologies. As is often the case, these ideologies are sustained by simple and graphic metaphors. These metaphors include the "thin blue line," "crime fighting," and the "criminal justice system."

Metaphors and images have been knowingly or unknowingly used by individuals, groups, and institutions to propound one point of view or paradigm, while suppressing others. Dominant metaphors have been used to illustrate or teach the "proper" business of organizations and occupations: police are crime "fighters." Metaphors have staked claims: crime control is the business of a criminal justice system. They have fed professional myths and "war stories" about what "real" policing is all about. They become powerful tools in the creation and maintenance of political, organizational, or professional ideologies: they define how one "ought" to think about crime and the functions of police and criminal justice agencies.

When, for example, Cresap in Houston advises governmental leaders that the business of policing is apprehending criminals and responding rapidly to calls for service, we are seeing the persistence of an ideology that has been unsupported by research, experience, or common sense, and that has ignored demands by citizens and neighborhoods for qualitatively different policing. This ideology has been supported, however, by powerful metaphors that trap police and other criminal justice practitioners and academics into conventional ways of thinking and responding.

Those rejuvenating policing have to take the metaphors of the past seriously and understand that their continued use only perpetuates poor popular and professional thinking. Policing is not law enforcement; law enforcement is one means that police use. There is no criminal justice system; there is only an amalgam of agencies that often operate at cross purposes. The crime problem is not simple; the nuances of nonstranger crime, disorder, and stranger crime are as subtle and perplexing as financial and white-collar crime. Finally, treating line police officers as dummies who are incapable of managing the subtleties of the crime problem becomes a self-fulfilling prophecy. The consequences of such thinking is that patrol remains a terribly underutilized police resource. Many police departments are beginning to move away from traditional policing and innovate. Police executives, unionists, line personnel, and academics must find new metaphors for policing that capture the imagination of police and communicate what constitutes effective policing to citizens and political leaders.

Notes

1.   In the case of the subway, the predominant street crime is robbery, most often some form of "snatch" of jewelry. Some assaults, rapes, and robberies occur, generally at a relatively low level, but almost always attended by high levels of publicity. Burglaries, of course, are virtually non-existent as are many other forms of theft typical of streets.

2.   Considerable attention was given to establishing the base of authority for dealing with problems of disorder. Farebeating was less of a problem, it was clearly illegal. Yet, even for farebeating, efforts were made to ensure that draconian measures were not taken for the theft of service worth $1.15. Special arrangements were made to expedite booking and release for those who were arrested for farebeating and who were not carrying a weapon or named in outstanding criminal warrants. Nevertheless, for many persons involved in fare scams the amount in question was considerable and warranted serious response. In the subway, rules of conduct created by the MTA board established the minimal levels of behavior that police would enforce. Some of these rules were tested in court, and although the prohibition against panhandling was at first suspended as a result of court action, subsequent appeals supported the prohibition.

3.   Complaints against police have not increased against either the New York City TPD or the LIRR Police Department. This is despite the constant monitoring of order maintenance activities by the New York Civil Liberties Union and, in the case of the TPD, an increase in ejections out of the system from 10,473 during the first five months of 1990 to 45,551 during comparable months in 1991.

References

Biderman, A. et al. (1967). *Report on a pilot study in the District of Columbia on victimization and attitudes*. Washington, DC: U.S. Government Printing Office.

Bittner, E. (1990). *Aspects of police work*. Boston: Northeastern University Press.

Bouza, A. V. (1985). Police unions: Paper tigers or roaring lions. In William A. Geller, *Police leadership in America: Crisis and opportunity*. American Bar Foundation. New York: Praeger Publishers.

Cresap report. (1990). Houston: Houston Police Department.

Dennis, R. (1980). Homicide among Black males: Social costs to families and communities. *Public Health Reports*, 95(6), 556 (Nov.-Dec.).

Glazer, N. (1979). Subway graffiti in New York. *Public Interest*, 54 (Winter), 3-11.

Goldstein, H. (1979). Improving policing: A problem-oriented approach. *Crime and Delinquency*, 25, 236-258.

Goldstein, H. (1990). *Problem-oriented policing*. New York: McGraw-Hill Inc.

Jacobs, J. (1961). *The death and life of great American cities*. New York: Doubleday.

Kelling, G. L. (1991). Reclaiming the subway. *NY: The City Journal* 1(2), 17-28 (Winter).

Kelling, G. L. & Moore, M. H. (1988). The evolving strategy of policing. *Perspectives on policing*. Washington, DC: U.S. Department of Justice, Office of Justice Programs, National Institute of Justice, 4 (November).

Kelling, G. L. & Stewart, J. K. (1991). The evolution of contemporary policing. In W. A. Geller (Ed.), *Local government police management*. Washington, DC: International City Management Association.

Klaus, P. & Rand, M. R. (1984). Family violence, *Bureau of Justice Statistics, Special Report*. Washington, DC: Bureau of Justice Statistics, U.S. Department of Justice, (April).

Lagan, P. A. & Innes, C. A. (1986). Preventing domestic violence against women, *Bureau of Justice Statistics, Special Report*. Washington, DC: Bureau of Justice Statistics, U.S. Department of Justice, (August).

Lewis, D. & Salem, G. (1986). *Fear of crime: Incivility and production of a social problem*. New Brunswick, NJ: Transaction Publishers.

New York Times, August 8, 1991.

Skogan, W. G. (1990). *Disorder and decline: Crime and the spiral of decay in American neighborhoods*. New York: The Free Press.

Sloan-Howitt, M. & Kelling, G. L. (1990). Subway graffiti in New York City: "Gettin up" vs "Meanin it and Cleanin it." *Security Journal*, 1, 131-136.

U.S. Department of Justice, Bureau of Justice Statistics. (1989). *Criminal victimization in the United States, 1987*, National Crime Survey Report NCJ-115524. Washington, DC: Government Printing Office, Table 34.

U.S. Department of Justice, Federal Bureau of Investigation. (1988). *Crime in the United States, 1987*. Washington, DC: Government Printing Office, p. 11.

Weingart, S. N. (1989). *Adding insult to injury: Domestic violence and public policy*, Dissertation, Harvard University, Cambridge, MA, (October).

Wilson, J. Q. & Kelling, G. L. (1982). Police and neighborhood safety: Broken windows. *Atlantic Monthly*, 249, 29-38 (March).

Chapter 7

Stability Amid Change

Gary W. Sykes

Change in Law Enforcement: Paradigm Choices, Risks, and Possibilities

It is commonplace to say that the world in which we live is in constant change. It is also commonly said that changes are accelerating. Talk to most futurists and one can get a feeling of uneasiness about the extent to which the world seems propelled by forces not completely understood, or at worst, out of control.

Without necessarily challenging these observations about change, it is important to keep in perspective that large-scale changes occur relatively slowly, especially in organizations and institutions and sometimes take decades before they are discernible. Most changes in organizations tend to be incremental over time as the structure learns about and adapts to changes in its environment. If the organization cannot or will not respond to change, the process of ossification develops and the stage can be set for a rupturing change. In the private sector, failure to adapt to market shifts can lead to bankruptcy and severe economic hardship for all concerned. The public sector, however, is a different story and operates in a different environment.

In the United States, the public sector is highly fragmented and decentralized. Various organizations performing the same function exist at different levels of government. The significance of this point for this discussion is that law enforcement agencies function in a very narrowly defined and decentralized environment. Consequently, agencies experience different rates of change as well as different types of change. As such, it is very risky to say general things about change in law enforcement organizations given this diversity.

Most of the literature about change, or the lack of change, is based on the largest urban departments. Most of the research focuses on cities with populations of 100,000 or more. Smaller departments, especially in the suburban rings around larger cities are becoming more heterogeneous in their demographic patterns and are beginning to experience the same problems found in the larger urban departments (Redlinger, 1991). For this article, the focus is on change in the larger departments, but it must be kept in mind that even though smaller agencies may be in a more stable environment with less pressure for change, the problems appear to be spreading from the urban centers outward.

For most law enforcement agencies changes come slowly and primarily after a considerable increase in evidence demonstrating the need for change. Unlike the private sector, the failure to change does not mean a threat to the physical survival of a police organization, but it may result in a decrease in its functions; e.g., it may no longer command center stage in its budget position *or* other institutions may begin to absorb or take over some of its functions. Police organizations do not go bankrupt or wither away; instead, they tend to shrink while other sectors of society assume an increasing role in maintaining order and enforcing the law.

The growth of private sector policing, e.g., private security, "moon-lighting opportunities," and "rent-a-cop" services, indicates a major part of the public security function has already moved beyond the traditional police agency (Shearing and Stenning, 1987). In fact, by some estimates, it is the fastest growing dimension while the public sector continues to decline. Although it might be an exaggeration to discuss the "failure" of public policing, the trend toward private policing suggests essential changes in the nature of the business, if not a crisis.

Change in Law Enforcement

In *Powershift* (1990), by Alvin and Heidi Toffler, the idea is proposed that "the entire structure of power that held the world together is disintegrating." The power base is shifting to one in which power gravitates to those who control and understand the new information-based age. They refer to this as the "super-symbolic economy." Production techniques change from mass-based to niche-based and are driven by computer-based processes. Knowledge becomes power by giving the advantage to those with access to sophisticated information.

The Tofflers suggested that "we are standing the principle of mass production on its head" and that the old theories, models, and methods designed for the "smokestack era" are no longer relevant. To illustrate those changes, they pointed out,

These changes have torn the belly out of some industrial giants that once dominated the economy and wielded enormous clout in Washington. The same changes have also shrunk the power of the mass-production labor unions. The same de-massification process has undercut the three giant TV networks, fragmenting their audiences as cable and other media arose to serve new niche markets.

As part of this de-massification, the power tends to shift to those who understand and control the new information-based environment. Decentralization becomes important. They concluded, ". . . the rigid, uniform structure of the firm must be replaced by a diversity of organizational arrangements." Flexibility and speed to adapt to changing conditions were required in a world in which information determines who succeeds and who fails on a global scale.

If the Tofflers are correct in their forecast, then the information age will bring about fundamental changes in the public sector, including law enforcement. In thinking about such changes, an outline of these information-related changes is now apparent. Long-term trends widely discussed in the literature suggest the need for a new way of thinking about law enforcement and future directions.

Observers over the past decade have discussed major changes in the openness of law enforcement agencies (Goldstein, 1990). Earlier writings described law enforcement organizations as self-contained, isolated, insulated, and distant from the other agencies of local government (Skolnick, 1975). It was common to find police departments described as internally focused and with a unique culture that made them different from other public organizations. However, as the Law Enforcement Assistance Administration sponsored research and later NIJ-sponsored research focused on law enforcement, the situation changed dramatically (Petersilia, 1987).

Even an overview of law enforcement texts dealing with administration serves as evidence for the change from closed to open systems. The traditional texts focused on internal supervision, control, discipline, and related functions within the organization. The newer textbooks focus on the public sector and the environment of law enforcement agencies. The chapters on police management now encompass areas such as media relations, policy development, community organizations, information systems, and legal concepts growing out of risk management (Swanson et al., 1988). In short there has been a dramatic shift from the closed internally focused isolated police organization to a more open-integrated unit as part of the local government services network.

Another trend that is related to the closed/open dynamic is the increasing emphasis on the use of research and information to guide policy (Petersilia, 1987). In other words, it is more likely today to think of performance-based organizations and to be concerned not only about efficiency, but effectiveness. If the more traditional kind of policing could be characterized as militaristic in symbols and structure, the performance-based organization has more of an organic set of symbols and structures. The change from a mechanistic view of the organization to a view of the organization as a team to be nurtured, developed, and managed is characteristic of the shift. Goldstein's (1979) first major article on problem solving focused on the need for performance. Any performance-based system requires extensive information about not only internal activities, but the impact of those activities on external problems and ultimately communities. This perspective led him to conclude in his most recent work that organizational cultural change is now a necessary condition to do problem-solving policing (Goldstein, 1990).

Goldstein's argument fundamentally challenges the ideas of the O. W. Wilsonian model that constitutes the conventional wisdom in law enforcement. Although diverse in its application across the organizational landscape, the older approach emphasized form over function, i.e., structure and formal organization instead of outcomes. Performance was assumed without critical examination.

Another way to characterize this trend in law enforcement relates to the numerous discussions arguing for proactive rather than reactive policing. Proactive as a term conjures up an image of an organization reaching out to impact its environment rather than simply responding to change. In short, over the past several years the language in law enforcement has shifted dramatically to reflect the importance of information as part of decision making and program development. This is not meant to conclude that law enforcement actually has implemented this change and has moved very significantly in this direction, but the thinking about where it needs to go now emphasizes the performance or proactive dimensions that rely on the use of information.

The development of police administration beyond the traditional approach was discussed as a significant trend in the growing complexity that characterizes management in an information age (Sykes and Taylor, 1991). They argued that police leaders must be capable of accessing a vast array of information concerning both internal and external problems that demand the ability to understand data from a management information perspective. Police executives must be able to link information to decision making aimed at planning, forecasting, and other management functions. In short, a major emphasis on open systems is essential if you are information dependent and law enforcement is moving rapidly in that direction.

This new information age will also require police managers to have specific skills in order to understand how to plan, research, and evaluate programs. Administrators must work routinely within a dynamic environment characterized by rapid change, information overload, and political ambiguity. Rather than seeking to be isolated and removed from political interference, integration is necessary. To function effectively this police administrator must be knowledgeable about the public process, have an understanding of public finance, relate well to the media, work as a member of a government services team, and be highly informed about the impact of his or her agency on the community. All of these activities require an extensive information system.

And finally, leadership in this setting requires a sophisticated approach that uses research and information to develop new ways of doing old activities. "Flying by the seat of your pants" gives way to the more rational and deliberative processes that are part of running a complex and sophisticated organization (Sykes and Taylor, 1991).

Another important indicator of the changes in law enforcement has to do with the increasing use of civilian employees for high-level positions in law enforcement organizations. One trend appears to be the expanding role of public safety directors and assistant city managers in day-to-day management decisions. In addition, there is increased use of civilians in high-level positions in budgeting, research, and finance. To the extent that information is central to the functioning of modern organizations, civilians play an increasing role at the center of law enforcement. The impact of this trend substantiates the importance of information and the difficulty of finding such talent within the sworn ranks; however, its effect is not known.

The high turnover rate of chiefs in larger agencies continues and suggests the instability brought on by changes within the law enforcement environment. The fact that chiefs in larger agencies tend to be recruited from the outside further reinforces the point that cities and towns are recruiting administrators with credentials and expertise in administration. It is becoming more common to think in terms of analyzing and evaluating performance, including the performance of chief executives.

Obviously there is no single factor fueling the trend from a reactive-based to a performance-based organization. Scarcity in the public sector certainly requires people to use resources more efficiently and creates an expectation of performance. The growing public expectation that more effective strategies in crime control should yield a lower crime rate are part of the pressure that police administrators experience.

Goldstein (1990) and others call for a new way of policing in response to the demand for performance. Their critique of traditional or the so-called "incident-based" policing in favor of problem-solving and community-based policing questions some of the most fundamental assumptions that operate in law enforcement to drive the allocation and distribution of resources. They advocate nothing short of a revolution aimed at changing the professional model of policing (sometimes called the crime-fighting model) that nurtured incident-based policing. Such changes are often called "paradigm" shifts when fundamental and accepted ideas are challenged. To explore these ideas about change, a discussion of paradigms is in order.

Paradigm Change

In one of the most influential and seminal books, Thomas S. Kuhn (1962) outlined the sociology of revolutionary and evolutionary shifts that occur in community belief systems. Although he analyzed the scientific community, a number of scholars use his ideas in sorting out and understanding community change. Kuhn defined "community" as a group committed to shared assumptions or an agreement about fundamental values within a group. These basic assumptions about reality and knowing constitute a powerful framework or a given set of categories that filters perceptions.

These assumptions, Kuhn argued, constituted a "worldview" or "paradigm." He further pointed out that paradigms remained stable over time, were relatively efficacious at explanation, and provided the basis on which models, theories, and, ultimately, behavior rest. In another sense, the paradigm was the cultural framework through which a community came to know itself, its boundaries (what separated it from other communities), and provided the basic explanations of reality. As such, a paradigm provided the "givens" necessary for social life and preserving it was tantamount to the survival of the group itself.

Kuhn's ideas define the source of change as coming from ongoing experience, or in other words, reality testing. Most accumulated experiences, if not irrelevant or irreverent to the prevailing explanations, reinforce the "givens," i.e., the consensus-based assumptions on which the accepted models of explanation and theories of reality rely. However, accumulated experience over time often produce "anomalies," i.e., basic facts and discoveries (new information), that contradict the expectations within the prevailing paradigm and cannot be dismissed very easily. As anomalies surface, for a variety of reasons, some political in nature, they may or may not contribute to a sense of crisis within a community.

In response to accumulated or persistent anomalies that challenge the given assumptions, Kuhn distinguishes three possible responses. First, the prevailing paradigm can be reified and anomalies ignored. In political terms, any challenges can be repressed and the contradictory ideas ridiculed, dismissed, or discredited in some way. This course maintains the status quo.

Second, a movement may be initiated to modify the existing assumptions in light of experience, or at least put forward alternative theories or models to account for the discrepancy between the paradigmatic expectations and the anomalous experience. Consequently, in the second pattern, the basic assumptions are modified and the theories and models shift to account for the unexpected experience. This is the road to reform and evolutionary change.

The third outcome, namely a revolution, radically alters the *status quo* by replacing the prevailing assumptions. As such, revolutionary change is fundamental, causes enormous turmoil as it begins to challenge the prevailing belief system, but the turmoil gives way to a celebration when the efficacy of the new paradigm is demonstrated. During the period of challenge, careers, reputations, movements, and new institutions rise and fall depending on the outcome of the challenge.

Community Policing: A New Paradigm

Basic thinking about law enforcement in the United States is changing. Broad-based reform ideas can be characterized in several ways (Greene and Mastrofski, 1988). Goldstein (1979), in a well-known article on improving police, advocated that practitioners change from reactive to performance-based approaches and provided part of the conceptual foundation for a movement variously labeled "community-based," "neighborhood-oriented," "problem-solving," and/or just generally "community policing." Another strain of reform, providing some of the impetus for reform, came from the ideas of James Q. Wilson and George Kelling (1982). They declared that changing police strategies from enforcement (a function of random preventive patrol) to order maintenance held the promise of salvaging a role in crime deterrence and intervention (Sykes, 1986).

At the heart of this community policing collection of ideas is the yearning that police and citizens can have an intimate, cooperative, and nonauthoritarian relationship (Manning, 1984). However, this kind of policing says Manning ". . . would require a change in the uses of the law; in the standards used to apply law and order enforcement; in the overall contracts governing police and the public and the degree of centralization, structure, hierarchy and formalization of such matters as recruitment, evaluation, promotion and rewards in police departments" (p. 226); in short, a fundamental or revolutionary change in the police role, function, and organization.

As a paradigm, community-based policing could be characterized as a proposed alternative to the prevailing bureaucratic/professional paradigm (Sparrow et al., 1990). Despite its diverse nature, community policing is the movement of the 1990s. It holds out the promise of salvaging the police role from the growing criticism and disillusionment that emerged in the past twenty years.

The dominant characteristics associated with the professional paradigm are captured in words such as hierarchical, authoritative, militaristic, and impersonal — i.e., bureaucratic. The proposed ideas of community policing are expressed in words such as decentralized, sensitive to community needs, and service oriented — i.e., personal policing. In fact, this use of language implies that police are no longer to be understood as a coercive force in society, but as service deliverers who "respond to" customers. They are defined "problem-busters" rather than "head-busters." There is little doubt that the thrust of community-based policing is revolutionary — i.e., to fundamentally alter the police role as defined within prevailing paradigm.

Accreditation: Salvaging the Professional/ Bureaucratic Model

Another significant movement in policing is the accreditation efforts by the Commission on Accreditation of Law Enforcement Agencies (CALEA). It has gathered momentum to the extent that at this point in time over 900 agencies have made the initial efforts to begin the process and over 200 have received the "stamp of approval" by the accrediting body.

Through policy and procedure standardization based on written criteria (over 850 explicit standards), the accreditation proponents believe that improvements in law enforcement are largely a function of organizational reform. To some extent this viewpoint represents a complementary movement to the military-based professionalism that prevailed in the 1960s from the early part of this century (for a history see Fogelson, 1977; Johnson, 1981; and Sykes, 1985).

Through centralized administration and policy standardization, CALEA's canons may be perceived as an attempt to salvage many of the reforms of the O. W. Wilsonian professional model in light of its alleged failures to penetrate agency culture beyond the superficial level and its limited effectiveness in crime control, i.e., efficient law enforcement (Sykes, 1985).

Although for a law enforcement agency there may be some economic benefits flowing from accreditation, such as increased leverage in an agency's budgetary process, less exposure to liability risks (potential civil actions), and less vulnerability to drastic changes in insurance liability costs, its vision of reform remains enigmatic.

The commission's criteria, in fact, were deliberately the result of various compromises between large and small agencies, between the interests of municipal and sheriff's departments, and among diverse groups of regional interests. As such, the multitude of standards was largely devoid of substantive measures that articulate "how" an agency should perform or what kind of outcomes are to be sought.

In other words, CALEA's standards specify form, not function, means rather than ends. There is no alternative paradigm, i.e., there is no vision of the "good" police organization with the exception how it should "look on paper." The normative questions and ethical ends are left to the agency.

In sum, the movement to accredit law enforcement agencies lacks both a critique of the present and a normative vision. In addition, it can be largely defined as an extension of more traditional concerns. Therefore, for purposes of this article, it will not be considered as a reform movement to change the prevailing paradigm, rather it resembles a complement to the *status quo* of military professionalism. Indeed, one can almost see O. W. Wilson smiling approvingly from heaven as he watches the accreditation movement expand.

Order Maintenance Policing: The Untried Alternative

The ideas on order maintenance policing, referred to as OMP, espoused by Wilson and Kelling (1982) and others (for a brief history, Sykes, 1986), have yet to become established beyond the debate level among academic researchers and scholars. Its major contribution appears to be as an argument in *debunking* the prevailing assumptions of incident-driven or crime control policing that dominated law enforcement as a reform movement over much of this century.

Although OMP is not as expansive as the community policing movement, it does articulate a vision of a future police role. It does not celebrate the O. W. Wilsonian values of legal and administrative due process, nor does it propose an extensive overhaul of the role expectations suggested by community policing advocates. OMP views the prospects for substantive change in law enforcement as incremental rather than revolutionary (see Kelling and Klockars, 1985).

The activities described as community-based policing are diverse (Trojanowicz and Bucqueroux, 1990; Greene and Mastrofski, 1988).   For purposes here, the distinction will be made between community policing as a strategy for problem solving and as a reform ideology. The experiments sponsored by PERF emphasize policing as "process" or *technique*. The organizational context and the basic role of the officer is not changed in order to implement this information-based strategy. It is a system to guide operations rather than a change in the organization and role expectations (Eck and Spelman, 1987).

In fact, on the operational side, problem-oriented policing contains several benefits that hold definite promise for law enforcement. If one views it primarily as a strategy to focus and use resources more efficiently, not aimed at changing the police role, it may in fact encourage more emphasis on systematic information gathering, research, program evaluation, and conscious strategic thinking. In other words, this approach as a management tool nurtures the development of a scientific information system as part of police administration.   It is long overdue that systematic planning and program evaluation become the norm within the law enforcement community. Research is needed to determine the most effective and efficient use of resources in the administration of law enforcement services and problem-oriented policing is an approach that clearly exhibits these attributes (Manning, 1984).

However, the more ideological advocates of community-based policing such as Goldstein (1979) characterized this idea as more than mere *technique*. He argued that unless the performance-based or problem-oriented approach became departmentwide, it was likely to have the same impact as the police-community relations movement. Specifically, Goldstein suggested that unless community policing permeated departmental culture, it would become a specialized separate unit within agencies and the basic role of the officer would remain unchanged. Goldstein's suggestion was that this approach was aimed at a basic change in the role of police.

Manning (1984) viewed community policing as a *metaphor* expressing a yearning for service personalization that cannot be fulfilled by the bureaucratic and professional model of policing. He argued that it was, and is, based on the belief that communities in the past were organic, that the police function was legitimate, and that close community bonds between the police and the public led to efficient and effective policing.

Stability Amid Change: Alternative Futures

Police executives are at a critical time in law enforcement. There appears to be a paradigmatic crisis that creates both threats and opportunities. It is not likely that many administrators have the choice to do nothing and continue to function in the traditional ways. The idea of "if it ain't broke, don't fix it" is probably not an option for many given the changes that demand performance.

One alternative future, of course, is accreditation through CALEA. David Couper, chief of the Madison, Wisconsin Police Department, put it succinctly when he said, "accreditation is great for a department that needs to bring itself into the 1960s." In other words, there are many agencies that are so tradition-bound that they must bring clarity and a sense of purpose to the existing chaos of their organization. Accreditation is concerned with means, i.e., processes, standards, and criteria. Formal and explicit organization is perhaps to be preferred over the informal norms and procedures that have grown through unconscious development over the years.

The accreditation future does not usher in a new era as much as it attempts to bring a sense of order and security to the old one without confronting the ambiguity and uncertainty of exploring fundamental questions. This pathway reifies the O. W. Wilsonian model by making it more explicit. It is grounded on the bureaucratic professional model of policing and does not address the problems raised about performance. In fact, an accredited department is concerned with means being explicit, not with the ends to be achieved. Therefore, it actually is an extension of the present into the future.

The future vision of community policing may or may not be revolutionary. Problem-solving policing, according to Goldstein (1990), can be applied in two distinct ways. As a process that can be divorced from the organization, it can be understood as simply a more efficient way to do police work. In other words, it enlarges the role of the officer by expanding his or her responsibility to do problem solving employing the proposed techniques. In this format, it can be attached to almost any organizational culture to improve productivity.

Implicitly, however, the advocates of community policing want it to be more than a mere efficient process. They see this approach requiring a vast array of organizational changes that reflect the long-standing critiques of the structure of police organizations that they view as repressive of officer autonomy and creativity. They see this process as the vehicle to create a revolution from within the organization. The word "empowerment" is often advocated both directly and indirectly, or the concept of "ownership" is employed in a way that would turn the organization upside down (Braiden, 1987). The organization should serve the officer, from this vantage point, rather than the other way around. The difficulties with this kind of revolutionary change are only beginning to be realized.

Stability Amid Change: Strategic Approaches

Both the accreditation movement and the community policing movement differ in how they see change implemented. CALEA seeks to "sell" its approach by providing support to chiefs who are committed to moving beyond the "folk culture." It promises to provide a more efficient organization without large-scale change in the nature and responsibilities of the rank structure. Many of its published standards are silent about the content of policy or how various roles are to be played, they only specify that agencies *must* have stated policies and trained personnel with certain defined tasks in order to be approved.

The accreditation movement does not have a clearly articulated vision of what the "good" department should look like except that all of the processes and procedures are written or exist in some form. Their strategy for change begins with a committed chief who can successfully convince his or her political agency to provide the resources for implementation of the standards and the cost of the accreditation process itself. It does not require any fundamental change in the role of the line officer, or even the active involvement of the rank and file. What is required is an accreditation manager, chosen by the chief, who initiates and manages the extensive work in preparing the appropriate documentation for the visit by the accrediting team. Whatever actual reform comes out of the process is fortuitous.

The advocates of community policing believe that top-down organizational reform is of limited value based on the experience of previous efforts that have failed, e.g., team policing. Their strategy for change begins by changing the nature of the police officer's role through both job enrichment and enlargement, i.e., greater responsibility and more responsibilities. Goldstein believes that if this change is authentic, it will lead to a major restructuring of the organization to serve the needs of the problem solvers on the street.

There is some disagreement about how much the culture of the organization must be changed in order for the street officer's role to change. In other words, are there organizational reforms that must be achieved before enrichment and enlargement can take place? This question of whether the organizational culture must change first, or can be changed *while* the officer's responsibilities are changing is an important strategic question without a clear answer.   There is no shortage of implementation issues when a revolutionary change is sought.

Stability Amid Change: Human Resource Issues

Central to the concerns of CALEA is training. Its standards imply the belief that a fundamental problem in law enforcement is the lack of specialized training for personnel. In this sense, it attempts to require a career development system for the many roles and responsibilities it defines as important in law enforcement agencies.   Consequently, it extends the professional model's emphasis on task specialization and requires agencies to implement and document their training programs.

CALEA's criteria reinforce the traditional view of human resource management by attempting to make the recruitment, selection, and training functions central to the organization.   More important, however, it may require agencies genuinely to implement what has largely been "lip service" to the training function.   In fact, as this movement expands, it is spawning major growth in the "training industry."

Community policing also shares a commitment to human resource development, but with different goals in mind. The skills necessary to do problem-solving policing rely heavily on educational rather than training skills.   Where traditional training emphasizes memorization, recall, and identification skills, community officers are required to develop expertise in analysis, synthesis, and evaluation.   The latter are most often associated with higher education and the social-behavioral sciences.   Research skills become important, and the role of the officer requires creativity as innovation and necessary complements to problem solving and community mobilization.

The community policing advocates understand that a major effort will be necessary to recruit a different kind of police officer. College-educated officers motivated by altruistic values will be required to implement this kind of service-oriented policing. A complete overhaul of the training curriculum as it now exists would be necessary to implement community policing.

The impact of this set of values on the traditional human resource structure is nothing short of breathtaking. To illustrate, an article that discussed the need for an open organization by Cordner (1989) created a strong reaction from CALEA advocates. Cordner suggested that the extensive written "don'ts" within policing need to be replaced to allow for officer discretion and autonomy consistent with employee empowerment. This argument seemed to challenge the CALEA efforts to require more extensive and detailed policies and procedures.

Stability Amid Change: Technology

The Tofflers' discussion of change in the information-age is relevant to any discussion of technology. Computer-based information systems are likely to be more important as a factor producing change than the emphasis on law enforcement hardware, e.g., DNA testing, weapons development, and detection-oriented innovations. Rapid social changes nurtured by the economic polarization of the emerging "super-symbolic economy" lead to shifts that give rise to disorder and violence.

The development of information systems that provide almost instantaneous feedback on performance can be expected to promote greater expectations from the public for both service and efficiency. Public policing is likely to undergo enormous scrutiny because of the availability of information. Alternatives to public policing are only beginning to expand and various forms of privatization will continue to grow. As the new-age society now expects quality and performance for the public resources expended, the pressure will be on law enforcement to stay current with this trend.

Stability Amid Change: Managing Change

Community policing calls for a visionary kind of leader as a change agent to implement long-term radical changes in the nature of the police business. Accreditation reform is not revolutionary and therefore does not require the nurturing of a new set of values for the organization. Trying to do both within the same organizational setting runs the risk of creating confusion. Whether or not a police manager should pursue change is a question that cannot be answered without some detailed understanding of the nature of the department and the community it serves.

For example, there are different types of law enforcement agencies. Is community policing or accreditation the appropriate model for a highway patrol agency? There are also different types of communities. Is community policing appropriate to an affluent bedroom suburb with a relatively low crime rate, strong community institutions, and little disorder? Or, can community policing values be implemented in a high-crime area where officers are stacking calls that cannot be answered and the city tax base will not allow for additional resources? Such questions point to the unique nature of change in policing due to its narrowly defined and decentralized environment.

The broad choices for change seem to fall between two general alternatives: (1) improvement of the *status quo* (accreditation) and (2) community policing that is essentially a fundamental change in the values of policing. If the Tofflers are right about the emerging powershift, then many, if not most, law enforcement agencies will undergo a major paradigm change as they move into the next century. Short of the risk and turmoil associated with such dramatic efforts, the accreditation movement offers the promise of an organizational house cleaning that will make what exists work better.

The difficulty with the more conservative course is that many of the problems associated with traditional policing, i.e., the shortcomings of the crime control model, may not be addressed. To put it another way, reforms aimed at salvaging the *status quo* run the risk of doing too little too late. The result could be the continued shrinkage of public law enforcement as a major player in providing for public security. It must be remembered that the emergence of community policing is a search for something that performs, a search for a more effective form of policing. The prevailing model of military and bureaucratic policing is on the defensive.

Revolutionary times are exciting times. The decade of the 1990s should hold the answer as to what path most law enforcement administrators will choose.

References

Braiden, C. (1987). *Community policing: Nothing new under the sun.* Edmonton: Edmonton (Alberta, Canada) Police Force.

Cordner, G. W. (1989). Written rules and regulations: Are they necessary? *FBI Law Enforcement Bulletin.*

Eck, J. E. & Spelman, W. (1987). *Problem solving: Problem-oriented policing in Newport News*. Washington DC: Police Executive Research Forum.

Fogelson, R. M. (1977). *Big-city police*. Cambridge, MA: Harvard University Press.

Goldstein, H. (1979). Improving policing: A problem-oriented approach. *Crime and Delinquency, 25*, 236-258 (April).

Goldstein, H. (1990). *Problem-oriented policing*. New York: McGraw-Hill Inc.

Greene, J. & Mastrofski, S. (Eds.). (1988). *Community policing: Rhetoric or reality*. New York: Praeger Publishers.

Johnson, D. R. (1981). *American law enforcement: A history*. St. Louis, MO: Forum Press.

Kelling, G. L. & Klockers, C. G. (1985). Order maintenance, the quality of urban life, and police: A line of argument. In W. A. Geller (Ed.), *Police leadership in America: Crisis and opportunity* (pp. 296-308). New York: Praeger Publishers.

Kuhn, T. S. (1962). *The structure of scientific revolutions* (2nd ed.). Chicago: University of Chicago Press.

Manning, P. K. (1984). Community policing. *American Journal of Police, 3*(2), 205-227.

Petersilia, J. (1987). *The influence of criminal justice*. R-3516-NIJ. Santa Monica, CA: The RAND Corporation.

Redlinger, L. W. (1991). Presentation to the third annual Advanced Management College, Southwestern Law Enforcement Institute, The University of Texas at Dallas Campus, Richardson, TX.

Shearing, C. D. & Stenning, P. C. (1987). Private policing, *Sage Criminal Justice System Annuals*. Beverly Hills, CA: Sage Publications Inc.

Skolnick, J. H. (1975). Why police behave the way they do. In J. H. Skolnick & T. C. Gray (Eds.), *Police in America*. Boston: Little, Brown & Co.

Sparrow, M. K., Moore, M. H., & Kennedy, D. M. (1990). *Beyond 911: The new era of policing*. New York: Basic Books Inc. Publishers.

Swanson, C. R., Territo, L., and Taylor, R. W. (1988). *Police administration: Structures, processes and behavior* (2nd ed.). New York: Macmillan Publishing Co.

Sykes, G. W. (1985). The functional nature of police reform: The "myth" of controlling the police. *Justice Quarterly*, 2(1), 51-65.

Sykes, G. W. (1986). Street justice: A moral defense of order maintenance policing. *Justice Quarterly*, 3(4), 497-512.

Sykes, G. W. & Taylor, R. W. (1991). The new police administrator, *Police yearbook*. Gaithersberg, MD: International Association of the Chiefs of Police.

Toffler, A. & Toffler, H. (1990). *Powershift: Knowledge, wealth and violence at the edge of the 21st century*. New York: Bantam Books.

Trojanowicz, R. C. & Bucqueroux, B. (1990). *Community policing: A contemporary perspective*. Cincinnati: Anderson Publishing Co.

Wilson, J. Q. & Kelling, G. L. (1982). Police and neighborhood safety: Broken windows. *Atlantic Monthly*, 249, 29-38 (March).

Chapter 8

Alternative Futures

Allen D. Sapp

Introduction

This chapter is an attempt to do that most difficult of tasks — to look into the future and to arrive at some logical conclusions about the shape of things to come. The study of the future, usually referred to as "futuristics" or "futures research," is always limited. Futures research is limited in three significant ways: (1) the future is neither fixed nor predetermined; (2) the future is not predictable; and (3) individual choices and actions can influence and change the future (Tafoya, 1990). Some forecasts are too pessimistic while others are too optimistic. All too often, forecasts of the future are given more weight, perhaps, than they merit. As a result, changes are made today that affect tomorrow and the forecasts become factors in shaping the future. The concept of "the self-fulfilling prophecy" is well known and always a potential when delving into the unknown and unknowable.

Some future conditions can be accurately predicted based upon extrapolation of trends and empirically validated evidence. Other conditions, particularly those involving abstract constructs, can only be estimated, while still others can be little more than an educated guess. None of these methods are infallible and all are subject to error. When futures research is extended beyond the theoretical exploration of trends and patterns into "applied futures," the problems are compounded. Applying futures research to specific problem areas requires a change in the traditional methods of problem solving. Any attempt to apply forecasts of the future requires unique perspectives, based on trying to understand the unknown, to see the "unseeable" and to predict the possible alternatives. Additionally, the problem of applying futures research requires the implementation of changes that are easily accepted and often seen as unnecessary by those less confident of the value of futures research.   Resistance to change is characteristic of human behavior and dogmatic clinging to traditional methods and activities tend to be particularly problematic in law enforcement.

Tafoya (1990) notes that three goals for futures research are needed if future outcomes are to be influenced:

> Futurists accept these three goals for futures research: (1) form perceptions of the future (the possible), (2) study likely alternatives (the probable), and (3) make choices to bring about particular events (the preferable). If future outcomes are to be influences, perceptions of the future must be formed. Fresh new images must be generated, identifying the opportunities as well as the risks. This goal is image driven and requires breaking the fetters of one's imagination. This is the vital, creative goal of futures research . . . . Thus, the future is best anticipated in an imaginative, analytical, and value-conscious manner (pp. 202-203).

Futures Research in Law Enforcement

Very little has been written about the future of law enforcement in America, although considerable research has been offered on the future in general terms (Toffler, 1970, 1980; Toffler and Toffler, 1990; Naisbitt, 1984; Naisbitt and Aburdene, 1990, among others).   Bennett (1987) offered predictions for the future of crime in America.   William Tafoya, Federal Bureau of Investigation, has been the leading investigator in futures research in law enforcement (1986a, 1986b, 1987, 1990). In 1991, under his leadership, the Federal Bureau of Investigation sponsored a conference on futures and law enforcement, the first of its kind. At that conference, a number of perspectives on futures were presented.

Tafoya's work (1986b) has been widely noted, particularly his predictions of future changes in law enforcement and in society that will drive some of those changes. Using a Delphi technique, Tafoya brought together a panel of experts in law enforcement that provided a series of forecasts. Among those forecasts, with the predicted date of expected occurrence, were

> 1995 - Community involvement and self-help (such as community- and goal-oriented policing) will become common practice in more than 70 percent of the nation. Domestic political terrorism (acts committed within the United States) will increase in number by more than 50 percent.

1997 - State of the art technology will begin to be employed in combatting crime.

1999 - Massive civil unrest and civil disorder are expected to plague America.

2000 - Local law enforcement could be overwhelmed by sophisticated crimes, using high technology, and may be reduced to taking preliminary reports.

2025 - Formal education will become the standard for entry and advancement in more than 70 percent of all police agencies. The majority of law enforcement executives will have changed their leadership style to reflect a proactive, goal orientation. Traditional, autocratic management will largely be abandoned.

2035 - Private security agencies will assume more than 50 percent of all present day law enforcement responsibilities.

2050 - The long-awaited mantle of professionalism is expected to be bestowed on law enforcement. (1987, pp. 17-19).

Overall, the prediction made in Tafoya's work offer a combination of hope and concern. Predictions about the changes that result in more professional and community- and service-oriented policing are encouraging. Those predictions that center on terrorism, civil unrest, and technological crime suggest that police administrators should be concerned about these areas. It is important to realize that these are predictions of the future and the predictions can be affected by actions and plans made now to change the future. The predictions focus on internal and external environments of law enforcement. The remainder of this chapter will review some of the trends in the external and internal environments of law enforcement and some areas where planning may influence the outcomes of these predictions.

Trends in External Environment

Trends in the external environment of policing include the changing demographic characteristics of the United States, among which are the aging of the population, mobility of Americans, and increasing affluence. Another obvious trend is in the area of technology where new advances are made almost daily. A third trend that will affect law enforcement is the shifting of American society from an industrial, manufacturing society to a technological, information-based society. These trends result in disproportionate and disparate rates and influences of change for different segments of society.

Demographic Changes. Perhaps the most dramatic or noticeable trend is the changing demographic characteristics of American society. According to the Bureau of the Census (1985, p. 53), the United States will reach zero population growth in the year 2050. By the year 2025 over one-fourth of the population will be age sixty or older, more than doubling the number of people who were in that age category in 1980. At the same time we are experiencing larger numbers of older citizens, the life expectancy is also increasing. Between 1970 and 1984 the life expectancy of a male rose from 67.1 to 71.1 years, while that of a female rose from 74.7 to 78.3 years. This trend toward an aging population is expected to continue and become significant by the year 2000 because the largest increase in age brackets has occurred for the 24- to 44-year age groups, while both the 5- to 7- and 18- to 24-year old age brackets have been decreasing in size (Bureau of the Census, 1985, p. xix).

Not only are Americans living longer, but their affluence is increasing. Between 1970 and 1984, disposable personal income increased from $695 billion to $2,577 billion per year. (Bureau of the Census, 1985, p. 14) They are expending more money on what might be considered luxury items and expect a better quality of life. For example, by 1990, revenue growth in the cable television industry is expected to rise from the 1980 level of $2,436 million to $18,505 million (Bureau of the Census, 1985, p. 157).

Over the past two decades Americans have been a fairly mobile society and the trend is not expected to change. Between 1960 and 1984 the percentage of the total population that had moved to a different house during the two-year reporting periods ranged from 16.6 percent to 20.6 percent. By the year 2000 the largest increase in population will occur in the western (18.1 percent) and southern (12.8 percent) regions. At the same time the northeastern and midwestern regions of the country will experience a decrease in population (Bureau of the Census, 1985, p. 14).

Increasingly, our society is becoming better educated. Between 1970 and 1984 the percentage of persons age twenty-five or older who had attended high school four or more years rose from 52.3 percent to 73.3 percent. During that period, college attendance of four or more years rose from 10.7 percent to 19.1 percent of the total population.

In addition to changes in the demographic makeup, there are other trends that have the potential to impact law enforcement. America is shifting from an industrial to a service-oriented society, while at the same time moving from a nationally based economy to a world economy. As this restructuring occurs there will be a corresponding decrease in the use of traditional or bureaucratic management styles as businesses come to rely more on networking and flexible organizations that allow them to adapt to rapidly changing economies and demands for services (Naisbitt, 1984).

As the nation moves toward service-oriented industries, it will be increasingly necessary to rely on technology to rapidly process information. This shift is already evident in the phenomenal growth in computer literacy. Research shows that in 1984 51 percent of full-time college freshmen had written a computer program within the past year and 40 percent had taken a computer-assisted course of instruction. This rapid increase in computer literacy becomes apparent when those figures are compared with the data from just two years earlier. Only 27 percent of full-time freshmen had written a computer program and only 17 percent had taken a computer-assisted instruction course (Bureau of the Census, 1985, p. 151).

One foreseeable consequence of the move toward a service-oriented society in which technology is rapidly changing and developing is the increasing emphasis placed on professionalization of the work force and the use of specialists. In turn, specialization and professionalization, trends in their own right, will have a direct effect on the organizational characteristic of law enforcement agencies, will require diverse types of personnel, and will increase the need for education and training.

The changes taking place in the population will have significant effects on organizational structure of law enforcement agencies in the twenty-first century. The population of America will increasingly become more mobile as workers and their families move more frequently and longer distances. Significant population relocation will continue as Americans live longer and the percentage of elderly persons in the population increases. Workers are going to be better educated, more informal, and more humanitarian in their work relationships. International events will continue to affect population movements in America.

Although we have great difficulty in reaching a consensus on what causes crime, arguments about reliability of the data aside, it is apparent that those who commit street crimes are typically younger offenders. As the mean age of the population increases, there should be a corresponding decrease in those offenses. To the extent that this occurs, the offenses that will concern law enforcement will be of a more technical nature and less violent or confrontive. It is highly probable that police in the future will be required to expend less effort on traditional forms of theft and find it necessary to concentrate their efforts on crimes that are committed by individuals in a position of trust or those that have specialized knowledge or expertise.

Mobile workers will increasingly agree to, and seek out, relocation to work sites perceived as more desirable. More major employers will yield to labor demands and pressures to relocate in sunbelt states and areas with a better quality of life. As these moves take place, law enforcement agencies will be required to expand to provide necessary services in the relocation areas.

As recent events in the energy field have so clearly shown, population movements will continue to be greatly influenced by world events outside the United States. The oil and gas boom of the late 1970s, triggered primarily by production and price controls established by the Organization of Petroleum Exporting Countries (OPEC), led to major population relocations to the oil-producing states. The collapse of OPEC production controls in the 1980s led to an oil glut and plummeting prices. In turn, the oil states in America are losing much of the population gained during the boom years.

As workers become better educated, law enforcement agencies will increasingly be confronted with decisions on organizational issues related to education. Workers are likely to have more choices of employment, to seek more informal organizational structures, and to demand more humanitarian and less bureaucratic organizations. Workers with more education have traditionally demanded better compensation, working conditions, and fringe benefits.

The rise in educational levels among the overall labor force will, of course, not include all of that force. There will continue to be a group of mostly young, poor, and largely minority workers who will be left outside the mainstream of the labor force. These people, who will be either unemployed or underemployed, will be considerably less mobile. If the trend toward an aging population with more formal education continues, the young or less educated will find it increasingly difficult to obtain a position in society. The obvious difficulty created by the shift in demographics for these people will be in their inability to relate on a personal basis to an older, more affluent, and better educated general work force. Demographics aside, other trends in our society may serve as even greater impediments to this segment of the population obtaining employment.

Changes in Technology. The computer revolution will force changes in the priority of law enforcement departments. It will not be uncommon to find all of a company's personnel records, planning documents, and research and development information stored in a computer that can be accessed from a remote terminal. Theft, sabotage, or inadvertent loss of these data will be of increasing concern to managers.

The cashless society will be close to a reality by the year 2000. Automated teller machines have become the norm rather than the exception, even in the smallest of communities and banks. Typically, these machines are connected to one of several nationwide computer systems, making them vulnerable to theft and fraud. Although the idea has met with some skepticism, several financial institutions have begun to offer electronic banking services that can be accessed by the customer's personal computer. An individual can complete routine banking transactions over the telephone by using an inexpensive modem. Increasingly, corporations are relying on the computerized transfer of funds. This computerization has led to a centralization of financial transactions. At the same time, more people have access to computer terminals who have an increased knowledge of how computer systems can be manipulated.

As the median age of society increases, one would expect to see a decrease in the number of the more traditional forms of theft that have previously been correlated with younger offenders. Although one can only speculate, it is probable that there will be an increase in the so-called "white collar" crimes, one of which would be theft by computer. Even if age proves not to be a factor, the movement toward a cashless society and computerized financial transactions would logically lead one to believe that the methods of stealing would shift toward the use of the computer out of sheer necessity.

The greatest potential for loss (barring destruction of the central computer) will be in unauthorized access. This will require the recruitment of computer programmers and experts with the technical ability to detect unauthorized entry into the system and illegal transactions. The training and education requirements of this type of employee are obviously vastly different from those engaged in traditional law enforcement work. If the past is any indication, sophisticated technology that has been developed for military and other governmental services will continue to be adopted by private business concerns.

In addition to adapting and improving existing technology, future developments and advances may provide greater opportunities for law enforcement. Automated Fingerprint Identification Systems (AFIS), DNA identification techniques, enhanced communications, and computer access are just some of the many technological advancements that will enhance policing in the near future.

Development of a Service-Oriented, Post-Industrial Society. In the United States, the percentage of the population engaged in industrial or manufacturing jobs has declined dramatically in the past thirty years. The number of farm workers in the 1980s was less than one-fourth the number in the 1950s. U.S. Department of Labor figures reflect a growth in service industries from 30 percent of the work force in the early years of this century to 70 percent in 1980. By the year 2000 that trend will level to 8.5 to 9 service workers for every 1 to 1.5 industrial workers (Department of Labor, 1970).

Typically, service workers require more education and training than industrial workers. Entry level job requirements have increased and most service occupations require at least some college education for entry today. This trend is likely to continue and the labor force in the year 2000 will have more education than the force today. With increased education is likely to come increased demands for economic rewards for college-educated employees. Colleges and employers alike are increasingly faced with demands for pragmatic and relevant education and training that has immediate payoff rather than long-term benefits for the student and employee.

Law enforcement is not exempt from the changes taking place as this conversion to service takes place. In fact, much of the growth in private security is a direct reflection of increasing public reliance on service industries and businesses. Much of the growth of private security will likely be in areas formerly controlled by local, state, and federal governments. Services that have traditionally been considered the sole responsibility of law enforcement are likely to become increasingly privatized. If law enforcement agencies are not capable of providing the necessary services for an information-oriented, technological society, private industry will move into the gap and provide those services.

Other External Trends. A number of other trends should be mentioned that will affect the external environment of law enforcement in the future. Our society is becoming more pluralistic as immigrants arrive from countries that have not traditionally been represented in the American "melting pot." Many observers of the American scene note that moral fragmentation is becoming a characteristic of our society. We need only reflect on such issues as race relations, abortion, and drug usage to see the divisions present on these issues.

There appears to be a growing underclass based on individuals and families that are caught up in a vicious cycle of devastating poverty and hopelessness. As the gap between rich and poor widens, the development of a permanent underclass is likely. The more the hopelessness and the futility of trying to join the wider society, the greater the likelihood that the underclass will resort to violence, drugs, and civil disturbances to attempt to attain relief from the intolerable situations in which they exist. The problems of the unattached, the homeless, the mentally ill, the addicts, and the increased violence of gangs and drugs are all factors in the external environment of law enforcement in the future.

Converging Cultures. During the next fifty years there will be four distinct cultures vying for control of our society. This should come as no surprise as these groups are already well represented in our nation. Their growth, both in population and political power, however, assures us that they will each play a significant role in the setting of national and local priorities. These are the Orientals (predominantly Japanese), Hispanics (from Mexico, Central America, and Cuba), Afro-Americans (blacks), and Caucasians (whites) (Holden and Sapp, 1991).

Historians and political scientists tell us we are a melting pot; that all cultures blend into a single identity — as Americans. Increasingly we are learning that this assumption may not be true. Cultures of similar race have tended to blend and intermarry. Racial groups, however, have generally shunned intermarriage and have attempted to maintain separate identities along racial lines. There has been a minimum of cultural blending and that may pose a serious problem for the future (Holden and Sapp, 1991).

As racial groups congregate, they establish a political power base. This power is often translated into attempts to institutionalize the group's cultural values and rituals. Rather than be absorbed by the larger culture, the groups attempt to change the prevailing culture by absorbing local, smaller cultures slowly over time. This process is accelerated in places where there is a high influx of immigrants — legal or illegal. We can already see that the political atmosphere in Miami, San Antonio, and Atlanta is politically different from in other cities farther north (Holden and Sapp, 1991).

This is not an indictment and it does not mean these cities are managed any better or worse than others. It means times are changing. Already the National Mayors' Conferences resemble a meeting of the United Nations more than a traditional meeting of local government officials. In the future that trend will increase, along with a comparable shift in racial representation at the state and national levels of politics.

To understand where we are going, we need to understand the cultures and values of each of these major groups. Each group is establishing its own agenda and, to a much lesser degree, its own territory. Each group also contributes different strengths and weaknesses to American society. In composite, they all represent what we as a society will become.

As the differences in a culturally pluralistic society increase, the police will see an increase in bias and hate-motivated crimes. Increases in intercultural as well as intracultural hate-motivated crimes will be evident. Recent clashes between blacks and Jews in New York are just one indicator of such activities. Some of these hate-motivated crimes will come from organized groups, while others will be the result of bigotry and prejudices in individuals. Regardless, the law enforcement community will be called upon to solve the crimes and arrest the perpetrators.

An area where law enforcement will be expected to provide added services is that of environmental crimes. This type of crime will have several aspects. There will continue to be increased concern over the environment, including such issues as air pollution, use of limited natural resources, landfill problems, noise pollution, the ozone layer, animal rights, and others. Information crimes will also require law enforcement attention. Information crime includes such diverse activities as theft of trade secrets and counterfeiting and piracy of software and hardware.

Trends in the Internal Environment

Several internal trends will have an impact on law enforcement in the future. These trends include specialization of services, professionalization of law enforcement, higher education issues, and labor relations issues.

Specialization of Services. Law enforcement will be competing with a wide range of other service industries for skilled technicians and specialists. Increasingly, the technology of today and the future will be computer-based, with resultant requirements for specialists. While diversification frequently increases the demand for generalists rather than specialists in industry, such is not the case in service fields. As service industries diversify into new areas, more specialization is required. More emphasis is likely to be placed on investigation services and technology. Training for specialists will likely involve some cross training of both investigators and technicians to provide integrated services. Specialized training will be more individualized and require a longer time to complete. In-service training on new and changing technologies will be an important task of management. Since employees will have a wider range of employment choices, training prospects are likely to become an important aspect in recruiting and retaining specialists. Similarly, specialists are much more expensive and demand more humanitarian and interpersonal management. Participatory management styles are far more likely to succeed in the future than bureaucratic management. Increasingly, work assignments will be made in relation to specialized training, skills, and personal preferences of the employee.

One of the dangers of specialization is the creation of jobs filled by employees who are unable to do anything else. Specialization that becomes too narrow is likely to lead to increased turnover in employees as well as boredom and carelessness on the part of those specialists who remain on the job. Specialists must be permitted to apply their particular expertise in as many different areas as possible. To provide such opportunities increases the need for in-service training and flexibility in management.

Specialization requires an increase in the number of employees and leads to larger organizations. Size is clearly one of the most important factors in management-employee relationships with larger organizations being at a distinct disadvantage. With more professional personnel, this problem is aggravated. Increased communication and personal contact with management are needed to keep specialists and professionals satisfied with their jobs.

Dissatisfaction of employees, for whatever reason, is most often expressed in demands for higher salaries and increased benefits. Even when such demands are met, dissatisfaction remains high if other needs of employees are not met. Law enforcement administrators will have to adapt to meet the challenges of dealing with the size of the organization as well as changes in employee needs. Labor relations will increasingly be an important part of the law enforcement milieu (Sapp and Carter, 1991).

Professionalization of Law Enforcement. As technology increases and more diverse and complex services become the norm in law enforcement, professionalization of police officers will inevitably follow. Professionalization invariably results when sophisticated equipment and specialized personnel become the norm in a field. Professionals will develop professional education programs, highly specialized training and begin to assume the identity of a profession, which includes adopting high standards of performance and ethics. Professionalization will extend from management to the lowest levels of the law enforcement agency where specialized skills will require a college education and lengthy training.

The implications of professionalization are many for law enforcement. Traditional management styles will be inadequate to cope with the needs and demands of a professional work force. Bureaucratic management will yield to more participatory styles, often involving variations of a "team" approach to decision making and business ventures. Professionals resent imposed management, particularly management perceived as less knowledgeable about day-to-day operations than are the professionals.

As technological applications increase in range and complexity, increasingly professionals will be required to handle the diverse equipment and activities of the field. Professionals are frequently concerned with job enlargement and job enrichment. Thus, law enforcement will be required to seek and use more diverse job assignments to maintain morale and productivity of the professional staff. Just as specialization leads to an increase in the need for more frequent in-service training and education, so does professionalization. In addition, professionals are more likely to seek release time and reimbursement to attend professional association meetings and professional training seminars.

Law enforcement will move to a more professional work force for reasons beyond that of technology and diversity of services. Crime is becoming more professional with career criminals accounting for a large share of major economic crimes. Computer literacy is a term used increasingly in all fields of endeavor and realistically one must consider that criminals will also become computer literate and add technology to their careers. Criminals will more often attempt to use technology and technological expertise to defeat security systems.

The increase in the demand for professionals will be evident across most jobs in society and law enforcement must be prepared to compete with other service industries for the available personnel resources. The demand of a professional education leads to delayed entry into the work force and requires higher entry level salaries and benefits. Since the population is aging, there may well be a large pool of retired professionals who will be available for limited part-time professional employment. However, this source of professionals is likely to be limited in many areas where climate and/or quality of life does not attract large numbers of retirees.

The greatest effect of professionalization is likely to be in the area of personnel. Competition will be the driving factor that requires law enforcement to offer compensation packages far different from those in use today. Career ladders that offer job enlargement and merit based advancement will be required if law enforcement is to hire and retain the quality of professional employees needed to operate the diverse and complex jobs of the future.

Postemployment training and education programs will become the rule in all professional-based occupations. Technology producers will be required to include training programs as part of the sale price of the technology. Law enforcement will increasingly turn to the colleges and universities to provide both preservice and in-service education and training.

Higher Education. In the late 1960s there was a flurry of activity related to higher education and law enforcement. The impetus for this activity was a result of several factors: civil unrest, the nature of the police response to unrest and disorder, police relationships with minorities, increasing interest in law enforcement research, changes to the "reform" management style in policing, and a vision of "professionalism" in law enforcement. Perhaps most significant, however, was the 1967 publication of reports from the President's Commission on Law Enforcement and Administration of Justice, followed by passage of the Omnibus Crime Control and Safe Streets Act in 1968.

The President's commission recommended that police educational standards be raised, with the ultimate goal of requiring a baccalaureate degree as a minimum standard for employment (President's Commission, 1967). The basis for these recommendations was the increasing complexity of police tasks, coupled with police officers' need for a strong foundation on which to base many critical decisions while policing the community. To facilitate these recommendations, one provision of the Omnibus Crime Control Act was the creation of the Law Enforcement Education Program (LEEP):

> LEEP was a program to stimulate criminal justice personnel to attend college. In the case of the police, the belief was that better-educated law enforcement officers would provide more responsive, more comprehensive, and more insightful police service. In the long term, as college-educated officers rose into police leadership positions, they would explore new

approaches, with more creativity and better planning (Carter, 1989, p. 167).

Thus, the recommendations of the President's commission and the financial incentives available through LEEP, formed the nucleus of a movement in support of law enforcement education. Colleges and universities developed law enforcement and criminal justice degree programs; police departments began to establish incentive pay, educational leave, and other educationally related policies.

Interest in police education grew, characterized by increased research, growth in organizations related to criminal justice education (such as the Academy of Criminal Justice Sciences and the American Society of Criminology), and large enrollments in criminal justice programs. Further incentive was given when the National Advisory Commission on Criminal Justice Standards and Goals (1973) set target dates by which police departments were to establish formal educational requirements.

Higher education seemed to be a good idea for the police; it appeared to be a logical evolutionary step for a profession in its adolescence; many people believed that the college experience would make officers perform better. Cautionary observers of the education movement urged contemplation, however, expressing concerns that curricula and policy were based on emotion and intuition rather than on empirically tested hypotheses and behavioral criteria (Roberg, 1978; Schick, 1978; Swanson, 1977; Wycoff and Susmilch, 1979). In fact, these criticisms were largely true. Arguments presented in support of the President's commission recommendations, the LEEP standards, and the National Advisory Commission's goals were generally rhetorical rather than empirical.

Just as concerns were expressed about the general value of higher education for the police, other criticisms were directed toward the quality of curricula and instruction in college criminal justice programs. Most noteworthy in this regard was the Police Foundation-sponsored National Advisory Commission on Higher Education of Police Officers. The essence of the commission's inquiry — that came to be known as the "Sherman Report" — was that law enforcement education had serious limitations. It was suggested that even if the arguments in support of police college requirements were valid, the overall benefits of college would not be realized because of qualitative inadequacies in academic course inventories, course content, and faculty credentials (Sherman and National Advisory Commission, 1978; National Commission on Higher Education of Police Officers, 1979).

Many of the Sherman Report's criticisms were correct. Standards were low, in-service people received "life experiences" credits, and, in many cases, police training hours were converted to academic credits. There were also charges of "academic profit-taking" where institutions were accused of taking advantage of LEEP and large criminal justice course enrollments to offset funding and enrollment shortages in other areas. Unfortunately, since law enforcement and criminal justice was not viewed as a "true" academic discipline, institutional standards for both faculty and students were lower than one would find in other fields (Carter et al., 1989).

As a result of these concerns, increased research on educationally related issues in law enforcement emerged, generally beginning in the early 1970s. Research on issues related to higher education included officer characteristics (Cohen and Chaiken, 1972); officer performance (Cascio, 1977; Smith and Ostrom, 1974); officer attitude (Dalley, 1975); discretion (Finckenauer, 1975); professional identity (Greene et al., 1984); ethics (Lynch, 1976); cynicism (Regoli, 1976); authoritarianism (Smith et al., 1970); decision making (Trojanowicz and Trojanowicz, 1972); deadly force (Sherman and Blumberg, 1981); minority recruitment (Peirson, 1978); police department policies (Ostrom, 1978); the role of higher education in policing (Bell, 1979); criminal justice in the educational institution (Felkenes, 1975); faculty productivity (DeZee, 1980); curricula (Kuykendall, 1977; Hoover, 1975); and syllabus design (Culbertson and Carr, 1981). This list does not purport to cite all the research on police education, but it illustrates the wide range of inquiries over a relatively short period (Carter and Sapp, 1991b, 1990a).

The results varied, but certain trends began to emerge in the research. Although not conclusive, the research suggested that higher education provided a number of benefits for law enforcement. In sum, the research found that college education achieved the following:

- Developed a broader base of information for decision making;
- Provided additional years and experiences for increasing maturity;
- Inculcated responsibility in the individual through course requirements and achievements;
- Through general education courses and coursework in the major (particularly a criminal justice major), permitted the individual to learn more about the history of the country and the democratic process, and to appreciate constitutional rights, values, and the democratic form of government;
- Engendered the ability to handle difficult or ambiguous situations with greater creativity or innovation
- In the case of criminal justice majors, permitted a better view of the "big picture" of the criminal justice system and a fuller understanding and appreciation for the prosecutorial, courts, and correctional roles
- Developed a greater empathy for minorities and their discriminatory experiences. This understanding was

developed both through coursework and through interaction in the academic environment;

- Engendered understanding and tolerance for persons with different lifestyles and ideologies, which could translate into more effective communications and community relationships in the practice of policing;
- Made officers appear to be less rigid in decision making, to tend to make their decisions in the spirit of the democratic process, and to use discretion in dealing with individual cases rather than applying the same rules to all cases;
- Helped officers to communicate and respond to the crime and service needs of the public in a competent manner, with civility and humanity;
- Made officers more innovative and more flexible when dealing with complex policing programs and strategies, such as problem-oriented policing, community policing, and task force responses;
- Equipped officers better to perform tasks and to make continuous policing decisions with little or no supervision;
- Helped officers to develop better overall community relations skills, including engendering the respect and confidence of the community;
- Engendered more "professional" demeanor and performance;
- Enabled officers to cope better with stress and to be more likely to seek assistance with personal or stress-related problems, and thereby to be more stable and more reliable employees;
- Enabled officers to adapt their styles of communication and behavior to a wider range of social conditions and classes;
- Tended to make officers less authoritarian and less cynical with respect to the milieu of policing;
- Enabled officers to accept and adapt to organizational change more readily (See Carter et al., 1988, pp. 16-18; Carter and Sapp, 1990a).

A recurring question arises whenever higher education for police officers is discussed. The question is whether college-educated police officers are better and it is a question for which a straightforward "yes" or "no" answer is usually sought. Unfortunately, the research evidence simply does not permit such a conclusive response. The research has addressed the effects of college on a wide range behavioral variables (as described above). Thus, a decision on the effects of college on police performance has to be made in view of one's interpretations of these collective findings. People have different interpretations of what makes an officer "good." For example, the research indicates that officers with college are less authoritarian and cynical—the authors feel this is a positive effect. Yet, some would argue that officers must be authoritarian and cynical (this being viewed as "not gullible") therefore, college would be interpreted as a negative effect (Carter et al., 1989).

Community Policing. The entire debate of the effect of college education on policing has an important new dimension that was not even an issue when the education movement took off in the 1960s — community policing. In the past decade the philosophy of community policing has experienced explosive growth (Kelling, 1988). As a new philosophy of both operations and management, community policing has drastically changed the way law enforcement views itself and its approach to accomplishing goals. As a result, line level police officers are given broader responsibilities and are charged with performing their jobs in creative and innovative ways. In addition, officers are urged to be proactive in program development in their duties and are given even broader discretion. In many ways, community policing views officers as being professionals less paternally than did traditional policing (Trojanowicz and Carter, 1988).

Given the mandates of this change in policing philosophy, the issue of college education appears to be even more critical. The knowledge and skills officers are being asked to exercise in community policing appear to be tailored to college preparation. Community policing is a *philosophy* of management and service delivery that must be tailored to each community individually (Eck and Spelman, 1987). While there are certain practices that may be transferred between departments, even these practices must be amended to meet the characteristics of specific jurisdictions. Community policing requires administrators, managers, supervisors, and officers to think about their responsibilities differently. Reactive and "incident-driven" policies are cleared away for implementation of proactive, innovative, "problem-driven" officer behaviors. There are different names for the community policing philosophy around the country as well as different ways the philosophy has been implemented. Beyond the question of the types of activities (or tasks) community police officers perform, there is significant variability in allocation and deployment schemes — some departments use community policing departmentwide while others are experimenting with the philosophy based upon shift or location (Carter, 1989).

There are a number of definitions available for community policing. For this discussion, the definition used is

> Community policing is a philosophy, not a tactic. It is a proactive, decentralized approach to policing, designed to reduce crime, disorder, and fear of crime while also responding to explicit needs and demands of the community. Community

policing views police responsibilities in the aggregate, examining consistent problems, determining underlying causes of the problems, and developing solutions to those problems. (Adapted from Trojanowicz and Carter, 1988, and Eck and Spelman, 1987).

Among the synonymous terms for community policing are Problem-Oriented Policing, Community Problem-Oriented Policing, Neighborhood-Oriented Policing, Police Area Representatives, Citizen-Oriented Patrol Experiment, Experimental Policing, Neighborhood Foot Patrol, and Community Foot Patrol.

What Can Be Done?

The future will be affected by all the trends discussed above. However, that future is still uncertain and still to be formed. Law enforcement does not have to sit idly and await the events that are suggested by the trends and the analyses of futurists. Instead through careful planning and positive steps, many of the events can be influenced and changed.

The policy directions discussed below are intended to be advisory in nature. The policy directions do not represent policy standards, as such, nor are they intended to be prescriptive in nature or tone. Instead, they highlight current issues in the field of police futures and suggest directions for policy development. Each law enforcement agency must evaluate these statements in terms of its own environment, needs, and resources.

Law Enforcement Policy Directions

As the twenty-first century draws near, apparently law enforcement personnel will continue to face complex social problems and increasingly sophisticated criminal behavior. The demands for police service will increase, along with demands for accountability, efficiency, and effectiveness. No law enforcement agency can fail to recognize the changes that are taking place in policing today. Among those changes are an increase in the educational level of citizens and police programs that are based on significantly increased police-citizen interactions. These two developments alone are sufficient to require review of law enforcement educational policy (Carter and Sapp, 1990b).

The question for the twenty-first century is not whether college education is needed for police officers, but rather how much and how soon. Based on individual department decisions, the needed policies may be phased in over a number of years and ultimately require a baccalaureate degree. Regardless of the policy developed, any police department establishing a college education requirement for employment should develop a policy paper validating college education as a bona fide occupational qualification as it uniquely relates to the department. If such a policy paper is developed as the first step in the establishment of a college requirement, the department is fully prepared for any challenges to the new requirements. Failure to develop such a statement of policy invites challenges and leaves the department in a less than favorable position to defend itself (Carter et al., 1988). Moreover, the policy paper will aid the police department in determining realistic educational standards considering available resources and community characteristics.

Policy development should also include input from all levels of the agency. Of particular importance is inclusion of the local police officer organization(s) in the preliminary discussions and policy development. Involving all levels of the agency leads to common understanding of the rationale for the policy, enhances acceptance, and expedites implementation.

If the general educational requirement for entry into policing is to be raised, then the promotional process should be also reviewed. As more highly educated officers enter policing, there will be a concomitant need for more highly educated supervisors, managers, and police executives. As a suggested starting point, police departments could develop policies leading to a plan requiring a minimum of sixty hours of college credit for promotion to sergeant, a baccalaureate degree for promotion into mid-management ranks, and a graduate degree for promotion to command ranks (Carter et al., 1989).

Simply developing a policy without standards for the educational experience is insufficient. All educational requirement policies should specify that college credits and degrees be awarded from a college or university that has received accreditation from one of the major regional accrediting organizations. Additionally, for college credits to be accepted, they should be based on a minimum grade average of C (2.0 on a 4.0 scale); credits less than a baccalaureate degree should be calculated on a semester hour basis to enhance consistency and to minimize confusion (Carter et al., 1989).

Additional policy standards that should be considered include the requirement that all college credits earned be directly in pursuit of a degree and consistent with a valid degree plan at the educational institution attended. This type of policy ensures that courses in liberal arts and/or general education are required in addition to courses in a major area. Departments developing policies requiring college education should define college majors that are in a job-related area, such as law enforcement, criminal justice, public administration, business administration, sociology, psychology, or other fields that can be demonstrated to be directly related to the practices and needs of policing.

When requirements are established for graduate education and degrees, even closer limits should be placed on the type of courses and majors permitted.   All courses in graduate work should be directly related to management issues and skills. Such courses are typically found in graduate programs focusing on criminal justice/police administration or management, business administration, management, or public administration. Particularly, policies should require graduate degrees to include such areas as budgeting, personnel management, planning, policy development, and other skills required to command a modern police department. The value of graduate education in other areas is fully recognized, but other areas of study may not provide the skills needed for organizational leadership and career development in law enforcement (Carter et al., 1989).

In addition to graduate course work and degrees, candidates for command positions should be encouraged or required to attend in-service programs and seminars that stress executive development and managerial skills. Such programs as Law Enforcement Executive Development Seminar (LEEDS), the Senior Management Institute for Police (SMIP), the command college of California, and the Texas Law Enforcement Management Institute are examples. Agencies should also consider developing scholarships and fellowships, perhaps in conjunction with local business and industry, to provide for attendance at executive development programs.

A sensitive question that has both philosophical and pragmatic implications involves the issue of whether a higher education standard for law enforcement is discriminatory. Philosophically, police administrators do not want to discriminate against minority groups nor do they want organizations that do not represent the total community. Pragmatically, if the police organization has discriminatory policies, they are liable for a lawsuit. The complete answer to this question is somewhat complex. Yes, college is a discriminatory requirement. The reason is that minority group members have disproportionate access to a college education as well as having lower college graduation rates as a result of poorer preparation in the public schools as compared with whites. However, college can still be required for police employment (Carter et al., 1989).

In the case *Davis v. Dallas*, the Fifth U.S. Circuit Court of Appeals held that the Dallas Police Department requirement of 45 semester hours of college with a "C" average was a bona fide occupational qualification considering the unique responsibilities of the police and the public responsibility of law enforcement. (See Carter and Sapp, 1991b; Carter et al., 1988; and Carter and Sapp, 1990b for further discussion of these issues.) This decision does not mean that discrimination is no longer an issue. Rather, law enforcement agencies must base a college requirement on a firm policy foundation. Moreover, innovative efforts should be made to recruit minorities who meet these requirements.

The findings of a recent Police Executive Research Forum study showed that overall, minority representation in American law enforcement agencies approximates the general population (Carter and Sapp, 1991b; Carter et al.,

1989). Moreover, educational levels of minorities in law enforcement are virtually the same as those of white officers. Thus, it is not an impossible mandate. A college-educated police force that is racially and ethnically representative of the community can be achieved. Such an accomplishment can only make the police department more effective and responsive to community needs.

Law enforcement agencies and colleges and universities must communicate with each other on a regular basis to ensure that curricula address the long-term problems and needs of law enforcement. Law enforcement must recognize the role of a college education, the concept of academic freedom, and the responsibility of challenging traditional assumptions and methods. Continuing dialogue can close the information gap between colleges and law enforcement agencies. This study found that both academics and law enforcement officials are eager for such exchanges, but each waits for the other to initiate the interaction. Only through a dialogue can colleges and universities learn of the concerns and the needs of policing. Only through a dialogue can law enforcement learn the strengths and limitations of the colleges and universities.

Dialogue should lead to clear understanding of what each can and cannot do. Police departments must be prepared to teach the physical and vocational skills needed for policing and expect academic preparation from the colleges and universities. In turn, the colleges and universities must accept the responsibility of shaping academic preparation to fit the needs of law enforcement.

There is much variance in criminal justice curricula and the quality of instruction in criminal justice programs. The Sherman Report (1978) pointed out the many problems, and although a number of those problem areas have been addressed and improved, many of the basic criticisms offered by the Sherman Report are still of concern today. Colleges and universities with criminal justice programs should explore alternatives for program review, resource assessment, and quality control. As the twenty-first century arrives, twentieth century models of education and law enforcement must be refined.

Affirmative Action and Education

Attracting qualified women and minority candidates continues to be of major concern to police executives. Those concerns are valid and police departments must continue to be vigilant in recruiting and retaining women and minority police officers. It is increasingly evident, however, that there is no need to limit entry or promotional educational requirements for minorities as long as innovative and aggressive recruiting programs are in place. As an area of policy development, police departments should explore the use of innovative and flexible recruiting programs that have been successful in recruiting minorities into police service (Carter and Sapp, 1991b).

Affirmative Action/Equal Opportunity plans must continue to be used for entry and promotion in order for police departments to achieve demographic parity with their respective communities. The results of this study indicate that such parity is within the reach of the agencies included in the study, without reducing educational or other substantive requirements. The goal will not be reached without clear-cut policies and well-planned programs, however.

Other Policy Directions

Law enforcement agency accreditation is likely to become increasingly important in the next century. To maintain its value, accreditation must reflect current trends in the field. As educational requirements rise, so must accreditation standards. Law enforcement administrators should carefully evaluate the benefits and costs and plan to join the accreditation movement.

Police departments should consider developing visiting fellowship programs. With support from grants, appropriations, or endowments from private foundations, police departments could appoint college faculty members to departmental positions (such as planning, training, research, administrative support, or similar positions) for up to one year. Similarly, colleges and universities could invite qualified police personnel to participate in academic activities, including teaching, curricula planning, and research, for periods of up to one year. "One for one" exchange programs might be developed whereby each agency would pay the salary and benefits for its own employee while he or she works with the other agency.

Every law enforcement agency needs to study and evaluate the many models of community alliances that are being employed across the country (Trojanowicz, 1989). Community policing is clearly the law enforcement philosophy of the future and offers great hope for improving policing, quality of life, and greater community investment in crime problems.

Labor relations will continue to be a major concern for labor and management in the future (Sapp et al., 1990). Emphases in labor demands are likely to focus on fringe benefits and on areas of traditional management prerogatives (Sapp, 1980, 1990; Sapp et al., 1990; Carter and Sapp, 1991a). As police management moves to more participatory styles, labor's role in management will necessarily increase. To prepare for such changes, law enforcement agencies could begin management intern programs to develop better understanding of management problems among the officers who will eventually become part of the management team.

Conclusions About the Future

A number of conclusions can be drawn from the discussions above. Clearly, law enforcement must adapt to changing conditions and respond to those trends affecting the field. Major changes are most likely to be required in the broad areas of organization and personnel and in education and training. Organizational changes are required to deal with an aging population, world events, geographical mobility, and the change to a service-based economy. Similarly, organizational structure will be affected by increased use of technology that in turn leads to specialization and professionalization. As the types of personnel change, so must the organization change to become more participative in style, more team-oriented and less bureaucratic. As the work force ages and becomes better educated, it will also become more mobile, more specialized, and more demanding. Career ladders, desirable work locations, and participation in career decisions will be among the demands for compensation and benefits.

Workers will have a great diversity of backgrounds and education requiring broader understanding of their needs. Services to employees will increase in cost as job enlargement and job enrichment demands increase. More professional police officers and specialists will be needed. Employees will have more autonomy, use more discretion, and face new liabilities and legal definitions and procedures.

These changes will require different types of training and more education. Specialized and professional staff will, for the most part, have college degrees at entry into the field and in-service training will become increasingly complex. Provision of cross-training to provide for job enrichment and job enlargement will become a necessity. Training will be more individualized, will last for longer periods of time and costs will increase dramatically.

Overall, the future of policing in America remains uncertain. There are clouds on the horizon, and some would suggest that the storm will break soon. Others point out the positive changes taking place in law enforcement today and place trust in technology and the dedication of law enforcement officers. However, neither technology nor dedicated officers can stem the trends that will affect policing in the future. What is needed is understanding and planning. Understanding of trends and events that will shape the future is required. Planning is required to effect the changes that are needed to influence the trends and future. The need for change is evident. Survival of law enforcement dictates change and only those willing to seek, find, and understand change will survive and succeed.

References

Bell, D. J. (1979). The police role and higher education. *Journal of Police Science and Administration, 7,* 467-475.

Bennett, G. (1987). *Crimewarps: The future of crime in America.* Garden City, NY: Anchor/Doubleday.

Carter, D. L. (1989). Methods and measures. In R. Trojanowicz & B. Bucqueroux (Eds.), *Community policing* (pp. 165-194). Cincinnati: Anderson Publishing Co.

Carter, D. L. & Sapp, A. D. (1990a). The evolution of higher education in law enforcement: Preliminary findings from a national study. *Journal of Criminal Justice Education,* 1(1), 59-85.

Carter, D. L. & Sapp, A. D. (1990b). Policy issues related to higher education and minorities in law enforcement. Paper presented at the annual meeting of the Police Executive Research Forum, Washington, DC.

Carter, D. L. & Sapp, A. D. (1991a). The current status of police collective bargaining: A national management survey. In *The future of police,* Washington, DC: U.S. Government Printing Office.

Carter, D. L. & Sapp, A. D. (1991b). *Police education & minority recruitment: The impact of a college requirement.* Washington, DC: Police Executive Research Forum.

Carter, D. L., Sapp, A. D., & Stephens, D. W. (1988). Higher education as a bona fide occupational qualification (BFOQ) for police: A blueprint. *American Journal of Police,* 7(2), 1-27.

Carter, D. L., Sapp, A. D., & Stephens, D. W. (1989). *The state of police education: Policy direction for the 21st Century.* Washington, DC: Police Executive Research Forum.

Cascio, W. F. (1977). Formal education and police officer performance. *Journal of Police Science and Administration, 5,* 89-96.

Cohen, B. & Chaiken, J. (1972). *Police background characteristics and performance.* New York: The RAND Corporation.

Culbertson, R. G. & Carr, A. F. (1981). *Syllabus design and construction in criminal justice.* Washington, DC: Joint Commission on Criminology and Criminal Justice Education and Standards.

Dalley, A. F. (1975). University and non-university graduated policemen: A study of police attitudes. *Journal of Police Science and Administration,* 3, 458-468.

Davis v. Dallas, 777 F.2d 205 (5th Cir. 1985. Certiorari denied to Supreme Court May 19, 1986).

DeZee, M. R. (1980). *The productivity of criminology and criminal justice faculty.* Washington, DC: Joint Commission on Criminology and Criminal Justice Education and Standards.

Eck, J. E. & Spelman, W. (1987). *Problem-solving: Problem-oriented policing in Newport News.* Washington, DC: Police Executive Research Forum.

Felkenes, G. T. (1975). The criminal justice component in an educational institution. *Journal of Criminal Justice,* 7, 101-108.

Finckenauer, J. O. (1975). Higher education and police discretion. *Journal of Police Science and Administration,* 3, 450-457.

Greene, J., Bynum, T., & Webb, V. (1984). Patterns of entry, professional identity, and attitudes toward crime-related education: A study of criminal justice and criminology faculty. *Journal of Criminal Justice,* 12, 39-60.

Holden, R. N. & Sapp, A. D. (1991). The evolution and future of bias motivated extremism in America. In *The future of policing.* Washington, DC: U.S. Government Printing Office.

Hoover, L. T. (1975). *Police educational characteristics and curricula.* Washington, DC: National Institute of Law Enforcement and Criminal Justice.

Kelling, G. (1988). Police and communities: The quiet revolution. In *Perspectives on policing,* No. 1. Washington, DC: Department of Justice, National Institute of Justice.

Kuykendall, J. L. (1977). Criminal justice programs in higher education: Courses and curriculum orientations. *Journal of Criminal Justice,* 5, 149-164.

Lynch, G. W.   (1976).   The contributions of higher education to ethical behavior in law enforcement. *Journal of Criminal Justice*, 4, 285-290.

Naisbitt, J. (1984). *Megatrends*. New York: Warner.

Naisbitt, J. & Aburdene, P. (1990). *Megatrends 2000*. New York: Avon Books.

National Advisory Commission on Criminal Justice Standards and Goals. (1973). *Police*. Washington, DC: U.S. Government Printing Office.

National Commission on Higher Education for Police Officers. (1979). *Proceedings of the National Symposium on Higher Education for Police Officers*. Washington, DC: Police Foundation.

Ostrom, E. (1978). *Police department policies toward education*. Washington: Police Foundation.

Peirson, G. (1978). *Higher educational requirements and minority recruitment for the police: Conflicting goals?* Washington, DC: Police Foundation.

President's Commission on Law Enforcement and Administration of Justice. (1967). *Task force report: Police*. Washington, DC: U.S. Government Printing Office.

Regoli, R. M. (1976). The effects of college education on the maintenance of police cynicism. *Journal of Police Science and Administration*, 4, 340-345.

Roberg, R. R. (1978). An analysis of the relationships among higher education, belief systems, and job performance of patrol officers. *Journal of Police Science and Administration*, 6, 336-344.

Sapp, A. D. (1980). *An exploratory and descriptive analysis of grievance procedures in law enforcement collective bargaining*. Unpublished doctoral dissertation. Sam Houston State University, Huntsville, TX.

Sapp, A. D. (1990). *Public safety labor contract grievance procedures*. Huntsville, TX: Justex Systems.

Sapp, A. D. & Carter, D. L. (1991). Indicators of future developments in law enforcement collective bargaining agreements. In *The future of police*. Washington, DC: U.S. Government Printing Office.

Sapp, A. D., Carter, D. L., & Stephens, D. W. (1990). *Law enforcement collective bargaining agreements: Preliminary findings from a national survey.* Washington, DC: Police Executive Research Forum.

Schick, R. P. (1978). *Structural and attitudinal barriers to higher educational requirements for police officers.* Washington, DC: Police Foundation.

Sherman, L. W. & Blumberg, M. (1981). Higher education and police use of deadly force. *Journal of Criminal Justice, 9,* 317-331.

Sherman, L. W. & National Advisory Commission on Higher Education of Police Officers. (1978). *The quality of police education.* Washington, DC: Jossey-Bass Inc., Publishers.

Smith, A. B., Locke, B., & Fenster, A. (1970). Authoritarianism in policemen who are college graduates and non-college police. *Journal of Criminal Law, Criminology, and Police Science, 6,* 313-315.

Smith, D. C. & Ostrom, E. (1974). The effects of training and education on police attitudes and performance: A preliminary analysis. In H. Jacob (Ed.), *The potential for reforms in criminal justice.* Beverly Hills, CA: Sage Publications Inc.

Swanson, C. R. (1977). An uneasy look at college education and the police organization. *Journal of Criminal Justice, 5,* 311-320.

Tafoya, W. L. (1986a). Law enforcement beyond the year 2000. *The Futurist, 20,* 533-536.

Tafoya, W. L. (1986b). *A delphi forecast of the future of law enforcement.* Unpublished doctoral dissertation, University of Maryland, College Park, MD.

Tafoya, W. L. (1987). Into the future . . . Looking at the 21st Century. *Law Enforcement Technology,* (September/October), 16-20, 82-86.

Tafoya, W. L. (1990). Futures research: Implications for criminal investigations. In J. N. Gilbert (Ed.), *Criminal investigation: Essays and cases.* Columbus, OH: Merrill Publishing Co.

Toffler, A. (1970). *Future shock.* New York: Random House Inc.

Toffler, A. (1980). *The third wave.* New York: William Morrow & Co. Inc.

Toffler, A. & Toffler, H. (1990). *Powershifts: Knowledge, wealth, and violence at the edge of the 21st century.* New York: Bantam Books.

Trojanowicz, J. M. & Trojanowicz, R. C. (1972). The role of a college education in decision making. *Public Personnel Review,* (January) 29-32.

Trojanowicz, R. C. (1989). Serious threats to the future of policing. *Footprints,* 1:3 and 2:1.

Trojanowicz, R. C. & Carter, D. L. (1988). *The philosophy and role of community policing.* East Lansing, MI: National Center for Community Policing.

U.S. Bureau of the Census. (1985). *Population projections for the United States.* Washington, DC: U.S. Government Printing Office.

U.S. Department of Labor. (1970). *The U.S. economy in 1980.* Washington, DC: U.S. Government Printing Office.

Wycoff, M. A. & Susmilch, C. E. (1979). The relevance of college education for policing: Continuing the dialogue. In D. M. Peterson (Ed.), *Police work: Strategies and outcomes in law enforcement.* Beverly Hills, CA: Sage Publications Inc.

Chapter 9

Strategic Approaches

Dennis J. Kenney

The past few decades have produced a virtual explosion of information about the police and what works in policing. To some, this growth was the inevitable outcome of a series of investigative commissions — usually federal — that explored the corruption and conflicts that seemed inherent throughout the 1960s. These commissions (President's Crime Commission on Law Enforcement, 1967; National Advisory Commission on Civil Disorders, 1968; and the National Advisory Commission on Violence, 1969) each noted that departments were unable to attract and retain quality candidates, that minorities were seriously underrepresented in most agencies, and that most of the civil disturbances that had become common were precipitated by some incident involving the police. Recommendations were offered and the federal government launched a major effort to both improve the people in police work and provide massive financial and technical assistance to criminal justice in general and the police specifically. Billions of dollars were spent and the foundations, both technical and human, were laid for a "research revolution" to follow.

To others, the movement to improve and innovate came from within as policing began to evolve toward professional status during the 1970s. Aided by the federal efforts, these observers note that as a new generation of more sophisticated managers began to come to authority, participatory management, collective representation, and innovations such as quality circles and work teams came into vogue. Increasingly, evidence of effectiveness and efficiency became important. Crime analysis and research and planning units (see Reinier et al., 1977) appeared and the police themselves began to challenge many traditional methods, offering outside evaluators inside access (see, for example, Kelling et al., 1974). In short, the police began to see the development and dissemination of a body of knowledge about themselves and their work as important. As their interest in such information grew, many officers and agencies became not only supportive of research but eager to participate.

The proliferation of outside research and evaluation groups also accounts for much of the recent development. Created by the Ford Foundation in 1970 with a mandate to "innovate and improve" American policing, the Police Foundation may have paved the way. Able to fund massive projects, the Foundation's early work with departments in Dallas (organization development), Kansas City (patrol), and San Diego (patrol staffing) raised important questions and challenged traditional assumptions about the ways we police our communities. Member organizations such as PERF and, more recently, groups such as the Crime Control Institute have continued the tradition with research and assistance in significant tactical and operational areas.

Regardless of where the credit belongs, the important point is that a body of knowledge about what works and doesn't work in policing has begun to accumulate. While much has failed to make its way into policy, the overall course of American policing has nonetheless been changed with a momentum that has become clearly visible. This chapter is intended to examine that body of knowledge as it relates to strategic approaches and to consider the extent to which it is policy relevant.

The Strategies of Change

Walker (1989), who has written extensively on police history, attributes recent police development to a broad-based movement at reform. These reforms, which he groups into general categories according to their primary focus, were propelled by a combination of court decisions, police-community conflicts, and significant increases in serious crime — each thrusting the police into national focus where they frequently became political issues.

Unfortunately, while each of these change agents may have overlapped and interacted with each other, Walker (1989) goes on to point out that they were frequently at odds. For example, at the same time professionalism and educational standards similar to those in law and medicine were being promoted, reformers simultaneously sought to limit officer discretion and increase bureaucratic controls. Similarly, while considerable interest and attention has been directed at the creation and experimentation with tactical programs, far less has been devoted to the overall strategies under which those tactics are employed. As such, specific programs such as surveillance, stings, and repeat offender targeting have each been tested extensively but largely within a strategic vacuum. In all then, we have seen uneven development proceeding in different directions, addressing different problems, and often building upon competing assumptions. That the results have often been disappointing or conflicting and not easily generalized to other settings should hardly be surprising.

Strategies Versus Tactics

Undoubtedly the area of police development to receive the greatest attention has been the creation and experimentation with crime attack programs. In general, these approaches focus on deterring or interrupting crimes, apprehending offenders, or, in some instances, better managing order-maintenance and other service-oriented problems. Included here are those tactics mentioned above, along with various targeted crackdowns.

Although interesting, most of this research consists of evaluations of programs undertaken within fairly narrow contexts. As a result, while promising results may have been achieved by Minneapolis officers who arrested abusive spouses (Sherman and Berk, 1984), when the research was replicated in settings where the demographics, legal environment, and agency components varied, the earlier successes were not repeated (Dunford et al., 1990). Nonetheless, by the time these differences were understood, almost half of the major police agencies in this country had already adopted policies of mandatory arrest for such crimes. Surprisingly, the majority of agencies surveyed who had recently changed to a policy of arrest reported doing so at least partly because of the Minneapolis research (Cohn and Sherman, 1986). From this, we should conclude then that the significance of tactical police development is greatly limited without an understanding of the strategic and environmental framework within which it occurs.

From the Beginning: Patrol in Kansas City

As most students of policing are undoubtedly aware, much of what we assume about policing today is built upon the Kansas City Preventive Patrol Experiment (Kelling et al., 1974). Recall that the Kansas City Police Department, needing personnel available for assignment to other duties, set about to test the efficacy of traditional preventive patrol. To do so, fifteen closely matched patrol areas were selected and grouped into five groups of three patrol districts each. Within each of the five groupings, the department then removed normal patrol in one area, doubled or tripled patrol in a second, and held the third at traditional patrol levels for control. With funding, technical, and evaluative support from the Police Foundation, the experiment was continued for twelve months so that the impact of patrol on crime, fear and the perception of crime, self-protective measures, and citizen attitudes and satisfaction could be observed. The results and conclusions from the research were both dramatic and controversial.

Specifically, the project's evaluation found that the increased patrol presence did not reduce the number of crimes committed nor did the virtual elimination lead to crime increases. Additionally, the variations in activity had no effect on citizens' fear of crime, on the measures for self-protection they took, or on the extent to which they were satisfied or dissatisfied with police services. Finally, there was no evidence that crime had been displaced to districts outside the experimental areas. As former Kansas City police chief Joseph McNamara wrote in the project report's preface, the experiment showed that "routine preventive patrol in marked police cars has little value in preventing crime or making citizens feel safe" (Kelling et al., 1974). Despite challenges to the experiment's methods and criticism that it had examined only one kind of patrol, many scholars and practitioners alike concluded that the traditional, undirected, response-oriented strategies of policing were ineffective. If that was so, then new strategies would be needed.

The Split-Force Concept

The split-force concept is based on the recognition that the patrol division of an urban police department is primarily responsible for two of the four major police functions: namely, the call-for-service (CFS) response and the crime prevention functions (Tien et al., 1978).

Recognizing the dual roles of the police patrol officer, by the mid-1970s some police theorists began to hypothesize that the patrol functions could be carried out more effectively and efficiently if handled by distinct patrol units. As such, they proposed splitting the traditionally generalist patrol division into two separate groups to allow each to concentrate on a single patrol function. These new patrol units would no longer be like their predecessors who fit preventive patrol among their calls for service. With the split-force concept, patrol would become specialized.

In fact, the split-force approach was already evolving informally on its own. Several cities, such as Worcester, Massachusetts, were already experimenting with patrol service aides — civilians who handled non-critical calls for service. Kansas City, Missouri and New Haven, Connecticut, were testing a directed patrol force that they freed from calls-for-service to concentrate on area-specific crime problems. And strike forces formed to respond to specific crime problems were, by then, fairly common (Tien et al., 1978). Far beyond these early efforts, however, what was proposed for testing in the Wilmington, Delaware, Police Department was a significant advance in the concept and by 1975 the idea for the Wilmington Split-Force Experiment became a reality.

What evolved in Wilmington was a unique bifurcated patrol division with one component dedicated exclusively to calls-for-service response (Basic Patrol Force) so that a second component (Structured Patrol Force) devoted to crime prevention could be formed. Of course, to do so the police bureau recognized that substantial increases in call-for-service efficiency would be necessary. The now much smaller Basic Patrol Force would, after all, have to handle the same work load that the traditional patrol unit had managed if the integrity of the split-force idea was to be maintained.

To increase efficiency, a number of important steps were taken. First, it was decided that more sophisticated temporal deployment of the Basic Patrol units would be necessary. Instead of the standard three equal shifts, officers in the newly formed Basic Patrol Force would be scheduled around-the-clock in proportion to the occurrence of service requests. Additionally, patrol beat reconfiguration was undertaken so that officers could be deployed according to where calls were occurring (spatial deployment). Each request for police service was also given a priority designation (differential response) so that calls could be dispatched first according to importance and then within priorities on a first-come, first-served basis. This way, when necessary, noncritical calls could be formally delayed. And finally, patrol roll call procedures were streamlined so that shift transitions could occur more smoothly with less backlogging of service requests. This was coupled with a curtailing of the department's traditional preference for two- over one-officer patrol units (Tien et al., 1978). Clearly, a series of well-thought-out tactical improvements were undertaken simultaneously to ensure that the new strategic approach could succeed.

Unlike the Basic Patrol group, however, the new Structured Patrol Force was left largely undefined. Offered few tactical guidelines for support, this unit's only real guiding principle was the knowledge that they were dedicated to a goal of preventing crime and that they were to be directed in their activities. Additionally, these officers remained aware that when required they would continue to provide backup to Basic Patrol units and, if necessary, they would respond to critical calls for service.

To accomplish their primary mission the officers of the Structured Patrol Force agreed with the traditional view that the identification and apprehension of criminals was the best way to accomplish crime prevention. Unfortunately, this limited view of their responsibilities reduced their tactical options such that the activities employed by the unit gradually evolved to include only directed, problem-oriented patrol and immediate, incident-oriented investigation (Tien et al., 1978). As a result, while the arrest-related statistics of the Patrol Division as a whole rose significantly, the creativity in activities that was hoped for did not occur and the tensions that had been found in many of the earlier split-force style efforts were all but assured. Briefly, however, let's review the methods that were used by the Structured Patrol Force.

Directed Problem-Oriented Patrol

Structured patrol in Wilmington was actually little more than what agencies today refer to as directed patrol. In Wilmington, the police bureau created a two-officer Special Operations Unit whose duties consisted primarily of rudimentary crime analysis. After reading the previous day's police reports each morning, these officers maintained color-coded pin maps showing all robberies, burglaries, and some types of thefts for the preceding fourteen days. Preventive patrol areas were then designed for day and nighttime shifts and Structured Patrol officers were assigned as staffing levels permitted.

Prior to a shift's beginning, each officer was briefed on the crime trends in his or her assigned area and was given a complete description of any identified crime patterns for guidance. Structured Patrol Force supervisors then chose the tactics for their officers to employ in the belief that the officers themselves lacked the day-to-day street knowledge for such decision making (Tien et al., 1978). Given the process, it should not be surprising that the tactics used were neither new nor innovative — not even for Wilmington. Still, the department was more flexible in the use of its tactics and, drawing from the lessons of the Kansas City patrol experiment, its efforts were now directed toward specific crime problems rather than being random in the hope that general deterrence would occur.

Incident-Specific Initial Investigations

Equally important during the planning process was the desire to have Structured Patrol officers respond rapidly to in-progress felonies. Immediate response would surely increase the probability of on-scene arrests leading to increased deterrence. Even when offenders were gone, by placing the responsibility for the initial investigation with the Structured Patrol officers it was believed that delays and duplication would be greatly reduced and leads would be followed more thoroughly by these officers with their uninterrupted patrol time. The detectives, who had previously investigated all felonies, could now be freed for the more complex and difficult investigations leading to greater effectiveness and efficiency all around. In short, it was thought that the Structured Patrol officers would become a bridge of sorts between the traditional functions of the Patrol and Detective Divisions where cases were often lost in the transition.

In a sense, the idea of the immediate patrol investigation worked as designed. Over one-half of the Structured Patrol officers' daily responses were to in-progress felonies:

> If the offenders escape from the scene before the Structured officers arrive, the officers seek to obtain sufficient information from the victims and witnesses in order to identify the offenders and begin their investigation. The combination of immediate response and follow-up investigation after each felony incident has been the key reason for the increase in the Patrol Division's arrest related statistics, especially the clearance statistics (Tien et al., 1978).

While the Patrol Division's statistics may have improved, many detectives reported feeling that the Structured Patrol unit had become little more than "a Patrol Division detective force without the benefit of training, proper supervision, or efficient records and files" (Tien et al., 1978). An equally likely concern, however, was that the Patrol Division's successes left the detectives in an awkward light since the activities of the Structured Force officers increased the Patrol Division's overall arrest rate by 4 percent, charges per arrest by 13.2 percent, and clearances by an impressive 105.5 percent. While little data are available concerning the quality of patrol arrests and investigations, it was clear that the Patrol Division's arrest-related productivity had increased remarkably.

Unfortunately, most of the patrol increases appear to have come at the expense of the detectives. Officers from the two units rarely worked together on cases or shared common sources of information. Formal communications were severely hampered by an organizational structure that included the chief as the only commander common to both units. As a result, plans were seldom shared and conflicts arose as officers from each unit suddenly discovered each other conducting surveillance on the same suspect or crime scene. Finally, while the Structured Patrol officers, who arrived first, were able to assume responsibility for the easier cases, the detectives found their productivity declining significantly. Indeed, offsetting the improved patrol clearances were equally dramatic reductions of over 61 percent in Detective Division clearances. The net effect was a decrease of 28 percent in the police department's overall clearance rate. Certainly, much can be explained by the more difficult and complex caseloads left for detective follow-up. Much should also be attributed to the tensions that developed between the units almost from the beginning. Evaluators noted, for example, that at times detectives would refuse to interview arrested suspects about other pending crimes because of alleged "contamination" by the Structured Patrol officers handling the initial investigation and arrest.

The Conclusions From Wilmington

Overall, the evaluation of the experiment considered it a qualified success. Oddly, although at the experiment's conclusion a majority of Wilmington's officers reported that they considered the split-force concept an effective strategy, about two-thirds nonetheless did not want use of the approach to continue. Specifically, officers were concerned about the divisiveness that had developed from the growing conflicts between the detectives and the Structured Patrol Force officers. A divisiveness that had plagued other split-force efforts as well. The lack of beat identity caused by the constantly changing beat designs developed by crime analysis was also of concern to the Structured Patrol unit's officers. And last, the project's evaluators noted that the inertial resistance to change typical to such projects and an underlying morale problem in the department resulting from labor contract disagreements may have contributed to the officers' attitudes as well.

From an administrator's perspective, however, the department's officials were very pleased with the project's results. By specializing the patrol functions, supervisory personnel reported that their command and control had improved, leaving each of the patrol components more accountable for their specific functions. Indeed, the department's new police chief, who was not appointed until the close of the experiment, decided to continue with the approach past the experimental period. This decision is especially significant in light of the fact that in his previous position, the new chief was captain of the Drug, Organized Crime, and Vice Division — a detective unit involved in many of the conflicts with the Structured Patrol Force.

Finally, the clients of the Wilmington police, those citizens requesting police services, do not seem to have perceived any differences due to the experiment.

Neighborhood Team Policing

Undoubtedly, neighborhood team policing has the distinction of being known as the single biggest failure of all experimental police approaches. In reality, however, the team policing concept is a significant and innovative advancement that contributed heavily to the strategies in policing being developed today.

In the broadest sense, team policing is a management concept intended to decentralize the delivery of police services by institutionalizing line level discretion into autonomous work groups. Each group is assigned around-the-clock responsibility for a specific police problem or, more often, a specific geographic area. Within broad guidelines, individual groups can then develop their own procedures, work rules, strategies, and tactics for their specific sphere of responsibility. In short, the groups can largely control their own destinies.

In theory, at least, team policing should have resulted in a number of positive outcomes. For example, the police services provided by a neighborhood team should be more personal to community members and should result in improved relations between the two. Since each team member is more fully involved in his or her duties, greater work satisfaction, creativity, and innovation should be expected. Accountability should also be enhanced since individual goals can more easily be set and results more easily measured. Simultaneously, the sharing of information and knowledge and the constant peer review of work and ideas should encourage professionalism and commitment among officers. Efficiencies should also be possible since most patrol and investigative functions can be merged within a single team. If so, the chain of command can be shortened and the conflicts and communications gaps between investigators and patrol reduced. Finally, team policing was also expected to increase community involvement with crime prevention and detection (Thibault et al., 1985).

In practice, however, the results were far from consistent. In fact, like many of the strategies today, team policing was all too often little more than a broad label applied to a variety of programs — some having little to do with decentralization and the sharing of decision making.

Models of Team Policing

After observing varied programs throughout the early 1970s Gay and colleagues (1977) grouped those they studied into four general categories. First were the *Basic Patrol Teams* concerned only with the delivery of traditional patrol services. The officers on these teams were not concerned with community relations or investigative duties but concentrated instead on preventive patrol, calls for service, and traffic duties. These programs were found in Richmond, Virginia; North Charleston, South Carolina; St. Petersburg, Florida; Syracuse, New York; and San Bruno, California.

The second category, which Gay labeled *Patrol Investigative Teams,* combined the features of the basic patrol teams with the responsibilities for initial investigations of most crimes. Rochester, New York, developed perhaps the best known model of this approach where patrol officers conducted complete preliminary investigations and often were assigned the entire follow-up. Similarly, the *Patrol Community Service Teams*, Gay's third category, coupled community relations duties with those of the basic patrol teams. Here, officers became involved with job referrals for the unemployed, medical referrals for the ill, and liaison services between the community and local service agencies. In San Diego team members combined their efforts by working directly with community service officers from a central community relations office.

It was the *Full-Service Teams* that became the most controversial. In full-service, virtually all aspects of police service were broken down into the team format. In the multispecialist form, patrol and specialist officers worked together within a team to provide the full range of service: patrol, investigations, and community services. Under a generalist approach, all team members were expected to perform both patrol and specialist duties. Some full-service teams chose to wear blazers as their uniforms to avoid a militaristic image. Others established storefront sites for closer contact with their neighborhoods. In all cases, however, the team established complete jurisdiction over assigned areas — patrol units from other areas entered the team neighborhood only for backup or in pursuit of suspects. In return, team members did not respond to calls outside of their own jurisdiction (Thibault et al., 1985).

Regardless of the approach, each of these four varieties of the team concept had a clearly defined organizational structure with corresponding goals. As the concept grew in popularity and spread nationwide, however, many agency administrators failed to understand that team policing amounted to a philosophical change in the way police services were organized and delivered. As such, many agencies confused the team concepts with tactical or directed patrol, strike forces, or crackdown operations. In these cases, the necessary emphasis on territorial exclusivity, ties with the community, participatory planning and management, and a results orientation were absent. That the outcomes from the efforts were inconsistent should hardly be surprising.

The Lessons From Team Policing

With the promise so great, how is it that the reputation for team policing can be one of such failure? From the early team policing projects, evaluators gave mixed reviews finding successes in some communities (San Diego and Rochester), failures in others (New York City and Albuquerque), and inadequate evaluative data to reach conclusions in most. Even in those cities most extensively evaluated (Cincinnati and Los Angeles) the results were inconclusive with some indicators showing improvement while others went largely unaffected (Gay and colleagues, 1977). Despite this rather inauspicious beginning, however, by the mid-1970s many police administrators turned to team policing as a panacea to the building pressures to attack rising crime rates and improve police-community relations in innovative ways. As the concept spread across the nation, important obstacles were all but overlooked.

Ironically, perhaps the primary underlying error can be placed with the early perception of success. In the rush to adopt team policing, many departments introduced programs they didn't fully understand, hadn't adequately planned for, or both. As such, while some agencies were fully committed to the concept, others introduced little more than the slogans. Of course, failure under these conditions occurred often.

Early successes also posed problems for the departments involved. In discussing this concern, Walker (1991) notes that the Los Angeles team policing project is arguably the most successful in the nation. Despite its reputation as among the most highly bureaucratized of American police organizations, decentralization was achieved and Los Angeles officers were brought into the planning processes at all levels. The early successes were quickly abandoned, however, when the administration decided to make team policing a political issue by offering citywide expansion of the concept in an effort to support substantial increases in the police department's budget. As the program grew in scope, planning and training all but disappeared and much of what had been gained was soon lost.

Equally troubling was the failure to anticipate the extent of opposition from within. As the structure of agencies was altered from traditional chain-of-command to participatory decision making relying on peer review, mid-level managers often found their positions and authority at risk. Suddenly, they were irrelevant to important departmental processes. Gradually, their resistance became apparent by their failure to address problems that arose and their tendency to undermine the efforts with misinformation. Eventually, in many departments top management was confronted directly with outright opposition.

Nor was resistance limited only to displaced managers. In some cities as team policing acquired a positive reputation, patrol officers excluded or not fully informed about the goals and procedures grew resentful and suspicious. In other instances, resentment grew out of the perception of unequal work loads. Walker (1991) explains that while sophisticated work load analysis often accompanied team policing assignments, other areas of the same cities did not receive similar support. The result was that the team policing areas often appeared to be overstaffed at the expense of those officers not involved in the project. As such, Sheehan and Cordner (1989) have observed that resistance to such radical organizational change, while quite normal, posed even greater difficulty for many team policing efforts.

Finally, despite efforts to the contrary, the limitations of centralized dispatching systems were in obvious conflict with the decentralized team policing orientation. Sherman et al. (1973) report that in New York City's program, team members spent nearly one-half of their duty time outside of their team areas. In Detroit the same was true one-third of the time. Recall that both of these experiments were considered failures, at least partly because the integrity of the strategy's neighborhood focus could not be maintained.

Obviously, these issues — occurring individually or together — pose serious obstacles to the ability of the team policing approach to survive. Despite these early experiences, however, as we will see, team policing serves as a foundation for much of our current strategic development. Because the potentials of team policing and the significance of the lessons learned are so important and relevant today, we should be careful that they not be ignored.

Problem-Oriented Policing

As he reviews the police efforts and reforms of the recent past, Goldstein (1990) concludes that the developments, new insights, and research findings have brought us to a "new era in policing." The more progressive practitioners, he writes, are now asking important questions, participating in research, and seeking new strategies to achieve greater results during times of diminishing resources. Among the considerations they confront is the balance between the reactive and proactive aspects of their work as well as the steps necessary to engage more effectively both the community and line-level officers in the task of getting the police job done. To meet these challenges, many police managers and researchers have begun to explore variations of the concept now widely known as problem-oriented policing — a strategic approach Goldstein (1979) himself first proposed over a decade ago.

To Eck and Spelman (1989), problem-oriented policing is about effectiveness. As officers respond to incidents, they frequently deal only with the most obvious and superficial aspects of what is often a much deeper problem. A problem-oriented policing approach expects more, requiring that officers do more than simply respond as though each service request is an isolated and individual occurrence. Instead, officers are to examine the scope and nature of the incident as well as the underlying problems that gave rise to its inception. The objective, of course, is to reduce or eliminate the problem or, at least, to provide a better means of handling it.

The problem-oriented approach is actually a four-step planning process that provides a systematic approach for officers to use in addressing an incident or problem. During the initial *scanning* stage, officers set about to identify the various neighborhood issues and concerns — determining which are to be considered problems appropriate for further work. Issues of interest might be as diverse as street crimes, vandalism, drugs and their availability, or the lighting or general accessibility of community facilities. Next, in the *analysis* stage the officers will find and collect varied information about the problems selected. As Eck and Spelman (1989) describe the process, "the goal is to understand the scope, nature, and causes of the problem." Sources of information available should include not only official police records but interviews, surveys, presentations, and outside opinions. Obviously, the heart of the process involves a careful and indepth analysis.

During the *response* stage, the officers and their problem-solving partners from the community will build upon their analysis to develop and implement solutions. Here, they may call upon police resources, involvement from the community, private and government service organizations, or assistance from other outside sources. In short, instead of relying upon traditional responses alone, anyone who can help will be invited to do so.

Finally, during the *assessment* stage, the officers will again collect data and evaluate the effectiveness of their responses. The results of these evaluations will be used to revise the response, collect new data for added analysis, or even to redefine the problem (Eck and Spelman, 1989). From this guided process, real solutions to important community problems are expected to present themselves and be discovered. Figure 1, below, displays the process as it has appeared to date.

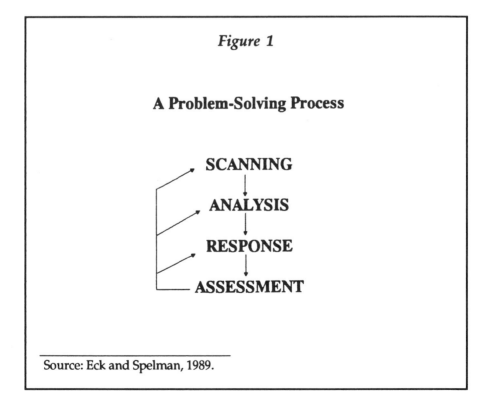

Figure 1

A Problem-Solving Process

SCANNING

ANALYSIS

RESPONSE

ASSESSMENT

Source: Eck and Spelman, 1989.

The Problem-Oriented Approach — Does It Work?

Although the problem-oriented approach was initially tried to a limited degree on specific problems in both Madison, Wisconsin, and by the London Metropolitan Police, the first real test of the concept's potential began in 1982 in Baltimore County, Maryland. Operating as the Citizen-Oriented Patrol Enforcement (COPE) Project, the county police initiated their test with the creation of three special teams (each with fifteen officers) to work with local neighborhoods to reduce the fear of crime. While the project was generally declared a success, what is perhaps more useful than the overall conclusions is the evaluation's attention to the problem-oriented process as it evolved among the COPE officers.

In its first two phases, the COPE project was limited by the tendency of its officers to rely only upon the traditional tactics with which they had considerable experience. For example, during the initial project phase, routine and directed patrol were the primary methods chosen. After being reminded of their mandate, in the second project phase the COPE teams made far greater use of crime prevention methods. Here too, however, the approach used was chosen for its traditional importance rather than because it had been deemed the most effective in reaching the goal of fear reduction.

Only during the third and final phase of the project was a problem-oriented approach adopted. As the COPE teams became more adept at collecting information about their communities, the identification of problems and the development of alternative responses became possible. Cordner (1985) reports that one clear difference during this phase was the willingness to make greater use of both private and external government resources in response to the problems identified:

> If a vacant lot was at the center of neighborhood problems, COPE officers marshalled park and recreation, zoning, sanitation and other public agencies to address the problematic conditions or force the property's owner to make improvements. If broken street lighting concerned neighborhood residents, COPE pressured the electric company, apartment complex management or whoever else had the authority to correct the problem. If a particular individual or group was terrorizing neighborhood residents, COPE adopted enforcement tactics to directly address the problem (Sheehan and Cordner, 1989).

The important point to note is that during this final phase of the project, COPE officers became aware of the need to select their methods based on analysis instead of simply relying upon more familiar tactics regardless of the problems being addressed.

The success from COPE clearly changed the nature of problem-oriented policing and gave impetus to the concept. Still, it was a privately funded project to test the approach in a limited application. As such, it would take additional projects in Newport News, Virginia, and, most recently, Minneapolis, Minnesota, to develop the idea more fully.

Problem-Oriented Policing in Newport News

Building upon the earlier problem-oriented programs, the Newport News study was initiated in 1984 with evaluative support from PERF and funding from NIJ. Critical of the earlier reliance on problem solving as a strategy for special units or projects only, officials in Newport News were determined to expand their version of the concept agencywide. For NIJ this was ideal since they too were committed to a problem solving system available to officers of all ranks and from all units of the police department (Eck and Spelman, 1989).

By 1986 the police department had completed the planning for its program and was prepared to implement the four-stage problem-solving process. Two dozen problems appropriate for police attention were identified and analysis, response, and assessment by officers from throughout the department were begun. Among the wide array of problems chosen were both crime and order maintenance concerns — some confined to specific neighborhoods and others having citywide impact. While the process and the diversity of problems selected confirmed the viability of the Newport News approach, PERF's research staff began a secondary examination of the effectiveness of the responses that resulted.

Of the many problems identified and responses undertaken, three were selected for systematic evaluation. Satisfied with the results, the PERF staff reported that

- Burglaries in a major apartment complex were reduced by 35 percent. Eventually, tenants were relocated to better dwellings and the complex was torn down;

- Responses to a prostitution problem in the central business district reduced robberies in the area by 40 percent; and

- Thefts from vehicles parked outside Newport News Shipbuilding were reduced by 55 percent.

Clearly, such conclusions are encouraging. Unfortunately, because the project did occur agencywide, experimental controls were limited, leaving open the strong possibility of competing explanations for outcomes, the existence of confounding variables not examined or explained, impact decay, or even residual or unintended consequences. Nevertheless, enthusiasm for the problem-solving approach mushroomed following the project, leading many to adopt the strategy as the best hope for modern policing.

RECAP: Policing "Hot Spots" in Minneapolis

Although not typically mentioned as a test of problem-oriented policing, the Minneapolis Repeat Call Address Policing (RECAP) experiment was undertaken in an effort to test the ability of the police to solve the problems generating repeat calls for police services. From his earlier work in Minneapolis, Sherman (1989) learned that only 3 percent of that city's estimated 115,000 addresses and intersections accounted for 50 percent of the police department's requests for service. Conversely, nearly 60 percent of the locations produced no calls to police at all. To Sherman, this highly skewed concentration of police calls into a relatively few locations suggested the need to focus police efforts on finding solutions to the underlying problems at these chronic, repeat call locations. If successful, officers could at once be responsive to their most frequent consumers' needs while reducing the overall demands upon their limited resources.

To accomplish this goal, a special unit of five officers was assigned 125 residential and 125 commercial addresses to which the police were known to have responded repeatedly during 1986. The RECAP officers then applied a variety of problem-solving tactics. At the residential locations these included meetings with landlords, supporting petitions for evictions, providing technical and inspirational advice on tenant problems, and delivering "napalm letters" (contact requests) to sites of repeated domestic disturbances (Sherman, 1990).

After six months of program efforts, the experiment's evaluation found that the targeted residential addresses had 15 percent fewer service calls than in the same period during the previous year — a significant difference relative to the trends in the project's control areas. By the end of the second six months, however, virtually all of these gains had been erased. Perhaps partly due to differences in RECAP team procedures and partly because of increased citywide attention to domestic violence arrests, by the project's fourth quarter the targeted residential addresses actually were producing more calls for service than their control group counterparts.

In discussing this apparent decay in project effect, Sherman (1990) suggests that the impact from RECAP officer contacts and recommendations may have worn off as those contacts grew more routine. If so, then the findings may indicate that the benefits of a problem-oriented approach may be primarily short term. An operational policy of rotating targets or target areas may produce optimal effects with long-term targeting being an unwise investment of limited resources.   This, in turn, would suggest that the problem-solving strategy may

> be better suited to a task-force approach to specific community problems than to the day-to-day handling of myriad routine calls for service, reported crimes and emergencies.   Also, problem-oriented policing recommends a process for analyzing community problems, but does not specify what alternative solutions to chose.   Resource constraints, legal considerations, and finite human creative abilities all limit our ability to identify innovative, effective strategies (Sheehan and Cordner, 1989).

Community-Oriented Policing

By the mid-1970s it had become fairly apparent that smooth relations between a community and its police could not be guaranteed by the efforts of public relations specialists, regardless of how creative and well trained they were.   Further, research into how the police solve crimes (Greenwood and Petersilia, 1975) was leaving little doubt that a police-community partnership, heavily influenced by encounters between the two, was essential for the police to be effective in their crime-fighting role.   In response, within the past decade many departments have begun to adopt a community-oriented model of policing that emphasizes "diversification of the kinds of programs and services on the basis of community needs . . . and where there is considerable involvement of the community with police in reaching their objectives" (Reiss, 1985).   As evidence of the strategy's growing popularity, from a recent survey of 366 police departments serving cities with populations of 100,000 or more, the Portland Police Bureau found that 165 (45 percent) had already or were implementing some version of the community-oriented approach (Wycoff and Kenney, 1990).

Despite its popularity, the concept of "community policing" has been defined only loosely and is used to describe a variety of programs, many having little in common with each other.   Included, but not a complete list, are Neighborhood Watch programs, mini- and storefront police stations, liaisons with gay and minority communities, unsolicited visits by patrol officers to homes, media campaigns, foot and directed patrol, and police-sponsored lectures, dances, and athletic leagues (Wycoff and Kenney, 1990).   Unfortunately, few of these efforts have been subjected to careful and rigorous evaluations leaving us little information about the effectiveness of the individual tactics they employed.

Comparing Team and Community Policing

Aside from the issues of effect, today's community-oriented approach is conceptually similar to the earlier team policing efforts in important ways (Walker, 1991). For example, both are focused at neighborhoods and are critical of traditional centralized command and control styles of police supervision. Because both seek to change the manner in which police services are delivered at the neighborhood level, neither can have an add-on, or special project, approach.

Additionally, both team and community policing require a different conception of the police role from both the public and the police. With both strategies, successful officers must analyze their environments, be planners, develop solutions to address the problems they identify, and reach evaluative conclusions about success. While the planning requirements may be greater with community than team policing, both require a similar approach that is quite different than those we traditionally identify with policing.

Finally, both strategies give recognition not only to the importance of fighting crime but to the role of order maintenance and quality of life concerns as well (see Wilson and Kelling, 1982). To do so, both place a heavy emphasis on community in problem identification and program development while placing the ultimate responsibility for each at the line rather than command levels. In her review of the efforts to date, in fact, Wycoff (1988) found that despite the multitude of differences among the varied programs wearing the label of "community policing," all did appear to have in common "the belief that police and citizens should experience a larger number of nonthreatening, supportive interactions." These should include efforts by police to

- Listen to citizens, including those who are neither victims nor perpetrators of crimes;

- Take seriously citizens' definitions of their problems, even when the problems they define might differ from ones the police would identify for them; and

- Solve the problems that have been identified.

Obviously, this differs greatly from the traditional styles of police decision making that centralized planning and policy development and sought to insulate officers from the public as a means of reform and corruption control.

What Lessons to Be Learned?

Given the similarities, why have we been so reluctant to compare our policing past with the future? In discussing this question, Walker (1991) offers three possible explanations.

First, is the sheer passage of time. Although versions of team policing date back at least to the late 1940s (Thibault et al., 1985), the concept reached its peak in the early 1970s and then quickly faded away. That means that most officers today — and a good deal of researchers and criminal justice professors — have no first-hand acquaintance with the strategy. Team policing, therefore, is for much of the criminal justice community little more than a matter of history.

Equally important is the aura of failure surrounding team policing. Many of those who do have knowledge may consciously be avoiding direct analogies out of fear of being tainted guilt by association. Advocates of the community-oriented concept may simply be attempting to avoid casting a cloud over current efforts by comparing those efforts with earlier programs widely considered to have failed. As Walker (1991) notes, however, "while this explanation may apply to police administrators, it is no excuse for the failure of the academic experts."

And last is undoubtedly our limited experience at learning from the past. As we saw earlier, the body of knowledge about policing has only begun to accumulate quite recently. It may be that we are slow to apply the lessons from team policing to our current strategic approaches because of our lack of practice at the process of building upon the past.

In fact, however, there are several important lessons that should be applied. Although community policing doesn't alter the organizational structure as team policing did, considerable independent decision-making authority is delegated to line-level officers. The fear, suspicion, and opposition generated among middle managers during team policing programs could well reappear today. Also troubling are the issues of peer resentment and the perception of unequal work loads. Walker (1991) notes that since community policing involves a radically different approach to policing, officers not involved may resent being excluded and soon conclude that their community-oriented colleagues are not doing their fair share of the "real" police work. Given the changes that will undoubtedly occur, the non-traditional duties of community policing will almost certainly pose serious problems for all involved in the process — officers, their supervisors, and the public requesting services from the police.

Finally, the problems of unclear goals and expectations may be especially difficult for community policing projects. As officers continue to confront growing numbers of calls for service, limited dispatching technologies, and public pressure to increase the fight against crime, the pressures to return to more familiar methods and tactics will be considerable. "Unless community policing officers have a clear sense of what they are supposed to do and receive the necessary support from their supervisors (who presumably also know what this new role involves) the tendency to drift back into a traditional role will be great" (Walker, 1991). From conversations with officers involved with the Houston community policing programs it appears likely that each of these problems may already be developing in that city's police department.

Strategic Approaches: A Few Concluding Thoughts

During the past three decades of police reform, research, and development much has occurred and even more has been learned. We know more about who the police are and what they do and have a far better understanding of what does and does not work. While some of what has been tried has failed terribly, even then the "body of knowledge" about policing has grown considerably. Still, a few cautionary observations are possible:

- Much of what has occurred over the previous thirty years is uneven and inconsistent. Driven by often conflicting goals of better law enforcement, improved police-community relations, and greater efficiencies in police operations, we have shifted among efforts to improve our officers, change the environment in which they work, and alter the nature of policing and the organizations from which it occurs. All too often this has led to inflated expectations and objectives that were counterproductive. With the current experiments in problem- and community-oriented policing, we have the opportunity to avoid these past mistakes that frustrated so many of the earlier efforts.

- As we explore new approaches to policing, the distinction between strategies and the tactics they produce should be continually stressed. The measure of an effective strategy — such as community policing — should not be whether a specific crime or order problem is reduced. Success is achieved if the strategy results in an atmosphere where appropriate tactics are developed, applied to specific problems, and refined as needed. Because an individual tactic fails does not necessarily mean that the strategy that produced it did.

- We should remind ourselves that much of what we "know" about policing — the conventional wisdoms we rely upon — may, in fact, be quite incorrect. That police patrol has little impact on crime or fear is routinely accepted yet the Kansas City preventive patrol study upon which this "fact" is based has been neither replicated nor have the findings been reproduced by comparable research. Nonetheless, many remain certain of patrol's ineffectiveness as well as that most police work involves little crime fighting, that patrol time is uniformly uncommitted, and that investigators are largely irrelevant to the solution of crimes. Given the knowledge gaps that remain, caution should be exercised as research is translated into policy so that the tendency to seek panaceas offering easy solutions to complex problems can be avoided.

References

Cohn, E. & Sherman, L. (1986). *Police policy on domestic violence, 1986: A national survey*. Washington, DC: Crime Control Institute.

Cordner, G. (1985). *The Baltimore County citizen oriented police enforcement (COPE) project: Final evaluation*. New York: Florence V. Burden Foundation.

Dunford, F., Huizinga, D., & Elliott, D. (1990). The role of arrest in domestic assault: The Omaha police experiment. *Criminology*, 28(2), 183-206.

Eck, J. & Spelman, W. (1989). A problem-oriented approach to police service delivery. In D. Kenney (Ed), *Police and Policing: Contemporary Issues*, New York: Praeger Publishers.

Gay, W., Day, H., & Woodward, J. (1977). *Neighborhood team policing*. Washington, DC: Department of Justice, U.S. Government Printing Office.

Goldstein, H. (1990). *Problem-oriented policing*. New York: McGraw-Hill Inc.

Goldstein, H. (1979). Improving policing: A problem-oriented approach. *Crime and Delinquency*, 25, 236-258.

Greenwood, P. & Petersilia, J. (1975). *The criminal investigation process, volume I: Summary and policy implications.* Santa Monica, CA: The RAND Corporation.

Kelling, G., Pate, T., Dieckman, D., & Brown, C. (1974). *The Kansas City preventive patrol experiment: A summary report.* Washington, DC: The Police Foundation.

Moore, T. N., Wycoff, M. A., & Kenney, D. (1990). *Facilitating organizational change from the bottom: Democratic planning in the police workplace.* Washington, DC: The Police Foundation.

Pate, T. (1989). Community-oriented policing in Baltimore. In D. Kenney (Ed.), *Police and policing: Contemporary issues.* New York: Praeger Publishers.

Reinier, G., Greenlee, M., Gibbens, M., & Marshall, S. (1977). *Crime analysis in support of patrol.* Washington, DC: Department of Justice, U.S. Government Printing Office.

Reiss, A. J., Jr. (1985). Shaping and serving the community: The role of the police chief executive. In W. Geller (Ed.), *Police leadership in America: Crisis and opportunity.* New York: Praeger Publishers.

Sheehan, R. & Cordner, G. W. (1989). *Introduction to police administration.* (2nd ed.) Cincinnati: Anderson Publishing Co.

Sherman, L. (1990). Police crackdowns: Initial and residual deterrence. In M. Tonry & N. Morris (Eds.), *Crime and justice: A review of research.* Chicago: The University of Chicago Press.

Sherman, L. (1989). Repeat calls for service: Policing the "Hot Spots." In D. Kenney (Ed.), *Police and policing: Contemporary issues.* New York: Praeger Publishers.

Sherman, L. & Berk, R. (1984). *The Minneapolis domestic violence experiment.* Washington, DC: The Police Foundation.

Sherman, L., Milton, C., & Kelly, T. (1973). *Team policing: Seven case studies.* Washington, DC: The Police Foundation.

Thibault, E., Lynch, L., & McBride, R. (1985). *Proactive police management.* Englewood Cliffs, NJ: Prentice Hall.

Tien, J., Simon, J., & Larson, R. (1978). *An alternative approach in police patrol: The Wilmington split-force experiment.* Washington, DC: Department of Justice, U.S. Government Printing Office.

Walker, S. (1991). *Does anyone remember team policing?: Lessons of the team policing experience for community policing.* Unpublished manuscript, University of Nebraska at Omaha.

Walker, S. (1989). Paths to police reform — Reflections on 25 years of change. In D. Kenney (Ed.), *Police and policing: Contemporary issues.* New York: Praeger Publishers.

Wilson, J. Q. & Kelling, G. L. (1982). The police and neighborhood safety: Broken windows. *The Atlantic Monthly*, 29-38 (March).

Wycoff, M. A. (1988). The benefits of community policing: Evidence and conjecture. In J. Greene & S. Mastrofski (Eds.), *Community policing: Myth or reality.* New York: Praeger Publishers.

Wycoff, M. A. & Kenney, D. (1990). *Facilitating organizational change from the bottom: Democratic planning in the police workplace.* Washington, DC: The Police Foundation.

Chapter 10

Human Resource Issues

Gary W. Cordner

Introduction

Because the police business is so labor-intensive, the management of *human resource issues* occupies a central position within the domain of police administration. Typically, 80 percent to 90 percent or more of police department budgets are allocated to salaries and benefits — to paying *people* for the time they devote to their jobs. The important aspects of police work are performed by employees, not by machines. Police management is much more concerned with directing and controlling police officers than with fiscal administration, purchasing, or information systems development. Clearly, when compared with other kinds of organizations, police departments stand out as examples of organizations that are particularly dependent for their success or failure on the effective management of *human* resources.

Recognition of the crucial importance of human resources for achieving police effectiveness is not new. One of Sir Robert Peel's principles for the London Metropolitan Police in 1829 emphasized the essential role of "securing and training proper persons." Arthur Woods, a reform police commissioner in New York from 1914 to 1919, stressed the need for better training and promotional practices (Woods, 1919). August Vollmer, the first in a long line of California police reformers, advocated higher intelligence and education standards for police recruits as well as extensive training (Vollmer, 1936). The professional model of policing that has guided our thinking for much of this century gives prominence to education, training, and the selection of employees on the basis of merit rather than political or personal connections (Fogelson, 1977). National inquiries since the

Wickersham Commission in 1931 have consistently called for improvements in the quality of police personnel. From 1968 to 1980 the Law Enforcement Assistance Administration (LEAA) used federal dollars to encourage widespread upgrading of police education, training, and personnel practices. In the 1990s, Congress continues to consider Police Corps legislation intended to attract young people to police service and to provide them with a college education.

Because the crucial contribution of human resources to police organizational effectiveness is so universally accepted, it is perhaps appropriate to caution the reader that upgrading police personnel is no panacea (Walker, 1989). Anyone familiar with at least a few police departments can probably identify one that is a complete mess despite being staffed with high-caliber people. As observed by Herman Goldstein several years ago,

> A large number of police agencies that have succeeded in carrying out most of the standard suggestions for upgrading their personnel have nevertheless not achieved the kind of overall improvement in the quality of their service that it had been assumed would automatically follow (1977).

How can this be true? One possibility is that we have yet to identify correctly the kinds of people best suited for police work or the most effective approaches to police education, training, and career development. Another is that we have typically made personnel improvements without changing either the nature of the police job or the nature of the police organization. In many instances, the effects of the job and the organization have been so powerful that they have diluted or nullified any changes in the kinds of people hired by police departments. Lurking behind these possibilities are the endemic issues in policing — the basic issues that we have generally failed to acknowledge or grapple with despite our attempts at police reform. Unfortunately, therefore, much of the herculean effort designed to upgrade the quality of police human resources has been subverted by "the passivity and limited horizons of those in administrative positions combined with the incredible naivete of those — both within and outside police agencies — who commonly overestimate what can be achieved by personnel reforms alone" (Goldstein, 1977).

After a brief description of a framework for getting a handle on police human resource issues, some observations on the current state of police human resource management, and a discussion of current human resource issues in policing, this chapter concentrates on the interface between the endemic issues in policing and the human resources perspective on police management.

Police Human Resource Planning

A framework for the consideration of police human resource issues can best be delineated by reference to the managerial activity termed *human resource planning*, the objectives of which can be described as follows:

> Ensuring that the agency has, and will continue to have, the right numbers and kinds of people doing the right things at the right times in the right places.

This simple-sounding description begs some exceedingly difficult questions and glosses over some very tough problems, but it makes a tremendous contribution by clearly articulating what we should be trying to accomplish as we carry out police human resource management. It implies that we must (1) figure out how many and what kinds of people we need to have doing what things at what times and in what places, and then (2) take steps to achieve what we have figured that we need. In other words, we must devote our energies both to personnel-related research and planning and to personnel administration. The definition also highlights several component questions:

- What functions, roles, and tasks must (should) personnel be prepared to perform?

- What kinds of people are best suited to perform the various police jobs?

- How can personnel be best prepared to perform the various police jobs?

- How many people are needed to fulfill the responsibilities of the police agency?

- How should police personnel be allocated and scheduled to take maximum advantage of their time and talents?

- Where should police personnel be deployed to take maximum advantage of their time and talents?

- To what extent, if any, will the answers to these questions be different in the foreseeable future?

This is definitely a complex situation, since the answers to these questions, taken separately, are far from obvious, and since the answer to one question is often contingent on the answer to another. The situation is further complicated because, even if a police department could determine the "correct" answers to the questions, its ability to achieve them through personnel administration would be greatly constrained by a whole host of organizational and environmental factors, including characteristics of the labor market, economic conditions, budgets, civil service regulations, labor contracts, legal mandates and prohibitions, and political considerations. One might expect that, given these conceptual and practical difficulties, police managers would throw up their hands in surrender. Such has not been the case, although some managers may very well be retreating.

The available evidence indicates that, first of all, police departments obviously undertake the component activities of personnel administration, including recruitment, selection, assignment, evaluation, and promotion, and they necessarily allocate, schedule, and deploy their personnel on some basis. A few police departments have complete control over these activities, most share responsibilities with host government civil service, merit system, or personnel departments, and some are completely dependent on host government services. Many police agencies go a step beyond mere personnel administration, however, and engage in analytical activities designed to produce relevant information for human resource decision making and planning — activities such as job analysis, selection validation, training needs assessment, work load analysis, and labor market analysis. One study found that the more that police agencies engaged in these kinds of human resource planning activities, the more they felt able to attract and retain the kinds of people they needed (Cordner et al., 1982).

This same study concluded, though, that it is the rare police organization that really takes human resource planning to heart. Most simply carry out the rudimentary components of personnel administration. Those that do engage in specific personnel-related analytical activities such as job analysis or training needs assessment typically do so to alleviate narrowly defined problems, to support narrowly conceived decisions, to respond to immediate crises, or to meet externally imposed requirements. That is, while some police departments undertake *operational-* or *tactical-level* human resource planning, very few give their human resource planning a *strategic* focus. To put it another way, the fundamental "right numbers and kinds of people doing the right things at the right times in the right places" question hardly ever gets any direct or serious attention.

Why would this be the case? First, day-to-day decision making and crisis handling tend to deflect attention away from strategic thinking in most areas of management, including human resource management. The need to get people hired, to get them trained, and to get them evaluated always seems more pressing than the need to think about what kinds of people the agency really needs. Strategic thinking and planning can almost seem like luxuries, frills, amidst the demands of daily personnel administration.

Another reason is that strategic thinking is hard, demanding, and dependent on an ability to see the big picture. Grappling with the "right numbers and kinds of people" problem is tough, as is trying to answer such component questions as "How can personnel be best prepared to perform the various police jobs?" It is much easier to stay within the confines of the status quo, to accept current kinds of personnel and current personnel practices as satisfactory, than to try to figure out what would be better. Just as a full appreciation of problem-oriented policing requires a realization that law enforcement is but a means to some other end (Goldstein, 1990), so to does an appreciation for strategic human resource planning depend on realizing that personnel administration activities are merely means to some larger end. Unfortunately, many managers get caught up in the personnel process and completely lose sight of what they are supposed to be trying to accomplish.

Also, a number of activities within human resource management, such as selection validation and manpower allocation, are sufficiently specialized and technical that executives responsible for strategic thinking are sometimes scared away. This tendency to leave technical matters to technical experts is understandable and of course somewhat necessary. However, a subtle shift often takes place. Instead of the executive specifying the goals and values that are to be pursued, and the technician figuring out how best to achieve them, over time the technician frequently assumes (or the executive abdicates) the responsibility for setting policy and deciding what objectives will be pursued.

An analogy to police information systems can be made here (Sparrow, 1991). We frequently let computer-aided dispatching and 9-1-1 technologies determine what patrol strategies we can adopt, instead of forcing the technologies to support patrol strategies chosen because they most promise to accomplish the goals of the department. Similarly, we sometimes let personnel technicians tell police executives what kinds of people can be hired, rather than having the technicians find the kinds of people that the executives believe are needed (admittedly, some legal constraints are also applicable). And we frequently let analysts and their patrol allocation models set the parameters that determine which operational strategies are feasible, instead of instructing the analysts to allocate personnel in accordance with strategically derived plans and programs.

In part because of the general lack of a strategic approach to human resource management in police organizations, most of our attention gets directed toward *current issues* rather than *endemic issues*. Usually, these current issues turn out to be subsets or symptoms of more basic problems. Ten current human resource issues in policing are briefly identified in the next section, after which attention is turned to more endemic issues.

Current Issues

Lengthy descriptions of the police personnel process and informed discussions of current police human resource issues can be found in several recent texts (see Swanson et al., 1988; Gaines et al., 1991; Nowicki et al., 1991; and Gaines and Kappeler, 1992), attesting to the central role of human resource management in police administration. Among the most widely recognized current issues concern the employment of women, minorities, and the disabled, the desirability of higher education, the importance of intelligence, the viability of psychological and physical fitness testing, the use of assessment centers, chronic complaints about performance evaluation, and debates over patrol scheduling.

Women in Policing

The employment of women as sworn police officers has increased dramatically in the past two decades and has spread beyond matron and juvenile officer duties to regular patrol and virtually all other types of positions. As a proportion of all police officers, the number of women police has increased nearly fivefold since 1972. Still, no more than about 10 percent of all police officers are female, and representation in higher ranks and in many state and federal law enforcement agencies is even lower (Martin, 1990).

Although most research has indicated that women and men perform comparably in various police positions, a considerable amount of resistance to the use of women in patrol and other physically demanding assignments lingers (Hale, 1992). Some of this resistance is expressed by citizens, but most comes from male police officers. These officers often cite the inability of female officers to control combative subjects and their lack of confidence in the effectiveness of female officers as backup assistance. Others dispute these claims, arguing that with proper training female officers can learn techniques to control physically uncooperative subjects, and further that women police can often use their superior communication skills (and lack of male ego) to avert such physical confrontations in the first place. Thus, although the issue of whether women will be used widely in police work has apparently been resolved, other issues regarding appropriate assignments, proper training, and organizational resistance remain salient.

Minorities in Policing

The most recent national data indicate that the employment of racial and ethnic minorities in sworn police positions closely approximates minority representation in the total population (Carter and Sapp, 1991). A tremendous increase over the past two decades in the number of minority police executives, particularly in large cities, is also apparent.   Therefore, although various forms of generally subtle discrimination persist in many police agencies, widespread employment of minorities in American policing has become a reality.

Nevertheless, many individual departments have few minority employees and are under severe pressure from community groups, human relations commissions, regulatory agencies, and the courts to increase their employment of minorities (Sullivan, 1989). In these situations, issues related to affirmative action, differential standards, and reverse discrimination are often hotly debated (see Gaines et al., 1989). Departments frequently compete vigorously with each other to recruit minority candidates, especially those with military or college backgrounds, and are not above hiring officers away from other police agencies.   The issue most on the minds of police administrators, then, is how best to attract and retain well-qualified minority candidates without unfairly discriminating against majority candidates.

Employment of the Disabled

The federal Americans with Disabilities Act of 1990 (ADA) has thrust the issue of employment of the disabled squarely before police administrators (Schneid and Gaines, 1991). This act prohibits discrimination against disabled persons unless it can be clearly shown that they are unable to perform the functions of the job. Inasmuch as there are currently serving police officers to be found who have very poor eyesight, who are obese, who suffer from epilepsy and other diseases, who employ prosthetic devices, and who are current or recovered drug and alcohol abusers, police managers probably will not succeed in ducking the ADA simply by generally asserting the physical demands of the police job. The issue should then probably focus on distinguishing between those disabilities that prevent satisfactory police performance and those that do not, and on determining what accommodations police organizations should make to facilitate employment of the disabled. It will likely be several years before the impact of the ADA on policing becomes completely clear.

Higher Education

After a decade or so of relative dormancy, the issue of higher education for police officers has reappeared.   While the empirical evidence demonstrating that a college education leads to better police performance remains relatively weak (Hayeslip, 1989; Worden, 1990), the courts seem ready to accept a college requirement for police employment as reasonable

(Carter et al., 1988). An influential recent report by PERF (Carter et al., 1989) has called for more widespread adoption of college requirements and documented a variety of programs and policies used by police agencies to support higher education.

Although one noted commentator has concluded that "it is necessary to lay to rest the spurious debate about the merits of a college education" (Bittner, 1990), it is doubtful that the argument will end anytime soon. The desirability of requiring college education for police continues to have its fervent advocates and many equally convinced, if less vocal, skeptics. As the debate continues, though, it seems likely that the overall educational level of police officers will continue to creep upward, whether because of higher social status accorded police work, maturation of the police higher education industry, or educational trends in the larger population.

Intelligence

The question of just how intelligent one needs to be to perform police duties raises many of the same issues as the higher education debate, but in addition, the difficult problems of defining and measuring intelligence come up. In recent years, many police agencies have shied away from using both intelligence and aptitude tests in their selection processes, for fear that they were culturally biased, discriminatory, and not clearly job related. Some level of intelligence is obviously required in police work, however, and proposed alterations in the nature of the job, such as problem-oriented policing, may demand more intelligence (Kenney and Watson, 1990), leading some observers to predict that intelligence testing may soon return to the battery of police selection techniques.

Psychological Testing

Many police departments have adopted psychological testing of applicants in recent years (Benner, 1989; Inwald and Kenney, 1989). Some have implemented psychologically based tests as their primary written examinations in the initial selection process, in place of aptitude and intelligence tests, in the belief that they are less discriminatory toward minorities. Others use psychological tests later in the selection process to weed out candidates with undesirable personality characteristics. A wide variety of types of tests are used, including projective, self-report, situational, interest, and attitude tests (Johnson, 1990). Unfortunately, the predictive validity of most of these tests is highly suspect (Wright et al., 1990) — thus, though they may not be discriminatory, the value of psychological tests in selecting the best candidates for police work, or even in weeding out unsuitable candidates, is largely unproven. Their use is bound to continue, though, if only to avert discrimination suits and as a hedge against civil liability claims of negligent hiring.

Physical Fitness Testing

A great deal of litigation and controversy has surrounded the use of physical fitness tests in police selection in recent years. Largely because women score lower than men on most traditional fitness measures, many departments have eliminated their fitness tests, lowered their passing scores, or moved to differential standards. Two basic models seem to be vying for supremacy at present: the use of job-specific physical tests, such as dragging an average-sized body away from a burning building; and the use of general wellness and fitness tests of strength, endurance, and flexibility. Justification for the former model is based on its job-relatedness — validation difficulties emerge, however, due to the relatively rare occurrence of physically demanding duties in police work. The latter model is usually justified more on the basis of sustained employee health and wellness, and on expert opinion that police officers need to be of about average fitness. The use of this model almost invariably requires differential standards based on age and gender norms, though, often to the consternation of fit young males.

Assessment Centers

Dissatisfaction with traditional promotional systems based largely on written tests and/or oral interviews has led many police agencies to adopt the use of assessment centers. These assessment centers typically utilize trained assessors who evaluate candidates' performance on exercises that simulate aspects of the job to which the candidates aspire. Ideally, the end result is a much more accurate estimation of each candidate's future job performance than can be obtained from written tests or interview boards.

Assessment centers are not without their critics, however. Often the exercises are too artificial to elicit truly realistic behavior from candidates, and frequently assessors are not sufficiently trained to guarantee reliable ratings. When candidate performance on exercises is rated according to such criteria as appearance, attitude, and maturity, the result can be more of a beauty contest than a simulation of job-related behavior. When vague rating criteria such as judgment, decisiveness, and initiative are used, assessor ratings can be so subjective that they are unreliable and meaningless. For reasons such as these, the experience with assessment centers in police promotional testing has not always been as positive as it could have been.

Performance Evaluation

At any point in time, a good bet for a burning human resource issue in policing, or for that matter in any other sphere of work, would be performance evaluation. Typically, the only organizations not upset with their methods for evaluating performance are those that do not even bother to evaluate (and this failure to evaluate performance can be counted upon to upset many employees). Most supervisors dislike having to evaluate their subordinates, and most workers are unhappy either with their evaluations or with their supervisors' unwillingness to discuss them.

Research indicates that many police departments (1) use evaluation forms borrowed from other organizations, (2) rely on evaluation of traits rather than behavior, (3) provide little or no evaluation training for supervisors, and (4) make little use of performance evaluations in subsequent decisions about pay, assignment, or promotion (Walsh, 1990). It is little wonder, then, that nearly everyone hates performance evaluations, they create a lot of grief for supervisors and officers, and they rarely fulfill any important purposes.

Patrol Scheduling

Schedules are a naturally hot topic. From a labor standpoint, they specify the days and hours when workers must put themselves at the disposal of the organization. From a management standpoint, they are a principal tool for optimizing resource utilization. Invariably, scheduling brings the interests of workers and management into conflict.

Several specific issues are typically debated in police patrol scheduling. Since patrol work load is often heaviest on weekend days, the proportional allocation objective held in highest esteem by resource managers conflicts with officers' preferences for desirable days off. Similarly, heavy work loads during evening hours create demands that conflict with many officers' desires to work the day shift as do other people. From a somewhat different perspective, minimum staffing on the late night shift, based on low levels of patrol work load, gives rise to safety concerns among those few officers unfortunate enough to draw such assignments.

Debates also ensue over permanent versus rotating shifts and over fixed versus variable days off. Perhaps the most heated arguments take place between advocates and detractors of the 4 x 10 schedule. This schedule, which uses a four-day work week of ten-hour days, became quite popular in policing in the 1970s, and remains in use in many agencies. Its defenders cite positive benefits for morale (officers have three days off each week) and the advantages that can be derived from the overlap periods built into the schedule. Its critics point out that the extra personnel available during overlap periods are often used inefficiently, and that the 4 x 10 schedule results in fewer personnel on duty during nonoverlap periods. Unfortunately, positions in this debate have hardened and many police executives are now either true believers in the 4 x 10 or rabid opponents. Few seem to recognize that this argument should really hinge on a comparison of costs and benefits — in particular, on whether in any specific situation enough benefit is derived from the extra personnel available during overlap periods to outweigh the cost of reduced personnel at other times. This determination will vary according to work load patterns and other situation-specific considerations; the 4 x 10 schedule is not inherently either more or less efficient than any other forty-hour work week schedule.

Endemic Issues

As interesting, topical, and, in some cases, persistent as these current issues may be, it is important to recognize the more profound and fundamental issues from which they spring. (For more general discussions of the basic issues and problems confronting police in a free society, see Berkley, 1969; Bittner, 1970; and Goldstein, 1977.) When we start peeling away layers from any of these current police human resource issues we are apt to find our way to more endemic issues. For example:

- The issue of the suitability of women for various aspects of police work centers not only on womens' rights and roles but also ultimately on a largely empirical question — what is it that police actually do? — and on a related but somewhat more philosophical question — what should be the police role in a free society? Many disagreements over women in policing really come down to disagreements over what "policing" is or should be.

- Arguments over minority employment issues in policing often boil down to different conceptions of police work and differing priorities for police goals. Those who hold mechanistic or scientific views of policing and who give highest priority to crime control and efficiency goals argue that we should simply hire those candidates who score highest on professionally devised selection tests. Such tests usually favor those with more education and produce personnel well suited to handle the legalistic and bureaucratic aspects of the police job. But other observers, recognizing the community service and order maintenance elements of policing, give higher priority to the need for personnel who are representative of, and who empathize with, all segments of society. These observers take a more organic and political view of policing and give higher priority to accountability, justice, and public tranquility goals.

• In the modern era, allocation and scheduling alternatives have been evaluated according to the criterion of work load proportionality. Recently, though, some have argued that existing patrol schedules interfere with attempts to implement community policing and problem-oriented policing. The real issue, of course, goes to the mission and priorities of the police. In retrospect, it is obvious that proportional allocation and scheduling have implicitly granted highest priority to the call-handling aspect of the police mission. Thus, some of the debate over allocation and scheduling is motivated by a desire to reorient the police mission away from mere call handling and more toward community service and problem solving.

We could go on and on. Clearly, issues related to hiring of the disabled, higher education, intelligence, psychological testing, and physical fitness testing eventually devolve to questions about the nature of the police job and the kinds of people best suited for it. Debates over assessment centers and performance evaluation partly hinge on disputes over what constitutes good police work and good management. Many issues in police training boil down to questions about the duties and roles for which trainees are to be prepared. And so forth.

In the sections that follow, an attempt is made to sketch out several of the most fundamental issues that underlie police human resource management.

Matching Structure to Objectives

It is critically important in any reasoned discussion of the police to acknowledge the existence of multiple legitimate objectives. In a free society we expect the police to control crime, maintain order, and provide a variety of services in a manner that is efficient, legal, and accountable to political authority and the public. This complex set of objectives creates a number of problems for police administration: to which objectives to attach high and low priorities; how to treat conflicts between objectives; how to choose among alternative strategies with mixed effects; how to react to changing public preferences among objectives; and so on. Moreover, each objective contains its own complexities. For example, there are many varieties of crime to be controlled; public opinion about the seriousness of different crimes is varied and changing; levels of crime are difficult to measure; the police are but one of many social institutions with responsibilities for crime control; and the methods available to the police for controlling crime are constrained in important ways.

What is the interface between these complications and police human resource management? It is axiomatic in organization theory that structure should be designed to match objectives. Personnel are part of organization structure. Therefore, police human resources should somehow match the objectives of police organizations. When we say that we need "the right numbers and kinds of people doing the right things in the right places at the right times," our use of "right" means "in order to maximize attainment of our objectives." Calculating a solution to this problem might be feasible if we had one clear objective. Little precision can be expected, however, when it is a complex set of conflicting and dynamic objectives to which human resource needs and other aspects of structure are to be matched.

Some police administrators have sought to simplify this very difficult problem by putting blinders on and asserting that police departments are simply agencies for law enforcement, period. They have dealt with the complexity of policing by ignoring it and by substituting a method of policing (enforcing the law) for the true if untidy objectives of the business. This approach, while it brings a certain amount of comfort to police executives, police officers, and the public, is destined to fail in the long run for the obvious reason that it neglects all of the important objectives for which police agencies were created and sustained.

It would clearly be mistaken to base police human resource management on the single objective of maximizing law enforcement. Unfortunately, the preferred alternative is difficult to specify with any precision. In determining the numbers and kinds of people that they need, though, and how best to use them, police agencies need to be conscious of their multiple objectives. They need officers who can maintain order in tense situations and also provide services with a smile. Within the organization, they need the capability of controlling traditional and high-technology crimes. They need to allocate patrol resources in a manner that is responsive to crime, disorder, fear, and other problems.

The result is bound to be a messier and more subjective approach to human resource management than many police administrators would prefer. By recognizing and giving serious attention to the multiple objectives of policing, however, we will come a lot closer to matching structure to objectives, and we will be in a much better position to figure out what kinds of human resources we need and how best to use them.

Community Alliance

The issue of community alliance intersects police human resource management at several levels. If we accept that ordinary police officers should work closely with citizens to identify and solve community problems, as posited by many modern strategists, then we may need to recruit certain kinds of people, provide new kinds of training, devise new performance evaluation systems, and allocate personnel according to different criteria (see Williams and Sloan, 1990). If we decide to give greater weight in personnel selection to local community knowledge and understanding of community problems, we may need new tests and imaginative approaches to their validation. Serious efforts toward police-citizen "co-activity" and "co-production of public safety" might have substantial implications for the numbers of police personnel needed (the numbers might go down if citizens accept greater responsibilities) or the numbers of different categories of police personnel (we might need fewer patrol officers but more problem solvers and community organizers).

A greater role for the community in defining police human resource needs might also be anticipated. Traditionally, we have determined the kinds of people we needed by conducting job analyses, which largely rely on current police officers reporting the tasks that make up their jobs and the kinds of qualities that are needed for successful performance. In truth, this technique usually produces a biased, self-serving, and superficial picture of what the job "is." Alternatively, we might seek greater community input in defining what the job "ought to be," as a guide to selecting the kinds of police officers we would like to have. Ideally, a mixture of information from job incumbents, experts, police executives, and the public could produce a better picture of "the right kinds of people" needed to police any particular community.

Some limits on community influence will always be necessary, though. From time to time the community's view of the preferred role of the police may be one that is so misguided, politicized, or downright illegal that it must be ignored. Similarly, the community's views on the kinds of people that ought to be hired may be so irrational or unlawful that police administrators must resist them. We see here nothing more or less than the classic problems of balancing politics and administration, of limiting democratic excesses, of achieving professional yet responsive policing.

Enriching Traditional Roles

How best to structure the role of the individual police officer is another issue that has implications for many aspects of human resource management. If individual roles are narrowly drawn, selection can focus on a few specific qualities, training can be very directed, and performance evaluation is usually simplified. Overly narrow jobs can lead to problems of low job satisfaction and high turnover, however, as well as to the need for multiple training programs and career tracks. Broader roles may be more challenging for initial selection and training, but may produce a more flexible personnel pool and more variety in the workplace.

The modern trend toward broadening and enriching the police role, a trend that seems to have its parallels elsewhere in public and private management, may also have implications for the numbers of people needed by police organizations. With the elimination of unnecessary specialization and divisions of labor, some productivity savings might be expected. More important, if job enrichment leads police employees to greater effort and accomplishment, fewer people might be required to complete the same amount of work.

If the police role is enlarged to include more and more activities such as community organizing, multipurpose problem solving, providing services to juveniles, supervision of probationers and parolees, and the like, the implications both for the numbers and kinds of people needed could be profound, as could implications for training, evaluation, and resource allocation. At a very fundamental level, the role that police are expected to fulfill has obvious implications for every aspect of human resource management. And needless to say, the role of the police in our society is currently anything but static or well defined.

Activity Trap

Most organizations fall prey to the activity trap — their attention becomes focused more and more on process and less and less on the achievement of their objectives. They count activities instead of results. They reward employees for generating activity and following the approved process, even if the desired outcome was *not* achieved. They punish employees for deviating from standard practice, even if desired results *were* obtained. Over time they come to train employees to process without educating them about results. Eventually, goal displacement occurs — for all intents and purposes, the process becomes the purpose of the organization.

Arguably, this has happened in many police agencies. Individual productivity is measured in terms of calls handled, arrests made, and tickets issued. Promotions go to those who play it safe and always abide by written rules. Discipline goes to those who break the rules, no matter how trivial the rule or how good the intention. Implicitly, if not openly, many agencies have adopted "call handling" and "law enforcement" as their operative objectives, in place of crime control, order maintenance, and other genuine objectives. Often, the net effect is a bureaucratically efficient police agency that accomplishes its true objectives only by accident, if at all.

If one took this problem seriously, the implications for police human resource management could be dramatic. Training, evaluation, and resource allocation would all have to be redirected toward goal accomplishment and away from simply following procedures and producing activity. Recruitment and selection would need to target results-oriented people rather than compliant rule followers and enforcers. And since police objectives are so mushy and complex, these results-oriented people would need to be ones who could tolerate a good deal of frustration and ambiguity.

Lest the implications of the activity trap seem too straightforward, we should quickly point out that in the pursuit of results and objectives the police are inextricably bound to abide by a whole host of rules and laws designed to protect individual freedom. In fact, police agencies are to some extent inevitably process oriented. Constitutional limitations on police power must be honored. Evidentiary rules must be followed if crime is to be controlled through successful prosecution and adjudication. Police departments must guide police use of force, police driving, and the release of confidential information though rules, procedures, and policies. Employees must abide by a variety of standard processes to prevent organizational chaos.

The trick is to keep process and outcome in their appropriate places and not to suffer goal displacement. Among other things, that means distinguishing between sacred and ordinary rules, between good and bad intentions, and between meaningless activities and those that really contribute to the attainment of the objectives of the police organization. For human resource management, it means selecting, training, and evaluating people on the basis of both appropriate effort and results. Easy to say, harder to do.

Creativity With Accountability

A more expanded police role, and one that seeks to avoid the activity trap, may be one that demands more creativity of police officers. In truth, many police officers have always found opportunities for creativity as they handled disputes, conducted investigations, or simply engaged in routine patrol. But other officers, probably the majority in most departments, found little reason to be creative when simply choosing whether or not to enforce the law in a given situation.

Should police departments decide that creativity is what they want, adjustments in selection, training, and evaluation would probably be necessary. Basic police jobs and a variety of organizational policies and systems may also need revision, of course. Moreover, if creativity is to be evidenced largely through problem solving and community interaction, changes in allocation and scheduling may be required, in order to give officers more opportunities to meet with citizens during normal waking hours and to prod public and private agencies during normal business hours.

This recent interest in creativity raises the same kinds of alarms as the assault on the activity trap. More so than in the private sector or even in most other public agencies, police departments are really only interested in creativity within certain rather inviolate boundaries. There are times when police officers must follow exact orders rather than free-lance. There are situations in which the room for creativity is severely restricted. Even when opportunities for creativity are fairly broad, some options are proscribed by law, others by policy, and still others by social convention. Police work may well call for more creativity than many other kinds of work, but at the same time it presents a host of constraints and limitations.

To some extent in this discussion of creativity we might as well have been discussing police discretion. This brings up a basic dilemma facing police administrators — whether to admit publicly the existence of widespread discretion in police decision making, which opens up a Pandora's box of issues and controversies centering on individual fairness versus equal application of the law. In reality, of course, police officers fill a quasi-judicial role in which they exercise a substantial amount of discretion, a situation probably recognized by most citizens, or at least those with driving privileges. If given the chance, these citizens would most likely choose creativity in policing over efficient law enforcement. They would probably also choose to be policed by people selected, trained, and evaluated on the basis of thoughtful and creative use of discretion.

Stability Amid Change

As complex a set of issues as are faced in trying to ensure that a police department has the right numbers and kinds of people doing the right things, the situation is further complicated by change. Society changes, police organizations are forced to change by external pressures, police departments initiate change intentionally, and individuals change. Just when police administrators think that they have gotten a good grip on things, something slips, and the chase is on again.

Change affects human resource management in many ways. Personnel change, requiring new hires, promotions, and the like. Jobs change, requiring new selection criteria, new training programs, and new evaluation systems. The professional field of human resource management changes, bringing new theories and new standards. Changed laws and administrative regulations may require adjustments to personnel processes. Changed politics may bring

new ideas about the right numbers and kinds of people and what they ought
to do.

One interesting ramification of the quickening pace of change in modern
society is that police officers probably need to be more flexible and more
adaptable than ever before. Today's police recruit is likely to be using
radically different technologies and handling much different problems ten
years from now, not to mention in twenty or thirty years. What kind of person
should be hired in light of this inevitable but not entirely predictable
change? What kind of training should recruits be given now in order to best
prepare them to be successful throughout a career full of changes? Will
continuing education and training become more important elements of police
human resource management, or will officers be able to adapt and learn what
they need to know on the job?

The issue of change and its effect on policing is interesting to consider in
light of the inherently conservative, status quo role played by the institution
of policing. A primary mission of the police, after all, is to protect people's
lives and property and the instruments of government against all illegal
threats. One might expect, as a result of this basic function, that police
agencies would be quite resistant to change. Most observers seem to agree,
however, that over the past twenty years police departments have become
among the most open and willing to change of any organizations.

Conclusion

The most basic issues affecting police human resource management are
embodied in the objective of ensuring that the police organization has the
right numbers and kinds of people doing the right things. This objective
should be kept firmly in mind by police personnel administrators and other
managers as they make decisions and carry out the personnel process. It
should also be part and parcel of all strategic planning done by police
executives (see Moore and Stephens, 1991). Beneath the first tier of police
objectives (the overall goals of the organization, such as crime control and
order maintenance), this human resource objective deserves prominence, since
it so clearly and forcefully affects an agency's ability to attain its overall
objectives.

Any serious attempt to pursue this human resource objective is bound to
be frustrating, since it is so difficult to resolve such matters as what police
work is, what it should be, what kinds of people are best suited for it, and
how many police are needed. In truth, these matters cannot be "solved" in
the sense that operations researchers find optimal solutions to complex
logistical or transportation problems, partly because our science of people is
poorly developed, but mostly because these are not entirely scientific matters
anyway. These are practical, dare we say political issues that can only be

resolved (and only tentatively at that) through a combination of science, reason, discussion, negotiation, compromise, horse trading, and trial and error.

This is not to say that police administrators should not work at it. The logical starting point is to document carefully the nature of the police job as it is currently constituted. In conjunction with that largely empirical task (which can be aided by a substantial body of research on the nature of police work that is not typically integrated with job analyses — see Cordner, 1989, and Greene and Klockars, 1991), administrators must explore among themselves and with the community just what the police job should be. These two projects will rarely result in a nice clean picture of the police role, because people differ in their expectations and preferences. But it will result in a more complete and useful picture of the police job than is produced by the typical superficial job analysis.

Next, administrators should draw upon various kinds of practitioners and experts to determine the kinds of people best suited to perform the job and role as outlined above (again, research on police behavior can be helpful — see Muir, 1977, and Broderick, 1987, for example). At the same time, the administrator and the community should identify the kinds of values and philosophies that police personnel should embody (see Delattre and Behan, 1991). Combining these two products — the more objective and conventional determination of knowledge, skills, and abilities needed to perform the job and the more subjective description of the kind of person wanted — will provide a more well-rounded picture of the satisfactory candidate than is produced by reliance solely upon modern pseudoscientific psychometric techniques.

Figuring out the kinds of people wanted in policing is only the first step in the human resource planning and management process, of course, but perhaps the most challenging. In the past decade or two we have become so ensnared in well-meaning scientific approaches to personnel selection, so overwhelmed by technical issues, and so timid in the face of equal opportunity and civil liability concerns, that we have often misplaced our ability to think clearly about the kinds of people to whom we want to grant the enormous authority and responsibility of police service. One way to begin to regain our practical capabilities is to rivet our attention on ensuring that we have "the right numbers and right kinds of people doing the right things."

References

Benner, A. W. (1989). Psychological screening of police applicants. In R. G. Dunham & G. P. Alpert (Eds.), *Critical issues in policing:*

Contemporary readings (pp. 72-86). Prospect Heights, IL: Waveland Press Inc.

Berkley, G. E. (1969). *The democratic policeman*. Boston: Beacon Press.

Bittner, E. (1970). *The functions of the police in modern society*. Washington, DC: U.S. Government Printing Office.

Bittner, E. (1990). Some reflections on staffing problem-oriented policing. *American Journal of Police*, 9(3), 189-196.

Broderick, J. J. (1987). *Police in a time of change* (2nd ed.). Prospect Heights, IL: Waveland Press Inc.

Carter, D. L. & Sapp, A. D. (1991). *Police education & minority recruitment: The impact of a college requirement*. Washington, DC: Police Executive Research Forum.

Carter, D. L., Sapp, A. D., & Stephens, D. W. (1988). Higher education as a bona fide occupational qualification (BFOQ) for police: A blueprint. *American Journal of Police,* 7(2), 1-27.

Carter, D. L., Sapp, A. D., & Stephens, D. W. (1989). *The state of police education: Policy direction for the 21st Century*. Washington, DC: Police Executive Research Forum.

Cordner, G. W. (1989). The police on patrol. In D. J. Kenney (Ed.), *Police and policing: Contemporary issues* (pp. 60-71). New York: Praeger Publishers.

Cordner, G. W., Greene, J. R. & Bynum, T. S. (1982). Police human resource planning. In J. R. Greene (Ed.), *Managing police work: Issues and analysis* (pp. 53-74). Beverly Hills, CA: Sage Publication Inc.

Delattre, E. J. & Behan, C. J. (1991). Practical ideals for managing in the nineties: A perspective. In W. A. Geller (Ed.), *Local government police management* (3rd ed.) (pp. 537-553). Washington, DC: International City Management Association.

Fogelson, R. (1977). *Big city police*. Cambridge, MA: Harvard University Press.

Gaines, L. K. & Kappeler, V. E. (1992). Selection and testing. In G. W. Cordner & D. C. Hale (Eds.), *What works in policing? Operations and administration examined* (pp. 107-123). Cincinnati: Anderson Publishing Co.

Gaines, L. K., Costello, P., & Crabtree, A. (1989). Police selection testing: Balancing legal requirements and employer needs. *American Journal of Police*, 8(1), 137-152.

Gaines, L. K., Southerland, M. D., & Angell, J. E. (1991). *Police administration*. New York: McGraw-Hill.

Goldstein, H. (1977). *Policing a free society*. Cambridge, MA: Ballinger.

Goldstein, H. (1990). *Problem-oriented policing*. New York: McGraw-Hill Inc.

Greene, J. R. & Klockars, C. B. (1991). What police do. In C. B. Klockars & S. D. Mastrofski (Eds.), *Thinking about police: Contemporary readings* (pp. 107-123). New York: McGraw-Hill Inc.

Hale, D. C. (1992). Women in policing. In G. W. Cordner & D. C. Hale (Eds.), *What works in policing? Operations and administration examined* (pp. 125-142). Cincinnati: Anderson Publishing Inc.

Hayeslip, D. W., Jr. (1989). Higher education and police performance revisited: The evidence examined through meta-analysis. *American Journal of Police*, 8(2), 49-62.

Inwald, R. & Kenney, D. J. (1989). Psychological testing of police candidates. In D. J. Kenney (Ed.), *Police and policing: Contemporary issues* (pp. 34-42). New York: Praeger Publishers.

Johnson, E. E. (1990). Psychological tests used in assessing a sample of police and firefighter candidates: An update. *American Journal of Police*, 9(4), 85-92.

Kenney, D. J. & Watson, S. (1990). Intelligence and the selection of police recruits. *American Journal of Police*, 9(4), 39-64.

Martin, S. E. (1990). *On the move: The status of women in policing*. Washington, DC: Police Foundation.

Moore, M. H. & Stephens, D. W. (1991). *Beyond command and control: The strategic management of police departments*. Washington, DC: Police Executive Research Forum.

Muir, W. K., Jr. (1977). *Police: Streetcorner politicians.* Chicago: University of Chicago.

Nowicki, D. E., Sykes, G. W., & Eisenberg, T. (1991). Human resource management. In W. A. Geller (Ed.), *Local government police management* (3rd ed.) (pp. 272-307). Washington, DC: International City Management Association.

Schneid, T. D. & Gaines, L. K. (1991). The Americans with Disabilities Act: Implications for police administrators. *American Journal of Police,* 10(1), 47-58.

Sparrow, M. (1991). Information systems: A help or hindrance in the evolution of policing? *The Police Chief,* (April), 26-44.

Sullivan, P. S. (1989). Minority officers: Current issues. In R. G. Dunham and G. P. Alpert (Eds.), *Critical issues in policing: Contemporary readings* (pp. 331-345). Prospect Heights, IL: Waveland Press Inc.

Swanson, C. R., Territo, L., & Taylor, R. W. (1988). *Police administration: Structures, processes, and behavior* (2nd ed.). New York: Macmillan Publishing Co.

Vollmer, A. (1936). *The police and modern society.* Berkeley, CA: University of California. Reprinted 1971 by Patterson Smith, Montclair, NJ.

Walker, S. (1989). Paths to police reform — Reflections on 25 years of change. In D. J. Kenney (Ed.), *Police and policing: Contemporary issues* (pp. 271-284). New York: Praeger.

Walsh, W. F. (1990). Performance evaluation in small and medium police departments: A supervisory perspective. *American Journal of Police,* 9(4), 93-109.

Williams, J. & Sloan, R. (1990). *Turning concept into practice: The Aurora, Colorado story.* East Lansing, MI: School of Criminal Justice, Michigan State University.

Woods, A. (1919). *Policeman and public.* New Haven, CT: Yale University. Reprinted 1975 by Patterson Smith, Montclair, NJ.

Worden, R. E. (1990). A badge and a baccalaureate: Policies, hypotheses, and further evidence. *Justice Quarterly,* 7(3), 565-592.

Wright, B. S., Doerner, W. G., & Speir, J. C.   (1990).   Pre-employment psychological testing as a predictor of police performance during an FTO program. *American Journal of Police,* 9(4), 65-84.

Chapter 11

Technological and Material Resource Issues

Peter K. Manning

Introduction

This chapter reviews selectively changes that can be anticipated in policing in the next ten or fifteen years as a result of the introduction of new information technologies (systems that permit individuals to process, store, and retrieve data). After characterizing both internal and external sources of change in policing, police organization and modes of decision making, and the role of information and record keeping in policing practice, this review considers ethnographic research on the impact of information technologies on police roles and organization. A framework for assessing changes in police organizations as a result of the introduction of information technologies is outlined. Five assumptions that guide information use in policing organize a discussion of ethnographic observations on the uses and distribution of information. The chapter concludes with a few observations on implementation and tentative generalizations concerning the expected consequences of information technologies. Given the current state of research, the degree and kinds of change are as yet unclear. The weight of evidence suggests that traditional practices are changing.

Changes in Policing in the Past Twenty Years

Many changes have occurred in the external environment of American urban policing in the past twenty years.[1] These include changes in police budgets, the pattern of public support for their actions, their involvement with the media, and their links to reform groups. I review these in a manner that links setting changes in police information technologies to a context.

Internal and External Environments of Policing. The infrastructure of cities has deteriorated even as city budgets have grown massively, and the costs of governance exceed the capacity of the taxpayers to meet them. As a result, the police continue to face serious budget cuts, layoffs, and hiring freezes in many large cities. These affect morale and command loyalty, as well as increase personnel turnover.[2]

The degree of support for policing, especially in urban areas, has declined and concurrently the public's fears of violent crime and drugs have increased. In spite of police efforts, unanticipated and negative consequences have resulted.[3]

The media have played an ever larger role in policing and social control. The media focus on policing and police figures (see Ericson, 1989, 1991) has made the quality of police leadership and police leaders national issues. Police have developed sophisticated media skills and create "media reality" by manipulating the conventions of the media, e.g., providing predigested "sound bytes," granting "in-depth interviews" (three or more minutes in length), and "on-the scene" statements for mini-cameras, and providing formatted press "releases" (Ericson, 1989; Altheide and Snow, 1991). The police have orchestrated and amplified the media-driven "moral panics" associated with drugs and violent crime. The police have developed links with strong political allies and reform movements. Organizations such as PERF, The Police Foundation, NIJ, International Association of Chiefs of Police and the National Council of Mayors influence policing, shape police leadership, and provide rhetoric. Reform movements such as "community policing" (see chapters by Manning, Mastrofski, and Bayley in Greene and Mastrofski, 1988, and Trojanowicz and Bucqueroux, 1990), and problem-oriented policing (Goldstein, 1990) have had a wide, if not deep, impact on the rhetoric of policing in virtually every town in America. The degree to which police practice has changed remains to be established. In total, these external changes increased public awareness of the limits and constraints upon policing while sensitizing police to the need for reform (see Cordner, 1990).

Important changes are seen *within* policing as well. These include changes in the level of education of officers (Mastrofski, 1990), changes in the conception of police, the role of the law in policing, and the social roots of the police mandate.

Police are now viewed by many observers as businesses rather than public service agencies. One indication of this is the surfeit of mannered euphemisms and the jargon of business management now used to describe policing. Police chiefs are seen as analogous to CEOs, managing businesses and taking risks within a market context. Seminars are offered on "Advanced Management for Law Enforcement Executives" by Southwestern Law Enforcement Institute, Richardson, Texas on the Campus of the University of Texas, Dallas, and on "Law Enforcement Management" by the Law Enforcement Management Institute and Sam Houston State University. Policing is termed a "service," analyzed using the concepts of market strategies and tactics, viewed as competing for a precarious market niche, and called "corporate" in character (Moore and Trojanowicz, 1988). No longer a secure monopoly, police do in fact compete with private security firms, community action groups, and the media for the right to provide legitimate application of social control. Researchers raise questions of efficiency and effectiveness in policing (Clarke and Hough, 1980) and innovations are advocated on the grounds that they will increase efficiency or reduce policing costs (Hough, 1980a, 1980b; Tien and Colton, 1979).

Both criminal and civil law have grown as determinants of police practice. Procedural aspects of criminal law continue to shape policing practice. The role of the civil law has also expanded. Once protected from civil suits, police are now liable, and out of court settlements and legally required restitutions are now major expenditures in large cities (Mastrofski, 1990).

As a result of these changes, the traditional (some might say "sacred," Manning, 1977) bases of the police mandate — commitment to maintaining the collective good, serving with honor and loyalty, and observing tradition — are in conflict with pragmatic obligations, concern for avoiding legal liabilities and civil suits, and budgetary constraints. The mandate is less "tightly coupled" (Weick, 1979) to society's moral core, and loosely linked to considerations of practical management and administration.

Demand for Policing and Communications Technology. Having reviewed the above, it should be pointed out that one of the most important trends in policing in the past twenty-five years is the rising demand for police services. An endemic issue in policing is how to ration and distribute a collective good to which all have a right, in the context of literally and figuratively shrinking resources (Samuelson, 1954; Lipsky, 1980). In the past thirty years or so, a variety of technologies, ranging from weapons to computer software, have been adopted by police, but the most important, arguably, is information technology.[4]

The police have always viewed advanced communications, from the first telephone to mobile two-way radios, hand-held radios, and computers, as a solution to the problem of responding equitably to public demands and crime control.   Since 1967 the police have attempted to deal with rising demand by increasing their communicative capacity by means of computer-assisted dispatching.   They sought, often with federal governmental assistance, to develop enhanced means of receiving and processing calls and to produce systematic, patterned, and considered response to these calls.

This focus on communication was keynoted by the President's Commission's *Report on Science and Technology* (1967).   This document, written primarily by computer scientists and engineers, claimed that information technology, namely computer-assisted dispatching, would reduce many of the vexing problems of policing, including crime control, strategic planning, evaluation and record keeping. Originally focused on crime control, on the grounds that more rapid police response would increase the probability of an arrest and thus deter villains and reduce crime, researchers continued to shift focus and rationales (reviewed below) to achieve an impact on policing.   In point of fact, information technologies, the means by which "data" or "raw facts" are transformed into useful and actionable information, have an enormous and as yet unrealized potential to shape the future of policing.

The Role of Technology in Organizational Change

Although technology is often defined in a restrictive sense as the material or physical means by which work is accomplished, any technology also has a symbolic dimension because it is defined and acted toward on the bases of symbols and language. Meanings arise from the terms used to label the technology.   This labeling process produces general meanings of technology, shapes questions of agency and purpose, defines spatial-temporal uses of technology, and builds selves. Let us review these quickly.

Labels give technology meaning. The imagery of a kind, benevolent despot who knows and sees all is evoked when the term, "big brother," a common term for the computer system in Britain, is used. The discourse used to define the purposes of technology also outlines the parameters of discussion. For example, the language of command and control and efficient decision making set technology's political and economic meanings in policing. The physical settings where it is housed, for example in the front dashboard area of a police vehicle, constrain or limit alternate or additional uses of that space. Finally, the process of labeling technology produces selves, or ways people define their own actions.   Officers in a British force, finding themselves responding to an increasing number of radio-transmitted calls, referred to themselves as "blue mice." They viewed themselves as acting in a frenetic, almost random manner, responding to unknown pressures and forces outside their control. Technology, in these ways, is socially constituted and granted meaning in an organizational context (Pfaffenberger, 1991; Barley, 1986).

Clearly, the physical properties of any technology will have instrumental consequences; constrain tasks, making them easier or more difficult to achieve in a given time period; shape roles, or expectations of work performance; and modify interactions. Technology, such as the omnipresent two-way police radio, mediates face-to-face communications. However, ". . . as one moves away from the 'man-machine' interface to higher levels of analysis, it becomes increasingly untenable to claim that a technology's ramifications are reducible to its physical properties" (Barley, 1988).

Technology has symbolic as well as instrumental consequences. Technology has the potential to alter a field of authority relations because it can increase or decrease choice, or autonomy, increase or decrease a span of control, or provide on-line supervisory information (Barley, 1988). A new technology brings with it new skill requirements for some workers, even while it may "de-skill" others. Any technological innovation introduces new uncertainties in the work flow and in role relationships. It may also stimulate responses designed either to restore the status quo or to modify it (Pfaffenberger, 1991). In these ways, technology can alter social relations within an organization.

Focus and Limitations of This Chapter

Some qualifications are necessary to place this review in proper research context. The evidence considered is drawn primarily from fieldwork and published systematic evaluation studies.[5]

Researchers have variously approached the analysis of technology. According to the conventional wisdom, some researchers and practitioners begin with the available technologies and speculate logically about their potential for modifying or changing policing (see Larson, 1989). This position is often hopeful and prescriptive in the sense that it outlines a set of problems for which, in theory, the technology has solutions. The position adopted here, an alternative to the focus on potential, begins with the known constraints of police organizational structure. These include the roles and tasks of officers, especially patrol officers, patterns of police deciding, the nature of information flow through the organization, its storage, and retrieval. The primary objective is to assess the known evidence of technology's effects when applied to central or thematic problems of policing. This latter approach requires assembling ethnographic knowledge and close observation of the actual workings of police. Ironically perhaps, such an ethnographic approach is conservative, emphasizing contradictions between rational plans and practices, and restraints, and seeking to illuminate the bases of the *status quo ante*.

The studies cited here are systematic and analytic comparative evaluations. Single case studies, descriptions of the workings of information technology, and nonevaluative works are omitted. Some general police ethnographies are relevant for their insights into police command and practices (Skolnick, 1966; Brown, 1981; Rubinstein, 1973; Wilson, 1968; Van Maanen, 1983; Davis, 1983; Reiss, 1971; Westley, 1970; Ericson, 1981, 1982). Only one detailed, comparative cross-cultural study of police communications exists (Manning, 1988), although some comparative works are of seminal importance (Punch, 1983; Wetheritt, 1989; Clarke and Hough, 1980). Unfortunately, available reviews of information technology in policing (Tien and Colton, 1979; Colton et al., 1979) are somewhat dated, and contain no analyses of the direct or indirect consequences of information technology on the social organization of policing.

Within the set of focused studies of police communication systems (PCS), a limited range of types of systems is included. These are basically two- and three-tiered systems in which messages are received by an operator and then forwarded to units (two-tiered) or received by operators, sent to zone controllers or dispatchers, and then broadcast to officers (three-tiered). The physical locations of the subsystems within a PCS also vary. Operators and dispatchers may be closely joined in a large room sending jobs to officers, or operators can be separated and dispatchers and officers joined in physical proximity (in precincts, for example).

The information technology employed in these studies varies. Not only do the computers used vary in speed, memory, capacity, and other engineering design features, they are products of different manufacturers. Departments sometimes find themselves with incompatible equipment, bought at different times, or with design features that never worked or were never developed because of budget constraints. These technical matters are not reviewed here.

Little research has been done on public expectations of computer-assisted dispatch (and 911 more specifically) and the consequences of installing such a system for the perceived quality of police responses to the public. Some research has been published on reasons why, when, and from where the police are called, and the patterns of call processing (Spelman and Brown, 1981). The impact of several social factors on demand (primarily, but not exclusively, telephone calls from the public) is not well understood. The impacts of variously organized social networks from which calls arise (alarms, internal calls, "hot spots" from which a disproportionate number of calls arise [Sherman, 1987], and the general public), population density, the number of phones per 1,000 people, increase in the number of phones, and ecological factors on patterning response (compare Bercal, 1970) are only sketchily understood. How these external factors affect work loads at various points within a PCS, and classification routines and practices is not known.

One of the reasons it is difficult to establish the impact of external sources on demand is that the internal system "buffers" the organization from the environment, and screens and reduces the load to a manageable level for officers. My estimate, based on work in three police communications systems, is that the operators and dispatchers reduce the potential by about 75 percent. That is, about 25 percent of the calls answered by operators are assigned to officers. What proportion officers actually attend varies, but a good estimate is about one-half.

The *interpretive work* accomplished in the PCS is of central importance in this buffering process, and is a window into police practices. Interpretive work requires quickly grasping (in thirty seconds to two minutes) both the *core* (words or phrases that define the meaning of the message) and *fringe* (contributory, but not essential aspects of the message for police purposes) meanings of a communication, classifying a message in a formal system of categories (e.g., 245 "disturbance"), and acting upon it. Interpretive work done by operators and dispatchers (see Gilsinan, 1989; Jorgenson, 1981; Heal and Ekblom, 1981; Ekblom and Heal, 1982; Manning, 1988; Percy and Scott, 1985; Shearing, 1984) is not addressed in detail here, nor is the complex and nuanced understanding of patrol officers of calls, shaped by the occupational culture, explicated (see Manning, 1988a, chapters 4 and 5 for details). The manipulation and control of types of output, such as arrests, is also detailed elsewhere (Coleman and Bottomley, 1979; Seidman and Couzens, 1973; McCleary et al., 1982).

In many studies of PCS, the interest is in improving public policy, or reducing errors, or exploring the functions of the various role players in the PCS (see Shearing, 1984; Percy and Scott, 1985; Ekblom and Heal, 1982). The aim of this chapter is to illuminate with ethnographic data the workings of the PCS. Even with the introduction of new information technologies, the interpretive work accomplished by patrol officers is the field in which police decisions are made and from which police information is generated.

Given these limitations, what inferences can be drawn concerning how information technology shapes police organizations?

Police Information Technologies

Information technologies in policing include the hardware and software that permit (1) centralized call collection, usually based on a three-digit number such as 911 or 999; (2) computer-assisted dispatching (CAD), which uses computers and functionaries to screen, classify, prioritize, and distribute calls to units (most large urban departments now collect and queue calls using computers, and have adopted some form of CAD);

(3) management information systems (MIS) employed for collection and analysis of data for strategic, short- and long-term planning, creation of positions or functions, and determining the depth of personnel assigned to given functions; (4) computer networking that facilitates data sharing via direct links between state and local police computers and FBI computers in the National Crime Information Center (NCIC) (Tien and Colton, 1979; Stevens, 1989). It took many years for these innovations to spread, and even now, they are restricted to large and middle-size cities.

The first full-time computer-assisted system of dispatching was installed in St. Louis, Missouri, in the 1960s. These early systems featured a two-part process. First, a telephone operator, not usually a sworn officer, screened calls and took handwritten notes (usually including the name and address of the caller and the nature of the incident) about accepted calls on a small card. Second, either the telephonist or a dispatcher, usually a sworn officer, dispatched the call to a unit using two way radio.

A second innovation occurred in the early 1970s. Funded by LEAA, a few large departments (New York, Detroit, and Chicago among them) experimented with automated CAD systems that utilized models of queueing and stacking of requests for service. The program was designed to select the nearest available unit for assignment to a job. These programs were soon abandoned because they could not meet design specifications. Nevertheless, by 1980 the principle of automated dispatching was widely adopted. At least 800 911 systems are now in place, and a 1981 PERF survey found that 45 percent of the larger departments used it (Mastrofski, 1990:42).

The third important innovation was the introduction of enhanced 911 (E911) systems. Around 1980 departments, among them Tampa-St Petersburg, Florida, and Wichita, Kansas, acquired programs that displayed on the operator's screen the phone number and address from which a call was made (Larson, 1989). By 1989, 89 of the 125 largest cities in the United States had E911, and some 36 states are required by law to adopt it in the next few years (Larson, 1989). Currently, these systems have several functions. CAD serves to allocate assignments quickly. It is also designed to permit police operators, dispatchers, and officers to create useful potentially applied information from "raw data." Information systems of this type can be used to gather and store in retrievable format(s) information about a caller (phone number, address), the call (time of day, day of the week, etc.), the operator (identification number, time spent processing the incident), and the incident (once accepted by the operator), its routing, assignment, and disposal. They also serve to allocate once-screened calls to dispatchers responsible for a given area of the city, record assignments and current work load of officers, and permit brief (a few weeks at most) storage of records on a mainframe computer. In addition, E911 permits an operator to characterize the call, the address from which it was made, and display data on the screen for all previous calls to the ten-block area from which the current call came. The operator's classification of those calls, the assignment made, and any police response is also shown. Phone lines can be held open while a response is made to an address. An enhanced system simplifies data gathered from distressed callers. In effect, message-call processing functions to screen, evaluate, and assign work to officers, and to permit on-line or retrospective re-creation of some aspects of message processing and police action: that which is written, spoken, and recorded in some fashion.

Some anecdotal evidence has been published about the rise in traffic tickets written, and in the number of police inquiries made to central communications as a result of CAD, but no systematic cost-benefit analysis of a police CAD system is available (see Tien and Colton, 1979). The only systematic evaluation of CAD was based on the extent to which the system met design specifications and longevity requirements. The evaluation concluded that the CAD installations did not yield promised results (Colton and Herbert, 1978; Tien and Colton, 1979).[6]

A political consensus on the potential utility of CAD remained nevertheless, and a series of experiments involving aspects of computer-driven policing were devised and funded. These experiments, focused on patrol activities, discovered the minimal impact of rapid response on arrests (Spelman and Brown, 1981) and citizen satisfaction (Pate et al., 1976). Hypercube or Patrol Car Allocation Models of dispatching designed to track and allocate units to calls by proximity to the incident failed to become fully operational and were never adapted (Tien and Colton, 1979). It was then suggested that patterns of supervised patrol would focus police officers and increase their "productivity" — it did not (cf. Tien et al., 1978) — and that combining CAD with vehicle locators would increase officer safety — it failed (cf. Larson et al., 1976; Tien, 1977). Rather sophisticated differential response systems, based on prioritization of calls and aligning response on the severity and urgency of the event, were tried. They have produced promising results (Sumrall et al., 1981; Worden, 1989). Schemes designed to "suppress" or discourage calls for service (Sherman et al., 1989), seem unlikely to control citizen demand. Some technological innovations, such as mobile digital terminals (MDT in many large cities), laptop computers (used in Los Angeles and in Houston), cellular phones, and artificial intelligence and expert systems, have not been subject to published evaluations. Applications of information technologies to detective work and drug enforcement are still under evaluation (see Manning, forthcoming).

The Social Organization of Police Information

There are three major sources of influence on the nature and amount of information that police gather, process, and store; police organization, occupational culture, and the information technology employed. First, policing is ecologically dispersed work (see Jermier and Berkes, 1979; McNamara, 1967) carried out in a "rule-oriented" structure. Historically, a large proportion of the uniformed personnel are concentrated in the lowest rank and distributed in space to maximize the probability that they will encounter or respond to citizens' requests. The work is carried out by rather low-skilled, unsupervised, largely male lower participants who exercise wide discretion. Almost any task can be performed by any officer with very brief training. Second, police occupational cultures, not reviewed in detail here, are an important determinant of police behavior (see Manning, 1977; Worden and Mastrofski, 1989; Jermeir et al., 1991). Third, the primary raw materials processed in policing are human beings, human interactions, and group relationships. Police traditionally rely on verbal skills, persuasion, and violence to accomplish their ends. More sophisticated means of communicating have been used primarily to manage officers and improve the administration of police work, rather than to enhance the quality of police-community relations. Be that as it may, any technology or technique, for example, for establishing the "solvability" of cases, for checking outstanding warrants using remote digital terminals in patrol cars, or for converting files and records to computer files, will alter role relationships. In order to view the impact of technology on the social organization of police work, the systematic use of information in deciding and interactions with new technologies have to be considered jointly.

Police Deciding. The known patterns of police decision making are profound and stable, and constitute fundamentals of the occupation (see Manning and Hawkins, 1989). Patterns of police decision making determine (1) the nature, quality, and amount of raw data that are (2) "processed" or converted into meaningful information, and (3) marked as officially known and stored in the institutional memory, files, and/or data banks. Officers' common-sense assumptions and practices screen and filter information entered into any formal record-keeping system, thus shaping what is taken to be primary data.

The information considered command and control or "operations relevant," is based on "street decisions." The quality of subsequent police decisions, in detective work, in other specialized units, and at the command level, is a function of the quality and texture of the information so generated. Of course, all officers, having received a report from the patrol division, can seek and create new information and often do. However, the initial decision to arrest someone places the person in the criminal justice system and this arrest requires further processing and decision making by other officers, e.g., whether to charge and how to charge, interviews by detectives concerning other crimes, further detective investigation, court appearances, and so on. The gatekeeping function of the patrol officer is fundamental in this respect, even if additional information is sought and obtained by other officers.

Police Information. Any information is only as good as its theory. Police information is based on what might be called "fundamental and taken for granted knowledge" (Bittner, 1990). This knowledge is believed to be constituted from the context-dependent facts gathered on a scene and understood best — in most veridical fashion — by those who attended that particular scene. The phrase, "you had to be there" is a truism for most officers. For example, in a domestic disturbance, officers can define an incident variously as a "family fight," "assault," or "neighborhood disturbance" or reporting the outcome in generalities by labeling the incident as "closed, no action required." As a result, quite a range of detail can be omitted or reported, depending on the label used to gloss the event (Davis, 1983; Ferraro, 1989).

This fundamental knowledge also embeds the formal reporting system. While police computer records purport to be universal, trans-situational, and comparable over time, police knowledge is substantive, detailed, concrete, temporally bounded, and particularistic in nature. These two types of knowledge are in uneasy alliance in policing. This contradiction between street knowledge and decisions and formal records and command decisions is not lost on officers. It is not possible to report all that was done and why, nor to rule out the various possibilities for further investigation. Command decisions often require making sense of detailed officers' reports and abstracted planning and budget documents (Mayo, 1985), yet these contain very different kinds of knowledge. Criminologists often uncritically use one as a surrogate for the other, and the validity of police crime statistics remains one of the central problems of criminological research (see McCleary et al., 1982).

The installation of huge computers for record keeping not withstanding, the information retained in police departments can be characterized as systematically decentralized, individualized, and quite personalized. Police information is nowhere organized into a uniform, formatted and comprehensive set of cross-referenced retrievable data files available to all officers (Bittner, 1990).[7] The occupational culture elevates the importance of the individual officer's actions even while seeing police work as teamwork. While the officer may cooperate occasionally within a widely dispersed network of invisible colleagues, the focus on individual actions sustains the pattern of information retention and secrecy at the bottom. Information is gathered in an environment officers perceive as risky or as having the potential to produce negative outcomes. Among other things — such as the degree to which features of the technology reduce paperwork, provide a means to conceal potentially troublesome or risky decisions, is easier to apply (such as the use of faxed warrants), or is fun — technology is assessed by patrol officers according to its potential to reduce personal risk. The job is learned as an apprenticeship, so notions about the nature of knowledge and risk are passed on from role models to young rookies in the context of direct encounters with the public. Paperwork, because it reflects a abstracted and generalized perspective rather than the clinical or context-dependent nature of information gathered at the original scene, is generally discredited or distrusted. Personalized authority and information, when combined with secretive guarding of knowledge, and an exaggerated emphasis upon work tasks ("jobs") that are closed (quickly) without paperwork, means that police street decisions are largely unreviewed and probably unreviewable.

There are additional reasons why police records are often truncated, elliptical, and uninformative. Mastrofski writes (personal communication, August 1991), "One is simply the time and trouble it takes to document what you do. [Another is] . . . the more information you provide, the greater the likelihood you will get in trouble for what you did. As is the case with income tax forms the police maxim is 'provide the least necessary to satisfy the authorities.'" Policy is rare in policing, and matters usually handled informally on the basis of tacit understandings are explicated or refined retrospectively; after a consequential event has transpired. Extant policy is minimal. One officer told me wryly that his chief had two unwritten policies: "Don't fire warning shots" and "Don't be a dummy." The latter principle would appear to cover most decisions, albeit without direction. Policy flows "downward," while most decisions are taken on the basis of facts gathered at the officer and sergeant level. Little information flows up the line by way of "feedback," correction, or validation. On the other hand, attempts to control or limit high-speed pursuits and constrain the use of fatal force by policy seem to work.[8]

No formal theory of human nature or administrative function drives information gathering and analysis, nor clarifies the conditions under which information will be entered into the police communications system. An example of the unwillingness to speculate in this way or develop a basis for information gathering is police refusal to develop systematic understanding of the causes of crime or disorder. The chief of police in Detroit, Mr. Stanley Knox, in response to a wave of auto thefts carried out through threats with weapons to drivers, said, "I am too busy fighting this new crime wave [the auto thefts] to worry about what causes it" (WKAR Radio, East Lansing, Michigan, August 30, 1991). Another Detroit officer was quoted in the *Detroit Free Press* (September 1, 1991), likening the same series of thefts to ". . . a fire that just has to burn itself out." Often, information is gathered and merely stored without reference to its potential for planning, policy, or evaluation. It is possible, as drug intelligence systems are put in place, that a clear rationale for information on a given network of importers and dealers might stimulate more general rules for data entry and use (see footnote 8, above).

In summary, in an important sense, the street basis of most deciding, the low quality of information entered into formal records, the absence of extensive policy guidelines, and a theory of information use consistent with applying knowledge outside the street context tend to mitigate centralized information use. Unlike the Weberian model of bureaucracy that features centralized, formatted, and accessible records and files, policing remains informationally highly decentralized (see McNamara, 1967). Information clusters into a few richly textured and coherent islands isolated from other islands of information. Only under certain specified conditions, usually when a crisis draws together police resources, does police information become accessible, understood, generally shared, reproducible knowledge held collectively in organization records. In an important sense, police commanders eschew responsibility for forward planning and rationalized data bases. The unwillingness of command personnel to specify in advance the nature of information needed and to ensure that it is gathered and processed means that most police information remains aggregated, context-dependent knowledge. This, of course, reduces their responsibility to supervise and blurs lines of accountability.

Impacts of Technology on the Social Organization of Police Work

Information technologies were introduced into policing, as was noted above, as a result of decisions made by scientists, politicians, and civil servants in conjunction with police command personnel (Hough, 1980b). Their belief was that increased use of available information technology, some of it adopted from the military, would enhance police efficiency and effectiveness. Exploration of the impacts of information technologies in an ethnographic context will perhaps illuminate why and how these decisions were flawed.

Assumptions Made About Information Technologies. The central assumptions of those who sponsor the introduction of information technologies into police are that (1) *rational systems development occurs* (Hirschheim and Newman, 1991) and (2) *information gathering, processing and transmittal and organized, long-term rationality guide all organizational actions* (See Hough, 1980a, 1980b). In general, information has been seen as key to police operations (Willmer, 1970), and the basis for explanations of the number, nature, and quality of police "outputs" such as "crime," "seizures," "traffic tickets," and "clearances." Virtually all administrative literature assumes that information is the basis for police actions. Researchers have assumed also that police decisions are taken on the basis of information (for a balanced overview on this question, see Reiss, 1974). Perhaps more accurately, one should make alternative guiding assumptions about the role of technology in organizations. Questioning these assumptions suggests further investigation of the following ideas: (1) The use of messages, files, cases, reports, and records in police work is based on sanctioned traditional police practice and organizational interests, not on the informational content of a message; (2) information flow, as information and systems theories of organization might claim (Hirschheim and Newman, 1991), is not the primary basis for organizational structure; (3) self-reflexive officers, actors who adjust their actions to the imagined consequences of their choices, take an active and self-interested role in shaping and subjectively constructing the uses of information technology; (4) unanticipated consequences of adaptive organizational practices play central roles in all technological innovations; (5) efforts will be made by those who use it to constrain technology to reduce its threat to their power position, or at least to ensure that it confirms in a new way the *status quo*. These five assumptions reflect a social constructionist view of technology, and are attuned to the observed consequences of officers' definitions and routine uses of it.

Ethnographic Evidence on the Impact of Information Technologies. The above-mentioned assumptions guide this section of the chapter on the impact of information technologies on police roles.

1.   **Information use in policing is based on matters other than the veridicality and accuracy of information.** Data or calls from the public are transformed by the police into workable and useful information. Manning (1988) and Ericson (1982) show how this happens. "Raw data" are first processed (classified, encoded, interpreted, placed in computer files) into primary information by operators and dispatchers. It is then converted into "secondary information," when used by detectives. Command decisions, in theory, are based on "tertiary information," the abstract, generalized policy-based analytic information that MIS and CAD provide. In each of these transformations, but especially the first one, information becomes, metaphorically at least, "police property." In other words, calls, or "citizen demand," are reshaped by the organization and police responses are based on these new interpretations.

This is most dramatically seen when calls from the public are reclassified either at the scene or subsequently (or without an officer ever having visited the scene) using euphemisms like "all quiet on arrival," "services rendered," or "advice given" (Meyer, 1974; Davis, 1983; Meehan, 1989). These glosses serve to cover the actions, if any, taken by the police. They are organizational ploys designed to avoid accountability, reduce work load, and maintain control of the pacing and quality of patrol work. Meehan (1989) has shown, conversely, that work of a particular type can be easily generated by officers if they convert "nuisance" and "noise" complaint calls received by radio into "gang calls." They can then attend these calls, take the necessary actions, and generate reports on their efforts to control and suppress "gang activities." Patrol officers thus display to their supervisors, politicians, and the public that "juvenile gang control" is being accomplished.

In *Narcs' Game* (Manning, 1980) it was shown that the information received by drug police was evaluated on the degree to which a source or source's source was trusted. A distrusted informant (source) or a distrusted piece of data from a known and trusted source would "contaminate" the entire message. Untrustworthy leads from phone calls were dismissed out of hand. The manipulation of trust works in another way within policing. If an officer in the London Metropolitan Police Department had a "shakey" affidavit for a search warrant, he or she would take it to a judge who was "pro police" and was inclined to sign anything for which the police vouched. Hierarchical relations produce apparent compliance that looks like trust. This is exemplified by a recent Detroit case. An officer received a call from an anonymous informant about a drug dealer. She agreed to say that the information came from a numbered and named informant (in order to have an affidavit signed by a judge) when her sergeant, in effect, ordered her to do so (*Detroit Free Press*, August 17, 1991). She and the sergeant were eventually convicted of perjury when the named informant refused to testify in court that he had given this information. Observers (Cain, 1973; Manning, 1977; Chatterton, 1975; and Hunt and Manning, 1991) found that both British and American officers felt that they owed loyalty to sergeants and inspectors and frequently covered for them by lying and omitting pertinent information. Chatterton (1991) claims that "It is implicitly understood that personnel above the rank of Chief Inspector expect to be protected from the contradictions and ambiguities inherent in routine police work and from the knowledge of the practical solutions adopted to deal with them." Thus, constables operate on a belief that they would only pass on information if there was a need to know established. If handled on the ground, or at the scene, skillfully, an incident will not rise to other levels in the bureau. Solutions are found at the lowest possible level. Thus, the few incidents that do rise are not representative of information known and problems solved on the ground, and in fact conceal the range of routine police work. Incidents that come to command attention are seen from below as signs of their failure to contain them, rather than as the necessary products of observing proper reporting procedures. As a consequence, supervision arises *ex post facto*, and is seen as unpredictable and capricious.

If one considers these examples further, it can be amply appreciated that by avoiding problems, keeping a low profile, and not "rocking the boat," officers avoid trouble. Failing to report serves the apparent dual organizational function of "protecting the higher ups" and "covering one's back."

2. Information use is not the exclusive basis for organizational structure. The police organization is designed to maximize the number of officers on patrol, rather than to engage them in information processing and analysis. Specialized units such as vice and narcotics are usually placed under the chief directly as staff units. They are not directly linked informationally to other detective units nor to the information generated by CAD from the patrol division, unless an arrest involving drugs is made. (Typically, credit for any seizures and arrests are given to patrol.) Files on drugs arrests and charges, affidavits and search warrants served, informants and payments, and seizures are kept separately in the unit, not stored on computers with general access, and often systematically kept incomplete or inaccurate to preserve unit secrecy and obscure plans and targets. Contact with other agencies, unless a task force has been formed, is *ad hoc.* Thus, the flow of information does not structure the placement of the unit. It would appear that the fear of corruption and the need to preserve secrecy are the primary reasons for the placement of vice units.

Chatterton (1991) evaluated officers in a community policing scheme in five divisions in the north of England who had too little time to assess the information they were given (in the form of printouts of incidents made by dispatchers). Furthermore, they had little inclination to analyze it in detail and were given no rewards for doing so. The same point can be made generally about police patrol officers; they have no desks, no quiet place in which to write reports, and no phones to which they have regular access. They are restricted in large part to their patrol vehicles or use space when and if it is available. This suggests that the police organization valorizes action over information, on the spot completion of tasks, and devalues paperwork other than that that can be completed with dispatch at the scene or shortly thereafter.

3.   Organization members take an active, self-interested role in using, shaping, and subjectively constructing information technology. In two drug police organizations, Manning (1980) found that in the absence of other rewards and supervisory pressure, officers would not create files on informants, register them with the department, or use available computer information to augment their personal styles of enforcement. Drug enforcement information, even if recorded and filed, did not become part of the departmental stock of available knowledge at hand until charges were filed. If the central resources of a drug unit — affidavits, evidence, seizures, and money — are not controlled centrally, individualized, ineffectual enforcement results. Further, as a result of this private knowledge base, link cannot be made between drug crimes and other crimes, and between drug problems and other order problems (Goldstein, 1990).

In 1981 the then commissioner of the Metropolitan Police (London), Sir Kenneth Newman, devised committees to set objectives and goals across the vast Metropolitan Police organization. The intent was to use these goal statements to assess and evaluate unit performance. Officers sitting on the goals and objectives committees in South London used rules of thumb such as predicting a 5 percent increase in arrests, a 10 percent increase in licensing visits, and the like. They did this in full knowledge that the average increases in previous years were higher than the figures they set to be attained.

In the English community policing research evaluation, Chatterton (1991) found that police constables did not use information from the micro-computer to set their objectives or evaluate performances:

> In fact, when they were interviewed about the quality of the information provided by [the] system relating to crime, area constables were highly critical of it. Yet they were content to accept the system. They were unable to target effectively [types of crimes they were to try to prevent] but they could still claim local knowledge to set objectives, content in the knowledge that supervisors were similarly disadvantaged and hence could not criticize their choice of objective.

In addition, supervisors on all save one subdivision avoided using the new system, preferring to remain ignorant while expecting the constables to conform to the demands of the information system. Neither higher nor lower participants changed their behavior. The lower participants were not effectively monitored, while the higher participants could rest easy behind the facade of electronic supervision.[9]

4.   Unanticipated consequences of change are important aspects of technological innovation. Any technological feature is shaped by organizational context or assumptions about the organization's mandate, strategies, and tactics. Technological work can be symbolically redefined and transformed by treating it not as a means to achieving organizational objectives, but as a source of expression. Any feature of an information technology can be redefined and used playfully (the experience of playing video games will serve young officers well in policing!) (Manning, 1988).

The Automatic Vehicle Locator (AVL), installed in St. Louis, Missouri, was designed to provide a sector quadrant location for any car so equipped. Evaluation found serious flaws (Larson et al., 1976). Cars were "lost" and could not be relocated. Dispatchers had to make radio calls to inquire about the car's position. The geographic location of the vehicles had to be reentered on the grid. Interviews with officers revealed the unseen dynamics behind the recurrent pattern of "lost" patrol vehicles. Despite the management's definition of the AVL as a means of ensuring officer protection and of checking on units that had not reported recently or that might be in unknown danger, officers perceived the AVL as a "Big Brother" surveillance device. They determined to foil it dramatically. The St. Louis officers discovered that if they switched off the motor on a bridge, the car's signal would disappear at the communications center and they would be "lost," and could not be "found" until they reported their current location. Obviously, once off the grid, it was possible for officers to respond and reposition themselves by reporting a false location, and continue to be a phantom misleading "blip" on the dispatcher's screen.

The aim of integrating the information and record-keeping systems of the police is not carried out in practice because, as mentioned above, detectives are not required to log in and out on the CAD system nor report their activities. By standing outside the system, they maintain their special higher status and maintain loose coupling with patrol activities.

5. **Every effort will be made to constrain and routinize the technology in traditional forms.** Mobile digital terminals (MDTs) were introduced in several large American police departments such as Dallas, Detroit, Houston, and Los Angeles in the mid-1970s. They were expected to increase officer efficiency, reduce paperwork, and reshape police response by encouraging proactive policing. In practice, it appears that officers use MDT much as they do the radio. They use it to inquire of the Department of Motor Vehicles about current vehicle ownership, registration, or the validity of a driving license; to inquire of the police department about an arrest record or outstanding warrant, or to ask that a "records check" be done with NCIC. These are requested because the computer is trusted to produce speedily useful and crime-related data. Ostensively, MDTs are faster, and speed is taken to indicate efficiency. (Tom Peters, in a PBS program on WKAR, East Lansing, Michigan, August 15, 1991, said, "Life is speed," referring to the virtue of speed in increasing efficiency.) It is likely that MDT will increase computer transactions because officers can "inquire" about a "suspicious vehicle" without stopping a citizen. They can play the computer, submitting data hoping for a "hit" — an outstanding warrant, a stolen car, a fleeing felon.

Detectives in a suburban Texas police department use computers as word processors to write their summary statements of investigations and to enter them directly by way of the mainframe into the police records system. When the deputy chief in charge of investigators was asked what detectives did with the time saved as a result, he answered: "They work on their other cases." In other words, more of the same. Most detective work is paper processing that seeks to dispose in the first instance of those cases with little evidence or no witnesses, and then to work on those seen as soluble (Ericson, 1981). Differential attention to cases is determined by internal factors judged by investigators (Brandl, 1991). As a result of computer technology, police may more quickly dispose of some cases and shift available time to more difficult cases. The question of whether time is gained as a result of more efficient inquiries or computer-generated statements remains moot. Evidence suggests that in the absence of changes in supervision and the pattern of rewards, the underlying character of police work — reactive, law enforcement focused, a historical response to suspected violations — will remain unchanged (Goldstein, 1990).

Finally, since this proposition or guiding assumption assumes that the technology does not radically alter the *status quo*, it should be noted that efforts are always made to alter the status quo by those with less power and to convert it to their own, change-oriented purposes.

Observations on Implementation

This ethnographic evidence contains some guidance for specifying the conditions under which information technologies will alter or shape police practice. Thus, one can comment on the ways in which endemic issues of technology can be managed to reduce their human costs. It is assumed that information technologies, combined with three-digit numbers and regional integration of dispatching services such as police, fire, and medical, will continue and that smaller cities will be required soon to devise computer-based information systems. If this is the case, what lessons can be learned from this review of ethnographic research on the impact of information technologies? It is clear that the assumptions of the officers on the ground must guide the design of the data gathering and inputting processes. As long as the nature of fundamental knowledge remains unchanged, ways must be found to capture this in sustainable record systems. It is possible that dictaphones, oral debriefing, or required, systematic training in computer use (especially in using laptops and MDTs) will facilitate more valid data. Given this, simple, context-based (not numerical) dispatching from local stations or precincts where face-to-face interaction can be maximized between officers and dispatchers is needed. The more clarification, feedback, and information given, the better. Reducing pass-through time and emphasizing speed is unnecessary in nonemergent situations and counterproductive in emergent situations.

Organizational integration is required. Specialized units and intelligence must be interfaced systematically with CAD data, and these data analyzed using analytic concepts rather than by organizational conventions such as incidents printed out by shift, day, time, month, or precinct. These categories have little meaning for establishing patterns of crime prevention or enhancing the capacity for order maintenance. Supervision must be based on detailed knowledge of events and actions derived in the first instance from CAD. However, and more important, supervisors should rely on independent reports, debriefings, and face-to-face interactions. Electronic supervision alone is inadequate. There is danger that CAD will erode the authority of sergeants and undermine the duties of lieutenants because it appears to entail close monitoring and surveillance, and gives supervisory authority to the dispatcher in effect. CAD and its capacity for electronic surveillance does not obviate the role of supervisors, it requires new kinds of training and knowledge to carry out supervision properly.

If organizational changes are to be affected, rewards must be made available to those with computer and analytic skills. Efforts should be made to retain these officers in patrol positions.

Conclusions

Changes in policing come slowly. Although the observed changes in the environment of American urban policing continue to alter budgets and resources, it is likely that information technologies will eventually substantially modify the material base of policing and, eventually, its practices. Because technology is social, constituted, defined, and acted toward as it is symbolized, it mediates between the material base of the organization and social relations. Thus, changes in technology, resources, and personnel will flow through traditional channels and be used in the established manner. It is likely, then, that the endemic issues of policing resources — the allocation of material and personnel to provide greater security for life and property as well as the sense of safety — remain.

The pattern of police deciding, the use and definitions of relevant information, and the constitution of technology sustain the discretion and autonomy of officers on the ground. Thus far, evidence suggests that officers use information technology in line with traditional practices. They reify the structure of authority, secrecy, and mistrust extant in policing. While the amount of data possessed by police has increased, it is not clear that information has. Converting data into information requires a theory of some kind to specify the uses and objectives of gathering or storing any bit, and to guide the transformation process. Thus, it seems likely that the character of and the *social distribution of the stock of knowledge remains substantially unchanged.*

It has long been argued that power lies at the bottom of the police hierarchy (Wilson, 1968). It is not clear how new information technologies have altered this. The balance of power within the organization may be reshaped. Most of the innovations seem designed to increase the surveillance of the officers and to increase the input of raw data. However, opportunities to use various channels of communication, to increase skills, to redefine the meaning of information, and to alter strategies to expand worker autonomy, all could offset increased managerial controls (Crozier, 1972). This review suggests that the underlying coding of information by officers (the rules they use to organize the meaning of the calls) is quite resistant to change. Given that they redefine information and give little feedback to dispatchers, there is an inherent conservatism in officers' practices that is not entirely overcome by the overlay of information technology. More evidence is needed about the ways in which computer technology alters the field of social relations in policing and how it affects officers' coding practices.

It is particularly important to note that rationales for policing information systems were and are based on claims that they will increase efficiency, or effectiveness, or make the police more responsive. Yet, they have been used primarily to increase surveillance of patrol officers, have made no impact on strategic planning or management, and have not produced evidence of crime-solving potential (Manning, forthcoming). The research reviewed here suggests that given the costs of this technology, the results have not been proven to have altered the everyday life chances of the vast urban population of this country. Furthermore, the entire technological edifice is based on the false and misleading assumption that policing is primarily about crime and crime control. As the research of the past twenty-five years has firmly established, policing is about differentially and situationally ordering the chaos of everyday life, providing a sense of neighborhood security, and responding to diverse human needs. Occasionally, speed and efficiency in information processing bear on these matters, for in rare events prompt response is required, but far more important is developing a police that provide a predictable presence and adequate responsiveness. This remains a matter for good judgment, restraint, persuasion, and tolerance rather than for increased capacity to process data.

Perhaps the thrust of science and information technology inevitably will reshape modern organizational life, but we are in the center of these changes, and perhaps unable to assess them accurately.

The social organization of policing is slow to change, and information technologies have been in place only slightly more than twenty years. The next ten years or so will tell whether the technological revolution will restructure policing.

Notes

1.   To the extent that these are international trends, they may apply to policing in New Zealand, Australia, Great Britain, and in North American. The pattern of policing found in these nations might be called "Anglo-American Policing."

2.   It is very difficult to assess to how well urban police departments have fared comparatively and over time in resource allocation. While between 1976 to 1986 the number of civilians working in police departments grew from 16.5 percent to over 20 percent, this rise is uncorrelated in aggregate

with increases in the number of sworn officers, which during the same period varied from 2.0 to 2.1 officers per thousand people (Mastrofski, 1990). Although justice employees grew some 5.6 percent a year between 1971 and 1974, they have grown 3 percent or less between 1974 and 1985 (McGarrell and Flanagan, 1985). Police have sustained their place, given inflation, in the total criminal justice expenditures. They account for 1.4 percent of all public expenditures, but half of all justice expenditures are for police. This supports about 20,000 agencies and 620,000 officers. Another way of saying this is that although police have grown in absolute numbers, they have not kept pace with the population, and there is some evidence that large cities are losing police services because of the increases in work load and crime and the rising ratio of officers to population. Policing is very expensive, whatever its worth, costing the taxpayer more than $20 billion a year (Moore and Trojanowicz, 1988). Further, most of these costs are relatively fixed: the cost of putting a patrol car on the road twenty-four hours a day is estimated to be $500,000 to $700,000 a year and 90 percent of police budgets are devoted to salaries, pensions, and fringe benefits (Larson, 1989).

3. I include here the videotaped, nationally distributed pictures of the brutal, vicious beating of Rodney King in Los Angeles, and beatings on videotape from Fort Worth, Texas, and Jackson, Mississippi. In Detroit, on two separate occasions in the past five years, narcotics officers shot each other or were shot in raids due to incompetence. The perjury trial mentioned in the text cost the Detroit police $3.15 million to settle. Former Detroit Chief William Hart is now (August 1991) under federal indictment for fraud and embezzling from the departments' secret fund, and his once deputy chief, Ken Weiner, was convicted of fraud and embezzlement in 1991.

4. It is not possible to survey technological innovations in policing in any detail here, let alone to evaluate them. Some of the more salient types include advances in the forensic technologies of crime solving such as laser technologies to lift fingerprints and computer-automated data bases for comparing patterns of prints; DNA typing; biochemical assays; and accident reconstruction. Many changes have appeared in the area of weapons and force-application techniques such as wider use of 9mm and 10mm and semi-automatic weapons and machine pistols; laser-guided weapons and night scopes; special weapons and tactics, hostage and anti-terrorist squads, and the proliferation generally of greater firepower per officer in the form of automatic shotguns, magnum load weapons, and even M-16 rifles. At the same time, nonfatal force techniques and modalities have been introduced and taught: several forms of Asian martial arts, aluminum batons (or nunchukas used in San Diego), and pepper mace. More training has been introduced in noncoercive persuasion techniques such as mediation, rape counseling, crowd control, and hostage negotiation. Means for enhancing the

data gathering and environment scanning capacity of departments and individual officers have been introduced. These include surveillance devices; miniature tape recorders; alcohol and drug testing kits; mobile video cameras mounted in patrol cars to record traffic stops; advanced laser guns for speeding that cannot be detected by drivers' radar detectors, and tools for systematic crime scene analysis. I am grateful to Steve Mastrofski for providing details of many of these innovations in correspondence.

5. The data cited were gathered in the London Metropolitan Police Department in 1979-1980 (see Manning, 1988); in London in 1973, 1979, and 1984 (Manning, 1977); and in the Boston Police Department in 1979, 1981, and 1984 (Manning, 1988a). Some additional materials were gathered at a Texas Law Enforcement Management Institute Seminar.

6. Only two in ten systems that adapted integrated systems of centralized call collection were considered operational and successful in an evaluation carried out in the late 1970s. Four of five such systems reviewed by Colton and Herbert (1978) failed to achieve acceptance. It is consistently noted that the social context within which the system is installed determines the degree of success of the system even when success is modestly defined as functioning for more than five years and merely meeting design specifications.

7. Data files may soon be more integrated and retrievable. Many departments now have access to computer-based information systems that allow them to network with federal agencies and other departments. These are complemented by huge geographically ordered data bases that include everything from the Census and land use patterns to the location of sewer lines and police precinct boundaries. The computer mapping potential (cf. Maltz et al., 1990) of several departments has been enhanced and the analytic techniques (the capacity to make lists, produce maps, and carry out statistical analyses) introduced by the Drug Market Analysis Project of NIJ in several American cities (San Diego, California; Kansas City, Missouri; Hartford, Connecticut; Jersey City, New Jersey) also suggests change potential. I am grateful to Steve Mastrofski for providing these examples in personal correspondence (August 1991).

8. If there are very few police policies, even fewer have been evaluated. It is possible that social researchers underestimate the impact of policies on police conduct.

9. Chatterton (1991) also details the "resistance tactics" employed by constables to account for their actions, and the complicity of the "higher ups" to maintain their own ignorance.

References

Altheide, D. & Snow, R. (1991). *Media worlds in a post-journalism era.* Hawthorne, NY: Aldine.

Barley, S. R. (1986). Technology as an occasion for structuring. *Administrative Science Quarterly*, 31, 78-108.

Barley, S. R. (1988). Technology, power and the social organization of work. In S. Bardach (Ed.), *Research in the Sociology of Organizations*, vol. 6, Greenwich, CT: JAI Press.

Bercal, T. (1970). Calls for police assistance. *American Behavioral Scientist*, 13, 681-691.

Bittner, E. (1990). *Aspects of police work.* Boston: Northeastern University Press.

Brandl, S. (1991). *The outcomes and processes of detective decision making in burglary and robbery investigations.* Unpublished Ph.D. dissertation, School of Criminal Justice, College of Social Science, Michigan State University, East Lansing.

Brown, M. (1981). *Working the street.* New York: Russell Sage Foundation.

Cain, M. (1973). *Society and the policeman's role.* London: Routledge, Kegan Paul.

Chatterton, M. (1975). *Organizational relationships and processes in police work: A case study of urban policing.* Unpublished Ph.D. dissertation, Department of Sociology, University of Manchester.

Chatterton, M. (1991). *Organizational constraints on the use of information and information technology in problem-focused area policing.* Unpublished paper presented to the British Criminology Conference, York, Great Britain.

Clarke, R. V. G. & Hough, M. (Eds.). (1980). *Organizational effectiveness.* Aldershot: Gower Publishing Co.

Coleman, C. & Bottomley, K. (1979). *Understanding crime rates.* Aldershot: Gower Publishing Co.

Colton, K. W. & Herbert, S. (1978). Police use and acceptance of advanced development techniques: Findings from three case studies. In K. W. Colton (Ed.), *Police computer technology.* Lexington, MA: D. C. Heath & Co.

Colton, K. W., Brandeau, M., & Tien, J. (1979). *National assessment of police command and control systems.* Cambridge: Public Systems Evaluation, Inc.

Cordner, G. (Ed.). (1990). Special issue: The future of policing. *American Journal of Police,* IX (3).

Crozier, M. (1972). The relationship between micro and macrosociology: A study of organizational systems as an empirical approach to problems of macrosociology. *Human Relations,* 25, 239-251.

Davis, S. (1983). Restoring the semblance of order: Police strategies in the domestic dispute. *Symbolic Interaction,* 6, 261-278.

Detroit Free Press, August 17, 1991.

Detroit Free Press, September 1, 1991.

Ekblom, P. & Heal, K. (1982). The police response to calls from the public. *Home office research and planning unit report,* no. 9. London: Her Magesty's Stationery Office.

Ericson, R. V. (1981). *Making crime.* Toronto: Butterworths.

Ericson, R. V. (1982). *Reproducing order.* Toronto: University of Toronto Press.

Ericson, R. V. (1989). Patrolling the facts: Secrecy and publicity in policework. *British Journal of Sociology,* 40 (June), 205-226.

Ericson, R. V. (1991). Mass media, crime, law, and justice, *British Journal of Criminology,* 31 (Summer), 219-249.

Ferraro, K. (1989). Policing women battering. *Social Problems,* 36, 61-74.

Gilsinan, J. (1989). They is clowning tough: 911 and the social construction of reality. *Criminology,* 27, 329-344.

Goldstein, H. (1990). *Problem-oriented policing*. New York: McGraw-Hill Inc.

Greene, J. & Mastrofski, S. (Eds.). (1988). *Community policing,*. New York: Praeger Publishers.

Heal, K & Ekblom, P. (1981). Coping with public demand: A challenge for police management. *Police Studies,* 4(3), 3-8.

Hirschheim, R. & Newman, M. (1991). Symbolism and information systems development: Myth, metaphor and magic. *Information Systems Research,* 2(1), 29-61.

Hough, J. M. (1980a). Managing with less technology. *British Journal of Criminology,* 20, 344-357.

Hough, J. M. (1980b). Uniformed police work and management technology. *Home office research and planning unit paper 1.* London: Her Magesty's Stationery Office.

Hunt, J. & Manning, P. K. (1991). The social context of police lying. *Symbolic Interaction,* 14, 51-70.

Jamieson, K. & Flanagan, T. (1987). *Sourcebook of criminal justice statistics.* Washington, DC: U.S. Government Printing Office.

Jermeir, J. W. & Berkes, L. (1979). Leader behavior in a police command bureaucracy: A closer look at the quasi-military model. *Administrative Science Quarterly,* 24 , 1-23.

Jermeir, J. W., Fry, L. W., Slocum, J. W., Jr., & Gaines, J. (1991). Organizational subcultures in a soft bureaucracy: Resistance behind the myth and facade of an official culture. *Organizational Studies,* 2, 170-194.

Jorgensen, B. (1981). Transferring trouble: The initiation of reactive policing. *Canadian Journal of Criminology,* 23(3), 257-278.

Larson, R. (1989). The new crime stoppers. *Technology Review,* X, 28-31.

Larson, R., Colton, K. W., & Larson, G. (1976). *Assessment of a police implemented AVM System.* Washington, DC: Law Enforcement Administration Assistance.

Lipsky, M. (1980). *Street level bureaucracies.* New York: Russell Sage Foundation.

Maltz, M., et al. (1990). *Mapping crime in its community setting.* Berlin: Springer-Verlag.

Manning, P. K. (1977). *Police work.* Cambridge, MA: MIT Press.

Manning, P. K. (1980). *Narcs' game.* Cambridge, MA: MIT Press.

Manning, P. K. (1988a). *Symbolic communication: Signifying calls and the police response.* Cambridge, MA: MIT Press.

Manning, P. K. (1988b). The drama of community policing. In J. Greene and S. Mastrofski (Eds.), *Community policing.* New York: Praeger Publishers.

Manning, P. K. (forthcoming). The police and information technologies. In M. Tonry & N. Morris (Eds.), *Modern policing.* Chicago: University of Chicago Press.

Manning, P. K. & Hawkins, K. (1989). Police decision making. In M. Wetheritt (Ed.), *Police research: Some future prospects.* London: Gower.

Mastrofski, S. (1990). The prospects of change in police patrol: A decade in review. *American Journal of Police,* IX (3), 1-79.

Mayo, L. (1985). Leading blindly: An assessment of chiefs' information about police operations. In W. Geller (Ed.), *Police leadership in America.* New York: Praeger Publishers.

McCleary, R., Nienstedt, B., & Erven, J. (1982). Uniform crime reports as organizational outcomes. *Social Problems,* 29, 361-372.

McGarrell, E. & Flanagan, T. (1985). *Sourcebook of criminal justice statistics.* Washington, DC: U.S. Government Printing Office.

McNamara, J. (1967). Uncertainties in police work: The relevance of recruits' background and training. In D. Bordua (Ed.), *The police.* New York: John Wiley & Sons Inc.

Meehan, A. J. (1989). *Gang statistics and the politics of policing gangs.* Paper presented to American Association Criminology, Reno, November.

Meyer, J. C., Jr. (1974). Patterns of reporting non-criminal behavior to the police. *Criminology*, 12, 70-83.

Moore, M. & Trojanowicz, R. (1988). Corporate strategies for policing. *Perspectives on Policing*. Washington, DC: U.S. Department of Justice and Harvard University.

Pate, T., Ferrara, A., Bowers, B., & Lorence, J. (1976). *Police response time: Its determinants and effects.* Washington, DC: The Police Foundation.

Percy, S. & Scott, E. J. (1985). *Demand processing and performance in public service agencies.* University, AL: University of Alabama Press.

Pfaffenberger, B. (1991). Technological dramas. *Technology, science and values.*

President's Commission on Law Enforcement and Administration of Justice. (1967). *Report on science and technology.* Washington, DC: U.S. Government Printing Office.

Punch, M. (Ed.). (1983). *Control in the police organization.* Cambridge, MA: MIT Press.

Reiss, A. J., Jr. (1971). *The police and the public.* New Haven, CT: Yale University Press.

Reiss, A. J., Jr. (1974). Discretionary justice. In D. Glaser (Ed.), *Handbook of criminology.* Chicago: Rand McNally & Co.

Rubinstein, J. (1973). *City police.* New York: Farrar, Straus and Giroux Inc.

Samuelson, P. (1954). The pure theory of public expenditure. *Review of Economics and Statistics*, XXXVI (November), 387-390.

Seidman, D. & Couzens, M. (1973). Getting the crime rate down: Political pressure and crime reporting. *Law and Society Review*, 8 (Spring), 457-493.

Shearing, C. (1984). *Dial-a-cop: A study in police mobilization.* Toronto: Centre of Criminology, University of Toronto.

Sherman, L. W. (1987). Repeat calls to police in Minneapolis. *Crime control reports, No 5.* Washington, DC: Crime Control Institute.

Sherman, L. W., Gartin, P., & Buegner, M. E. (1989). Hot spots of predatory crime: Routine activities and the criminology of place. *Criminology,* **27**, 27-55.

Skolnick, J. (1966). *Justice without trial.* New York: John Wiley & Sons Inc.

Spelman, W. & Brown, D. K. (1981). *Calling the police: Citizen reporting of serious crime.* Washington, DC: Police Executive Research Forum.

Stevens, J. (1989). Computer technology. In W. G. Bailey (Ed.), *Encyclopedia of police science.* New York and London: Garland.

Sumrall, M. R., Roberts, J., & Farmer, M. (1981). *Differential response strategies.* Washington, DC: Police Executive Research Forum.

Tein, J. (1977). *An evaluation report of an alternative approach in police patrol: The Wilmington split-force experiment.* Cambridge, MA: Public Systems Evaluation.

Tien, J. & Colton, K. (1979). Police command, control, and communications. *What works?* Washington, DC: U.S. Government Printing Office.

Tien, J., Simon, J. W., & Larson, R. (1978). *An alternative approach in police patrol: The Wilmington split-force experiment.* Washington, DC: U.S. Government Printing Office.

Trojanowicz, R. & Bucqueroux, B. (1990). *Community policing: A contemporary perspective.* Cincinnati: Anderson Publishing Co.

Van Maanen, J. (1983). The boss: First line supervision in an American police department. In M. Punch (Ed.), *Control in the police organization.* Cambridge, MA: MIT Press.

Weick, K. (1979). *The social psychology of organizing* (2nd ed.). Reading, MA: Addison-Wesley Publishing Co. Inc.

Westley, W. (1970). *Violence and the police.* Cambridge, MA: MIT Press.

Wetheritt, M. (Ed.). (1989). *Police research: Some future prospects.* Aldershot: Gower Publishing Co.

Willmer, M. A. P. (1970). *Crime and information theory.* Edinburgh: Edinburgh University Press.

Wilson, J. Q. (1968). *Varieties of police behavior.* Cambridge, MA: Harvard University Press.

Wolfe, J. L. & Heaphy, J. (Eds.). (1979). *Readings in productivity in policing.* Washington, DC: The Police Foundation.

Worden, R. (1989). *Differential police response: Response delays, telephone reports and citizen satisfaction.* Unpublished paper, Michigan State University, School of Criminal Justice.

Worden, R. & Mastrofski, S. (1989). *Varieties of police subcultures: A preliminary investigation.* Unpublished paper presented to Law and Society Association, Madison, Wisconsin, June.

Chapter 12

Organizational Communication

Mittie D. Southerland

Executives and managers at all levels of police organizations must be vitally concerned with the management perspective of organizational communication. It is through this perspective that the vision, values, goals, and objectives of the organization are spread. This chapter is devoted to a discussion of some of the key issues that surround organizational communication as they influence the quality of police service rendered.

Organizational and Interpersonal Communication

The vast majority of organizational communication occurs through the culture, climate, and management style of the organization; the system of rewards and punishments that exist organizationally; the symbols that are adopted for use in the organization; the adopted values, mission, and role that the organization is to pursue; the mechanisms and standards for measuring police performance; the mechanisms for governmental accountability for police action; and the expected relationship between the police and the community. Each of these shapes the range of possibilities for communication to occur as well as determining the forms and atmosphere of that communication. Each sets up a range of expectations and assumptions about the behavior of others, that is, both the police and the public have a basis for anticipating certain forms of response from each other. These expectations may be implicit or explicit and may be correct or incorrect.

Often unanticipated consequences result from a failure on the part of management to examine the implicit communication that occurs in the organization through the above-stated factors. Often police officers and citizens act on the basis of the implicit communication (what they believe will happen based on their interpretation of implicit communication) while ignoring the explicit communication (what they are told to believe through oral or written communication). This happens most frequently when the implicit and explicit communications are in conflict with each other.

The following scenario illustrates the conflict between explicit and implicit communication within the police organization. An officer has been told that the department wants to be more community oriented. The officer tells her supervisor, "Several citizens have expressed concern to me that broken street lights still have not been replaced even after the citizens had repeatedly reported the broken lights to the Public Works Department." The supervisor responds to the officer, "Broken street lights are not a police problem. You should not waste your time listening to this type of complaint." The supervisor's implicit communication is "The community's views of what we need to do really aren't important at all." (Operating behind the scenes here is the officer's knowledge that the supervisor does rate her and is in control of rewards and punishments.) Therefore, based on the supervisor's implicit communication, the officer disregards the official, explicit communication "let's be more community oriented out there." Such a circumstance is not infrequent and reminds us of the age-old saying "actions speak louder than words." Police agencies communicate much more loudly by what they value implicitly than by what is valued explicitly. It is crucial that the message in implicit and explicit communication be consistent with one another. Consistency of management and communication throughout the department was found to be one of the concerns at all levels of the Madison, Wisconsin, Police Department as it experienced change (Couper and Lobitz, 1991). There is a clear need for management and communication to be dependable. Even though the traditional model may not be the most effective communication model, it is a familiar one, and even though it may not be consistent in some ways, it is dependable. Dependability can sometimes work against change which creates anxiety even in the best of circumstances. Madison found that the lack of dependability during change was one of the most significant factors they had to overcome.

Implicit communication can also overrule explicit communication when psychological barriers intervene in the communication process. In such cases perceptions involving or implying stereotypes, which may have been created through media communication, personal past experience, or the past experience of acquaintances can cause filtering or blocking of communication between two parties. In such situations, interpersonal communication that occurs between officers, managers, and citizens has strong implications for the overall complex of organizational communication. Organizational messages may be blocked or filtered by psychological barriers.

The topic of interpersonal communication typically is concerned with the styles, forms, modes, and process of communication. It examines the various forms of oral and written verbal communication, nonverbal kinesic communication, active listening, barriers to communication, negotiation strategies, and directive versus nondirective approaches to communication. These will be discussed in this chapter only indirectly. Interpersonal communication has important implications for organizational communication and is indeed a part of organizational communication but has been covered well in a number of police administration texts.[1]

Open Versus Closed Organizational Communication[2]

Internal Implications. The traditional police agency uses a closed form of organizational communication. This means that when there is a decision to be reached management considers only management's view in reaching that decision. Ignored is the knowledge and view of the officers on the street. Ignored is the individual citizen's view or the views of the various communities incorporated within the department's jurisdiction.

The open model of organizational communication functions from a different perspective, i.e., one that is prescribed as the hope for quality policing (Couper and Lobitz, 1991; Sparrow et al., 1990). Decisions should be made not only in consideration of officer and citizen views but in consultation with them as full partners in the venture of policing. As problems or issues are encountered, potential sources of pertinent information or ideas regarding solution of the problem are identified. The problems or issues are then faced at the lowest possible level and resolution is sought with full input from those sources.

These open and closed models are polar extremes in decision-making style and in communication style. They require completely different management approaches. The open model of organizational communication cannot function in the traditional classical police organizational structure of top-down communication. It is problematic for open organizational communication to occur with the paramilitary symbols that are currently used in policing. The assumptions on which the classical structure and symbols of policing are based have specific implications for organizational functioning and expectations of rewards and punishment. For example, top-down communication indicates relative importance of ranks. Those who are at the top are more important than those at the bottom of the organization. The top carries more weight (authority and power) than the bottom. The top is paid more and has greater status. The top is where important and not so important decisions are made; the bottom is where they are carried out without question and without making waves. This type of symbolism carries much baggage when trying to get those people on the "bottom" to share their opinions and become involved in decision making. It is no wonder that they are skeptical and hesitant, at best, to participate in the early stages of any endeavor to change a closed system of communication to an open one.

Effective communication within the department is essential to quality improvements in the organization (Crosby, 1979; Couper and Lobitz, 1991). What we know in policing has typically resulted from quantification of information (data crunching, bean counting). Rarely have police agencies embarked on attempts to gain knowledge through qualitative research efforts. Data crunching often gives us no real knowledge about what is happening. There is a need in policing to begin to look at information gathering from the field research perspective. Our emphasis on bean counting has often ignored the wealth of information that exists in the memories of police officers and even in their narrative reports. All of this information has been vastly underutilized and mostly ignored. The police agency would benefit from field research (qualitative research) training for police personnel and their managers. The police officer should be trained to be the participant observer in the field of the community and to identify and facilitate the resolution of problems. The observations of the police officer should then be routed to a chief researcher (manager) who can put all the pieces together to see trends and perspectives on the observations. Police communication could then be approached as a master part of field research. Each member has a vital part in the research effort and the resultant understanding and knowledge gained depends on everyone participating as equals in the research process. Everyone observes, records, and interprets. At each level the process is repeated and the research never ends.

Another means to capitalize on the knowledge and information of police officers is through the use of committee structures to facilitate problem resolution and decision making in policing. The use of committees of police personnel, such as those used in Madison, Wisconsin (Couper and Lobitz, 1991), require the department to use an open communication style. Such committees tend to be similar to the quality circle concept that has been tried in several police departments around the country (Hatry and Greiner, 1986).

External Implications. The closed model is more readily apparent in the forms of communication used by a traditional police agency in dealing with its external environment than it is in its internal dealings. The traditional police agency has isolated itself fully from the community. It does not seek community input and when given input in the form of complaints or suggestions, the department often neither listens to nor heeds what the community tries to communicate. If the officers at the bottom of the organization have no status to participate in organizational decision making, the community has even less standing. The community lost its status when reformers sought to depoliticize the police as a move toward police professionalization. The symbols, regulations, and control systems of traditional (reform) police agencies mitigate against a closeness to the customer (the community) because the community has no status in decision making regarding police policies and practices much less the vision and values of policing.

Nevertheless, police leaders of today recognize that communication with leaders in the community and community members is vital to the health of the police organization. Such communication helps to keep the police organization on an even keel, focused on those factors the community sees as important. Police often find that the community and the police have very different views of what are important police responsibilities. Reform police tend to emphasize Part I Uniform Crime Report (UCR) crimes while citizens often focus on what police consider nuisance offenses (Sparrow et al., 1990).

Several methods for effective communication with the community have been used in policing. Regular contact with the community leadership is important for police to learn what of importance is happening in the various communities of the jurisdiction. There is widespread recognition that police executives should collaborate closely with the head of their local government but the research indicates that close to half of the executives studied in one research project made policy alone (Guyot and Martensen, 1991). Some chiefs have used committee structures to assist them in maintaining close communication with their customers. Open reporting mechanisms for dealing with print and electronic media are critical in supporting the open style of organizational communication. Regular surveys of the community have also been significant in helping some departments learn of community needs and reactions to departmental programs. Active listening on the part of police officers and dispatchers is also crucial. Some departments have totally revamped their dispatch and call-taking policies and procedures because of the need to be responsive to community needs and not merely have quick response to calls for service. These are a few of the strategies that have been shown as successful for departments that truly want to know what the community thinks and feels.

One of the primary organizational communication responsibilities of the police executive is to provide external leadership to the community. The chief must lead the community while listening to the community's concerns. The chief must provide the kind of leadership that assists a partnership role between the department and the community. The department must work with community leaders to identify problems and find solutions to them. Nevertheless, there is a line of demarcation over which the police executive must not allow the department to be drawn. The department must remain accountable to the public through political oversight while remaining independent from political interference.[3] Without political oversight there is no external control to ensure that the police perform their functions within the framework of the Constitution and other existing laws. Yet, political interference can result in corruption of the intent of police and violation of the constitutional mission of policing. Organizational communication controls these by establishing the framework for communication with outside parties. The boundaries of that communication are the constitutional limitations of police power and discretion. At times the police must explain why they are unable to perform unconstitutional actions requested by constituents or government officials. Typically, unconstitutional requests have to do with an individual or group wanting the rights of another group to be violated by the police for the benefit of the requesting group. For example, a group of property owners want the police to move a group of teenagers from a sidewalk where they congregate peacefully after school. If the police ignore the request the property owners will be unhappy. If they move the teenagers, the teenagers will be unhappy and will feel that the action violates their right to peaceful assembly. In such cases the police must attempt to find a solution to the conflict between these two groups while both acknowledging the rights of the teenagers and the emotions of the property owners.

There is a move toward partnership in policing. The potential for partnership exists not only between the police and the community but also with private security organizations, civic organizations, private business, and other governmental agencies (Williams, 1991; Sparrow et al., 1990).

Another organizational communication responsibility of police executives is to provide leadership to the profession. Part of this responsibility revolves around open communication with other police leaders and organizations, involvement in professional organizations, and sharing the knowledge base that is developing through an active involvement in speaking and writing. Openness means among other things being willing to examine the "party line." Some of the questions open leaders might ask follow: Are we doing the right things in policing? What could we do differently? Is the majority view, the correct approach? Not only will open leaders be willing to examine the party line but they will be willing to share the experiences of their police agencies openly with others. There is much to be gained by laying what you are trying to do on the line for others to give suggestions and critically examine. This type of professional leader also will be less concerned about what is happening in their police department than for what is happening in policing as a whole. These leaders will read and keep up with what is happening outside their department as well as inside their department. Their loyalty will be to the values of policing and not to covering or protecting their position in the particular department. They will strive hard to a avoid xenophobia and its negative results. The fear of outsiders can destroy an attempt to develop a police common culture that values partnership between police, their community, and their profession.

Williams (1991) suggests that police executives should fully utilize academic and research institutions. He also stresses the important role of police professional membership associations in supporting, nurturing, and setting the standards for professional conduct and for providing for professional development. By active involvement in these pursuits, the police executive has an instrumental part to play in the leadership of the profession.

Values and Culture

Values. Values are enduring beliefs that certain, specific modes of conduct are preferable (Rokeach, 1973). Organizational values are the beliefs, purpose, mission, and goals that define what is essential to the organization. The value system organizes these concepts into a framework that guides individuals to know the range and limitations on behavior in regard to means and ends, i.e., what *ends* are to be sought and what *means* are acceptable to achieve the ends. Organizational values include a set of beliefs about what kinds of strategies and techniques work well in the organizational setting (Ouchi, 1981). These beliefs identify the decision makers and the kinds of activities the organization should or should not consider doing. If new members of the organization are to understand and believe them, organizational values and beliefs must be expressed in concrete ways (Southerland and Reuss-Ianni, 1992). A major problem of police values is that the implicit values are often at odds with the explicit values of the police agency. "This breeds confusion, distrust, and cynicism rather than clarity, commitment, and high morale" (Wasserman and Moore, 1988).

Clear operational definitions of values are necessary to allow for personnel evaluation based on values (Cordner et al., 1991). Field research is a very useful and important strategy for evaluating management and officer behavior in terms of their effectiveness in carrying out organizational values (Steinman, 1986).

Peters and Waterman (1982) found that every excellent company they studied had a clear set of values and was serious about the process of shaping those values. They questioned whether it is possible to be an excellent organization without having the following set of seven values:

1. A belief in being the "best"

2. A belief in the importance of the details of execution, the nuts and bolts of doing the job well

3. A belief in the importance of people as individuals

4. A belief in superior quality and service

5. A belief that most members of the organization should be innovators, and its corollary, the willingness to support failure

6. A belief in the importance of informality to enhance communication

7. Explicit belief in and recognition of the importance of economic growth and profits (p. 285).

These seven values can be translated directly to policing if we modify the seventh one to say, "Explicit belief and recognition of the importance of upholding the Constitution and producing those outcomes that make our community safe and orderly."[4]   The police executive's leadership role is critical to transmitting values to members of the organization so that they become "bone-deep beliefs."   To that end executives should follow this advice:

Be confident in your beliefs.   Live them with integrity. Remember that the "small stuff" is all there is.   It's a pretty tough message.   If your convictions about people aren't all that clear and strong, then it's tough to be confident and consistent. Maybe that's the secret, for good or ill, after all   (Peters and Austin, 1985, p. 212).

Culture.   The symbols, ceremonies, and myths that communicate the organization's values and beliefs to its employees compose its organizational culture.[5]   "These rituals put flesh on what would otherwise be sparse and abstract ideas, bringing them to life in a way that has meaning and impact for a new employee" (Ouchi, 1981, p. 35).   When all personnel in the organization have the same set of values, a common culture results.

The common culture or shared philosophy results in everyone speaking the same language.   Each employee understands their rights and responsibilities as a member of the organization and they are aware of the degree to which they will participate in decision making.   These common understandings simplify the entire process of leadership and management.

The common culture develops as employees have a broad range of shared experience through which they can communicate subtly.   Due to the common culture, each is able to assume correctly responses and agreements without having to negotiate them.   This facilitates coordination and greatly simplifies decision making and planning.   Large numbers of people can be involved as active participants in decision making and planning because they have an underlying agreement on philosophy, values, and beliefs.   Shared responsibility is feasible only under the conditions of a common culture.

The common culture and its shared value system is extremely important to organizational success (Ouchi, 1981; Peters and Waterman, 1982).   Without a strong shared value system, it is highly unlikely an organization will be successful.   The common value system depends on a strong executive leadership that is committed to developing strategies for transmitting the values to all employees; to using tight control mechanisms when the values of the organization are at stake; and using loose or no control on all other matters.

The implicit values in community- and problem-oriented policing contradict the traditional orientation of the police culture.[6] There must be basic changes in the culture of policing if these new forms of policing are to take hold (Cordner et al., 1991).

Communicating Vision, Values, Goals, and Objectives Toward Common Culture

The order of presentation here is essential. These must be seen as a hierarchy of importance from vision as most important to objectives as least important. They must also be seen as fitting together as a set of puzzle pieces making up the whole. The whole is the vision. The pieces of the puzzle are various levels of the vision. The police executive is responsible for creating the puzzle and ensuring that the members have a clear understanding of the way the puzzle pieces fit together and the skills needed to put the puzzle together. Creating the puzzle begins with the whole board — the vision. In that board are the values that are carved from the vision. The goals are carved from the values. Objectives are carved from the goals. All action therefore is directly related to the vision and values of the organization since every puzzle piece is parented by them. This ordered approach is essential so that we can avoid, at all cost, the *means* driving the *ends*.

The vision provides the *ends*.[7] Organizations must decide how the accomplishment of the vision, values, goals, and objectives will be measured. Otherwise, the activities of the organization drive it to some undetermined destination that may be totally unacceptable to the community and/or the governmental authority to which the police are responsible. The activity trap is most easily fallen into when we fail to evaluate the activities being performed in reference to the vision we have for the organization. We must look beyond the calls that come into the organization through 911 to find the other concerns of the community. We must find other ways to communicate with the community concerning the problems and needs that exist there and the issues the department faces in attempting to be "all things to all people."

Also at stake is the manner in which the vision and the accoutrements of vision are developed. The police executive must have a vision but it should be developed neither in isolation from the department nor the community. The vision must be one to which all three can relate positively. It is most important initially that the community and the police executive see the vision as a favorable one. For best results the departmental members should also see the same vision, but often in organizations where there are problems of misuse of police power or corruption the department is in a state of crisis and must be led by the community and chief executive to a new state of being. In such cases major change is necessary.

By having a clear picture of where the department is heading (vision) and having identified methods to measure progress toward that end, the organization has communicated the outcomes that are expected. Activity then is counted only when it helps the organization achieve that end. The activity trap exists when we are performing activities that have no relationship to the desired outcomes of the organization. Organizational communication regarding what is desirable activity and a reward structure that clearly rewards the desired activities go a long way toward providing management that assists members of the organization to avoid the activity trap. People will select activities that are aimed toward accomplishing the vision and mission of the organization and therefore the activity that occurs within the organization will not be a trap at all, it will be essential to organizational outcomes.

The Menlo Park, California, experience clearly demonstrated that symbols make a difference in the behavioral choices made by police and the public (Tenzel et al., 1976). In all the organizational communication related to vision, values, goals, and objectives it is important to keep the symbols — words, colors, equipment — in mind so that there is no conflict between the explicit verbal messages being sent to organizational members and the public and the kinesic or implicit messages being sent through the symbols used.

The problematic nature of transmitting values throughout the police organization is evident from the following illustration of ineffective organizational communication:

> Departmental policy is often not clearly expressed or understood. Supervisors indicate sometimes subtly, sometimes directly — what they prefer by way of action. Officers are aware that what they normally do is not what "the sergeant" or "the lieutenant" would do. Officers cynically remark that calling a supervisor for assistance in a domestic fight usually produces "two domestics," one among civilians, another among police . . . (Bayley and Bittner, 1989, p. 91).

It is very difficult to translate the vision and values to all levels and throughout the department so that everyone can understand them in the same way, that is, so that a common culture is developed eventually.[8] Personnel selection is a logical starting point for ensuring that new employees can and will incorporate the organizational values into their belief systems. It is important to use the values of the organization as the basis for establishing the criteria and process for personnel selection (Peters, 1987).

All police personnel are responsible for implementing the policies and procedures of the organization. When the values and goals of the police agency are not shared by personnel at all levels of the organization (administrators, managers, supervisors, and officers), the police agency is in trouble; no one will really know what is supposed to be happening, much less what is actually happening. As a result the goals cannot be achieved or at best they will be achieved inconsistently and unreliably. Research on bureaucratic organizations repeatedly suggests that the behavioral intentions of personnel in organizations often diverge from the formally stated organizational objectives.

For Reuss-Ianni (1983), the organization of policing has no single culture. It is the interaction of two distinct cultures: a street-cop culture and a management-cop culture. The struggle between street-cop and management-cop values might be explained by the relative lack of participation of all except top management in organizational decision making and the punitive control structures evident in many police agencies. The inevitable result is conflict between the bosses and the cops.[9]

Values are transmitted in organizations through socialization. The socialization process occurs at all career stages, yet the effect of socialization during the breaking-in period is most significant for determining behavior due to the individual's vulnerability at this point — the officer has little operational knowledge, few guidelines to direct behavior, and too much or too little confidence. Numerous studies indicate that recruit socialization determines, to a great extent, the officer's later beliefs, attitudes, and behaviors (Van Maanen, 1978). This process of values transmission must be planned for. It is critically important that the values be accepted and appropriate behavioral responses occur throughout the organization. Strategic planning for values transmission must include clearly defined roles for mid-level and senior management in fostering a common culture based on the organization's value system (Cordner et al., 1991). The socialization of police recruits while in the training academy must be carefully examined and changed toward the outcome of facilitating the desired common culture.

Van Maanen (1978) found that the paramilitary environment of group reward and punishment in the *training academy* promotes peer group solidarity. The recruit learns quickly to support the peer group because the peer group will be the only dependable source of support the recruit will have. The recruit learns that formal rules and regulations are applied inconsistently and that when managers notice behavior, it will be to punish, not to reward. The traditional socialization or values transmission in policing observed by Van Maanen (1978) resulted in officers being pitted against supervisors and managers. If community-oriented or problem-solving policing are to become the rule of thumb in policing, training academies must be changed to develop an experience base that supports the concept of policing as a full-partnership endeavor.

Structure

Different structures of police organization bring about different forms of organizational communication for management and leadership. They also tend to set up different management and leadership approaches.

The structure gives off kinesic communication about the relationship and the nature of communication that is allowed in the organization. The more levels of hierarchy in the structure, the more barriers to communication and the less two-way communication the organization will have. The shorter the organizational structure the more likely there is to be multiway communication. Specialization creates limitations on the ability of units to cooperate for effective police service. Centralization means less democratic decision making and reduces potential for participation. A highly centralized structure tends to create more authoritarian approaches. Decentralization with geographic specialization creates a scale that lends itself to a team approach. Centralization virtually makes the team concept an impossibility due to the power and authority being placed in a single place and the large number of people that would have to be involved in any decision if attempting to operate from the team perspective. Big is not always better — especially when effective communication is at stake.[10]

Management and Leadership

Management is the tool through which police executives and other managers shape or mold, or sometimes assist beat officers to shape or mold the directions the department will take in the future. The type of communication used in management can have a powerful influence on the amount and quality of participation from officers in the lower ranks of the police agency. Style of management has everything to do with communication.

There have been dramatic changes in managerial thought in the past twenty years primarily because of three factors. First, the Japanese have had significant economic success relative to American companies by using a radically different managerial philosophy. Second, there have been a number of research findings on the managerial practices of successful private-sector organizations. Last, there has been a significant growth of a service economy at the expense of the production economy and organizations had to adjust to the changes required for success in the service industry (Moore and Stephens, 1991b).

Several questions need to be addressed here. Is there a best style of management for law enforcement to work best? Do particular management styles facilitate organizational communication? Do particular styles result in more goal accomplishment? At present we can only reply that there are a variety of management styles that have been proposed and examined in a variety of settings.[11]   The recent literature in police management and leadership recommends the adoption of open contingency models of management.

The management style sets the stage for what can be communicated. It determines the amount and effectiveness of delegation in an organization. A highly authoritarian management style will not allow for delegation of decision making to the bottom of the organization. Yet that style is more effective than a laissez-faire style of leadership since the laissez-faire leader will not follow up to see that the delegated assignment is completed.

Management styles are very closely related to the form of communication used in them. The management style is often very diverse within a police agency (see Van Maanen, 1989; Southerland, 1989, 1990). The challenge today is to determine the appropriate management philosophy for the environment and mission of the police agency. Many police experts are recommending management strategies that follow the general principles of Peters and Waterman (1982), Ouchi (1981), Peters (1987), and Peters and Austin (1985).

Hoover and Mader (1990) reported that Texas administrators are very supportive of the principles of excellence advocated in the private sector management literature, yet they feel impotent to implement the principles of excellence in their police agencies. It is hoped the more recent police examples found in Couper and Lobitz (1991) and Sparrow, Moore, and Kennedy (1990) will give impetus to new resolve to follow through on these challenging strategies.

It is important for a management approach of openness to be chosen for new forms of policing. Problem- and community-oriented policing require an open management approach. Different types of management style still will be necessary for different situations.[12] How much direction and support is needed is the question. Control is another issue. The new police manager shouldn't be in the business of control but of performance oversight. Southerland (1990) found that police officers wanted to know their mistakes so that they could correct them but they wanted to know what they had done wrong in specific terms. Oversight is directed at improving performance not just catching someone doing something wrong. A lot is communicated by the tone of voice and the manner in which the oversight is performed. It must be done in a positive manner toward improvement of performance, not toward punishment.

Coaching is an appropriate role model for police managers. A coach is a teacher, allowing mistakes to occur but using them as a means to teach improvement of skills. A coach is a cheerleader who is happy and proud of improved performance, doesn't gloat over mistakes, but focuses primarily on what was done correctly and helps to improve problem areas. A coach allows the person to grow and develop in their position and to need gradually less and less involvement by the coach. A coach always pays attention to performance of all players, even those who are highly skilled performers. Everyone needs some level of support and encouragement. Positive attention is the key.

Can traditional supervisory models be enriched or redesigned to be effective? They can be enriched by making them less authoritarian. The answer really depends on what we want as a desired result. If we want supervisory models to be more benevolent we can easily enrich and redesign them. But if we want them to be more productive, resulting in higher quality organizations, we must begin with a new and different conception of police vision.[13]

The New Management Style. Supervision in the new style focuses much less attention on the means of policing and more on the ends achieved. It looks for new ways to measure performance based on the vision and values of the organization. The Madison experience (Couper and Lobitz, 1991) gives us some assistance with understanding how this new strategy works. The New York City community-oriented policing supervision methods of evaluating police performance also broke new ground in finding ways to measure a police officer's knowledge of and relationship with the community (Weisburd et al., 1988).

Supervision in community-oriented, neighborhood-oriented, problem-solving policing must be different from traditional models. Why? Because the traditional models value crime control through the reward and control structure. Community policing must have other rewards. If we continue to reward only crime control, these experiments in a new form of policing are doomed to failure.

The new management manages with values instead of rules. The use of rules supports a "cover yourself" mentality that will not allow for innovation or risk taking of any sort. The rules become a viper waiting around the next corner or under some piece of paper to strike you dead for making a mistake. The new management uses values to set the limits of acceptable performance. Reasonableness within the range of constitutional limitations will be the guiding force for disciplinary action. Most supervisory response will be guidance and in support of values, not catching officers making mistakes.

The new management is seen in the organization's workplaces — on its night shifts, in the field. They help to do work and ask questions so they know in clear terms what their employees need from them to do a quality job as a manager. That is how they let their employees know they care about the quality of the work that is being done and that they are looking for ways to improve conditions and processes (Couper and Lobitz, 1991).

The new management requires impassioned leadership with a vision for the organization and an ability to translate that vision to the members of the organization and create a climate where members are rewarded for taking risks toward achieving the organizational vision.

The new management encourages creativity. One might ask, can current traditional supervisors and managers alter their styles and behavior to encourage rather than discourage creativity? It depends. The chief and structures must change. It is easier to accomplish such changes the less time one has been in a supervisory position. It is also easier the lower the supervisor is in the organization. The higher in the organization the more difficult it is to modify these styles because these supervisors have more to lose. Regardless, one has to be patient and expect a good deal of resistance to these types of changes. It will take time. There have been some demonstrated success in changing the management style in several departments around the country.[14]

Quality Leadership. Quality leadership may well characterize the new management approach. In the book describing the Madison, Wisconsin, experience Couper and Lobitz (1991) discuss the impetus and the methods that have been used there. They have not yet completed their experiment in policing and may never really feel that it is complete. However, the experience is instructive to any police executive who is considering this type of complete makeover of the police department and its vision. One of the key management differences between this department and traditional police management is that it forces managers to make delegation explicit. The committee structure used at different levels in their experiment defines explicitly who makes what decisions and who has input on what issues.

The principles of quality leadership are based on a commitment to people. It emphasizes that people must be treated with respect. This means all people, employees as well as consumers. The workplace is people oriented. Crucial to the principles of quality leadership is the belief that leadership can and does make a difference.

Quality leadership requires police leaders to put the needs of their citizens together with the answers from their employees. They must also look at a new role for their managers, that of coach and teacher, in order to develop the skills and abilities of their employees. Coaching is contrasted with the old role of scheduling and reviewing reports. The new supervisor assists the officer in focusing on outcomes not outputs (activities). When we focus on activities it is easy to get trapped into a mind set of activity and lose sight of the desired outcome. Then we have mere busyness, not productivity.

As it embarked on the journey toward quality leadership, the department purposefully chose to first create a vision. To do this they asked what is it that we want to be? Next, the management team asked how do we get there? What resources do we need to do this? How will we know when we are making progress? And finally, how will we know when we are making continuous improvement?

The department's managers then pursued the following steps in carrying out their plan:

1. They listened carefully to their employees and their citizen-customers.

2. They tailored a leadership style to meet those needs.

3. They trained all of their employees in a new way from the top to the bottom of the department.

4. They empowered, coached, and enabled managers and supervisors to be Quality Leaders.

5. They promoted, praised, and gave key assignments to the quality "champions" in the organization.

6. They settled down for the long term; they took risks and continually tried to visibly practice what they were preaching (Couper and Lobitz, 1991).

As they have moved along the journey toward quality leadership they have found that practicing the principles of quality leadership is much more difficult than getting consensus on the principles or getting people to agree to adopt them. It requires that one unlearn the traditional style and learn the new one. Breaking old habits takes a great deal of concentration and time.

Communicating for Change. One of the characteristics of the new management is its emphasis on change as a means to improve police effectiveness. One key to improvement is the identification of future needs. To accomplish this management must utilize all its resources. The police officer on the street is a very important resource as is the business community and the community leadership.

A vision of the future must drive any change attempt. It is very important that the police executives be able to communicate with their partners regarding the future. The vision of the future is continually modified due to changing environmental conditions. Technological advances can have very significant ramifications for police management.

In this world of rapid change and in a time of rapid change in a police organization it is very important to establish a variety of mechanisms to keep the membership of the organization informed about what is going on in the organization and where the agency is headed. These communication processes are just as important for the executives to learn what is going on in the organization and where it stands in its attempts to change the organization. Some of the strategies that are useful are MBWA (otherwise known as management by walking or wandering around), newsletters, memoranda, staff meetings, and personal meetings with various members of the organization.

When committees are used for decision making it is essential that they are open to the rest of the organization and community input. It is all too easy for the committees to become isolated and walled off due to getting wrapped up in trying to accomplish their function (activity orientation) and not by design or intention. Checkpoints to ensure that communication lines remain open must be carefully planned and implemented.

The chief and all management personnel should schedule time with employees regularly to keep in touch with them. This communication should be meaningful, that is, it must involve asking the right questions and listening, above all listening to employees.

Communication for change must involve both the community and rank-and-file input. Without the involvement of both these constituencies the chief may make serious mistakes and may not have the necessary support to accomplish the proposed change. Support for change cannot be developed without at least two-way communication and preferably multiway communication.

Summary

Organizational communication may be the most important managerial perspective for determining the productivity and quality of policing. Improvements in quality and productivity will only come about when police leadership is willing to innovate. The full acceptance of a partnership model between police executives, police managers, police officers, the community, business, and other government agencies is a necessary precursor to quality policing. The right sorts of values must be clearly adopted throughout the organization and the police executive must take an active role in ensuring that the organization is value driven toward quality policing.

Management helps create the activity trap through forms of direction and control. However, the activity trap can be limited by clearly identifying vision, values, goals, and objectives, and connecting all rewards, punishments, and direction clearly to them.

Notes

1.   For discussion of interpersonal communication in the police setting see Gaines, Southerland, and Angell, 1991, chapter 7; Lynch, 1986, chapter 3;

Sheehan and Cordner, 1989, pp. 299-307; and Thibault, Lynch, and McBride, 1990, chapter 6. Blair, Roberts, and McKechnie (1985) discuss the forms and approaches of organizational communication particularly as it relates to power, status, and decision making in private organizational settings. For an examination of bargaining as organizational communication in the private sector see Putnam (1985).

2. For a more thorough discussion of open and closed organizational models see Gaines, Southerland, and Angell, 1991, chapters 1 and 5, and Cordner, 1978.

3. For a discussion of the importance of independence from political interference versus accountability through political oversight see Moore and Stephens (1991b) and Guyot and Martensen (1991).

4. Delattre and Behan (1991) examine the relationship between the values of policing and the nation's constitutional foundations.

5. For an excellent review of the literature in organizational communication and its implications for organizational climates see Poole (1985). He also provides an excellent review of research methods for examining organizational climate from the context of communication.

6. For a treatise on the traditional culture of American policing see Drummond (1976).

7. Moore and Stephens' (1991a) book is devoted to a discussion of corporate strategy for policing, that is, the process of defining the organization's mission or purpose.

8. Couper and Lobitz (1991) describe the way in which the vision and values are being transmitted to develop a new police culture in the Madison, Wisconsin, Police Department.

9. The implications of internal value conflict between the cultures in policing are further examined in Southerland and Reuss-Ianni (1992). Not only is Reuss-Ianni's (1983) conceptualization of culture conflict examined, but also those of Van Maanen (1989) and Currie (1988a; 1988b).

10. If you are interested in learning more about the structural implications on organizational communication see Blair, Roberts, and McKechnie (1985), and McPhee (1985). These articles present different dimensions of the structural elements of communication from the general literature of organizational communication.

11.   For a review of this literature and an examination of what works in police management and leadership see Southerland and Reuss-Ianni (1992).

12.   See Southerland (1990); Hersey and Blanchard (1988); and Blanchard, Zigarmi, and Zigarmi (1985) to examine situational leadership that has relevance for police management and leadership. Also of interest is Weisburd, McElroy, and Hardyman's (1988) work on supervision for community policing.

13.   Couper and Lobitz (1991), Sparrow, Moore, and Kennedy (1990), Moore and Stephens (1991a), and Gaines, Southerland, and Angell (1991) give examples of this new form of police management.

14.   For recent examples of police change see Couper and Lobitz (1991) and Sparrow, Moore, and Kennedy (1990).

References

Bayley, D. H. & Bittner, E. (1989). Learning the skills of policing. In R. G. Dunham & G. P. Alpert (Eds.), *Critical issues in policing: Contemporary readings* (pp. 87-110). Prospect Heights, IL: Waveland Press Inc.

Blair, R., Roberts, K. H., & McKechnie, P. (1985). Bargaining as organizational communication. In R. D. McPhee & P. K. Tompkins (Eds.), *Organizational communication: Traditional themes and new directions* (Volume 13, pp. 55-78, SAGE Annual Reviews of Communication Research). Beverly Hills, CA: Sage Publications Inc.

Blanchard, K., Zigarmi, P., & Zigarmi, D. (1985). *Leadership and the one minute manager.* New York: William Morrow & Co. Inc.

Cordner, G. (1978). Open and closed models of police organization: Traditions, dilemmas, and practical considerations. *Journal of Police Science and Administration,* 6(1), 22-34.

Cordner, G. W., Fraser, C. B., & Wexler, C. (1991). Research, planning, and implementation. In W. A. Geller (Ed.), *Local Government Police Management* (pp. 333-362). Washington, DC: International City Management Association.

Couper, D. C. & Lobitz, S. H. (1991). *Quality policing: The Madison experience.* Washington, DC: Police Executive Research Forum.

Crosby, P. B. (1979). *Quality is free: The art of making quality certain.* New York: McGraw-Hill Inc.

Currie, C. (1988a). First-line supervision: The role of the sergeant — part one. *The Police Journal,* 61(4), 312-329.

Currie, C. (1988b). First-line supervision: The role of the sergeant — part two. *The Police Journal,* 62(1), 69-84.

Delattre, E. J. & Behan, C. J. (1991). Practical ideals for managing in the nineties: A perspective. In W. A. Geller (Ed.), *Local government police management* (pp. 537-554). Washington, DC: International City Management Association.

Drummond, D. S. (1976). *Police culture* (SAGE Professional Papers in Administration and Police Studies, Vol. 3, Series #03-032). Beverly Hills, CA: Sage Publications Inc.

Gaines, L. K., Southerland, M. D., & Angell, J. E. (1991). *Police administration.* New York: McGraw-Hill Inc.

Guyot, D. & Martensen, K. R. (1991). The governmental setting. In W. A. Geller (Ed.), *Local government police management* (pp. 431-464). Washington, DC: International City Management Association.

Hatry, J. P., & Greiner, J. M. (1986). *Improving the use of quality circles in police departments.* Washington, DC: U.S. Department of Justice, National Institute of Justice.

Hersey, P. & Blanchard, K. (1988). *Management of organizational behavior: Utilizing human resources* (5th ed.). Englewood Cliffs, NJ: Prentice Hall.

Hoover, L. T. & Mader, E. T. (1990). Attitudes of police chiefs toward private sector management principles. *American Journal of Police,* 9(4), 25-38.

Lynch, R. G. (1986). *The police manager: Professional leadership skills* (3rd ed.). New York: Random House Inc.

McPhee, R. D. (1985). Formal structure and organizational communication. In R. D. McPhee and P. K. Tompkins (Eds.), *Organizational communication: Traditional themes and new directions* (Volume 13, pp. 149-178, SAGE Annual Reviews of Communication Research). Beverly Hills, CA: Sage Publications Inc.

Moore, M. H. & Stephens, D. W. (1991a). *Beyond command and control: The strategic management of police departments.* Washington, DC: Police Executive Research Forum.

Moore, M. H. & Stephens, D. W. (1991b). Organization and management. In W. A. Geller (Ed.), *Local government police management* (pp. 22-58). Washington, DC: International City Management Association.

Ouchi, W. G. (1981). *Theory Z.* New York: Avon Books.

Peters, T. (1987). *Thriving on chaos: Handbook for a management revolution.* New York: Alfred A. Knopf Inc.

Peters, T. & Austin, N. (1985). *A passion for excellence: The leadership difference.* New York: Random House Inc.

Peters, T. J. & Waterman, R. H., Jr. (1982). *In search of excellence: Lessons from America's best-run companies.* New York: Harper & Row, Publishers Inc.

Poole, M. S. (1985). Communication and organizational climates. In R. D. McPhee & P. K. Tompkins (Eds.), *Organizational communication: Traditional themes and new directions* (Volume 13, pp. 79-108, SAGE Annual Reviews of Communication Research). Beverly Hills, CA: Sage Publications Inc.

Putnam, L. L. (1985). Bargaining as organizational communication. In R. D. McPhee & P. K. Tompkins (Eds.), *Organizational communication: Traditional themes and new directions* (Volume 13, pp. 129-148, SAGE Annual Reviews of Communication Research). Beverly Hills, CA: Sage Publications Inc.

Reuss-Ianni, E. (1983). *Street cops and management cops.* New Brunswick, NJ: Transaction.

Rokeach, M. (1973). *The nature of human values.* New York: Macmillan Publishing Co.

Sheehan, R. & Cordner, G. W. (1989). *Introduction to police administration,* (2nd ed.). Cincinnati: Anderson Publishing Co.

Southerland, M. D. (1989). *First-line police supervision: Assessing leadership styles.* Paper presented at the annual meeting of the Southern Criminal Justice Association, Jacksonville, Florida, October.

Southerland, M. D. (1990). *Police patrol supervision: The consequences of supervisory behavior on officer performance and satisfaction.* Paper presented at the annual meeting of the Academy of Criminal Justice Sciences, Denver, Colorado, March.

Southerland, M. D. & Reuss-Ianni, E. (1992). Leadership and management. In G. W. Cordner & D. Hale (Eds.), *What works in policing?: Operations and administration examined* (pp. 157-177). Cincinnati: Anderson Publishing Co.

Sparrow, M. K., Moore, M. H., & Kennedy, D. M. (1990). *Beyond 911: A new era for policing.* New York: Basic Books Publishers Inc.

Steinman, M. (1986). Managing and evaluating police behavior. *Journal of Police Science and Administration,* 14 (4), 285-292.

Tenzel, J., Storms, L., & Sweetwood, H. (1976). Symbols and behavior: An experiment in altering the police role. *Journal of Police Science and Administration,* 4(1), 21-27.

Thibault, E. A., Lynch, L. M., & McBride, R. B. (1990). *Proactive police management* (2nd ed.). Englewood Cliffs, NJ: Prentice Hall.

Van Maanen, J. (1978). Observations on the making of policemen. In P. K. Manning & J. Van Maanen (Eds.), *Policing: A view from the street* (pp. 292-308). Santa Monica, CA: Goodyear Publishing Company, Inc.

Van Maanen, J. (1989). Making rank: Becoming an American police sergeant. In R. G. Dunham & G. P. Alpert (Eds.), *Critical issues in policing: Contemporary readings* (pp. 146-151). Prospect Heights, IL: Waveland Press Inc.

Wasserman, R. & Moore, M. H. (1988). *Values in policing. Perspectives on policing.* Washington, DC: National Institute of Justice.

Weisburd, D., McElroy, J., & Hardyman, P. (1988). Challenges to supervision in community policing: Observations on a pilot project. *American Journal of Police*, 7(2), 29-50.

Williams, H. (1991). External resources. In W. A. Geller (Ed.), *Local government police management* (pp. 463-487). Washington, DC: International City Management Association.

Chapter 13

Executive Responsibility

Darrel W. Stephens

> The police administrator is a much more important figure in the
> overall structure of government than is commonly recognized. He
> is constantly being called upon to formulate policies that require
> the balancing of fundamental and often conflicting values. His
> decisions directly affect the quality of life in his community.
> Herman Goldstein (*Policing a Free Society*, 1977)

Increasing Complexity of the Police Executive Job

Overall, today's police executives are much better prepared to meet
the challenges of policing in the 1990s than were their counterparts of the
1970s and the 1980s. The police chief today has more education and
experience than those of twenty years ago. Among the education available to
the police executive in the past decade has been a higher quality and more
extensive training and more opportunity to learn from colleagues as
conferences, seminars, and written material on policing have increased.
Twenty years ago a police chief could place the entire library of police
literature on three or four bookshelves. There has virtually been an
explosion of written material on policing in the past two decades that
provides knowledge and help that were not available to the police executive
of 1970.

The police chief of 1970 had almost no empirical research to guide
decisions on what the police should do to improve their effectiveness. At
that time, few in policing questioned the efficacy of the basic crime fighting
strategy of preventive patrol, rapid response, follow-up investigation,

arrest, prosecution, and incarceration. The limitations of that strategy are better understood today, and the research of the past twenty years has provided executives with the support they need to experiment with approaches to addressing crime problems that do not place as much emphasis on traditional crime control methods.

Nevertheless, the already difficult job of the police executive has increased in complexity as the problems of policing have become more complicated. This may sound like an obvious truth, but it is at least theoretically possible that, as frontline workers' jobs become more complex and they become more adept at fulfilling their responsibilities, the jobs of their bosses could become simpler rather than more complex. But such has not been the fate of American police administrators. With the exception of a few years in the early 1980s reported crime has steadily increased (even though actual *victimizations* have not). A greater number of people abusing drugs and the introduction of powerful crack cocaine in the mid-1980s have produced a level of lethal violence in many of our urban areas that has surpassed anything that we have experienced before. Increased work load, fueled in part by police encouraging citizens to call for everything, has overwhelmed the capacity of many 911 systems and the ability of officers to respond personally to these calls. In many communities across the nation police complain that they have no time to do anything but respond to 911 calls.

The criminal justice system has been overwhelmed as well. Jails and prisons at all levels of government are well beyond their capacity in spite of a building program that has more than doubled the number of beds available in the 1980s. Whatever value incarceration has as a deterrent to others has been limited further because of this situation and, even in those cases where incapacitation is a viable alternative, opportunities to use it are restricted. In most jurisdictions, for one offender to enter jail or prison another has to be released. In many states, criminals serve only a small portion of their sentences in order to make the space available for new inmates. In addition to limiting the cost of criminality to the offender, this overcrowding also curtails the use of arrest as the cornerstone of the police response to crime problems.

Moreover, the problems of cities and counties have become more intractable in the past twenty years. Most urban centers have lost middle-class taxpayers to suburban cities and counties. Jobs and businesses followed them. The urban cities have been left with the problems of poverty, unemployment, health care, inadequate housing, and a crumbling infrastructure with substantially less financial ability to deal with these issues. The suburban cities and counties face the problems of developing an infrastructure (streets, transportation, educational facilities, etc.) to serve the overwhelming growth of these areas. The problems of local government in both settings have been further complicated by the edicts of state and federal government that carry little or no financial assistance with them. At the same time state and federal government have transferred greater responsibility to local government for dealing with problems like the homeless, mentally ill, housing, and highway construction that historically had been either handled at or paid for by the federal or state government. Many of these problems have become local government problems because that is where public officials can least afford totally to ignore them. Police executives, of course, are key players in the urban and suburban arenas and must cope with the attendant demands as the problems increase and the resources available to the police and other units of local government become more scarce.

Along with the increasing severity and range of the problems the police must face come the increasingly complex executive tasks of leading and managing the organization. In today's environment the police, like local government in general, must meet the basic challenge of doing more with less, or in the best of circumstances, handling increased work load with the same level of resources. To do that, given the labor intensive nature of policing, a minimum requirement is for the people in the organization to be both more efficient and more effective. In short the police must improve their productivity. An important, but difficult, responsibility of the police executive is to provide the leadership in the community and organization needed to achieve those productivity improvements.

Partly the task of leading and managing today's police organizations is a formidable challenge because even though the current executives are better prepared and educated than their predecessors, many have failed to recognize the full effects of the fundamental changes in their work force. Today's police work force is better educated, more diverse, and much more willing to question both the organizational status quo and any efforts to change it. They are willing and able to launch their questions and critiques within the organization and in the political arena through their employee organizations. Many of our police executives cling to the top down autocratic management styles that focus almost exclusively on control and have always failed to make the best long-term use of the skills and knowledge of the officer on the street. In some of our police organizations we have produced adversarial relationships with the very people we expect to deliver competent service to the community.

The effects of unions on leading and managing police organizations have been felt throughout the nation, even in those states where collective bargaining is not permitted. The effects have been both positive and negative. On the positive side, the unions have been the key factor in improving salary and benefits for police officers at all levels. In many cases they have also improved overall working conditions for officers and provided protection against the arbitrary decisions of police supervisors and managers. They have also forced police executives to consult the rank-and-file officers on issues that affect their working conditions.

The downside, for many police departments, has been the introduction of even greater obstacles to changing practices and procedures to meet today's demands for police service. In some communities the unions have greater influence over scheduling and resource allocation than does management. Labor negotiations without the active involvement and leadership of thoughtful police executives over the years have produced contracts that have placed severe limitations on the ability of police organizations to be flexible enough to introduce the type of changes in assignments and practices that would result in greater productivity. In an exercise of municipal myopia, management rights have been given to unions to avoid providing increases in wages and benefits.

To the extent that unions have failed to get power at the bargaining table, they have ventured further into the political arena at every level of government, where they have been relatively successful at obtaining the passage of legislation favorable to their membership. This adds to the complexity of leading and managing a police organization in at least two ways: (1) impositions enacted by the legislation, and (2) the subtle and sometimes not subtle costs of "losing" in the political process. Candidates for political office, especially at the local level, remember whether or not they received the union's endorsement and/or campaign contributions. While the union clearly "wins or loses" with the election or defeat of the candidate, the police executive, the department, and the citizens are almost always losers in this process regardless of whether the union-endorsed or -financed candidate wins. If the candidate wins, the union gets the benefit of a receptive ear for issues of concern. If the opposing candidate wins, almost anything dealing with a police issue (especially increases in resources) is often viewed as being helpful to the people who opposed the union's preferred candidate.

One additional area that has increased the complexity of the police executive's job is the growing interest on the part of citizens (particularly minority citizens who believe the police treat them differently) to have some input and/or review concerning officer behavior. Over the past five years some type of civilian review in the nation's largest fifty cities have more than doubled (Walker and Bumphus, 1991). The creation of these boards usually follows a particularly serious incident of police use of force or a series of incidents that occur within a short-time frame. These incidents serve as the basis for raising questions about the police ability to investigate themselves credibly. Right behind these questions follows the proposal for civilian review, which in some cities has taken the form of moving the complaint reception and investigative processes outside of the police department. These measures introduce new complications for the police executive in dealing with officer behavior. In Washington, D.C.; for example, the chief may have to wait two or more years before he can discipline, or clear, an officer in connection with a complaint filed by a citizen.

Clearly, the challenge of fulfilling the responsibilities of the police CEO in any community has always been demanding and continues to grow in complexity. In the following section these challenges will be discussed in the context of the responsibilities the police executive has long been delegated to fulfill. The first three responsibilities addressed below are important to all police executives — even those who reject the trend toward a community problem solving style of policing. The responsibilities are matching structure to objectives, avoiding the activity trap, and enriching traditional roles. The last three more deeply affect police executives who are actively moving their organizations and communities toward new roles and relationships. They are establishing an environment for creativity while maintaining accountability, introducing change with some semblance of organizational stability, and developing alliances with the community.

Police Executive Responsibility

Matching Structure to Objective: Setting the Direction

Among the most important responsibilities of the contemporary police executive is to define and articulate the purpose of the organization. This is a difficult task for many executives because of the common belief that the purpose of the agency has been well defined in the government charter and in the laws that have been enacted for the police to enforce. These official statements of purpose have essentially been translated to mean that the primary purpose of the police is crime control through law enforcement. Clearly, crime control and law enforcement are important responsibilities of the police. However, experience tells us that citizens seek the help of the police far more frequently to address matters that are not directly related to crime or law enforcement. Therefore, a police executive must look to both the internal (organizational capabilities, unions, etc.) and external environments (political setting, crime, and service problems) in addition to government charters and laws to set the direction for policing the community.

In charting new courses for police organizations, executives have been turning to the private sector and learning from their experience with the concept of strategic management. This concept requires that police executives look at their roles and responsibilities from the perspective of what their police organization can provide to community improvement. These new directions for the police are most often set through the development of a statement of mission, the articulation of values, and the establishment of goals and objectives for the organization that are consistent with the mission and values. In *Beyond Command and Control* Moore and Stephens suggest that for a particular strategy to be successful it must meet three tests:

> First, the articulated goals and objectives must describe a purpose that is plausibly valuable to the society. Some public value must be created, some conception of the public interest successfully pursued. Otherwise, the enterprise will be unable to justify its costs. Second, the purpose must be operationally feasible and should take advantage of the distinctive competencies and capabilities of the organization. It must use the organization and its accumulated investments well. Third, the purpose must be able to continue to attract support from those in political and legal positions who authorize the continuation of the enterprise. Otherwise, the enterprise will be ill-founded. If a proposed strategy fails any of these tests — that is, if the proposed purpose has little value to the society, if the proposed purpose cannot be achieved by the organization or if there is or if there is little political or legal support for the proposed purpose — then the strategy is not appropriate (Moore and Stephens, 1991).

Thinking through an organization's capabilities to produce something of value within the framework of the external and internal environments is a difficult and critical police executive responsibility. Once articulated, the guiding principles also require that the organization be structured to match the direction set forth in the mission, goals, and objectives.

The typical police organizational structure is the classic pyramid, with six or seven layers of supervision and management between the chief executive and the officer on the street. The dominant organizational theme in policing is the functional structure. That is, police departments are organized around the police functions — patrol, investigations, administration, and support. They are also quasi-military organizations; officers wear military type uniforms and use military titles to identify the various levels. The combination of the military trappings and the pyramidal structure creates a sense of close supervision, strong discipline, and the concentration of important decisions at the top of the organization. Although these organizational features have survived many years, it is becoming increasingly clear they are not the most appropriate methods of organizing today's police departments. And, as more is learned about the emerging community problem solving style of policing, the future will call for dramatic changes in the way police departments are organized.

A policing strategy that calls for street level officers and investigators to collaborate with citizens and other governmental agencies in the development and implementation of solutions to problems requires more flexibility and greater line officer authority than most departments currently allow. Police departments are going to have to decrease the number of layers in the structure and push down more authority and responsibility than officers and detectives generally have. Individual officers and groups might operate almost like a franchise in the private sector — they will have a specified territory in which to provide their service within the framework of an overall set of goals, objectives, policies, procedures, and standards. The organizational structure of the future will require a much closer fit with the organization's purpose than has existed in the past.

Activity Trap — Process Over Product

For many years police and citizens alike have gauged police performance on the basis of process measures rather than products (outcomes or effects). The primary focus of police performance has been numbers of arrests, response time, reported crime, numbers of calls, and crimes cleared. As the police became more involved with the community the number of speeches given, meetings attended, and the size of the audiences have been added as performance measures. These activities have become substitutes for outcome or effectiveness measures because it is usually much easier to count the number of activities than it is to determine if the activities had the desired results.

Before the research conducted in the 1970s on rapid response to crime calls, it was assumed that immediate police response produced (1) more arrests, (2) higher levels of citizen satisfaction, and (3) some degree of deterrence to potential offenders. The research clearly showed that in connection with FBI Uniform Crime Report "part 1" crimes, response time affected arrest only about 3 percent of the time. The research also indicated that citizen satisfaction was related more to what the police did when they got there than how fast they arrived. It was also related to whether the police arrived when the call taker *said* they would arrive. The focus on reported crime assumes that the activities the police engage in have an effect on the level of crime, while it ignores unreported crime and other governmental or criminal justice policies that may influence how much crime occurs in a community. The emphasis on the numbers of calls and the amount of time to handle them fails to take into account the quality of the officer's response. Each of the traditional process measures the police use have similar limitations when considered in isolation and when outcomes from the activities being measured are not taken into account.

It is an important responsibility of the police executive to begin moving the organization toward productivity measures that are more reflective of police effectiveness. The process measures are not unimportant, they just need to be placed in their proper perspective. It is important to measure activity levels, for this provides information on what individuals or units of the organization are doing. Activity levels also give some indication of the organizational work load. The problems occur, however, when the organization emphasizes the activity measures over the outcome measures.

The emphasis placed on arrests is perhaps the best example of where the focus on counting activities can get in the way of effectiveness. Since 1986 the police have made large numbers of arrests for drug violations. In fact, a basic strategy in some urban communities was to "sweep the streets" of drug dealers and users. It was assumed these arrests would serve as a deterrent to both dealers and customers, reduce the level of violence associated with the drug trade, and reduce the complaints from citizens about these activities. But according to Eck,

> sweeps produce a large number of arrests but the little evidence that exists suggests that this strategy fails as often as it succeeds (Kleiman, 1988; Zimmer, 1987; Hayeslip, 1989). The successes that are achieved are often fleeting (Barnett, 1988). The costs of maintaining these operations can be quite high. And it is difficult to protect the civil liberties of neighborhood residents (and offenders) who may inadvertently be caught up in these operations (Bouza, 1988). Experimental evidence suggests that local residents do not notice any positive effects and their fear of crime remains unchanged (Uchida, 1989) (1989).

Although some police executives might argue that the sweep tactic would have been more effective had there been jail space, the focus on arrests in the absence of quality and outcomes produces approaches that may create more problems than they solve. In some locales police efforts to destabilize the "balance of power" among street gangs may unintentionally trigger violent turf wars among those competing to seize the new leadership and entrepreneurial opportunities. This does not mean, of course, that police should tolerate illegal enterprises in their communities, but it does suggest the need to think carefully through plans of attack to avoid making matters even worse than they have been.

The challenge facing police executives is how to change the focus from measuring police performance in the traditional ways to one where results are considered as well. It is an enormous challenge that requires the introduction of different ways of thinking about what the police do and how that is communicated to the public. It also requires the development of a greater level of sophistication on how activities are measured and how this information is conveyed to both the public and the police organization. Avoiding the "activity trap" is an important aspect of the responsibility of the police executive to develop an effective organization.

Enriching Traditional Roles

In the traditional police organization, the emphasis of the police executive has been on management. Police executives have been expected to focus on the responsibilities of planning, organizing, staffing, and controlling. In handling these responsibilities one important expectation of the police chief executive held by elected and appointed officials has been to minimize the amount of public controversy about the police. As long as the chief ensures that officers respond to calls in a satisfactory manner, crime increases are limited, morale is high, and those who create embarrassing incidents are dealt with promptly the chief's job security is relatively high. The control responsibility of the chief, however, does not extend to the rest of the criminal justice system, to the police union, or to the myriad other things that affect police department operations. Police executives are not able to meet the traditional expectations by just being good managers. To be effective a police CEO must also be a leader.

Most police executives have acted as if management and leadership were one and the same. Traditionally, the emphasis has been placed on the management role. What is required of police executives now and in the future is greater emphasis on the leadership role. There are many definitions of management and leadership but Bennis and Nanus seem to have captured the difference between the two best. They define management as doing things right and leadership as doing the right thing. Obviously, an effective executive must ensure that the organization does most things right. The more difficult and often more risky (in the short run) undertaking for the police executive is to do the right thing (Bennis and Nanus, 1985).

Frequently in policing, "the right thing" is not always clear. An acceptable approach to addressing a problem to one group is often not the best solution to another. Leadership is the glue that a police executive must use to hold things together and advance the programs that have been developed to address the problems. Witham has identified five different arenas in which a police executive must work and exercise leadership: (1) community, (2) political, (3) organizational, (4) interorganizational, and (5) the media (1984).

Each arena is important. They are interrelated, and each requires thoughtful consideration by the chief executive advancing any new ideas for dealing with problems. The community must be convinced the new approach has a greater chance of successfully addressing the problem than the old methods. The political representatives must be convinced the resources they will invest in a program are going to be well spent and that the majority of the community will go along with whatever is being proposed. Employees in the organization must have a sense the new program will succeed where others have not. Other organizations the police interact with have to understand what effect the proposed program will have on their operations.

The police executive must also find a way to communicate effectively the new program, the new idea, or the change in procedures to all of the arenas. The news media usually provide one of the most effective vehicles for doing this. An effective police chief executive is able to provide leadership in all five of these arenas. That is, he or she influences, guides, and creates a vision of how things ought to be that is plausible to the majority of people in each arena.

The greatest opportunity that exists for enriching the traditional role of the police executive lies in placing much more emphasis on leadership than management. A key aspect of this emphasis on leadership is communicating a new "vision" of what policing should be. The attributes of a "vision" have been described by Kouzes and Posner thusly

> a unique image of the future;
> it is something that can be seen; it evokes images and pictures;
> it reflects a future orientation;
> it suggests an ideal, a standard of excellence;
> it is unique to the leader or the organization. (1987)

The current dominant vision of policing is the "professional model." This model emphasizes law enforcement and crime fighting objectives and places the police in a dominant position in determining how these objectives will be achieved. The developing vision of policing that has been called community policing, problem-oriented policing, community problem solving, and other names recognizes the contributions the professional model has made to addressing deficiencies of the past. It also recognizes and understands the limitations of an approach that almost exclusively focuses the energies of the police on the internal organizational arena. That focus helps create the situation where most police organizations are overmanaged and underled. The new vision requires an emphasis on leadership.

Creativity With Accountability

One of the greatest challenges of a police executive is establishing an organizational environment where creativity can flourish. Creativity is almost antithetical to the traditional police organization. In the name of accountability police organizations have become highly structured, rigid, and centralized. Employees are trained in the "department's" way of doing things that has been developed over years. The "department's" way is reinforced with lengthy manuals of policy, procedures, rules, and regulations. The "department's" way is rarely openly questioned by those who do the work even though they soon discover that much of what they do is not directly addressed in the manuals or the training. They also discover that those who do raise questions and offer different approaches are not the beneficiaries of the department's reward systems. Although the policing environments of today and the future demand new approaches, yesterday's problems serve as strong inhibitors to developing creativity in police organizations.

In order to develop an environment where creativity thrives police executives will have to overcome the strong barriers that currently exist. One of the greatest barriers to creativity in policing is the belief that the current strategy is the best approach. Most people recognize the current strategy is not meeting expectations, but it is believed to fall short only because there are not enough resources invested to make it work. So the current view is that there is no need to create something new; just more adequately endow current approaches. This view is a powerful impediment to creativity that can only be overcome through aggressive efforts by police executives to encourage and support employees in questioning the existing policies, procedures, and operating procedures.

Some police departments routinely use ad hoc task forces and committees made up of representatives of every rank and a variety of assignments to address specific issues. The work of these groups is often facilitated by individuals trained to help them think outside of the traditional boundaries, and they are encouraged to develop new approaches for dealing with old issues. Some departments have used problem solving as a way of encouraging creativity. In the problem-oriented policing approach implemented by the Newport News Police Department, officers were specifically trained to analyze problems and encouraged to seek "non-traditional" solutions to them. The search for nontraditional solutions was supported by a committee of individuals from all areas of the department that regularly met to review an officer's progress on the problem-solving effort. This committee provided reinforcement to officers who proposed solutions that were different or even in conflict with the department's established way of doing things. Other departments have used suggestion boxes, quality circles, and other methods aimed at involving the person doing the work in efforts to improve both efficiency and effectiveness. The important point is that the police environment cannot be made more conducive to creative thinking without the direct intervention of the chief executive to make clear that a new order of things is being established.

A second barrier to creativity in policing is that new ideas must be introduced and survive in a hostile environment. Without an active commitment to nourishing and supporting new ideas most will never get the consideration they deserve, and employees will be reluctant to advance them. The police organization is filled with people who have numerous reasons why something won't work. In fact, this is usually the first response to a new idea that has been proposed. A police executive that asks how can we make the idea work, puts a different emphasis on an idea, and communicates the message that the idea is important even if it turns out that it cannot be implemented.

A third barrier in policing to establishing a more creative environment is the concern that many police executives have that they will lose control, more mistakes will be made, and as employee freedom increases so will the opportunities for abuse. There is a prevailing notion that the most creative environments are those that produce the least accountability and that with decreased accountability, comes increased liability and risk of losing one's job. The truth is, though, that the current environment in policing creates more of an illusion than a reality of managerial control.

There are many examples in the current control methods of the abuses being concentrated in a small number of people. In Los Angeles the Christopher Commission points out that 5 percent of the officers accounted for 20 percent of the use of force reports (Independent Commission on the Los Angeles Police Department, 1991). In Washington, D.C., 1 percent of the officers accounted for one-fourth of the complaints made by citizens. Do the current control mechanisms influence the behavior of the other 95 percent to 99 percent of the officers in those departments? Or do they simply provide a basis for dealing with those who struggle with differentiating right from wrong or cannot seem to exercise their authority in a way that respects the dignity of those with whom they deal? How one answers those questions is important to overcoming the reluctance to establish environments that allow officers greater freedom in addressing the problems of policing. Granting greater freedom to police officers is not tantamount to discarding all the mechanisms of control. Police executives can establish environments where creativity can thrive without decreasing the level of accountability. In fact, an environment where creativity flourishes might increase the amount of accountability at all levels of the police organization. To do this, the primary focus must be on the work of the police — the problems with which citizens look to the police for help. A patrol officer, for example, would be given the time and encouraged to identify the public's problems, analyze them, and seek creative ways of solving them. That does not mean officers are cast out entirely on their own.

They still have patrol areas to which they are responsible. Those areas are the sources of the problems on which they will work. They are still responsive to the radio and for answering calls for service. The calls are often the basis for identifying the problems on which they will work. They are still responsive to supervision. In fact, supervision may be closer. To gain the time to work on problems that are identified and the authorization for implementing nontraditional solutions officers must interact more frequently with their supervisors. In order to understand fully the problems in their areas, officers must interact with members of the community who are affected by them. This produces a level of knowledge by the community about the officer that does not currently exist. Rather than being policed by a stranger in a patrol car, the community sees a person who is concerned about them. Establishing an environment where officers are allowed greater flexibility in the way they do their work seems to have as much potential for increasing accountability as it does for decreasing it. Experience suggests that this type of environment will result in greater creativity and job satisfaction among officers, and it has considerable promise for making the police more effective.

Stability Amid Change

As one scans the internal and external environments of policing it is clear the police have experienced considerable change over the past twenty years and that change will continue into the future. Some of the change of the past has come from within, but much more has been imposed from forces outside of policing. Developments in information processing technology have introduced a considerable amount of innovation in policing. The civil courts have imposed changes on the police in response to citizens concerns over police practices experienced through lawsuits. Employee unions have influenced changes in how workers are treated and compensated. Citizens have sought and gained greater influence in monitoring the behavior of police officers. As one thinks about change in policing and looks to the future, there seem to be some clear lessons that we can draw from the past.

First, change is inevitable. Police executives are going to have to understand that fact and increase their skills in managing change. The basic law of nature is that organisms that fail to change — to adapt continually to their environment — perish. The same is true of organizations. Second, employees are affected by change and will vigorously resist changes they do not understand or have not had an opportunity to help plan or implement. Third, police executives are going to have to be more responsive to citizen concerns about police practices because citizens have demonstrated the capacity to alter these practices through the courts and the political process. The imposed changes are not always in the best interests of the police department or the overall community. Finally, police executives are going to have to create more stable environments in the midst of constant change. It is clear, if somewhat paradoxical, that change requires stability (Kanter, 1983).

Making use of the lessons of the past requires a much a much better understanding of the change process than most police executives have demonstrated. In his book, *How To Manage Change Effectively*, Kirkpatrick identifies the common themes on managing change:

1.   Managers must understand the people who will be affected by the change. Their feelings and emotions will have much to do with the effectiveness of the change.

2.   Change should not be forced on people. Otherwise strong resistance will probably occur.

3.   Effective communications are a must. People must be informed in advance and must understand the reasons for the change. Feedback from employees must be encouraged and listened to. If the ideas are used, credit must be given. If not, the manager should explain why the idea was not used.

4.   People who will be affected by the change should be involved in the decision-making process.

5.   It usually takes time for changes to be accepted. The more resistance, the longer the time. Therefore, planning should include the speed at which change is introduced.

6.   Strategies for deciding on changes and getting them implemented must be developed. These strategies should be based on principles that will help make the best decisions and get them accepted by those affected. (1985)

These themes represent some basic principles that police executives could follow in dealing with change, whether imposed from outside or stimulated from within. Obviously, the more adept a police executive is at anticipating the need for change and in its implementation the less the organization will be negatively affected by changes imposed by the external environment. That will contribute to increased stability for the organization in a world of policing where change will be the rule rather than the exception.

Community Alliance

Police departments exist to serve the community. This is a simple straightforward statement with which most police executives would agree. Indeed, it led Canadian police leader Chris Braiden to express his befuddlement over the term "community policing": "It's like saying you're going fishing for fish," he declared. Only when one begins to ask questions — Who is the community? What services should they receive? How should these services be provided? How much influence should they have in the decisions concerning police service? What is the role of the police executive in dealing with the community? — does the statement that police exist to serve the community become enormously complex. In the emerging strategy of community policing the role of the community is much larger than serving as victims, witnesses, and financiers of the policing enterprise. Kelling has expressed a powerful critique of traditional, reactive policing strategies. "We use crime victims," he observed, "as bait to feed the criminal justice system" (see Kelling, 1991).

In the new, preventive strategy community members are being asked to help identify and prioritize the problems on which the police work. They are expected to play more active roles in the implementation of solutions that have been developed to address the problems. And, they are being asked to agree to changes in the way some services are provided to allow more time for officers to focus on the problems that have been identified. The role of the police chief executive is critical to forging this new relationship or alliance with the community.

Perhaps the most critical role of the police chief executive in developing a new community alliance is that of communicator. The chief has the lead responsibility for communicating the vision and for developing the support for implementation of the vision in the community at large and in the political arena. This is an important responsibility that all too often is not given sufficient attention by the chief. Frequently, "communicating the vision" to the community is a one- or two-page news release made at a news conference in police headquarters where the chief is not much more than a talking head. Although the news release and conference are important steps, they are barely the beginning of the efforts that are required to develop an understanding on the part of the community of how the changes in policing styles might affect them. To be effective the police executive must do much more.

Before the vision is communicated to the community the chief must be sure that the organization has a good understanding of what the new style of policing involves and, to the extent possible, how that will change the way police do things and when personnel can expect implementation to begin. It is as important for the chief to play a key role in the internal process of communicating the vision as it is in the external.

Once the employees have a good understanding of the vision, a thoughtful plan of action should be developed that identifies the key people and groups in the community that need to understand the change and what methods will be used to reach them. The news release and subsequent news media attention might create an interest in what the police are doing — but they are not likely to impart the necessary information to develop an understanding of what is involved and generate the necessary success. It is important that the chief and other police executives make personal contact with the key people and groups that have been identified. Through this contact the chief and his or her team can address specific questions about how things will be different. The rationale for changing the way calls are responded to can be presented, and feedback can be heard on how citizens feel about the changes. The community needs to know the process for implementation.

They should be told if the new approach will be implemented immediately throughout the city or if it will be phased in over a period of time. Through personal involvement in the communication process the chief is showing the importance of the effort and demonstrating a commitment to the new direction. Following the initial contacts with the people and groups identified in the plan, opportunities should be sought in the day-to-day operations of the department that show the value of the new approach.

Establishing and maintaining an alliance with the community is an important and difficult responsibility for the police chief. Communities are collections of many different cultures, values, and beliefs. Communities have differing expectations of the police. In one part of the community the police may be expected to strictly enforce the law. In another part of the community the expectation might be that the police exercise discretion and use the law as a means to an end — not an end in itself. Police executives have the responsibility to establish an environment where these differences in expectations can be sorted out so the police can be responsive to the community and responsible in light of legal and ethical obligations to policing without favoritism or discrimination.

This requires, of course, that alliances with the community be built around fundamental values. Communities must understand, and the chief must communicate in words and practice, that the police will not break the law to enforce the law. The chief must serve as the organizational symbol around which a relationship of trust can be established and nurtured. Trust is established through an honest and open relationship with the community. It requires the chief to acknowledge when mistakes have been made and to support employees when they make decisions they believed were right that turned out to be wrong. It requires the chief and other police department employees to seek out and create opportunities to discuss issues that affect them. Alliances with communities are strongest when the department personnel reflect the diversity of the community. When the work force does not, the chief must make a personal commitment to the community that diversity in the department is a high priority and demonstrate through hiring and promotion practices that the commitment is sincere, even if implementation will take some time. Alliances with the community must be based on the idea that integrity is the most valued characteristic of the chief and police department employees. Alliances built around fundamental values do not ensure smooth and conflict-free relationships. They do however, provide a basis for working together and building relationships that serve the best interests, of both the police department and the community.

Conclusion

The tasks and responsibilities of the police chief executive have always been complex. An examination of the external and internal environments of policing clearly indicates that the difficulty of the job is increasing as the complexity of the issues and problems the police are called on to address increase. The success of the police in addressing the persistent issues facing our business is directly related to the effectiveness of the chief in articulating an inspiring vision and providing the leadership needed to make it a reality.

References

Bennis, W. & Nanus, B. (1985). *Leaders: The strategies for taking charge.* New York: Harper & Row, Publishers Inc.

Eck, J. E. (1989). *Police and drug control: A home field advantage.* Washington, DC: Police Executive Research Forum.

Goldstein, H. (1977). *Policing a free society.* Cambridge, MA: Ballinger.

Independent Commission on the Los Angeles Police Department. (1991). *Report of the Independent Commission on the Los Angeles Police.* Los Angeles: City of Los Angeles.

Kanter, R. M. (1983). *The change masters.* New York: Simon & Schuster.

Kelling, G. L. (1991). *Crime and metaphor.* New York: The City Journal.

Kirkpatrick, D. L. (1985). *How to manage change effectively.* San Francisco: Jossey-Bass Inc., Publishers.

Kouzes, J. M. & Posner, B. Z. (1987). *The leadership challenge: How to get extraordinary things done in organizations.* San Francisco: Jossey-Bass Inc., Publishers.

Moore, M. H. & Stephens, D. W. (1991). *Beyond command and control: The strategic management of police departments.* Washington, DC: Police Executive Research Forum.

Walker, S. & Bumphus, V. W. (1991). *Civilian review of the police: A national survey of the 50 largest cities.* Omaha: University of Nebraska.

Witham, D. C. (1984). *The American law enforcement chief executive: A management profile.* Washington, DC: Police Executive Research Forum.

Chapter 14

Current Perspectives on Policing

Victor G. Strecher

Thinking about the future of policing and our attempts to influence it depend more than a little upon our knowledge of the beginnings and derivation of policing as a social institution and as a subculture. And the utility of our knowledge depends, in turn, upon the validity and comprehensiveness of our frame of reference.

Two of the common but generally conflicting conceptions of history are that (1) human societies proceed through *cycles*, or recurrent patterns, as if a great wheel turns and seemingly returns to familiar inevitable imprints, and (2) human history is a linear path upon which are found major epochs and major actors. The cyclic model is found in the common idea of the rise, flowering, and demise of civilizations, and in the works of Pareto (circulation of elites), Ibn Khaldun (nomadic and sedentary successions), and, more recently, Wilburt Moore (the sin and penance cycles of backslide and reform). This scheme is particularly attractive to those who view with alarm a Rome-like decline in our society. The alternative linear/epochal model is perhaps exemplified in Vico's ages of gods, heroes, and men, in which the style of society progressed from the theocratic to the heroic to the rational. It is also prominent in Marx's historical progressions, and essential to most ideologies of human social progress.

A generation ago it could be said that policing was an occupation without a written, generally known history and its academic counterpart a field with a one-book theoretical foundation. What was commonly known of policing penetrated the past barely beyond the collective memories of elderly police practitioners and journalists on the police beat. The few published works of the nineteenth century (e.g., Baker (1867), Savage (1971), Costello (1970), Flinn and Wilkie (1973), Hale (1893), Roe (1976) and early twentieth century (e.g., Fosdick (1969), Fuld (1909), Hamilton (1924), Hickey (1925), Maltby (1906), Peck (1903), Russell (1975) were largely anecdotal, richly subjective, and occasionally self-serving glimpses rather than systematic histories. The contemporary, serious study of police history had not yet commenced (although Hale (1893), Fosdick (1969), and Fuld (1909) did provide cross-sectional views of policing in their times).

Fortunately, the past fifteen years have seen the beginnings of a significant history of policing in the works of Gene and Elaine Carte (1975), Robert Fogelson (1977), Mark Haller (1976), Sidney Harring (1983), David Johnson (1981), Roger Lane (1967), Wilbur Miller (1976), Eric Monkkonen (1987), James Richardson (1978), John Schneider (1980), Richard Terrill (1989), and Samuel Walker (1977). Collateral historical insights have derived from works of Egon Bittner (1990), Peter Manning (1977), Arthur Neiderhoffer (1967), Louis Radelet (1973), Albert Reiss (1971), Thomas Repetto (1978), Jerome Skolnick (1966), and others.

But as enlightening and helpful as the historical treatments of policing have been, they have not provided the depth, breadth, scope, detail, and quality of insight that would adequately serve our needs. For these needs go beyond having a genealogy of bureaucratic structures or of critical events, roles, or political successions. We need a more explicit tracing of changes in American culture and in the police subculture, which can be extrapolated systematically into the future. Purposes include not only policy analysis and formulation, but also the design of continuing research into the development of policing.

The most serious shortcoming of existing historical materials is their failure to establish meaningful units of analysis, their tendency to select events as the major (or only) indicia of change, and a certain arbitrariness in the assessment of significance of events. Too often, too little is made of the social contexts within which policing and its management evolved. The method needs to move beyond historiography.

Conceptual Framework

What is proposed here is an alternative view of the development of policing in the United States. It is in many ways like the biological science of genetics, and will use the terminology of that science because of its aptness. But it is also like epistemology, the origin and derivation of ideas, and so will rely also upon the methods and concepts of Arthur O. Lovejoy, founder of the *Essays in the History of Ideas* (1955).

The ideas of genetics are now well known. The double helix segments of DNA, called genes, are visualized as tiny spots on chromosomes, which are larger threadlike structures located in all cells and which transmit characteristics of the reproducing organism to its offspring. An important aspect is that there are always many more possibilities of characteristics in the genes (DNA) than are actually passed forward. The notion of evolution, of course, is that DNA that helps the offspring to adapt and survive is more likely to let the offspring live long enough to reproduce and thus show up in successive generations. Originally biological, the idea of adaptability and survival eventually had powerful overtones of social survivability in the latter part of the 1900s and first decade of the twentieth century in the works of William Graham Sumner at Yale.

As for the transmission of ideas, Lovejoy asserted in *The Great Chain of Being* (Lovejoy, 1970, pp. 3-23) that "new" ideas are seldom new, but more often novel combinations of "unit ideas," most of which have appeared previously in different combinations. He compared the world of ideas to analytic chemistry, stating that the apparently countless number of different ideas may be more like the numberless chemical compounds that are composed of few more than a hundred elements in the periodic table. The new combinations, he says, are not always recognizable as new compounds of old elements. The same elements are often renamed, and old names, if used, may be used differently. These compounds, he adds, should be considered to be "unstable compounds."

In addition to the foregoing, three ideas of Lovejoy's (1933) will be used in this chapter:

- Implicit assumptions or unconscious mental habits operate in the thoughts of individuals or generations. These beliefs are so much commonplace and presupposed, not even formally expressed and argued for, that they establish a dominant intellectual tendency of an age.

- There are, in this sense, susceptibilities to various kinds of "metaphysical pathos . . . evocation of emotional reverberations" that operate below the level of conscious reasoning and contribute to new combinations of ideas.

- The most significant factor in the expression of new combinations of ideas may not be in the doctrine itself, but in the motives that led their authors to state them.

The most interesting aspect of Lovejoy's scheme is its similarity to genetics: both provide modes of transmission of biological traits or ideas from one generation to another.   The idea that there are innumerable traits available to be passed along to the next generation (but not necessarily reaching it) is immensely attractive in both the realm of physical traits and the values and knowledge base. Why? Because, like "good" theory, it seems to explain so much of what we can observe.

Social, Cultural, and Subcultural Change

The evolution of policing and of its management are forms of social change, and more particularly forms of institutional social change.   The institution of policing is merely one of the many institutions that have emerged in our complex social system to activate and sustain some of our more compelling and durable values. *Community safety* is a social value, while *policing* is one of the actualizing instruments of this value. In a simpler society the value alone, operating uniformly and consistently in the behavior of its members, might suffice to produce the social effect by means of the collective effort of that membership.   On the other hand, in complex societies, with their minutely detailed division of work, most of the important values eventually crystallize into social institutions, which give continuity to the fulfillment of these social values. These institutions, in turn, undergo social change as their social environment changes. Examples of other values that become institutions are education (schools), spiritual belief (churches), security for working people (labor unions), and monetary exchange (currency systems and banks).

But policing is more than just another social institution; it has been aptly termed a *subculture*, which implies for its membership more than a secondary, earning-a-living institutional relationship.

We are interested here, as the title implies, in identifying and tracking what might be termed the genetic material, or "Cultural DNA," of the policing institution, which leaves its imprint upon successive generations of policing.

But despite the ease of identifying policing as a modern *social institution*, it must be emphasized that social institutions do not by themselves carry cultural DNA material through the generations. To carry the analogy a step further, institutions might be considered only one of the kinds of "genes" that are imprinted with the nucleotides of former generations of American societies — a form of cultural memory.

If institutions are but one kind of gene, what are the others? The following are offered as elements of a conceptual framework for social change in general, and the evolution of policing as the subject of immediate interest. Obviously, because of the extensiveness of the topic, the method will be illustrated in this article rather than fully played out.

Genes of Social Change

The genes of social change consist of the "nucleotides" of a culture — the character of its essential building blocks. Just as the molecules of DNA, called nucleotides, consist of various combinations of the base elements adenine, guanine, thymine, and cytosine, so too any culture is a combination of certain basic elements. Some of these bases are physically observable features in a culture, such as:

- *Institutions* or *organizations* (e.g., for the culture as a whole, business, government, education, religion; for the police subculture, patrol force, detective bureau, police union, etc.)

- *Physical environments* or *habits* or other parts of the *social ecology* (e.g., for the culture, suburbs, office buildings, factories, farms, small towns, metropolises, Native American reservations, urban slums, parks; for the police subculture, beats in the "war zone" or the quiet suburb, the dope pad, fence, chop-shop, foot patrol, highway patrol, underwater recovery, etc.)

- *Technologies* (e.g., for the culture, steel making, all-weather air travel, X-ray diagnosis, telephones, television, beer brewing, desktop publishing; for the police subculture, Gamewell boxes, in-car computers, National Crime Information Center, radar, surveillance vans, etc.)

But others would be *ideas* of considerable variety, including:

- *Beliefs* or *social values,* the former referring to those of individuals, the latter to their aggregated distribution within groups or the entire culture

- *Values* and *social functions* in this discussion are often parallel concepts, sometimes equivalent in usage (e.g., for the culture, criminalization or decriminalization of substance abuse, freedom of speech, acceptance or rejection of sexual behaviors, for the police subculture, only the "thin blue line" keeps the peace, "we" need to control "them," keep secrets in the family)

- *Knowledge base* of a culture, comprising its intellectual, scientific, and artistic heritage, difficult in some cases to distinguish from its *technologies*, a somewhat more "realized" form of cultural invention (e.g., for the culture, everything we know; for the police subculture, Wilson's notion of "omnipresence," requiring patrol plans; "case linking," requiring crime analysis; national tracking of serial killers, requiring a VICAP data base

Still others would be observable only if conceptualized and deliberately observed in a scientific sense:

- *Economy* in the sense of arbitrary and symbolic systems exchange in modern cultures. Individual economic behaviors and those of institutions aggregate to patterns for the entire culture and, indeed, among cultures (e.g., for the culture, a bullish market, decision to buy a car this year or next, depression, 5 percent or 8 percent unemployment; for the police subculture, erosion of city's tax base, driving patrol car 120,000 miles rather than 60,000, no salary increases, freeze on hiring, etc.)

- *Social structure* represented in stratification or a cultural hierarchy based upon status indicators (e.g., for the culture, family, wealth, education, occupation, and ability; for the police subculture, rank, assignment, privileges, recognition. Structure is found in primary social groups, institutions, and in the culture as a whole. Social class or "socio-economic status" refer to social structure and to the indicators commonly used.

- *Social roles* that provide individual activations of social functions, often in *social institutions* (e.g., for the culture, there are common roles, such as teachers, maids, and judges, but there also inventors, politicians, and actors — roles that do not exist in some cultures. On the other hand, we no longer have court composers or a king's food taster. For the police subculture, there are patrol officers, detectives, ballesticians, undercover investigators, supervisors and chiefs)

Incidentally, the "base elements" of *knowledge base* and *technologies* are separated because most police histories fail to distinguish between what is known to be possible to do and the actual practices of policing. In this sense, historical accounts often move freely among disparate elements of practice and knowledge without noting whether they are connected with their ideational and activity counterparts. In many cases, it is suspected, no distinction is made because none is recognized or even suspected. In our time, all that's required to establish a distinction between knowledge and practice is to observe the variety of police operational forms and quality to be found among agencies within a single metropolitan area. From primitive to state-of-the-art modern and from corrupt, brutal, and inept to professional policing can be observed within a few miles of each other in many parts of the country.

A model of cultural change might look like the following (Figure 1), which, when drawn forward by time, involves a lively interaction of all the "bases" in the model. In this model *cause and effect* are difficult to establish.

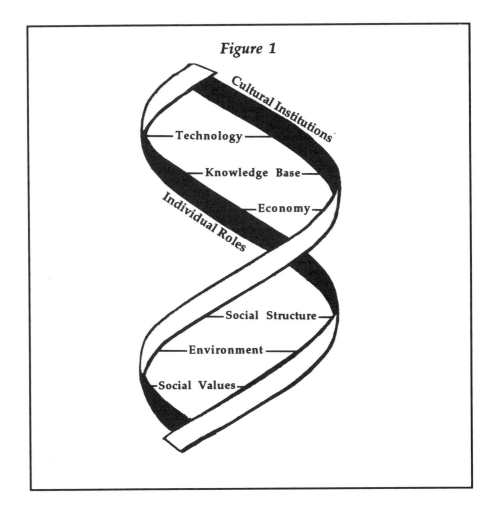

Figure 1

Cultural Institutions

Technology

Knowledge Base

Individual Roles

Economy

Social Structure

Environment

Social Values

The restless, continuous interactions of the "bases" of these "DNA" strands produces countless potentiating effects that almost immediately rebound upon their causes. Like biological genetics and evolution, continuous small-scale adaptations are hard to observe, but major points of mutation — introduction of new or changed DNA, often impelled by external events — is often strikingly observable.

Although simple cause and effect patterns of change have been described as elusive, it is often possible to hypothesize about the stimuli of major effects, although these relationships are sometimes open to alternative explanations. Following are some speculations about the evolution of policing and about the emergence and evolution of the *police subculture*, which would be one of the institutions in the cultural frame of the figure above.

Institutions are conceptualized here as crystallizations of pervasive and important social values (or functions) in the form of durable, organized efforts to provide continuity in the fulfillment of these values. Popular education in the United States is an example of an institution engendered by a value that is not found in some other cultures. So is policing.

Colonial American Policing

An enduring and lethal pairing of *value genes* entered the colonial New World, a genetic strain that has operated almost continuously, with varying degrees of intensity to the present time. The two genes are elements of America's earliest conflicted times, and may be described as *moralistic exclusivity* versus *frontier multiculturalism* This strain is often cast in a narrow framework of Puritanism against Enlightenment Rationalism or Deism, but Puritanism was not alone in claiming exclusive status. As early as 1643, even before the *Ratelwacht* was organized in New Amsterdam, there were twenty different nationalities and sects on Manhattan Island, speaking eighteen languages (Costello, 1970, p. 5). The colonists who came to America to escape oppression were not prepared to accept multiculturalism any more than their European oppressors were. In 1631 a decree of the Massachusetts General Court provided that only members of the established church would be extended the privilege of citizenship. This law was passed during a ten-year wave of migration into Massachusetts, during which only 4,000 of the 16,000 persons who entered the colony were church members. It seems a quite theocratic beginning for what was to become the most pluralistic nation in the world. The lethal pairing of Puritanical and rational and pragmatic values genes has plagued American politics and, as a consequence, American policing. For it is often at the street level that this symbolic clash of beliefs is played out.

The following is an attempt to portray the interaction of the moral value gene with other DNA in colonial times. It seems reasonable to assume that the felt need for community security (social value or function) in the earliest colonial settlements preceded the creation of the burgher watch and *Ratelwacht* in New Amsterdam (1650s) (Costello, 1970, p. 10) and the Boston night watch (1630s) (Savage, 1971, p. 8), which were minimal institutional responses to the perceived needs and the values attached to these needs. Once established, however, the reciprocal and rebounding effects of social change become apparent as the original mandate for arousing the populace if trouble arose was expanded to

- New Amsterdam, 1650s — ". . . interdicting the tapping of beer during the hours of divine service (on the Sabbath) or after ten o'clock at night; and brawling and all kinds of offenses; removal of hog-pens and out-houses from the highway, prohibiting trespass" (Costello, 1970, pp. 5-7).

- New York, 1702 — "A new duty was imposed on the Constables . . . . This was to visit every house, and see whether the inhabitants kept the number of fire buckets required by law . . . (also) to make a presentment of all such persons as shall neglect or refuse to clean their streets . . . (or) in any way break the Holy Sabbath" (Costello, 1970, p. 31).

At this early stage of maintaining order in the colonies these interactions of "base elements" might be depicted in Figure 2.

For Boston the interactions of "base elements" might be somewhat different, considering the following events (see Figure 3):

- Boston, 1769 — "In consequence of existing difficulties, the watch were ordered 'to patrol two together'" (Savage, 1971, p. 33).

But these are primitive examples of the institutionalization of public order, and long before anything resembling a police department, much less a *police subculture*, began.

Major Stimuli of Change in the Police Subculture

A comprehensive model of social change — one that would explain much of what is happening in our world — involves an ongoing but uneven

Figure 2

HYPOTHETICAL EVOLUTION OF POLICE FUNCTION IN COLONIAL AMERICA

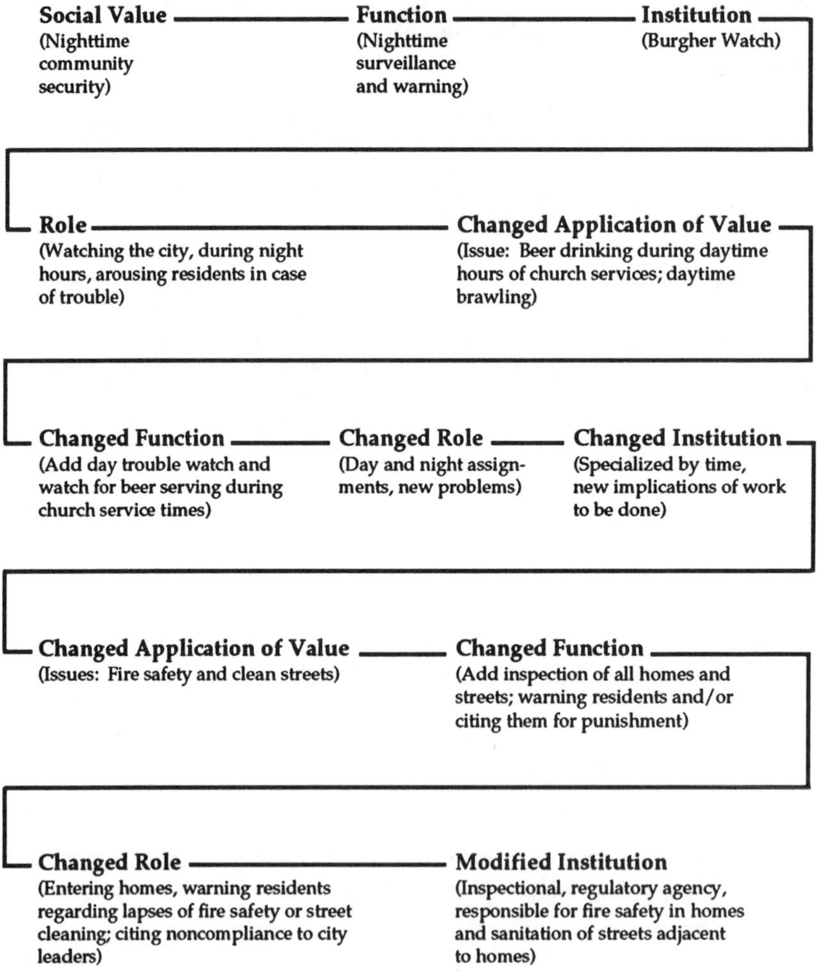

Social Value ——————— **Function** ——————— **Institution** ——
(Nighttime   (Nighttime   (Burgher Watch)
community   surveillance
security)   and warning)

Role ———————————————————— **Changed Application of Value** ——
(Watching the city, during night   (Issue: Beer drinking during daytime
hours, arousing residents in case   hours of church services; daytime
of trouble)   brawling)

Changed Function ——————— **Changed Role** ——————— **Changed Institution** ——
(Add day trouble watch and   (Day and night assign-   (Specialized by time,
watch for beer serving during   ments, new problems)   new implications of work
church service times)   to be done)

Changed Application of Value ——————— **Changed Function** ——————
(Issues: Fire safety and clean streets)   (Add inspection of all homes and
                                            streets; warning residents and/or
                                            citing them for punishment)

Changed Role ———————————————————— **Modified Institution**
(Entering homes, warning residents   (Inspectional, regulatory agency,
regarding lapses of fire safety or street responsible for fire safety in homes
cleaning; citing noncompliance to city   and sanitation of streets adjacent
leaders)   to homes)

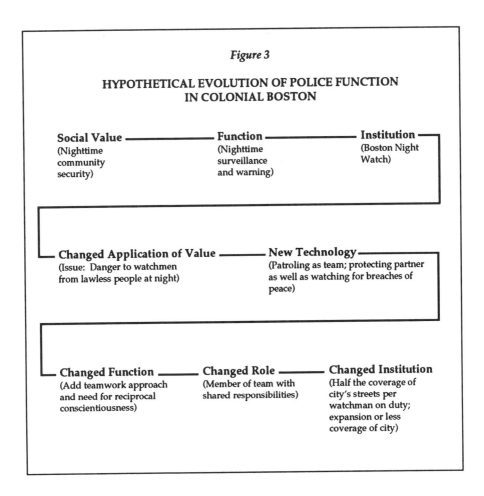

Figure 3

HYPOTHETICAL EVOLUTION OF POLICE FUNCTION
IN COLONIAL BOSTON

Social Value ——————— Function ——————— Institution ─┐
(Nighttime   (Nighttime   (Boston Night
community   surveillance   Watch)
security)   and warning)

┌─ Changed Application of Value ——————— New Technology ───────
│ (Issue: Danger to watchmen   (Patroling as team; protecting partner
│ from lawless people at night)   as well as watching for breaches of
│   peace)

┌─ Changed Function ——————— Changed Role ——————— Changed Institution
│ (Add teamwork approach   (Member of team with   (Half the coverage of
│ and need for reciprocal   shared responsibilities)   city's streets per
│ conscientiousness)   watchman on duty;
│   expansion or less
│   coverage of city)

interaction of the factors described in the model above. The "genes" or "DNA" or change are the specific inventions, values, structural features, ideas, economic conditions, status indicators, and ecological arrangements that continuously interact to shape a social system. Any major change in one of these factors — e.g., a technological change, such as the use of automobiles on patrol, or an ideational one, such as expecting the police to control crime, puts stress on the existing arrangement of these genes and induces change in them.

Incipient Policing and Its Genetic Content: 1830-1880

Early American policing was as intensely political as the very creation of the United States and its formation of other governmental institutions. It was, after all, a revolutionary beginning in a complex milieu of social perspectives and values, and a struggle between continuity and change in social institutions, structures, economics, and political development.

Knowledge Base Element

Peel's Reforms were known to the major cities, such as New York, Philadelphia, and Boston, during the 1830s. Even the London Metropolitan Police uniforms were widely imitated, often by individual officers before those cities adopted uniforms; badges, number tags, and cap pieces followed. Perhaps these were superficialities, but it is more likely they were the simplest of the Peelian reforms to imitate. Accounts of early police organizing in the major cities had overtones of Peelian ideas, and the Progressive Era reforms were strikingly like Peel's and found as far west as Cincinnati and Omaha.

Values Element

Some of the values and values disputes that entered the gene pool of policing at that time were the following:

> The *rural-urban values pair* is another bipolar combination that was clearly evident during Revolutionary times, a precursor of modern, partisan differences between Democrats and Republicans on such issues as central executive power versus local legislative power. It includes rural attitudes that agriculture is fundamentally good, while cities are inherently wicked; that rural work is healthful, while urban industrial work is detrimental to well-being that slave labor is an economic necessity, that the countryside is peaceful, whereas the city is foul with crime and immorality. City dwellers' values held country folk to be uneducated, superstitious, slothful, dependent upon slave labor, and culturally backward, while the city served as the repository of Western culture, higher learning, sophistication and technological development. Urbanites thought themselves energetic and quick to accept change, while rural folk lived in the past.

There is a tendency to equate the rural viewpoint with the southern states and the urban perspective with the northern states because of the respective predominance of agriculture and industry in those two regions. There were, however, crossover perspectives in both the northern and southern regions of the newly forming nation.

Institutional offshoots of these value differences were reflected in the rural sheriff becoming the more powerful institution of policing in the South, and the city police becoming the primary institution in the north. Here, too, there are obvious exceptions.

Political values entered the police gene pool most explicitly during the "Spoils Era of American politics" (1829-1883) (Germann et al., 1967, p. 68). A somewhat longer version of this period has been called the "Political Era" of American policing by Kelling and Moore (1988), thereby raising two implications about policing and politics.

First, it raises the question of whether policing was deviantly political or simply part of an era that was inherently political. Policing, after all, was merely one of many governmental services, functions, and processes being devised throughout that period. Was the emergence of services such as sanitation, waste disposal, water supply, fire protection, parks and recreation, street construction, welfare, public health, social services, and education also beset by political struggles? Were the associated functions of taxation, budgeting, public personnel administration, the emergence of civil service, land-use controls, and licensing politicized? Anybody cognizant of the histories of these governmental services and processes knows of the intense, protracted political influences and conflicts that attended their development.

Second, this labeling implies that politics were uniquely manifest in this period and that in later eras the influences of politics were eliminated, reduced, or displaced by some other social mechanisms. This is so clearly not the case that it merits only brief consideration. Kelling and Moore are hardly alone in having failed to distinguish between the primitive sorts of corrupt and dominating machine politics prevalent during the formative years of American local governments and the less controlling but still prevalent political incursions into policing commonly recognized through subsequent periods of development and to the present time. There is a crucially important distinction to be made between the "politics" that Wilbur R. Miller described in the early New York City Police Department (Miller, 1976): The appointment of police officers by aldermen of each ward, the continuing debt of those policemen to their individual aldermen, including the responsibility to work for their reelection to safeguard their jobs, and the several unsuccessful attempts to bring all police officers of the city under citywide executive authority. These events and their significance are in contrast to the less comprehensively controlling "politics" in policing encountered during Prohibition and in more recent times (e.g., Ahern's *Police in Trouble* (1972), regarding his experience as chief of the New Haven Police Department).

"Politics," in the context of the structure of American government — three branches of government and their interdependent accountability model — is an essential element of American local governance and thus necessarily part of the administration of policing. The question is not whether politics has a role in policing, but only what that role should be and when it is legitimately to be exercised. City councils have the duty to appropriate funds, but generally not a duty or right to decide who will be promoted within internal police ranks. Councils can pass licensing ordinances, but should not tamper with police inspection reports upon licensed premises.

The customary failure of conventional wisdom to distinguish between this kind of legitimate political involvement and the primitively corrupt machine politics of the nineteenth and early twentieth centuries introduces serious confusion into any discussion of a "political era" and the succeeding eras. If we merely mean the amount, nature, and intensity of political intrusion into policing changed, we should say that, but then we should recognize that inappropriate intrusions have continued to the present day.

This point needs emphasis. The design of American government requires politics at the executive level of policing. The pejorative labeling of "politics" during these early developmental times was carried forward and institutionalized. It eventually became a straw man symbol around which to organize policing's resistance to any form of political influence over its practices. This symbol of "politics" — assumed to be corrupt and inimical to the proper functioning of dedicated police officers — persists not only in the thinking of police officials but in the beliefs of middle-American culture as well.

Corruptibility was a mainstream component of policing during its formative generations, inasmuch as it was a creature of its politically corrupt social context. It could not have been otherwise, considering the power of the urban ward bosses in the North, the planters in the South, and the mine owners in the "company towns."

Brutality was simply a sidecar to the corruptibility gene, inevitable, considering the social context of early policing. This earliest time of development might be called the "primitive" era of government, and the title should be applied to all institutions of American government (and perhaps culture) rather than singling out the police.

As this discussion continues, it will be useful to remember that the evolution of policing (or of any social change) is not a linear developmental line, whether toward improvement or deterioration. Like biological genetics and epistemology, a characteristic of policing (an idea, technique, process, obsession, belief, organization structure, or ethos) can drop from sight and then reappear after an absence of decades. But those genes and ideas and social processes never really disappeared because they have been carried along in the germ plasm or the culture, and when they recycle it their reappearance is in a new body, a new social context.

"Eras" or "epochs" with their new ideas and conditions do not cause cultural knowledge to somehow disappear. Social change theory instructs us that social innovation is overlaid upon existing culture rather than destroying it. Culture is not thrown away. New ideas are continuously joined with old ideas in myriad combinations; values not only change, but become more diverse, subtle, and shaded in meanings. New institutions emerge from powerful social values (e.g., public education, paid policing) and then endlessly reorganize to reflect shifting values. Social innovation emerges out of complex interactions of technology, institutions, values, creative roles, and the human environment. An accurate reading of history would find social change to be a restless network of interaction among variables such as these.

Police Reform

General governmental reform began during the 1880s. Popular revulsion to the fiscal and personnel excesses of the Grant administration generated pressures for reform that eventuated in ethical constraints upon national, state, and local governmental practices. It was the assassination of President Garfield in 1882 that precipitated Congress's passage of the Pendleton Act, the first attempt to bring civil service and merit principles into federal government (ca. 1883). It was merely one of the signals of this movement. Fiscal reforms were set in motion, although they were not effective until 1910 in the case of New York City, and 1920 in the case of the U.S. government.

This initial reform thrust was aimed at blatant governmental corruption: nepotism, favoritism in awarding government contracts, bribery, and in general the use of political powers by elected and appointed officials as baronial prerogatives.

These years were notable for the number of police scandals that resulted in the removal of chiefs and moves to bring police operations under more central, executive branch control in the cities. George Hale's *Police and Prison Cyclopedia* of 1893 contains an astonishing set of commentaries from police chiefs in response to his survey report of 1893. Although there is plenty of rough and ready stuff here (as there would be today), it is more than offset by the articulate, socially pragmatic, and reform-minded tone of many chiefs' statements.

Some of the DNA that entered policing from its reform-minded social context of the time included (1) accountability to the law and ethics, but not to partisan politicians or conservative moralists outside the legal framework; (2) emphasis upon centralized executive command, supervision, and departmental rules and regulations; (3) communications between the station and the police beat, so that officers could be better managed and informed of the need for their services.

Values, Ideas, and Knowledge

Community, in the sociological sense (*gemeinschaft*, mechanical solidarity, shared values) was nearest to actual realization during the earliest days of New World policing during colonial times. The function of the early Watch was to spot disorder and summon all adult men to restore order. That was "community." As New World communities became culturally diverse, Watch members and later police officers were called upon increasingly to define "order" more arbitrarily in accord with the local rule makers. "Crimes" requiring a response from the Watch or (early) police were pretty generally considered crimes by the community. Even "crimes" of slaves (attempted escape, disrespect) were "community consensus" crimes in their specific cultural regions.

Dating from 1830 and the beginnings of institutionalized policing, however, definitions of "order" and "crime" became increasingly arbitrary and technical, and thus the gulf grew between the *values* of police officers and the *definition of the police mission*. Some of the cultural genes emerging during this era from the combination of the "bases" of values, ideas, and knowledge were

- *Experience mystique.* Only experience can teach a police officer what he or she needs to know, and only police officers are in a position to have that experience.

- *Use of force.* "No taint of official corruption or prostitution of authority attaches to any member of the force. Brutal clubbing, severity, and unkind treatment of prisoners, which are frequently noticed in the newspapers of other cities, form no part of the record of the Denver police."

- *Morality versus law as basis of enforcement.* "Police are not agents of creeds and sects, but of the law." (Cincinnati)

- *Civil service.* Civil service for urban policing was well established by 1893. Of 142 cities in Hale's survey, 49, or 35 percent reported being under civil service laws. This figure is on the low side, because some cities reported similar personnel systems maintained by police commissions. Considering the federal law dated from 1883, this diffusion of civil service across the country represents a rapid adaptation, one that might be termed a case of massive reform. Civil service cities were found in California, Connecticut, Illinois, Indiana, Iowa, Louisiana, Massachusetts, Michigan, Minnesota, New Jersey, New York, Ohio, Tennessee, Texas, Washington, West Virginia, and Wisconsin. Civil services was distributed about equally among all sizes of cities.

- *Buffering.* Buffering in several forms besides civil service entered the policing plasm during the Progressive Era, and would see a resurgence in the 1930s, when public administration flowered. It was clear, though, even in the 1883-1893 period that the police needed protection from inappropriate political interference and demogoguery.   Boards, commissions, and other buffering mechanisms containing police job protections came into existence as alternatives to civil service. All of these buffers were intended to shield the police from partisan politics. Atlanta, 1893: "The members of the force are kept out of politics as much as possible, and retain their position as long as they comply with the rules of the Board of Police Commissioners." Cincinnati, 1893: "Non-partisan force. Four Police Commissioners, two Democrats, two Republicans." Dayton, 1893: "Bi-partisan Board of Directors of the Police Department."   Fort Wayne, 1893:   "Four elected Police Commissioners, who serve one year."   Seattle, 1893:   "Four Commissioners, appointed by the Mayor: two Republicans and two Democrats, who serve four years" (Hale, 1893).

Technology and Knowledge

Emerging from the combination of technology and knowledge were

- *Bertillon system of identification* in use in Detroit.   Also photographing of all arrested criminals.

- *Pawn shop detail* was doing excellent work in Los Angeles.

- Gamewell boxes and other brands of police signal and telephone systems introduced improved *communications* to policing. Of the 142 American police departments that responded to Hale's survey of 1893, 52, or 37 percent of them reported having installed Gamewell boxes (or a few made by Pearce and Jones, Brewer and Smith, or Metro Duplex) (see Figure 4).

Figure 4

CITIES USING GAMEWELL BOXES — 1893

Population	No. Cities	Percent
Over 1,000,000	3/3	100
500,000-999,999	2/2	100
250,000-499,999	6/7	86
100,000-249,999	10/10	100
50,000-99,999	16/27	59
25,000-49,999	10/33	30
10,000-24,999	5/60	8

(From an analysis of all 142 responses of American police chiefs to Hale's survey of 1893, by V. G. Strecher, 1971.)

Social Structure of Environment

From the combination of the "bases" of social structure and environment were

- *Docks/wharves assignments to protect travelers* were instituted in Hoboken and other cities near points of entry for immigrants.

- *Ambulance service* demands upon police steadily increased after the police signal systems (Gamewell) were installed. Numerous cities reported this change in service demands.

- *Counseling and social work DNA* entered policing during its formative stage. Police (some in full-time specializations) served as truancy officers, counselors to immigrants after they left Ellis Island, counselors to troubled marriage partners, crime prevention advisors to business proprietors, rescuers of helpless inebriates ("lodging" in holdovers during inclement weather was the rule, rather than the exception).

A reading of Hale's (1893) sampling of the criminal justice system of his time leaves no serious doubt that the reform of policing was being vigorously pursued at the time of his survey.

Reform Chromosome: For Professionalism, Methods (1915-1960)

August Vollmer (1931) called it "a police system of thinking," and he taught it to his "college cops," who were recruited out of the University of California at Berkeley. These young people attended school half time and worked half time. One of them was Orlando W. Wilson, another was V. A. Leonard, who later headed the Washington State Highway Patrol, and still another was William Wiltberger, who systematized Vollmer's new "police science" in the Military Police Corps of the U.S. Army. Vollmer is sometimes credited with enunciating the value and leading the effort to insulate policing from politics, but as we have seen, that effort was already a generation old and plainly documented in Hale's 1893 survey. However, it is not exaggerating Vollmer's influence to observe that he was the first nationally credible proponent of a whole spectrum of values, ideas, technologies, and structural arrangements, a full-blown chromosome, for the professionalization of policing in the United States.

Values Genes

Certainly, Vollmer had a great deal to say about the values of modern policing. In fact his forthright and continuous urging that policing be insulated from partisan politics, and the more recent continuation of that theme by his disciples has persuaded many that Vollmer was the author of the idea, or that his student, O. W. Wilson, might have been. It is more clearly the case that the "politics DNA" came into policing during the 1880s or before, and simply popped up again with reinforcement during the next few generations. Carte and Carte (1975) as well as others have argued that Vollmer's position led to the isolation of the police from its clientele. In this connection it should be observed that Woodrow Wilson, as well as O. W. Wilson, advocated the separation of machine politics from the administration of public services. This is not to say that either of the Wilsons seriously advocated separating government services from the communities they served.

It should not be so hard to understand that they were both, Woodrow and O. W., seeking ways to preserve the intended constitutional distinctions among the three branches of government. The executive branch institutions, they were saying, should be permitted to do their work unimpeded by narrow, partisan, corrupt machine politics. Also, the line between legislative policy making and executive administration was to be preserved. The tendency of policing early in the reform days to define all politics as bad politics was an aberration of a time when nearly all politics were corrupt. But "politics," even at that time, surely did not refer to the whole electorate.

Reformers were not as concerned about their officers associating with the mass of householders and business people on their beats as with ward bosses and their runners, fixers, and thugs. It has been too facile, and perhaps disingenuous, an interpretation that police administrators' efforts to insulate their officers from dirty politics were intended to quarantine them from all the people living in the police jurisdiction. Perhaps a few police officials did intend that, but there is much to suggest the real concern of reformers was with dirty political interference in internal police administrative matters, which they correctly interpreted as a breach of the separation of powers, and essentially criminal in intent and practice.

Corruptibility/Deviance DNA. Where corruption had been normative during the mid-1800s, Vollmer's intensification of the Progressive Era reforms put the stamp of deviance upon the DNA of old, once-acceptable practices. He gave the depoliticization of policing a national showcase in his attempt to reform the Los Angeles Police Department in the 1920s, in his inaugural address to the IACP in 1922, and in his Wickersham Commission Report in 1931.

Brutality/Use of Force DNA. Here, too, Vollmer's influence mutated the DNA of the overuse of force, particularly by means of his documentation and condemnation of the "third degree" in the Wickersham Commission Report.

Altruism/Dedication DNA. Vollmer's tendency to imbue policing with the dedication of a religious vocation was taken seriously by his disciples and many of theirs following. Often viewed cynically by external observers, this bit of DNA operates to make many police officials utterly serious about their work.

Last Moral Man DNA. Another manifestation of the dedication DNA is the "thin blue line" connotation of policing. This complex of values makes it possible for police officers to see their role as that of modern knights.

Suspiciousness DNA. Systematically inculcated from Vollmer's time on; part of the "police system of thinking."

Police Function Genes

Crime control orientation or emphasis has often been attributed to Vollmer and his "professionalization" movement. Even a cursory look at accounts of colonial and primitive policing, however, should be enough to show that crime became a concern of the Watches in Boston and New

Amsterdam early on. It is probable that, as in modern times, the tool of the Watch turned out to be handy for more serious purposes than merely watching for disorders in the night. The process drove the discovery of new functions. What other social mechanism was out there on the street, so available for the added function?

It is probable that the following functions were assigned to the earliest forms of policing in the order given:

- Watch for disorder and arouse the residents to deal with it as a community, primarily at night.
- Deal with the disorder as a specialized institution, day as well as night.
- Provide services not related to order, such as inspecting streets for cleanliness, checking homes for fire buckets.
- Deal with minor crime, both day and night.
- Deal with major and minor crime, day and night.

By the time Vollmer arrived on the policing scene, about 1911, taking responsibility for preventing or, failing that, responding to major crime was considered a police function. More than a hundred years before, city councils were upbraiding the Watch for being asleep while burglaries were committed — a clear enough implication of police responsibility.

What Vollmer did accomplish, however, was to develop the concept of individual expertise in the crime control function.

Police Role and Status Genes

Bottoms-up Professionalism. Every officer was a police scientist on his beat — An expert in the causes of crime and its resolution.

Police Science. A bookkeeper by training, Vollmer revered the sciences when he discovered them at the University of California. Physicists there so captivated him that Vollmer decided there could well be a science of crime and policing, that its knowledge base could be as systematically compiled as those of the physical sciences, and as systematically taught in "police schools" throughout the country. He attempted to do all of that.

Police Technology Genes

Vollmer's police system of thinking encompassed the application of virtually all known technologies of his time to the needs of policing. He advocated police responsibility for the level of crime and for the identification of offenders. His ideas led to our present understanding of omnipresence and rapid response, tactics of surprise and control on the beat, patrol plans, communications, use of vehicles, training, education, fingerprinting and photographing all arrestees, police records of incidents, women in policing, self-regulation, national crime reporting, crime analysis, and forensic science.

Although Vollmer advocated science in policing, it is more accurate to observe that he and his disciples developed a craft of policing in two generations and wrote "cookbooks" based upon their experience in the craft. Unlike science, their books, although providing policing its greatest advancement in a hundred years, were place bound and time bound.

Reform for Planning and Purpose: Enter Science (1960s-present)

The introduction of systems science into the planning and management of U.S. Department of Defense operations by Secretary of Defense McNamara profoundly changed the administration of all other federal government operations as well. Thus, when President Lyndon Johnson appointed a commission to study crime and law enforcement in 1966, it was against a backdrop of "systems thinking" that had suffused the national government for some five years. When the President's Crime Commission had done its work and published its reports, the social context of the end of the 1960s (prosperity, increased higher education for police, improvement of the police occupational status and image, social values that supported crime control legislation, a strong presidency) was ready for a massive attempt to reform policing — unlike in 1931, when the Wickersham's proposed reforms found no sentiment or funding to implement them. The consequences of that juncture of opportunity and ideas are well known.

Over the next two decades more police research and development occurred than had been previously done in all the history of American policing. Expenditures were in the range of $1 billion per year during the early years of work. LEAA funded research and development, while LEEP funded higher education for the police. Where fewer than 4 percent of police officers were estimated to have some college education at the time of the Wickersham Commission Report, more than 80 percent were estimated to have completed some college work by 1985 (Strecher, 1988). Other follow-up commissions required states to establish goals and standards in all areas of police operations, administration, and management.

Most important, old doctrines were for the first time systematically examined. Science was actually brought to the study of policing. The very purposes of policing were freshly examined. Just a partial listing of research and development work would include the following:

- The NIJ police executive development programs administered by the University Research Corporation and the Police Management Association delivered new research findings to thousands of police executives in every region of the country. These workshops became a forum for the examination of old doctrines and new findings for a period of more than fifteen years.

- The research agenda of the Police Division of NIJ, LEAA, during the 1970s and 1980s addressed virtually every major issue of police operations, administration, technology, and management. The knowledge base, values, and ideas of policing were on the table for discussion.

- There were wide-ranging attempts to convert patrol from the random, blunt instrument Kelling reported upon in his study of the Kansas City patrol in the early 1970s, into a focused, goal-oriented strategy. The following are only a few of the studies engendered by skepticism about random patrol and called-for-service management:
  - New Haven Directed Patrol
  - Kansas City Directed-Interactive Patrol
  - Wilmington's Split Force Patrol Experiment
  - San Diego Field Interrogation Experiment
  - San Diego One-Officer, Two-Officer Patrol Experiment
  - Three Approaches to Criminal Apprehension in Kansas City
  - Differential Police Response in Birmingham
  - Crime Analysis in Support of Crime Control Developments
  - Police Car Allocation Model
  - Hypercube Beat Design Model
  - Police Performance Measures Research Project

- The RAND Study of the Investigative Process set in motion:
  - The SRI case screening model
  - The Rochester investigations management model
  - Investigative screening/optimization models
  - Offender-based investigative methods
  - Case purging criteria
  - Crime analysis in support of investigations
  - Concepts to integrate patrol and investigative operations

The years of the most recent wave of police reform produced the most durable kind of effect: policing now involved science. Here we are not speaking of microscopes and X-ray diffraction, but rather of bringing the traditional standards and methods of the sciences to the description, analysis, and planning of police operations. The management of policing would continue to be an art based upon sciences, but the old-fashioned cookbook versions of police administration would now yield ground to a more rigorous way of thinking about policing. George Kelling's (1974) Kansas City Preventive Patrol Study deserves recognition as the first carefully designed and executed scientific analysis of a long-standing police doctrine. Systems analysts often say that in order to ask the right question you have to know half the answer. That, indeed, was the situation in the early 1970s, when Kelling undertook his important research; many observant police managers were already questioning the utility of random patrol.

William Bieck's (1977) stunning analysis of response time in Kansas City not only upset rapid response doctrines, but also produced findings that dramatically overhauled our ways of visualizing the response time continuum and its implications. The most critical response delays were found not to be those in processes controlled by the police — dispatching and travel time, in which millions of dollars had been invested — but in complainants' delays in calling the police. The response time problem was suddenly deflected away from computer-assisted dispatch, automatic vehicle locator systems, mini-radios, fast cars, sirens and lights, and optimum response beat designs, and toward the problem of educating the victimized public to call sooner, if able. More scientific thinking was the durable effect of the reform and so-called professionalizing years. More to the point, this effect is one that continues and thus contradicts the notion that police reform has ended. Science suffuses not only the knowledge base of policing, but also its more recent approaches to operational analysis and development. The universities and colleges are no longer teaching cookbook doctrine about patrol being the backbone of policing, but instead are instructing students to consider the issues and problems of crime, order, and the delivery of services. They make use of the rigorous studies that have been conducted in analyzing these issues and problems. Gone is the old belief in doctrines. In its place resides a skepticism that raises hard questions for hard analyses.

Some of the science is not very good (for instance, not enough replication has been done), and the loss of large-scale federal support for research has been unfortunate. But a corner has been turned in two respects by the years of LEAA and LEEP:

- Rigorous thinking has found a place in policing.

- A market for higher education has been established within the police occupation, even without LEEP support.

Community Policing as a Future for Policing

The current emphasis upon community policing raises formidable issues of sociological credibility. As stated earlier, there may have been genuine "communities" in the early colonial days, and incipient policing may have had consensual support. But is necessary to see whether that very old community DNA is still viable in the knowledge base of policing or government. The beginning of community problem solving and the emphasis upon community consciousness in policing began in 1955 with the work of Louis Radelet (1973) and his police community relations programming at Michigan State University. The massive activities of the Center for Police Community Relations over the next generation included annual, international conferences attended by thousands of police administrators and police scholars, and generated values changes and institutional innovations. Most police agencies sprouted police community relations units, specialized personnel, and community support organizations. Most departments still have them. Radelet published his ideas and the output of these annual conferences and had the most profound influence upon police — international as well as American. If it had not been for Radelet's grand vision of community-oriented policing, it would be difficult to explain the origins of ministations, police store-front centers all over the country, and other measures to increase contact between the police and their communities, and to increase the involvement of members of the community in their own crime prevention and avoidance of victimization.

But is this new vision of community policing simply a turn away from one process-oriented policing (patrol, investigation) toward another? The substance of community-oriented policing is difficult to pin down. When officers assigned in the community-oriented policing mode are asked what they do, they paw the ground, shrug, and give answers such as, "walk and talk," "grin and chin," "chat and charm," "schmooze," and, most often, "maybe the brass will let us know." Peter Manning (1990), in a recent presentation at Sam Houston State University, described community-oriented policing as more of an ethos than a method or concept, an ethos driven by the academic establishment rather than by developments in policing. Others refer to it as a philosophy of policing. Either term leaves unanswered the question of what community-oriented officers actually do, how their activities differ from those of traditional patrol officers, and how these activities might be evaluated. As such, the community-oriented furor may only be another rung in the DNA ladder that determines the structure of policing rather than a brand new chromosome.

The most serious question is whether there is a residue of community DNA in American society, a genetic foothold for this new mode of policing. More detailed questions are these:

- Is American society moving toward community and carrying policing along with it?
- Is American government moving toward community outside the context of the general social trend, and carrying policing along with it?
- Is policing (in the form of some 17,000 local agencies) moving toward community on its own, outside the context of American society and government?
- Is academic criminal justice moving toward community on its own?

An "American community" is a warm, comforting phrase. In this concept there is the overtone of the small society, the community of neighbors who know each other (to the third generation), and whose offspring develop their self-awareness in an atmosphere of warmth, trust, and a wish to become like those who have gone before. Here is Toennies' *gemeinschaft*, and Durkheim's mechanical solidarity of society, and the small, simple, preindustrial, consensual, almost primitive aspect of community that does not require much secular law (especially *mala prohibita*), not much beyond the Ten Commandments — no big government, no regulatory laws and agencies, (certainly nothing as secular or commercialized as the Code of Hammurabi), no tension between the sermons heard in church and the high school curriculum.

Where do we find this small, uncomplicated, unspecialized, unstratified colony of believers who are clustered around an agreeable moral code? Chicago? Miami? San Francisco? Minneapolis? Maybe those are too large. Bangor? Rocky Mount? Wausau? Dothan? Waco? Nogales? Butte? Poplar Bluff? Bakersfield? Boulder? Eugene? Take a look at one of these smaller places. Determine for yourself whether any one of them has a basis for "community": a moral consensus, a definition of social order that will guide the police department — the "forces of order" in its daily activities.

Indicators show the United States becoming more, not less, of a mass society. There is increasing cultural pluralism and moral fragmentation. The underclass is growing, the middle class diminishing. High-transiency poor neighborhoods are known to be much harder to organize for purposes of community crime prevention and cooperative programs with the police than affluent neighborhoods. These poorer neighborhoods usually have higher rates of violent street crime than middle- and upper-class areas, and are most in need of police services. Add to that the traditional mistrust the poor have for the police and you have the unlikeliest of social settings for "community" policing.

American government, similarly, seems to be growing more distant from the mass society it serves. Smaller proportions of the electorate vote, and those strata that vote least are the poorest, the most victimized by crime, and most productive of offenders. Local, state, and national governments are increasingly polarized and cross-cut on a variety of issues. The trend is away from moral consensus, and though polls sometimes indicate a consensual concern over the extent of an issue such as crime, education, health care, transportation, or environmental damage, there is an abyss among advocates of conflicting policies and measures. There is nothing in the conduct of our many local governments to indicate they are carrying themselves or policing toward a more intimate relationship with their communities.

Is policing, then, moving closer to the community on its own, unsupported by a social or governmental trend? There is no example from history to suggest this is even possible, much less probable in our conflicted times. In almost all cases the police have been creatures of their social systems and times, rarely if ever presenting institutional forms, technologies, processes, or values different from those of their parent governments. The addition of a community-oriented value base may create a new gene, but if the environmental component rungs of the DNA ladder are missing, the mutation will fail to live long enough to reproduce.

There is no joy in this observation. The prospect of a stronger bond between community and police is intrinsically attractive. Sadly, however, one can visualize a whole new episode of the Keystone Cops rushing down the street to meet its "community," only to find nothing there. Or they might find a bewildering array of multicultural minicommunities that would overwhelm their naive comprehension of policing needs.

There is the possibility that academic criminal justice is defining an era of community policing on its own, and making of us a collection of police experiments and innovations to support the hypothesis. Community-oriented policing is sometimes said to include elements of foot patrol, vertical patrol, ministations, substations, store-front centers, special purpose patrols,fear-reduction efforts, premise security crime prevention programs, citizen patrols, problem-oriented policing, location-oriented policing, and a variety of other operations. Upon close inspection, community-oriented policing seems diffuse, difficult to define and describe, and comprising too great a variety of operational forms to be considered a typology. Most probably it is, as Manning has stated, an ethos that has yet to be defined operationally. Even among academics who would support its emergence, community policing provokes endless debate about its format, operations, utility, and whether it includes problem-oriented policing, location-oriented policing, neighborhood-oriented policing, known offender-oriented policing, or is, conversely, an element in one of the others.

If community policing is largely a reified concept at this time, a creature of the academic literature rather than a defined, measurable, and widespread approach among the 17,000 local policing agencies, a reason for the academic explosion on its behalf should be found. The energy being expended in producing community policing literature may be greater than the energy of community policing being expended on the streets of America's cities. Is there, in fact, a clamor for foot patrol, for a closer relationship between community and police? There is more reason to believe citizens simply want to be protected, by whatever means; have lost faith in the capacity of government to provide that protection; and want the situation corrected. There is less reason to believe citizens want to become involved actively with the police in order to protect themselves. Every attempt to sustain citizen motivation in community and police programming has verified the tenuous nature of citizen participation. In our age of highly specialized division of work, the idea of more personalized, intimate governmental services has a romantic and nostalgic note to it. What, then, motivates the community policing movement, if not verifiable successes?

An Alternative View

I wish all of the community policing scenarios were on target. What a better life in the cities of the United States that would portend. Unfortunately, the trends of social change and governmental conservatism seem not to support such a conclusion. Following are some thoughts about newer genetic material to revive the long-dormant community DNA. These new strands of powerful DNA may be expected to interact powerfully in shaping the future of policing.

Cultural Pluralism. This phenomenon is growing, particularly in the high-density cities of the nation. Standardized, citywide operations are poorly constituted to deal with the order-maintenance function in these multicommunities. Neighborhood policing that recognizes numerous, diverse definitions of community order may be the only way in which to address the growing complexity. Even then, there will be formidable obstacles to having neighborhoods policed largely by police officers from these ethno/linguistic groups. Separate but equal policing will not be acceptable. Community-oriented policing has not yet addressed this most serious of the looming urban questions, and remains an unwieldy concept to it.

Economic Distress in America's Cities. This factor is epidemic and irreversible for the near future. Revenue bases are shrinking; retrenchment is the new art of fiscal management. "Minimalist" public policing is a probable consequence.

Private Policing. This trend is growing and threatens to degrade the economic base of public policing. If the trend continues, the affluent alone will be able to afford high-technology policing, while the residents of high-density, high-crime areas will be provided either

- a scaled-down version of call-for-service policing (the leanest model of differential police response), accompanied by the investigation of only the most serious offenses (the leanest model of case screening), or
- an old-fashioned looks good, feels good foot patrol, schmoozing its way through each day, while the police operators tell callers why a car cannot be sent and why their burglary will not be investigated because it lacks sufficient "solvability factors."

Only the affluent will have access to the professional police services that have been well on the way to development during the past seventy years. It will be expensive, but worth it, and unavailable to a majority of citizens. The affluent will have an obvious interest in capping urban taxes to avoid paying for schmooze services they do not need. In time, public policing will become a lowest common denominator of service levels.

Information and Communication Technology. These technologies will improve, making it increasingly feasible to gather information about the actual events and behaviors relating to crime. The rules of evidence and due process requirements will not permit the use of most of this information, because of the sources and techniques of collection. The strain between intelligence and evidence will become almost unbearable for operating agencies. Public policing will not have the means to do much of this, nor will there seem much point in it. But private policing will certainly have reason to gather the information and to find private solutions to the crime problems of their clients. Due process may well suffer as a consequence.

Empirical Analysis of Policing. This activity will continue as will the technical reform of policing, but not in a public sector fixated upon the schmooze patrol. The science DNA is there, but private policing will probably become the major benefactor of this research and development, and may eventually conduct most research and development under proprietary sponsorship.

Process-Oriented Policing. This trend will continue in the public sector, because of the uncertainty and lag of diffusion to 17,000 jurisdictions. It will provide low-expectation jobs to working class men and women. Strong industrial-styled unions will set process quotas in the work of these public police officers.

Systems or MBO-Oriented Policing. This style of policing will grow in the private sector because it will specify deliverables, target its resources, deliver expensive services as specified, and satisfy its clientele. Private protection will become a major investment sector with a political agenda of its own.

End Note

Only if American policing undertakes a major territorial reorganization and commitment to policy-driven operations will the quality of services increase in public policing.

A confederated system of services ranging from state-level major crime services to urban neighborhood order-maintenance services might have the flexibility and scale of economy to adjust to the modern realities of costs, tax revolts, population distributions, cultural pluralism, the need for information technology, the need for continued systems development and an educated personnel to cope with it, and competition from the private sector. Public policing will not get to that model by adopting a simplistic, diffuse rhetoric as currently represented in community policing.

References

Ahern, J. F. (1972). *Police in trouble.* New York: Hawthorn Books.

Baker, L. C. (1867). *History of the United States secret service.* Philadelphia: L.C. Baker.

Bieck, W. (1977). *Response time analysis.* Kansas City, MO: Kansas City Police Department.

Bittner, E. (1990). *Aspects of police work.* Boston: Northeastern University Press.

Carte, G. E. & Carte, E. E. (1975). *Police reform in the United States: The era of August Vollmer, 1905-1932.* Berkeley: University of California Press.

Costello, A. E. (1970). *Our police protectors: History of the New York police from the earliest period to the present time* (1885 Reprint). Montclair, NJ: Patterson Smith.

Flinn, J. J. & Wilkie, J. E. (1973). *History of the Chicago police* (1887 Reprint). Montclair, NJ: Patterson Smith.

Fogelson, R. M. (1977). *Big city police*. Cambridge, MA: Harvard University Press.

Fosdick, R. (1969). *American police systems* (1920 Reprint). Montclair, NJ: Patterson Smith.

Fuld, L. (1909). *Police administration*. New York: G.P. Putnam.

Germann, A. C., Day, F. D., & Gallati, R. J. (1967). *Introduction to law enforcement*. Springfield, IL: Charles C. Thomas.

Greenwood, P. & Petersilia, J. (1975). *The criminal investigation process, volume I: Summary and policy implications*. Santa Monica, CA: The RAND Corporation.

Hale, G. W. (1893). *Police and prison cyclopaedia*. Cambridge, MA: Riverside Press.

Haller, M. (1976). Historical roots of police behavior: Chicago, 1890-1925. *Law and Society Review*, (Winter), 303-324.

Hamilton, M. E. (1924). *The policewoman, her service and ideals*. New York: Frederick A. Stokes Co.

Harring, S. L. (1983). *Policing a class society: The experience of American cities, 1865-1915*. New Brunswick, NJ: Rutgers University Press.

Hickey, J. J. (1925). *Our police guardians: History of the police department of the city of New York*. New York: Author.

Johnson, D. R. (1981). *American law enforcement: A history*. St. Louis, MO: Forum Press.

Kelling, G. L. & Moore, M. H. (1988). The evolving strategy of policing, No. 4 *Perspectives on Policing*. Washington, DC: U.S. Government Printing Office.

Kelling, G. L., Pate, T., Dieckman, D., & Brown, C.E. (1974). *The Kansas City preventive patrol experiement: A technical report*. Washington, DC: The Police Foundation.

Lane, R. (1967). *Policing the city: Boston, 1822-1885*. Cambridge, MA: Harvard University Press.

Lovejoy, A. O. (1955). *Essays in the history of ideas.* New York: George Braziller Inc.

Lovejoy, A. O. (1970). *The great chain of being: A study of the history of an idea.* (The William James lectures delivered at Harvard University, 1933). Cambridge, MA: Harvard University Press.

Maltby, W. J. (1906). *Captain Jeff; or, Frontier life in Texas with the Texas Rangers* (Some unwritten history and facts in the thrilling experiences of frontier life). Colorado, TX: Whipkey.

Manning, P. K. (1990). *Developments in Policing,* Beto Chair Lecture delivered at Sam Houston State University, Huntsville, TX.

Manning, P. K. (1977). *Police work: The social organization of policing.* Cambridge, MA: MIT Press.

Merton, R. K. (1936). The unanticipated consequences of purposive social action. *American Sociological Review,* 1.

Miller, W. R. (1976). *Cops and bobbies: Police authority in New York and London, 1830-1870.* Chicago: University of Chicago Press.

Monkkonen, E. H. (1981). *Police in urban America, 1860-1920.* Cambridge, MA: Harvard University Press.

Neiderhoffer, A. (1967). *Behind the shield: The police in urban society.* Garden City, NY: Doubleday Anchor Books.

Peck, W. F. (1903). *History of the police department of Rochester, New York, from the earliest time to May 1, 1903.* Rochester, NY: Police Benevolent Association.

Radelet, L. A. (1973). *The police and the community.* Beverly Hills, CA: Glencoe Press.

Reiss, A. J. (1978). *The police and the public.* New Haven, CT: Yale University Press.

Repetto, T. A. (1978). *The blue parade.* New York: The Free Press.

Richardson, J. F. (1978). *The New York police: Colonial times to 1901.* New York: Oxford University Press.

Roe, G. M. (1976). *Our police: A history of the Cincinnati police force, from the earliest period until the present day* (1890 Reprint). New York: AMS Press.

Russell, F. (1975). *A city in terror: 1919, the Boston police strike.* New York: Viking Press.

Savage, E. (1971). *Police records and recollection* (1873 Reprinted). Montclair, NJ: Patterson Smith.

Schneider, J. C. (1980). *Detroit and the problem of order, 1830-1880: A geography of crime, riots, and policing.* Lincoln, NE: University of Nebraska Press.

Skolnick, J. H. (1966). *Justice without trial: Law enforcement in democratic society.* New York: John Wiley & Sons Inc.

Strecher, V. G. (1971). *The environment of law enforcement.* Englewood Cliffs, NJ: Prentice Hall.

Strecher, V. G. (1988). Stimuli of police education. *The Justice Professional,* 3(2), 298-319.

Terrill, R. J. (1989). Police history: 1920 to the present. In W. G. Bailey (Ed.), *Encyclopedia of Police Science* (pp. 447-452). New York: Garland Publishing Inc.

Vollmer, A. (1931). The police executive. In *Wickersham Commission (National Commission on Law Observance) Reports, No. 14: Report on Police.* Washington, DC: U.S. Government Printing Office.

Walker, S. (1977). *A critical history of police reform: The emergence of professionalism.* Lexington, MA: Lexington Books.

CONCEPTUAL
FRAMEWORK

Conceptual Framework

As noted in the Preface, this book is organized around a conceptual framework in which police management is examined in terms of six endemic issues (matching structure to objective, community alliance, enriching traditional roles, activity trap, creativity with accountability, and stability amid change) each from six management perspectives (alternative futures, strategic approaches, human resource issues, technological and material resource management, organizational communication, and executive responsibility). The conceptual framework is best depicted as a matrix — see the following page.

The definition of each of the six endemic issues is as follows:

- **Matching Structure to Objectives** — maintaining flexibility in organizational format such that evolving agency objectives are best achieved;

- **Community Alliance** — accepting the premise that the culture of a police organization must be based upon a foundation that not only recognizes the value of citizen involvement, but also attempts to manage departmental affairs in association with such beliefs;

- **Enriching Traditional Roles** — debunking the mythology of traditional, bureaucratically based police roles in pursuit of redefining functional responsibilities that will enhance job satisfaction, improve morale, and increase operational and managerial efficiency;

- **Activity Trap** — avoiding a primary focus on the performance of activities without first recognizing how they relate to the satisfactory attainment of outcomes;

- **Creativity With Accountability** — providing individuals with opportunities to be creative within organizations characterized by a stringent accountability regimen;

- **Stability Amid Change** — striving to maintain a sense of order during the performance of day-to-day responsibilities while simultaneously initiating and managing the process of change (i.e., pursuing organizational development).

Conceptual Matrix

ENDEMIC ISSUES

MANAGEMENT PERSPECTIVES

	Matching Structure to Objectives	Community Alliance	Enriching Traditional Roles	Activity Trap	Creativity With Accountability	Stability Amid Change
Alternative Futures						
Strategic Approaches						
Human Resource Issues						
Technological & Material Resource Management						
Organizational Communication						
Executive Responsibility						

Each of the long-term, intractable, problems peculiarly associated with policing can then be examined from at least six management perspectives as follows:

• **Alternative Futures**	identifying, analyzing, and responding to different types of societal, communal, and occupational environments;
• **Strategic Approaches**	recognizing when and knowing how to utilize different analytical methods of planning and problem solving;
• **Human Resource Issues**	learning how to manage efficiently the development and utilization of people within an organization under varying conditions;
• **Technological and Material Resource Management**	identifying and utilizing available resources to optimize effective service delivery; knowing how different types of technology can be used to massage information to aid in the decision-making process throughout the organization;
• **Organizational Communication**	knowing when and understanding how to use various communicative systems to enhance operational efficiency;
• **Executive Responsibility**	creating opportunities amid diversity and competing demands.

The Texas Law Enforcement Management Institute Executive Issues Seminar Series has been organized around this matrix, each seminar addresses a single column or row in the matrix. With the addition of an introductory and conclusionary chapter, this book is likewise organized in terms of the matrix. After the introductory chapter, the next six chapters address sequentially the endemic issues listed, the subsequent six chapters each address one of the management perspectives.

On the following pages each "cell" in the matrix is defined in terms of the questions and issues raised at that juncture of the matrix.

Matching Structure to Objectives

Management Perspectives

Alternative Futures	To what extent do the objectives of law enforcement agencies vary (1) between different agencies, (2) between units within the same agency, and (3) over time? To what extent will the objectives and structures of law enforcement agencies be different in the future? What will they be? What structures work best in law enforcement? • Goal displacement • Basis for organization: process vs. purpose vs. teams • Rigid vs. flexible structures: temporary organizations, use of ad hoc groups, etc. • Vertical vs. horizontal differentiation: tall vs. flat organization structures

Strategic Approaches	How do you identify the objectives of a law enforcement agency? How do you determine how well a law enforcement agency is attaining its objectives? How do you determine what structure is best suited for attaining a particular set of objectives in a particular situation? • Priorities among objectives • Conflict among objectives • Measures, indicators, etc. • Structure follows function, or vice versa?

Human Resource Issues	What are the implications of differing law enforcement objectives for the kinds of people who should be employed and how they should be trained? What are the implications of differing law enforcement structures for the kinds of people who should be employed and how they should be trained? • Generalist vs. specialist officers: Can one person do it all any more? • Crime fighters vs. social workers • Military rank structures: authority based on position vs. expertise • Boot camp/stress training vs. police education

Matching Structure to Objectives — Continued

Management Perspectives

Technological and Material Resource Management	What are the implications of differing law enforcement objectives for the role and importance of new technology?
	What are the implications of differing law enforcement structures for the role and importance of new technology?
	Does technology adapt to law enforcement objectives and structures or vice versa?
	• Response technology vs. prevention technology • Functional forecasting • Enhanced management information systems for monitoring and feedback

Organizational Communication	What are the implications of differing law enforcement objectives for management, leadership, and organizational communications?
	What are the implications of differing law enforcement structures for management, leadership, and organizational communications?
	What styles and methods of management and leadership work best in law enforcement?
	• Linkage between strategy and operations • Communicating objectives • Outcomes vs. outputs vs. process • Communication barriers and filters

Executive Responsibility	What is the law enforcement executive's role in determining law enforcement agency objectives?
	What are the constraints and opportunities that confront law enforcement executives in setting agency objectives and creating organizational structures?
	• Autonomy, politics, community pressures, etc. • Sharing authority vs. the loneliness of command • Management team, executive board, etc. • Demystifying police organizational structure (rank, status, symbols, etc.) • Limiting the impact of information as power

Community Alliance

Management Perspectives

Alternative Futures	What is the nature of the "community" and its values and preferences for law enforcement? What is the proper "coproduction" of crime control and order maintenance between law enforcement agencies, community groups, and individuals? How will communities, and their law enforcement needs and desires, differ in the future? • Heterogeneous communities and their contradictory demands • Pluralism vs. assimilation • Politics vs. political input • Professional autonomy vs. public participation • Standardized vs. differentiated law enforcement • Integrity issues • Comparative perspectives

Strategic Approaches	How do you identify communities and determine what they want from their law enforcement agencies? Can the police deliver once communities say what they want? • Communities of geography vs. ethnicity vs. interest • Is formal PCR dead? • COP vs. NOP vs. LOP vs. POP • Structuring systematic community input • Reaching the "silent majority" • Responding to special issues/special events

Human Resource Issues	What kinds of people are best suited for community-oriented policing? Can currently employed law enforcement officers adapt their styles and behaviors to the community-oriented approach? • Recruitment, selection, training, evaluation, promotion, etc. to foster COP • Modifying supervision and management to fit COP • Changing police values • Mixing police functions: police agents, police officers, community service officers, etc.

Community Alliance — Continued

Management Perspectives

Technological and Material Resource Management	Are law enforcement technology and the community-oriented approach compatible?
	What technological applications could enhance the success of the community-oriented approach?
	• Police responsiveness and attentiveness vs. intrusiveness and harassment • Big brother computers and information systems • Remote headquarters vs. local ministations • Standard patrol cars vs. other means of conveyance

Organizational Communication	Under COP what information is needed by whom in the law enforcement agency and in the community?
	What methods can be used by the law enforcement agency to communicate effectively with the community?
	What styles and methods of leadership and management are best suited to the community-oriented approach?
	• Centralization vs. decentralization • Supervision within COP/NOP/POP • Setting policy parameters to guide discretion • Sharing community knowledge • Linking crime analysis to community responsiveness

Executive Responsibility	How does the law enforcement executive draw the line between appropriate community involvement/responsiveness and politics?
	Is the law enforcement executive's role different under the community-oriented approach than under the professional model?
	What is the appropriate political role of the law enforcement executive?
	• Law enforcement executive styles: administrator vs. top cop vs. politician vs. statesman • Following the community vs. leading it • Media relations • Institutionalizing COP: structure vs. deployment vs. philosophy • Surviving long enough to institutionalize COP

Enriching Traditional Roles

Management Perspectives

Alternative Futures	To what extent does the law enforcement role vary from place to place and over time? What will the future law enforcement role be? Will it be more of the same or radically different? • Historical perspectives • Comparative/international perspectives • Community problem solving • Centrality of the capacity and license to use force • Police/fire role consolidation
Strategic Approaches	How do you determine the most effective distribution of law enforcement duties and responsibilities among patrol, detectives, and other traditional functions? How do you measure and then enhance job satisfaction, morale, motivation, and commitment among personnel in law enforcement agencies? • Managing Patrol Operations, Managing Criminal Investigations, Integrated Criminal Apprehension Program • Generalists vs. specialists • Community Service Officers — cadets, safety offices, etc. • Split-force concepts — work redesign • Civilians, volunteers, auxiliaries, etc. • Career development and personal development • Reward without rank — master police officer concept • Police Corps
Human Resource Issues	What are the implications of differing role conceptions (expanded, redesigned, more specialized, etc.) for the kinds of people best suited to perform law enforcement duties? Can currently employed law enforcement personnel adapt to different roles and responsibilities? What roles are best suited for today's new employees from the "twenty-something, me" generation? • Education and training implications • Utilization of college-educated personnel • Desirability of higher education requirements • Management preparation implications • Cost implications of enriched/redesigned roles

Enriching Traditional Roles — Continued

Management Perspectives

Technological and Material Resource Management	To what extent are law enforcement roles determined by or constrained by technology? What technology and equipment would be needed to facilitate enriched or redesigned law enforcement roles? With enriched roles will computer skills and access to information systems need to be more widespread within law enforcement agencies? • Crime and operations analysis • Laptops, local area networks, etc. • Equipment implications of police/fire consolidation
Organizational Communication	What are the implications for law enforcement management and leadership of expanded/enriched/redesigned roles? Can traditional law enforcement supervisory and managerial roles be enriched or redesigned? • Making delegation explicit • Setting policy parameters • Managing civilians and volunteers • Managing with rules vs. values • Management and leadership styles
Executive Responsibility	To what extent can the law enforcement executive redesign roles that are shaped and reinforced by strong media and popular culture messages? Can the traditional role of the law enforcement executive be enriched or redesigned? • The executive as statesman and educator • Problems of motivation and reward within the agency — rewarding real performance rather than risk-avoidance • Avoiding least-common-denominator management (managing for minimum acceptable performance) • Linking self-development to job enrichment

Activity Trap

Management Perspectives

Alternative Futures	Do we want the police to emphasize ends over means? Is an emphasis on means necessary to ensure adherence to constitutional limitations on police authority and desirable limits on police intrusiveness? Can we develop the body of knowledge needed to select effective means for attaining chosen ends? • Feasibility of rational police planning • Functional and dysfunctional habit patterns • Identifying the real costs and benefits and traditional activities • Controversies over both means and ends in policing
Strategic Approaches	How do we identify desired outcomes (objectives to be attained or problems to be solved) in law enforcement? How do we weigh the relative costs and benefits associated with different alternatives in law enforcement? • Need for research • Need for environmental scanning • Need to identify priorities and community values • Applicability of Management By Objectives to law enforcement • Goals vs. problems in planning, strategy development, and operations • Problem-oriented policing
Human Resource Issues	What are the implications of a more ends-oriented approach to law enforcement for the kinds of people employed and their preparation for duty? Can currently employed officers adapt to a more ends-oriented or problem-oriented approach to law enforcement? • Implications for recruitment, selection, training, promotion, etc. • Superficiality of job analysis and selection validation: reifying the status quo • Evaluation: quantity vs. quality and objective vs. subjective • Measuring outputs and activities vs. measuring outcomes

Activity Trap — Continued

Management Perspectives

Technological and Material Resource Management	What has been the effect on law enforcement of technology that makes it so much easier to count activities and keep track of calls, reports, and arrests? Does technology generally encourage the activity trap in law enforcement? Can we develop measures, indicators, and information systems that monitor and evaluate outcomes rather than just outputs and activities? • Records systems vs. information systems • Computers that store information vs. computers that aid in planning and decision making • Monitoring vs. evaluation
Organizational Communication	What are the implications of a more ends-oriented or problem-oriented approach to law enforcement for police leadership and management? How can law enforcement supervisors and managers encourage their subordinates to avoid the activity trap? How can law enforcement supervisors and managers avoid the activity trap themselves? • Communicating the meaning of the activity trap and its alternatives throughout the organization • Management and leadership styles • Methods of direction and control • Coaching vs. scheduling and reviewing reports • Time management
Executive Responsibility	What is the proper balance between the internal and external roles of the law enforcement executive and between the management and leadership roles? Can the law enforcement executive maintain organizational control and ensure respect for civil liberties while emphasizing ends over means? • Constraint-oriented vs. ends-oriented police administration • Crime control vs. due process models • Avoiding reactive crisis management

Creativity With Accountability

Management Perspectives

Alternative Futures	To what extent is "creativity" an important and desirable element of law enforcement? What do we mean by "creativity" in policing? In what functions and in what situations is creativity particularly desirable or undesirable in law enforcement? • Basic nature of police work: profession vs. art vs. craft vs. routine • Does creativity = discrimination — i.e., individualized treatment vs. standardized treatment • Realities of police discretion
Strategic Approaches	How do we provide sufficient direction and control in police administration to ensure accountability without squashing all creativity? How do we distinguish between creativity and abuse of authority in law enforcement? • Incentives and rewards for creativity within traditional rank structures • Structures that encourage creativity (quality circles, profit centers, etc.) • Rules vs. values • Team building and horizontal work groups • Techniques for creativity: brainstorming, etc. • Institutionalizing creativity: research and development units • The experimental law enforcement agency
Human Resource Issues	What are the implications of an emphasis on creativity for the kinds of people we want to employ and how we prepare them? Can currently employed law enforcement personnel develop creativity (or resurrect their dormant creative abilities)? • Implications for recruitment, selection, training, promotion, and evaluation • Will frustration set in when we ask for creativity within narrowly constrained jobs? • Can people be trained to recognize when to employ creativity and when not to?

Creativity With Accountability — Continued

Management Perspectives

Technological and Material Resource Management	What are the implications of an emphasis on creativity for the technological and material requirements of law enforcement? Has technology generally constrained or enabled the development and exercise of creativity in law enforcement? Can we develop technology that will foster creativity in law enforcement? • Technology that limits major mistakes — i.e., nonlethal weaponry, body armor, improved personal identification systems, etc. • Command/control systems that permit more effective supervision without constraining creativity — i.e., cellular phones, automatic vehicle locators, etc. • Information systems that provide officers with accurate information on which to base decisions
Organizational Communication	What are the implications of an emphasis on creativity for law enforcement leadership and management? Can incumbent law enforcement supervisors and managers alter their styles and behavior so as to encourage rather than discourage creativity? • Rewarding and institutionalizing creativity while also limiting it and connecting it to the agency's mission, strategy, and policy • Handling creative excesses • Developing techniques for testing creative suggestions — i.e., market research, trial balloons, simulations, pilot programs, etc.
Executive Responsibility	How does the law enforcement executive balance the likely benefits of creative organizational behavior against the costs of likely mistakes? Does the police executive want to openly discuss the concept of creative police work (i.e., police discretion in dealing with the public)? • Risk management: improved effectiveness vs. increased liability • Enforcing the law vs. doing street justice • The Dirty Harry Problem: Ethical considerations

Stability Amid Change

Management Perspectives

Alternative Futures	Should law enforcement follow society or lead it? If the world is changing at a faster and faster rate, can police administration be a tidy and orderly endeavor? How much change is too much in police administration? • Future shock • Crime warps • Organizations without walls • Temporary organizations, ad hoc groups, task forces, etc.
Strategic Approaches	How do we choose between radical change and gradual change in law enforcement? What methods are most effective for implementing radical changes in law enforcement? What methods are most effective for maintaining the momentum of gradual change in law enforcement? • Institutionalizing change • Change agents • Transition periods • Unfreezing and refreezing • Traditional consultants vs. ongoing organizational development • Parallel staff to oversee changes • Role of planning and analysis units
Human Resource Issues	What are the implications of rapid, constant change for the kinds of people we employ in law enforcement and how we prepare them? Can we attract, develop, and retain a work force in law enforcement that can adapt not only to rapid change but anticipate and influence it? • Stress of change • Reducing the trauma of transitions • Leaving people behind — dinosaurs — and the agency's responsibility to them • Effects of change on turnover • Value of turnover for adaptation to change

Stability Amid Change — Continued

Management Perspectives

Technological and Material Resource Management	To what extent is rapid change in law enforcement merely a reflection of rapidly developing technology? Will technology enable law enforcement to adapt to rapid social change or make it more difficult to adapt? • Information systems for environmental scanning to detect changes • Information systems to monitor change within the law enforcement agency • Problem of keeping up with the latest technology • Technology becoming obsolete more and more quickly
Organizational Communication	What are the implications of rapid and continuous change for law enforcement leadership and management? Amid rapid change, how do you keep the entire law enforcement agency informed about what is going on and where the agency is headed? • Implications for management and leadership styles • Importance of symbols and pictures • Need to communicate a vision of the future and translate it to all levels • Problem of supervising those who get left behind or who choose not to come along
Executive Responsibility	What is the law enforcement executive's role vis-à-vis social and organizational change? How does the law enforcement executive tell when he or she has become an impediment to change rather than a change agent? What are the law enforcement executive's ethical responsibilities to those in the agency and in the community who are disadvantaged by changes? • Planned vs. incremental change • Adapting to change vs. encouraging it • Defending the agency against external threats vs. adapting to them • Change for change's sake • Shaking things up vs. lasting improvements

About the Authors

Chris R. Braiden is the assistant chief of police of the Edmonton, Alberta Police Service. Joining the department in 1964 he rose to his present rank in 1987. Superintendent Braiden commanded Edmonton's South Side Division until 1990, when he assumed responsibility for the department's community-based policing effort. He is known internationally for his writing and lectures on the professionalization of policing, particularly from a community-based perspective. He has served as a consultant to both Canadian and American agencies, including Colorado Springs, Houston, Madison, New Haven, Portland (Oregon), Regina (Saskatchewan), St. Paul, and Toronto. From 1984 to 1986 he was on assignment to the Canadian Solicitor General's Office as a special advisor on policing. He has also consulted with the Canadian Police College, Michigan State University, and the Police Foundation. His publications include numerous research monographs, a regular column for the Canadian police officer monthly magazine, and articles for *Law Enforcement News* and Michigan State's *Community Policing Series*.

David L. Carter is an associate professor in the School of Criminal Justice at Michigan State University who specializes in police administration and policing issues. He received his bachelor's and master's degrees in criminal justice from Central Missouri State University and a Ph.D. in criminal justice administration from Sam Houston State University in Huntsville, Texas. A former Kansas City, Missouri, police officer, Dr. Carter was Chairman of the Department of Criminal Justice at the University of Texas — Rio Grande Valley in Edinburg, Texas, for eleven years before his appointment at Michigan State. Dr. Carter has presented training sessions at the FBI National Academy and for the U.S. Customs Service and U.S. Parole Commission as well as serving as a consultant to the U.S. Drug Enforcement Administration. Dr. Carter is currently a member of the U.S. Attorney General's Working Group for Reducing Violence in America, and directed the congressionally mandated Toy Guns and Crime research project for the Police

Executive Research Forum (funded by the Bureau of Justice Statistics). He also provides technical assistance work for the National Center on Community Policing at Michigan State. Most recently he was project director of the Police and Higher Education research project of the Police Executive Research Forum (funded by the Ford Foundation). In addition to teaching courses at Michigan State, Dr. Carter is Director of the Criminal Justice Overseas Study Program to England. He is the author or coauthor of four books and numerous articles and monographs on policing issues. His fifth book, *The Police: Systems and Practices*, is forthcoming from Prentice-Hall.

Gary W. Cordner is an associate professor of police studies at Eastern Kentucky University and past editor of the *American Journal of Police*. He has coauthored texts on police administration and criminal justice planning, authored over twenty articles and book chapters on police topics, and is co-editor of the book *What Works in Policing?* (Anderson Publishing Company, 1992). He received his Ph.D. in social science and criminal justice from Michigan State University. Dr. Cordner began his police career as a police officer in Ocean City, Maryland, and later served for three years as police chief in St. Michaels, Maryland. In the early 1980s, he helped Baltimore County, Maryland, develop a repeat offender program and evaluate a community policing program. During the past few years, he has worked on projects with the Police Foundation, the RAND Corporation, and the Police Executive Research Forum, and conducted police executive training programs in Maryland, Ohio, Kentucky, Illinois, Florida, and Texas. He is currently evaluating a Drug Elimination Program in the public housing authority in Lexington, Kentucky, and a community policing program in Jefferson County, Kentucky.

Larry T. Hoover received his B.S., M.S., and Ph.D. from Michigan State University and has been on the criminal justice faculty at Sam Houston State University since 1977. Before that he taught at Michigan State University, served on the staff of the Michigan Law Enforcement Officers Training Council, and held assignments in the patrol, communications, and personnel divisions of the Lansing Police Department. A past president of the Academy of Criminal Justice Sciences, Dr. Hoover has directed several significant research projects in law enforcement and criminal justice. His specialty area is police personnel issues. Since 1980 he has been coprincipal of Justex Systems, a personnel relations consulting firm that markets promotional examinations for public safety agencies and publishes the newsletters *Police Labor Monthly* and *Fire Service Labor Monthly*. His publications include articles in the *Journal of Criminal Justice, Police Science and Administration, American Journal of Police, Texas Police Journal, Public Personnel Management, Security Administration, Liberal Education,* and a research monograph for the NIJ. He is also coeditor of the *Encyclopedia of Police Science*. Dr. Hoover has worked with the Texas Commission on Law Enforcement Officer Standards and Education on several projects, and is now directing the Sam Houston State University elements of the Law Enforcement Management Institute.

George L. Kelling is a professor of criminal justice in the College of Criminal Justice, Northeastern University, and a fellow in the Program in Criminal Justice in the Kennedy School of Government at Harvard University. He has his bachelor's degree from St. Olaf College, his master's degree from the University of Wisconsin-Milwaukee, and his Ph.D. from the University of Wisconsin-Madison. He has been involved in police research, consultation, and teaching since the 1960s. From 1971 to 1980, Dr. Kelling was director of field research for the Police Foundation. In that capacity he conducted the Kansas City Preventive Patrol Experiment and the Newark Foot Patrol Experiment. One of his most noteworthy publications was co-authored with James Q. Wilson in *Atlantic* and is popularly known as "Broken Windows." Dr. Kelling is currently involved in consulting with the New York City Transit Authority, where he has assisted in the development of strategies to deal with disorder, farebeating, and robbery in the subway. His current research focuses on the types of authority cities have, and are developing, to deal with disorder.

Dennis J. Kenney has over 18 years of experience in varied aspects of criminal justice — as a Florida police officer; as a director of research and planning in Savannah, Georgia; as a project director for the Police Foundation in Washington, D.C.; and as a university professor at both the Western Connecticut State University and the University of Nebraska at Omaha where he is currently an associate professor. He is the author, coauthor, or editor of numerous articles, monographs, and books including *Crime, Fear and the New York City Subways* and *Police and Policing: Contemporary Issues*. Additionally, Dr. Kenney has provided consulting services to police agencies around the country and has managed federally sponsored research and technical assistance projects. He is currently completing work on a textbook examining organized crime in America and has recently been appointed as editor of the *American Journal of Police*. Dr. Kenney holds a Ph.D. in criminal justice from Rutgers University, an M.A. from Rollins College, and a B.S. from Saint Leo College.

Dennis R. Longmire is currently the associate dean for academic administration at Sam Houston State University's College of Criminal Justice. He received his M.A. and Ph.D. degrees from the University of Maryland's Institute of Criminal Justice and Criminology and worked as a juvenile probation officer and an adult correctional officer in Maryland prior to pursuing his graduate degrees. In addition to holding faculty positions in California and Ohio, Dr. Longmire has been actively involved in research and evaluation projects examining a myriad of criminal justice activities including evaluations of multijurisdictional crime control projects and "small town" policing. He has published extensively in both academic and professional journals and is committed to the process of "translating research and theory into practice."

Peter K. Manning received his B.A. in 1961 from Willamette University; his M.A. in 1963 and his Ph.D. in 1966 from Duke University in Sociology, and an honorary M.A. in 1982 from Oxon). He is professor of sociology and psychiatry at Michigan State University. He was a research scholar at the Department of Justice, LEAA, Washington, D.C. (1974-1975), and has been a visiting professor at SUNY, Albany, MIT, and the University of Victoria. In 1990 he delivered a lecture in the Beto Distinguished Lecture Series at Sam Houston State University Criminal Justice Center. While at Oxford, he was a visiting fellow and then research fellow at Wolfson College, a fellow of Balliql College (1982-1983) and a senior research officer at the Centre for Socio-Legal Studies (1984-1986). He is author and editor of some twelve books and numerous articles and chapters in scientific publications. Most recently, he published *Seminotics and Fieldwork* (Sage, 1987), *Symbolic Communication* (MIT Press, 1988), and *Organizational Communication* (Aldine Press, 1991). His recent interests are in occupations and organizations, medical sociology and criminology, with special interest in fieldwork and qualitative methods. His recent research examines legal decision making (with Keith Hawkins), nuclear safety regulation, and psychosocial aspects of AIDS.

Timothy N. Oettmeier is an eighteen-year veteran with the Houston Police Department. He has served time in patrol, dispatch, and training. Additionally, he has served as an executive assistant to assistant chiefs of police and the chief of police. As a lieutenant, he is currently assigned to the Houston Police Academy. He has attained a bachelor of science degree, majoring in psychology, from the University of Houston (1975); a master of arts degree, majoring in criminology and corrections, from Sam Houston State University (1978); and a Ph.D., majoring in criminal justice, from Sam Houston State University (1982). He has also published several articles and written numerous reports on police management and operational issues.

Allen D. Sapp received his doctorate in criminal justice from Sam Houston State University. He also holds a master's degree in guidance and counseling from the University of Southern California and the bachelor's degree in sociology from the University of Nebraska at Omaha. He is a certified law enforcement instructor in several states and is a commissioned deputy sheriff and a member of the Central Missouri Rural Crime Squad. He has been a member of the criminal justice faculty at Central Missouri State University since 1982. He received the university's highest awards for Outstanding Research (1989) and Outstanding Scholarship (1990). Dr. Sapp has been a consultant to more than one hundred law enforcement agencies at local, county, state, and national levels. He was a member of the U.S. Attorney General's Working Group on Reducing Violence in America. Dr. Sapp is also a Research Fellow with the Police Executive Research Forum. He lectures frequently at the FBI National Academy and the Florida Center for Advanced Law Enforcement Studies. Dr. Sapp has published more than sixty articles, monographs, book chapters, and books on law enforcement education, training, conduct, labor relations, and the future. He also has published on elderly offenders, sex offender treatment programs, right-wing extremism, and child abuse. He has been the research director of several national law enforcement studies for the Police Executive Research Forum. These include studies on police education, issues in policing, labor relations, and a study on police responses to toy guns mandated by Congress. He currently is involved in a national assessment of police responses to the homeless and street people.

Mittie D. Southerland is associate professor of police studies in the Department of Police Studies at Eastern Kentucky University. She served previously as coordinator of Eastern Kentucky University's Fort Knox Programs for the College of Law Enforcement. Dr. Southerland earned her master of science in criminal justice at Eastern Kentucky University in 1973 and her Ph.D. in social and philosophical studies in higher education at the University of Kentucky in 1984. A former criminal justice planner and juvenile counselor, her expertise is in the areas of administration, management, and supervision with particular emphasis on organizational environments and change in the police setting. Dr. Southerland has served as consultant to a number of police agencies. Dr. Southerland is coauthor of *Police Administration* (McGraw-Hill, 1991) and has also published chapters and articles in the areas of police management and leadership, juvenile justice, and criminal justice education.

Darrel W. Stephens is currently the executive director of the Washington, D.C., -based Police Executive Research Forum, and has an extensive background as a police executive. Since beginning his career as a patrol officer in Kansas City, Missouri, in 1968, he has served in a number of police executive positions: first as assistant chief in Lawrence, Kansas, and later as chief in Largo, Florida, and Newport News, Virginia. While chief in Newport News, the police department gained national recognition for developing and implementing the problem-oriented policing concept. The department was also among the first in the United States to be accredited. Stephens, who also spent a year as a NIJ fellow, coauthored several books including *Beyond Command and Control: The Strategic Management of Police Departments; The State of Police Education: Policy Direction for the 21st Century;* and *Drug Abuse by Police Officers: An Analysis of Critical Policy Issues.* He holds a master's degree in public services administration from Central Missouri State University and a bachelor's degree in administration of justice from the University of Missouri at Kansas City.

Victor G. Strecher is a professor in the College of Criminal Justice at Sam Houston State University. He received his Ph.D. in 1968 from Washington University (Missouri) in Sociology. His main areas of instruction are criminal justice policy analysis, the analysis of American policing, systems theory, criminal justice systems organization and management, planning and finance administration, human resource development, crime analysis, and social and organizational change. From 1978 to 1985 he served as dean and director of the Criminal Justice Center. Dr. Strecher has lectured extensively throughout the United States on a variety of criminal justice topics, including managing patrol operations and managing criminal investigations. He was team leader of the National Field Test of Managing Patrol Operations sponsored by the NIJ, and was a former member of the Research Policy Review Board of NIJ. Dr. Strecher has served on numerous advisory commissions in Texas, including the Criminal Justice Policy Council and the Governor's Blue Ribbon Commission for the Review of the Texas Criminal Justice System. He has published extensively, including *The Environment of Law Enforcement* (Prentice-Hall), editor of *The Cyclopedia of Policing* (LEAA), and coeditor of *The Encyclopedia of Police Science* (Garland).

Gary W. Sykes currently directs educational programs in law enforcement administration at the Southwestern Law Enforcement Institute in Dallas, Texas, after joining the Institute in 1989. He received a bachelor's degree, a master's degree, and a Ph.D. (awarded in 1976) from the Pennsylvania State University. He also received a postdoctoral fellowship in criminology at the University of Virginia in 1977. In 1980 in the Superior, Wisconsin, Police Department he conducted research and was a fully sworn police officer. Dr. Sykes has conducted funded research projects and has authored numerous publications in professional journals, for the Bureau of Justice Statistics, U.S. Department of Justice; served as educational consultant to The Police Foundation and UNISYS Corporation; and served on the editorial boards of many criminal justice and law enforcement professional journals.

Elizabeth M. Watson joined the Houston Police Department in 1972. She earned the ranks of detective, lieutenant, captain, and deputy chief before being appointed chief of police on January 19, 1990, by Mayor Kathy Whitmire. Following the election of Mayor Bob Lanier she was replaced as police chief and currently holds the rank of assistant chief. Chief Watson implemented the department's first neighborhood-oriented policing program while serving as deputy chief of the Westside Command Station from 1987 to 1990. Her plan became the model for the department's citywide neighborhood-oriented policing initiative. During Chief Watson's three-year tenure as captain of the Auto Theft Division, the Houston Police Department was awarded the Anes Electronics Award. This distinction was given to the police department for having achieved the largest reduction in auto theft among competing cities throughout the United States. Apart from the Houston Police Department, Chief Watson is a member of a number of police and management associations, including the International Association of Chiefs of Police (IACP), where she cochairs the Civil Rights Committee. She is also on the editorial board of the *American Journal of Police* and the advisory board of the Southwestern Law Enforcement Institution and the University of Houston-Downtown Criminal Justice Center. In addition, Chief Watson works with several organizations outside the area of law enforcement. She is a member-at-large of the Board of Directors of the San Jacinto Area Girl Scouts and she serves on the University of Texas Health Science Center's Committee for the Prevention of Injury and Violence. Chief Watson is an honors graduate of Texas Tech University with a degree in psychology.

Police Executive Research Forum

The Police Executive Research Forum (PERF) is a national professional association of chief executives of large city, county and state police departments. PERF's purpose is to improve the delivery of police services and the effectiveness of crime control through several means:

- the exercise of strong national leadership;
- public debate of police and criminal justice issues;
- research and policy development; and
- the provision of vital management leadership services to police agencies.

PERF members are selected on the basis of their commitment to PERF's purpose and principles. The principles that guide the Police Executive Research Forum are:

- Research, experimentation and exchange of ideas through public discussion and debate are paths for development of a professional body of knowledge about policing;
- Substantial and purposeful academic study is a prerequisite for acquiring, understanding and adding to the body of knowledge of professional police management;
- Maintenance of the highest standards of ethics and integrity is imperative in the improvement of policing;
- The police must, within the limits of the law, be responsible and accountable to citizens as the ultimate source of police authority; and
- The principles embodied in the Constitution are the foundation of policing.